The Hill School Company, Limi[ted]

No. 635 **ORDINARY SHARES**

[INCOR]PORATED UNDER THE CEYLON JOINT STOCK COMPANIES ORDINANCES.)

[Ca]pital: Rs. 500,000 [...] 50,000 Shares of Rs. 10
Rs. 267,[...], Rs. 10

[Cert]ificate [...] Walke[r]

ent[y] five (25)

Shares of TEN RUPEES
COMPANY LI[...]

0614- 4231-5558

DATE AND PLACE OF ISSUE OF THIS TICKET

Agent I.D. 506039

0614- 4231-5557

[...] PLACE OF ISSUE OF THIS TICKET

Via Brindisi

Miss Hornby
Sandown
Waverl[ey]
Liverpool
England

CORR 64(M)

[...]PER.
[...]STON AVENUE.
[...]URGH.

146163

Please see instructions on reverse.

Date 3.6.44.

[...]KER,
[...]A) LTD.,
DELHI.

[...]bout me a bit more. I am doing
[...]ut in rickshaws a bit, and for
[...]e children are all most comfortabl[y]
[...]ery day, and so far all news is
[...]as sent - a recent very good
[...]& M. To you we have also sent
[...]an nor Tiffar is very good.
[...]n very interested. Susan can loo[k]
[...] to have Susan and Tiffar done
[...]ey cannot do a total collapse,
[...]top and very bottom cannot be
[...]ut they have a fairly satisfactor[y]
[...] of action. My tummy has still
[...]der, and Whyte is taking that
[...]one go here of pa[...]

Words 50 | Day 19 | Hour 9 | Minute 20 | From Ch[...]

To (Person)

Gladys
Olive Jack
Lemarchand To
William Watson & Co

Good bye and God b[...]
you Darlings a
and please [...]
You [...]

Carachi TELEG[RAM]

Children
of the Raj

Children of the Raj

Vyvyen Brendon

Weidenfeld & Nicolson

LONDON

First published in Great Britain in 2005
by Weidenfeld & Nicolson

1 3 5 7 9 10 8 6 4 2

© Vyvyen Brendon

A CIP catalogue record for this book
Is available from the British Library.

ISBN 0 297 84729 5

Typeset, printed and bound in Great Britain by
Butler and Tanner Ltd, Frome and London

Weidenfeld & Nicolson

The Orion Publishing Group Ltd
Orion House
5 Upper Saint Martin's Lane
London, WC2H 9EA

www.orionbooks.co.uk

To the memory of my mother,
Gladys Davis.

Contents

Illustrations

Endpapers

Hugs and Kisses from Dorothy Wilkins to her family (courtesy of Wilkins family)

Air Tickets for unaccompanied minors (courtesy of Anne Paylor)

Shares in Hill School, Ceylon (courtesy of Walker family)

Stamped envelope from Fyzabad (Author's possession)

Telegram, 1899 (Author's possession)

Wartime airgraph, 1944 (courtesy of Parker family)

Instructions to seaplane passengers, 1939 (courtesy of Pepita Lamb)

Illustrated envelope from Henry Thornhill to his grandson Teddy, 1922 (Thornhill family)

Between pages 170 and 171

Children in India

Iris, Susan and Jane Portal with servants, Bombay 1935 (courtesy of Sue Batten)

Brian Outhwaite, Dagshai, 1939 (courtesy of Outhwaite Family)

George, Robert and Beatrice Baker with syces, Travancore, c. 1919 (courtesy of Baker Family)

Rosie and Mavora Harrison, Pakistan, c. 1951 (courtesy of Rosie Gutteridge)

Pat Foster with family and friends, Nagari, 1928 (courtesy of Pat Harrison)

Grave of Alice, Lindsay and Georgiana Daniell, Pussellawa, Ceylon 1866 (courtesy of Sue Farrington)

Gerald and Richmond Ritchie with sepoy, Barrackpore, 1857 (from G. Ritchie, *The Ritchies in India*, 1920)

Boarding the boats at Cawnpore, 1857 (from M. Thomson, *The Story of Cawnpore*, 1859)

Hilary Johnston with servants, Himalayas, c. 1931 (courtesy of Hilary Sweet-Escott)

Eric Wilkins, Orissa, c. 1911 (courtesy of Wilkins family)

Robert and Beatrice Baker among friends, Kodai, c.1920 (courtesy of Baker family)

Major George Wemyss and Katherine Anson with sons Otto and Frank, Raniket, 1880s (courtesy of Anson family)

Henry and Charles Doherty with servants painted by Mrs Doherty, Bangalore, 1818 (India Office Library)

Self-portrait of David Wilkins with Haru, Orissa, 1944 (courtesy of D. Wilkins)

Self-portrait of David Wilkins with family, Landour, 1945 (courtesy of D. Wilkins)

Depiction of her father by Hilda Reid, Lahore early 20th century (courtesy of Alex Reid)

Hilda Reid on her father, Lahore early 20th century (courtesy of Alex Reid)

Children at school in India

Lawrence Military Asylum, Sanawar 1864 (Howard and Jane Ricketts)

St John's College, Agra (Author's photograph)

Arthur Jones and Hockey Team, Bishop Cotton School, 1949 (courtesy of A. Jones)

Margaret Hinds with her daughter Alison and friends, Gulmarg, c. 1934 (courtesy of Alison Newton)

Penny Elsden-Smith with friends, Kalimpong, 1943 (courtesy of Penny Francis)

Jim, Pat and Mick Butler, Mount Abu High School, 1935 (courtesy of James Butler)

Children back 'Home' in Britain

Constance Halford-Thompson, Amsterdam, 1938 (KLM)

Archibald Campbell, East Sheen, c. 1877 (India Office Library)

William Brown, Craigflower Prep School, c. 1930 (courtesy of W.Brown)

Letty, Tutu and Willie Beveridge, Southport, 1885 (India Office Library)

Leslie and Marjorie Wenger, 1916 (courtesy of Wenger family)

Explanatory Notes

INDIAN PLACE NAMES

The book refers to places by their old names, as used in the days of the Raj (e.g. Simla), except where reference is made to places today (e.g. Shimla).

WOMEN'S SURNAMES

In the first reference to married women who were children under the Raj both married and maiden names are given. Subsequently, the name by which the subject was known at the time of the reference is used. For those who are referred to only as children maiden names only are used.

QUOTATIONS

Occasional changes to punctuation and spelling have been made in the interests of clarity.

Acknowledgements

I owe a great deal to the many people who have helped me with the research and writing of this book.

The staff of all the British libraries and archive collections I have contacted or worked in have provided expert, patient and cheerful help. In particular I thank Allen Packwood, Natalie Adams and Andrew Riley of Churchill Archives Centre; Dr Kevin Greenbank and Mary Thatcher (retired) of Cambridge Centre for South Asian Studies; Rachel Rowe and Godfrey Waller of Cambridge University Library Manuscripts Department; Jill Geber, Jennifer Howes, Margaret Makepeace, Nisha Mithali, Hedley Sutton and Tim Thomas of the India Office Library; Roderick Suddaby of the Imperial War Museum; Kate Morgan of the Sound Archive at the British Empire and Commonwealth Museum; Anne Ward of Lambeth Archives; Sara Kinsey of the HSBC Archive; Paul Smith of the Thomas Cook Archive; Stephen Rabson of the P&O Archive and Anthony Pemberton of the Pemberton Archive. Richard Wildman of Bedford Modern School and John Brown of Streatham have given me valuable information.

On my visits to India I was treated as a welcome guest by the staff at schools, clubs, cemeteries and churches even when I arrived late, dishevelled or unannounced. My thanks are due, in particular, to Kabir Mustafi, Shusheela Prabhudas and P. K. Thakur of Bishop Cotton School, Shimla; Sunita John of Auckland House, Shimla; Christine McLeod of Woodstock School, Mussoorie; K. J. Parel and Praveen Vasisht of the Lawrence School, Sanawar; Lt.-Col. S. C. Narula of the Agra Club; Dr F. M. Prasad, R. B. Sharma and S. B. Sharma of St John's College, Agra; R. C. Sharma, who guided me around 'British Agra' and Babulal and Rajkumar, the *malis* (gardeners) who showed me the Skinner tombs at St James's Church, Delhi. These visits would not have been nearly so much fun without the companionship of my former colleague, Fleur Spore, whose geographical expertise came in very useful, and my son, George Brendon, who proved a most conscientious research assistant. Back in Britain another ex-colleague, Anne Beckett, and my other son, Oliver Brendon, patiently helped me to develop a few essential computer skills.

Many friends have helped me not only by their interest and encouragement but also in practical ways. Some gave me references arising from their own expert knowledge in relevant fields: Dr Mary Abbott, Professor Haroon Ahmed, Charles Allen, Professor Christopher Andrew, Dr Nicky Blandford, Rex Bloomstein, Mary Brown, Tim Cribb, Dr Alan Findlay, Pam Gatrell, Lawrence Goldman, Dr Felicia Gordon, Bill Greenwell, Tim Jeal, Sean Lang, Dr Peter Martland, Philip Macdonagh (formerly the Irish Ambassador to India), Patti Rundall, Dr Joan Stevenson-Hinde and Sister Ursula, IBVM. Others put me in touch with 'Indian children' of their family or acquaintance: Capt. Vivek Bhasin, Jaya Bolt, Dr Janet Bottoms, Clare Byatt, Shirley Cosgrave, Patricia Davis, Judy Findlay, Lizzie and David Fitzgerald, Goody Khan, Hope Gilbert, Dr Anasuya Grenfell, Alex and Stephanie Hamilton, Gill Harrison, Gwen Harrod, Hester Hinde, Dr Pam Hirsch, Jo Kirkpatrick, Belinda and David Marler, Professor James Mayall, Anna Murray, Dr Alison Newton, Gay Niblett, Suzy Oakes, Peter and Sybil Pagnamenta, Hazel Pritchett-Harris, Laura Ponsonby, Dr Tom and Ann Rosenthal, Henley and Penny Smith and Fleur Spore.

The 'Children of the Raj' themselves are listed in the Bibliography. I am indebted to them for their friendly reception, kind hospitality and generous sharing of sad or joyful memories. I hope they will approve of the use I have made of their precious material. Many of them lent me memoirs, letters and photographs. The following people also entrusted me with family papers which were in their possession: Andrew Best, Jaya Bolt, Graham Broad, Margaret Colville, Hilary Evans, Elinor Kapp, Vivek Kapp, Dick Perceval Maxwell, Alex Reid and Christine Usborne. In addition Patrick Higgins and Valentine Davies generously allowed me to see the unpublished fruits of their own research.

I am especially grateful to those who have read my chapters hot from the computer: Judy Findlay, the late Dr Brian Outhwaite and Henrietta Twycross-Martin. Without their tough criticism, helpful suggestions and steady encouragement the text would have been much the poorer. The faults and mistakes which remain are all my own. At Weidenfeld & Nicolson Anna Hervé managed the production of this handsome volume, Jamie Tanner designed the beautiful jacket and

Linden Lawson and Jane Birkett skilfully copyedited and proofread the text. And, of course, the book would never have appeared at all without the backing of my agent Laura Morris and publisher Ion Trewin. It has been a great pleasure and privilege to work with them both. I also thank my husband Piers Brendon for giving me the benefit of his experience as well as his time, support and love.

For permission to quote poems:

My Boy Jack and verse from *In Partibus* by Rudyard Kipling: A. P. Watt Ltd on behalf of The National Trust for Places of Interest or Natural Beauty.

Orphanage by Richard Murphy: the author and The Gallery Press, Loughcrew, Oldcastle, County Meath, Ireland.

Verse from *Indian Childhood* by Alan Ross: Collins Harvill

India! India! by Spike Milligan: Michael Joseph.

Every effort has been made to fulfil requirements with regard to reproduction copyright material. The author and publisher will be glad to rectify any omissions at the earliest opportunity.

Glossary

Anglo-Indian	Term used to describe British people resident in India, later used to describe people of mixed Indian and British race
ayah/amah	Children's nanny (or lady's maid)
baba log	Children
Begum	Title of high-ranking married Muslim woman
box-wallah	Pejorative word for people involved in trade or commerce (originally pedlar)
burra sahib	Important European
charpoy	Bed
chi chi	Term used to describe Eurasians or their lilting form of speech
country-born	Disparaging term for those who were not only born but also brought up in India
crannies	Clerks
dacoit	Robber belonging to an armed gang
dhooly	Covered litter
dhye	Wet-nurse (also spelt *dhaye*)
domiciled	Europeans whose families had made their home in India, often synonymous with Eurasian
Eurasian	Person of mixed Indian and European race
ferringhies	Indian term for Europeans (foreigners)
fishing fleet	Term used to describe British girls who went to India to find a husband among the bachelors working there
furlough	Period of leave, usually spent back in Britain
godown	Outbuilding, sometimes referring to servants' quarters

heaven-born	The higher ranks of the Indian Civil Service, the elite of the British in India
Home	Used with a capital letter by Anglo-Indians to refer to Britain
ICS	Indian Civil Service
John Company	Affectionate term for the East India Company
Kindertransport	Scheme for transporting Jewish children out of Nazi-occupied countries in Europe
maidan	Public open space
mali	Gardener
mofussil	Country districts
munshi	Teacher or tutor
nabob	Old term for an Anglo-Indian who made a princely fortune in India
pan	Betel leaves used as a drug or stimulant (or *paan*)
pani	Water
Presidency	Administrative area in India (e.g. Madras)
pukka	Originally meaning correct, it came to mean respectable
purdah	Women living in an area secluded from men
Raj	British sovereignty in India
Resident	Official representative of the British in an Indian princely state
rupee	Indian currency. I have taken ten rupees to be worth one pound.
sepoy	Indian infantry soldier serving the British
SPCK	Society for Promoting Christian Knowledge
suttee	Hindu rite of widow-burning
syce	Indian groom
thugee	Banditry
tonga	Light two-wheeled vehicle
writer	Junior grade in East India Company
zenana	Part of the house reserved for women

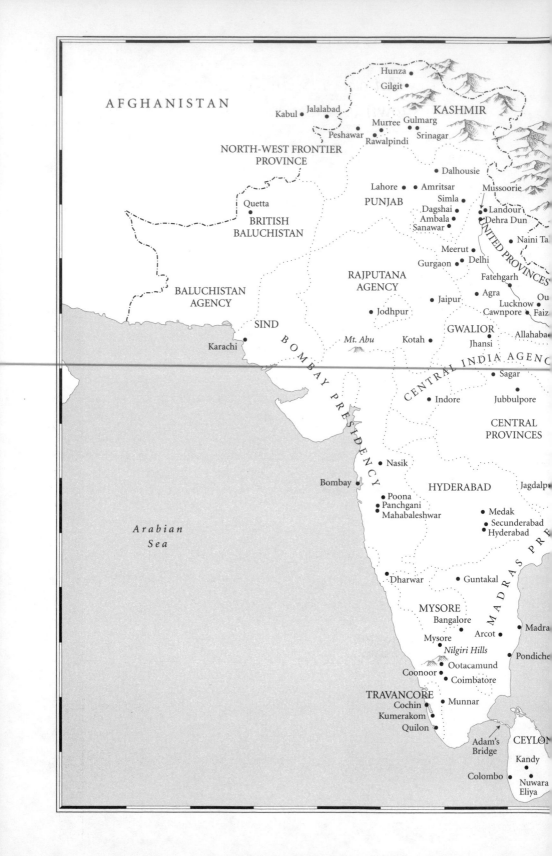

AFGHANISTAN

Hunza
Gilgit

KASHMIR

Kabul • Jalalabad

Murree • Gulmarg
Peshawar • Srinagar
Rawalpindi

NORTH-WEST FRONTIER
PROVINCE

Dalhousie

Lahore • Amritsar
Mussoorie

PUNJAB
Simla
Landour

Quetta
Dagshai
Dehra Dun

BRITISH
BALUCHISTAN
Ambala
Sanawar

Naini Ta

Meerut

Gurgaon • Delhi

BALUCHISTAN
AGENCY

RAJPUTANA
AGENCY

Fatehgarh

Agra
Ou

Lucknow
Cawnpore • Faiz

SIND
Jaipur

Jodhpur

GWALIOR

Karachi
Mt. Abu
Kotah

Jhansi

Allahaba

BOMBAY PRESIDENCY

CENTRAL INDIA AGENC

Sagar

Indore
Jubbulpore

CENTRAL
PROVINCES

Nasik

HYDERABAD
Jagdalp

Bombay

Poona
Panchgani
Mahabaleshwar

Medak
Secunderabad
Hyderabad

Arabian
Sea

Dharwar • Guntakal

MADRAS PRE

MYSORE
Bangalore

Arcot • Madra

Mysore

Nilgiri Hills
Pondiche

Coonoor • Ootacamund
Coimbatore

TRAVANCORE
Cochin • Munnar
Kumerakom
Quilon

Adam's
Bridge

CEYLO

Kandy

Colombo • Nuwara
Eliya

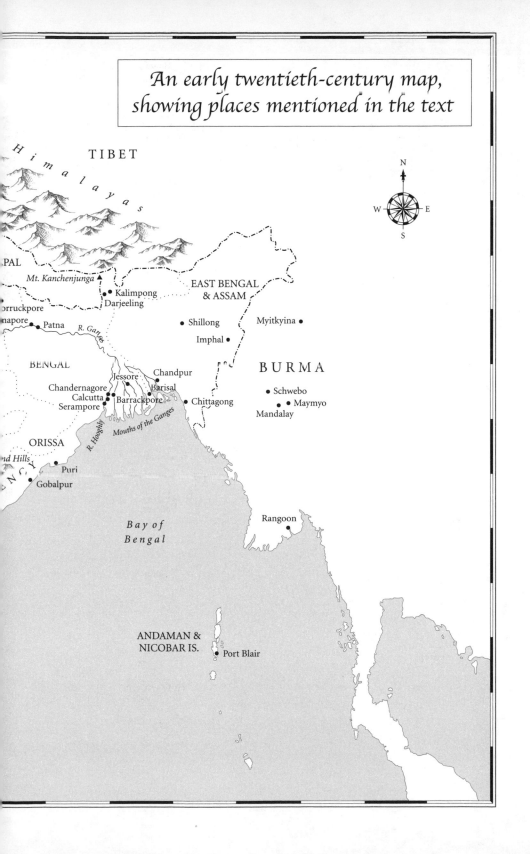

An early twentieth-century map,
showing places mentioned in the text

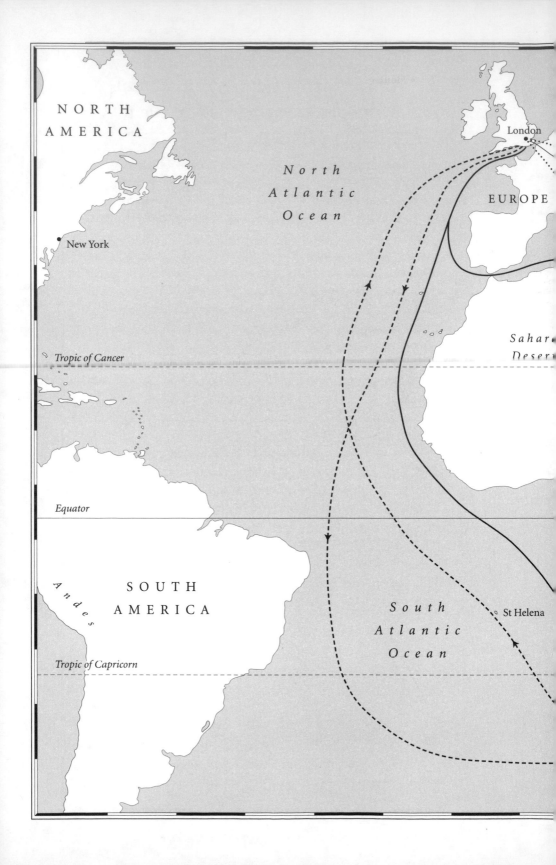

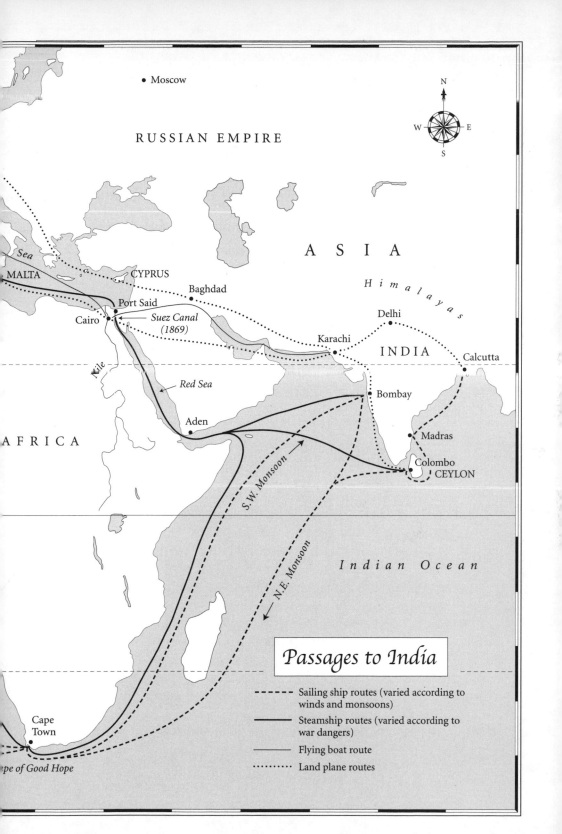

Moscow

RUSSIAN EMPIRE

N
W E
S

ASIA

Sea

MALTA
CYPRUS
Baghdad

Himalayas

Port Said

Delhi

Cairo
Suez Canal (1869)

Karachi

INDIA

Calcutta

Nile

Red Sea

Bombay

Aden

Madras

AFRICA

S.W. Monsoon

Colombo
CEYLON

N.E. Monsoon

Indian Ocean

Passages to India

– – – – Sailing ship routes (varied according to winds and monsoons)

———— Steamship routes (varied according to war dangers)

———— Flying boat route

·········· Land plane routes

Cape Town

pe of Good Hope

'We Indian Children'

The children of the Raj are legion. Over the whole period of British rule in India their numbers amounted to millions – so many that almost every family in the country has some Indian connection. And tens of thousands of those who spent their childhood under the British Raj are still alive, the youngest of them now middle-aged. I am not one of them. Yet in the course of my research for this book I have discovered ancestors who did work in India: Grenfells and Moyles who travelled from Cornwall to serve in Indian regiments, build railways or sit on medical boards. One, Colonel Charles Augustus Moyle of the Bombay Native Infantry, left a memoir which deals mainly with his fighting, shooting and pig-sticking exploits. But it does mention in passing the birth in various army camps of three 'little strangers'. Augusta, Agnes and 'a son and heir', in 1849, 1850 and 1851.¹ Sadly the Colonel died while writing the memoir, which ends in 1852, so I have been unable to discover the fate of these infants. A member of my husband's family, Patrick Brendon of the Indian Civil Service (ICS), also wrote a memoir which features in this book. Many who inquire into their family history discover similar links with the Indian sub-continent.

Nevertheless the story of Raj children has never fully been told, though it is one of compelling interest. It is dramatic and traumatic, involving dangerous voyages, vivid experiences in exotic places and profound emotions springing from the sudden, unexplained and lengthy separation of children from their parents. 'We Indian children', William Makepeace Thackeray called himself and his cousin, who were sent to England in 1817 aged five and four respectively, accompanied only by an Indian servant. It was a six-month journey broken by a stay on St Helena; here the boys caught a glimpse of the exiled Napoleon Bonaparte who, the servant told them, 'ate all the little children he could lay hands on'. They survived the hazards and ended up in a 'dreadful' school, where William's only hope of comfort was that he would dream of his mother.² The tragic plight of such youngsters is well illustrated by two celebrated fictional characters. Punch, in Rudyard Kipling's semi-autobiographical *Baa Baa, Black Sheep*, is deprived of his parents and victimised by his guardian during a five-year exile from India. And Mary Lennox, in *The Secret Garden*, is orphaned and transplanted abruptly from bowers of scarlet hibiscus to a bleak Yorkshire moor.

This book tells the true stories of many other 'black sheep' and 'disagreeable-looking' children. It encompasses all the territory of the Indian subcontinent, including what are now the separate countries of Pakistan and Bangladesh, but excluding the small French, Portuguese, Dutch and Danish enclaves retained at different times by Britain's erstwhile rivals. It extends to neighbouring Burma, which was part of the Raj between 1886 and 1935. It also includes Ceylon (Sri Lanka), virtually linked by Adam's Bridge to the mainland but a separate Crown Colony from 1815 to 1948. The book covers the period from the 1760s, when the British first began to colonise India, to the 1960s, by which time most British people had left the subcontinent. Its subject is the young progeny of traders, soldiers, civil servants, missionaries, planters, engineers and others working in India during this time. (In those days they were called 'Anglo-Indians', a term which later came to mean those of mixed race, who used to be known as 'Eurasians', and this book uses the terminology of the Raj.) The narrative begins in the unpredictable days of the East India Company's rule. It explores the dangers of the Afghan wars and the Indian Mutiny. It moves through the more settled era presided over by the Queen-Empress. It culminates in the twentieth-century conflicts leading to Britain's hurried exit. And it finishes with those who stayed on after the Raj was over. Against this changing background families struggled to find a *modus vivendi* and adopted different solutions to the problem of what to do with the children born during long periods of Indian service.

In making these decisions Raj parents were presented with an eternal dilemma, which gives the book a permanent relevance. Should they risk the happiness of their offspring for the sake of physical safety, material well-being or future prospects? The problem is as acute now as ever it was, preoccupying modern parents who also feature briefly in these pages: wartime families using overseas evacuation schemes; persecuted Jews saving their children's lives with the help of *Kindertransport*; West Africans currently seeking educational advantage for their children by having them fostered in Britain; Asian parents sending sons and daughters to British boarding schools; multinational business employees trotting the globe with their families; and hard-working Western mothers and fathers who 'are rarely, if ever, both home awake with the kids at the same time'. The mother quoted here loves her tough, well-paid job on a New York magazine but she 'will never be able to share the surprise [her two sons] feel when they find a cicada in the grass because stopping to marvel at the cicada means I will miss my morning train'.[3] Journalist Gary Younge recognised such parallels when he rebuked a British government minister who accused asylum-seekers of deserting their families for money: 'He could just as easily have been talking about the staff at the East India Company.'[4]

It is not hard to talk of East India Company staff separated from their families for they have left behind plentiful evidence, on which I have drawn heavily. As Francis Pemberton wrote to his sisters just after he had begun employment with the Company in 1771, they would all have 'to correspond and tell each other our thoughts and sentiments and wishes'.[5] This need did not diminish over the years of the Raj. Families often kept such letters, with their exciting and poignant evocations of life in India or their dutiful descriptions of school activities. They often contain illustrations. More recent ones have visual expressions of love in the form of noughts and crosses to represent hugs and kisses. Diaries, scrapbooks and photograph albums, compiled as a record for children or parents, have also been preserved, sometimes bearing the ravages of damp and decay, to say nothing of white ants. Many such records have been deposited in public archive collections like the India Office Library, Royal Commonwealth Society and National Army Museum or in county record offices. In addition some firms, Thomas Cook and Hong Kong and Shanghai Banking Corporation (HSBC), for example, have well-preserved archives which shed light on family life under the Empire. Other bundles of correspondence still rest in family attics but I have been lucky enough to see some of these too. One man arrived for an interview in a Bristol hotel carrying a suitcase full of his own schoolboy letters to his parents in India; until that very morning, when he had been exploring on my behalf, he had not realised that his father had kept them. Ephemera of other kinds have also come to light. One woman had preserved the aeroplane tickets by which she and her sister travelled to India as Unaccompanied Minors. They showed just how costly air travel was, even after the war.

Of course these records have their limitations. The adults who wrote letters and diaries had their own concerns and might not fully appreciate their children's feelings. Take the case of Lady Nugent, who accompanied her husband on a lucrative tour of duty to India from 1811 to 1815, leaving at home her four children, including a six-week-old baby. Just before her return she recorded in her journal the certainty that her trials (illness, anxiety and homesickness) had been worthwhile and that 'We have done our duty by our children.'[6] There is no evidence of how well George, Louisa, Maria and baby Edmund bore her absence. Children's letters, where they do survive, were often censored by guardians or teachers. In the early nineteenth century a governess insisted that one small child should dictate a list of the wrong and self-willed things she had done – to be sent to her parents. Some letters from school bear stern teachers' notes, such as this one added to a boy's appeal to his parents for money: 'He gets his pocket money every week and does not need any more.'[7]

Yet the authentic tones of lost generations of children echo down the ages. Their preoccupations range from the profound to the trivial. On a letter received from her mother in 1843 explaining that 'it was a great trial to both Papa and myself to leave you behind' a child has added a pencilled note: 'O dear Mamma.'[8] In 1905 a young girl says that she has broken her stays jumping off the garden wall; she wants to leave off this uncomfortable garment but does not know what she can pin her skirt to. She ends with an anxious appeal for help from her distant mother: 'What could I do about that do you think Darling?'[9] Sometimes the letters of a lonely child contain the 'anguished poetry' mentioned by Katie Hickman in a recent review. One wrote from England to her mother in India: 'Just now as I looked out of the window I saw a huge, big, perfectly round, red sun sinking behind the trees. I have told him to give you my love when he sees you in a few minutes. I hope he will do so.'[10] In such poignant extracts the youthful figures in sepia photographs are given a voice.

A good example of the importance of letters to writers, recipients and posterity are those of Sir Henry Thornhill to his grandchildren. Sir Henry had been a child in India, surviving a long siege at Agra during the 1857 Mutiny (which caused the death of many other members of the Thornhill family). After that he was sent to school in England, but only his orphaned cousin Henrietta seems to have preserved his schoolboy correspondence. He wrote her cheerful, ill-spelt letters, reporting that Eton was 'the joliest place I ever was at' once he had got over the initial period when 'I had no one to tell me what I ought to do'.[11] Henry followed his father into an Indian career, in the later stages of which he kept in touch with his grandchildren in England through letters, containing beautiful illustrations of Indian wildlife. Soon after he retired to England in 1914 his daughter's husband was posted to India and so the flow of letters across the seas continued, every word in them conveying 'a kiss from Kaka [Grandpa]'. As Sir Henry was now a lonely widower the letters consoled him as much as they did his grandchildren. On Christmas Day 1921 he wrote: 'I called out as I awoke, "A Merry Christmas to you all!"' Of special value to eight-year-old Teddy were the letters awaiting him at every port of call on his solitary voyage to England in 1922. Sir Henry continued to write to Teddy, who was not very happy at school, urging him to 'keep smiling and pegging away'. Eventually, of course, the boy became embarrassed to receive Kaka's letters in their painted envelopes. Nevertheless he knew that they came from 'the best friend I ever had'. The stock of over a thousand letters lay in the family attic for sixty years but a selection has now been published on a website, providing evidence not only of the imperial way of life but also of the emotions it inspired.[12]

In addition, those who have spent time abroad are particularly prone to write retrospectively about their childhood; whether published or in manuscript, polished or artless, these memoirs form another valuable source of information. Of course, the writers may be selective in what they record and they are likely to be middle-class people. But I do not agree with the American historian who argued recently for the rejection of these 'one-sided interpretations', hoping that they would soon 'become extinct along with the "tribe" of former colonizers'.[13] It is true that children of the Raj have tended to see their parents' Indian work in a favourable light, but that does not invalidate their childhood memories. In any case, as well as loyal defenders like M. M. Kaye and Iris Portal, there are more objective sons and daughters. Henry Beveridge concluded that his parents spent their lives working 'for a purpose which has not been accomplished'. Michael Foss quotes his father's verdict that 'we members of the Raj botched it ... because we lacked sympathy and understanding'.[14] It is quite wrong to claim that archivists and publishers have sought out only 'positive narratives'.[15]

What good autobiographies can do, as the literary critic Richard Coe suggests, is to present the child's angle of vision, capture the magical experience of childhood and convey the sense of 'moving and existing in a universe which is *full*; of being crowded in on all sides by sounds and colours, by flowers, butterflies and grasses'.[16] Because such self-revelations were usually written after the death of parents, aunts, guardians and schoolteachers (sometimes in an age which encouraged freer expression of feelings), they were more honest than juvenile letters could ever be. This does not mean that such writers have 'consistently depicted both parents and children as martyrs', creating 'much ado about family sacrifice' to the imperial cause.[17] Some, like John Harvey-Jones, do convey the genuine misery of years of separation and parents' 'woeful misunderstanding ... of how a child of six or seven perceives life'.[18] Others suggest gently that 'parents of Empire-born children ... never seemed to understand how much we loved the places where we spent our formative years'.[19] And many simply evoke the spirit of their childhood in glowing images like Hilda Reid's drawings of 'Father Being Happy' and 'Jungle Tales'.

More vivid than anything else, perhaps, is oral testimony. I acquired most of this by conducting over fifty interviews with Raj children from varying walks of life, tracked down by following up leads like a photograph displayed in a south Indian hotel converted from a family residence. It was four-year-old David Baker in a toy pedal car adorned with a Union Jack who first drew me to the children of the Raj. And I was eventually able to meet David's sister and sister-in-law. It has been more rewarding to talk to people than to rely on ready-made collections of interviews like Laurence Fleming's *Last Children of the Raj* (2004) or the oral history archives at the India Office Library and British Empire and Commonwealth Museum, useful though all these are. For I found that feelings were readily unlocked in the course of conversation. Two elderly sisters, daughters of a Hooghly River pilot, vied with each other to convey their far-off childhood experiences and both were reduced to tears by certain painful memories. As one woman answered questions about her missionary childhood in Calcutta she suddenly used some words of Bengali, a language she thought she had entirely forgotten. A man educated at a Roman Catholic school in India held up a bent finger which had been broken by the science master. Another ended by showing me a video of a moving service in the chapel of his old school at Shimla, which he and his wife had recently visited. After being interviewed separately three sisters said that the experience had 'started us talking about our childhoods in a way we never did before'.

Among the most valuable secondary sources are biographies of famous Britons whose youth was spent in India and in exile from it. Among them are the singers Peter Pears and Cliff Richard, actresses Vivien Leigh and Julie Christie, film-maker Lindsay Anderson, comedian Spike Milligan, broadcaster Mark Tully and many writers such as George Orwell, John Masters, M. M. Kaye, Rumer Godden and Tom Stoppard. It is sometimes difficult for biographers to weigh up the effects of a Raj childhood. Why did Lindsay Anderson film his 'startling social satire of the English public school system' (*If*, 1968) at Cheltenham College, traditionally a school for Anglo-Indian exiles like himself? Was the suicide of physicist Alan Turing anything to do with his painful early partings from India-based parents? Was Peter Pears's adult life affected by the fact that his real home as a boy was Lancing College, which he found 'very heaven'? And did Douglas Jardine learn the 'authoritarian approach' which characterised his cricket captaincy during his lonely years at Winchester College? This book provides a context for such questions.[20]

Historians of childhood have largely ignored the protracted separation which was part of Raj life and which was far more distressing than the common practices of sending children to boarding schools, to relations in the same country or into the nursery with nannies and ayahs. In 1974 Lloyd de Mause, an American 'psychohistorian', suggested that 'institutionalized abandonment' (such as the custom of apprenticing children in other households) died out by the eighteenth century. James Walvin's *A Child's World* (1982) does not mention separation at all, although it is concerned with many other forms of deprivation. Ivy Pinchbeck and Margaret Hewitt wrote about orphans being boarded out in barrack schools and young convicts being transported, but they did not suggest that anything comparable ever happened to upper- and middle-class children in English society.[21] Important works in the 1980s brought to light the practice of sending twentieth-century British orphans to Australia — a traumatic story but one involving far fewer children than are under scrutiny here.[22] Hugh Cunningham's *Children and Childhood in Western Society* (1995) mentioned but did not explore 'powerful forces ... which endorsed the separation from parents'.[23] Currently there is much interest among American sociologists in the offspring of expatriates, but these 'Third Culture Kids' differ from their Raj predecessors in that they are not usually parted from their parents.

In the course of my research, however, I consulted two unpublished academic dissertations which were relevant to my theme: Valentine Davies weighs up the psychological effects of an Indian childhood and Elizabeth Buettner examines 'the important role childrearing patterns and childhood experiences played in positioning families within cultural, racial, socioeconomic and geographical perimeters'.[24] (The latter also formed the basis for various articles and for a book, *Empire Families*, published in 2004.) My aim is simpler: to listen to children whose voices went unheard while parents were preoccupied by lofty matters of war, Empire, precedence and etiquette.

Fiction can help to reveal the secrets of a child's heart, especially when it is based on experience. Lee Langley's excellent *Changes of Address* arises from her own vagrant childhood with her alcoholic mother in India, while *Persistent Rumours* is based on lonely Anglo-Indian boys whom she knew. But some writers reject the stuff of childhood as subject-matter too mundane for adult fiction, as is illustrated by Carolyn Slaughter's recent novel, *A Black Englishman*. In an article she related the story of her grandmother, Anne Webb, who married a soldier soon after the First World War and went to live in India, where 'the harshness and loneliness of her life in the Punjab' gave her a nervous breakdown. Her husband promptly sent her back to Britain and consigned their two small children (including Slaughter's mother) to the same Himalayan military school which he had attended as a boy. 'Year after lonely year they endured its harsh discipline with no visits, no letters, no birthday cards or presents.'[25] Anne Webb managed to buy a passage back to see her children in India – only to be locked up in a mental asylum in Bihar. Carolyn Slaughter aimed to base a novel on her grandmother's life but, instead of using this touching story, she wrote a fast-paced romance with an unlikely plot in which the young woman has a love affair with an Indian doctor in the full glare of an army cantonment. The children do not feature in the novel at all.

Much more true to life is Jane Gardam's portrait of 'an emotionally crippled remnant of Empire' in *Old Filth*. Yet it does not equal Kipling's *Baa Baa, Black Sheep*, on which it is partly based. Gardam overdramatises the situation by introducing too many tragic factors: the child's mother is dead, his father never writes to him, his aunts will not have him to stay and his guardians abuse him. All these things happened to Raj children but they did not usually happen to the same person. And there was always some saving grace. 'It wasn't all misery', as Margaret Forster says in her fictional memoir of Thackeray. The young William forgot his homesickness when Aunt Becher bought him presents and took him on outings into the countryside where he took 'great pleasure in finding birds' nests and other boyish pursuits'.[26] He was cheered also by memories of India and drew for his aunt a picture of his house in Calcutta 'not omitting his monkey looking out of the window and Black Betty at the top drying her Towells'.[27]

Thackeray was not unusual in this source of consolation. Most Anglo-Indian children garnered something from the time they spent in India's 'large, warm embrace'.[28] This is true even for the two sad characters encountered in the second paragraph. Mary Lennox, whose Indian experiences are so bleakly portrayed by a writer who had never visited the subcontinent, could find in her memory a Hindustani lullaby to revive her sick cousin and the magic of her ayah's stories to enrich the secret garden. And Rudyard Kipling was able to use his vividly remembered time in India to convey in writing, as an Indian critic recognises, 'the many faces of that country in all their beauty, power and truth'. A paragraph from *Kim* typifies his achievement:

Kim was in the seventh heaven of delight. The Grand Trunk [Road] at this point was built on an embankment to guard against winter floods from the foothills, so that one walked, as it were, a little above the country, along a stately corridor, seeing all India spread out to left and right. It was beautiful to behold the many-yoked grain and cotton wagons crawling over the country roads: one could hear their axles, complaining a mile away, coming nearer, till with shouts and yells and bad words they climbed up the steep incline and plunged on to the hard main road, carter reviling carter. It was equally beautiful to watch the people, little clumps of red and blue and pink and white and saffron, turning aside to go to their own villages, dispersing and growing small by twos and threes across the level plain. Kim felt these things, though he could not give tongue to his feelings, and so contented himself with buying peeled sugar-cane and spitting the pith generously about his path.[29]

Images like these transcend the 'Raj nostalgia syndrome' decried by some modern historians.[30] For they were brought back in the hearts and memories of Raj children, to bring colour to a land they often found grey and comfortless. This book tells of the joys and the sorrows of a childhood divided between two continents.

ONE

'The Cure for the Heartache'

Children of the Nabobs

On the night of 1 May 1793 the Governor-General of India, Sir John Shore, had a terrifying dream. It was about his little daughter Caroline, whom he had left in England with his pregnant wife and their older daughter Charlotte. He dreamt that he was out walking with his 'dear girl' when, on stopping to speak to somebody, he found that she was missing.

> A ladder was erected against a house which was repairing, and I concluded she had ascended by it. I entered the house; and, on inquiring for the child, was told a coroner's inquest was sitting on the body of a dead infant. I hastened to the room, and was struck with the appearance of the dissevered limbs of a child, which I knew to be my own. I took up an arm; and the hand grasped my finger. I need not add that I awoke with a scream, and in an agony of tears.

Four months later, in September, a letter arrived by packet-boat from England telling him that Caroline and the new baby had died of measles on the very night of his dream. His only consolation, Sir John wrote to Lady Shore, was that the nightmare had helped 'to prepare and sadden . . . the heart, that it might not be broken by the sudden blow of so hard a calamity'. Already suffering all the 'pangs comprised in the word Separation', Sir John 'had a bitter time of it' for another year. Then his wife and Charlotte braved the 'risk of the climate and the dangers of the sea' to join him in Calcutta. For the rest of his five-year term of office this stern and humourless ruler was cheered by a child with a 'fund of spirits not to be tamed' and by two more babies who began their lives within the grand confines of Government House.[1]

The kind of trauma suffered by Sir John Shore was common to generations of Britons in India. They had first gone to the subcontinent, in the seventeenth century, not as rulers but as traders in the service of the East India Company. From its isolated trading posts the Company had established by the eighteenth century three areas of control (called Presidencies) around Calcutta, Madras and Bombay. Eventually Bengal, the hinterland of Calcutta and the largest of the conquered territories, gained ascendancy over the other two Presidencies and its Governor became known as the Governor-General. He wielded influence also in some independent Indian princely states, where his representatives were known from the 1790s as Residents. In the Company's three major cities and in the surrounding countryside employees served in its offices, armies, law courts, hospitals and churches – but not in schools, which the Company saw no need to supply. Both civil servants and military officers were allowed to engage privately in 'country trade' between India and other parts of Asia; thus a Calcutta surgeon, Andrew Hunter, admitted in 1771 that 'as well as serving the Company,' he was a 'fortune maker'.[2] The rewards were often so rich that their envious compatriots nicknamed Anglo-Indians *nabobs*, after *nawabs* (Indian princes). Like rajahs they lived extravagantly, dispensed lavish patronage to friends and relations, and expected to pass their rank and fortune on to their heirs. This last ambition gave rise to the acute difficulty which confronted Sir John Shore and all other Company officers: how to do the best for their offspring. Believing that children could not acquire in India the gentility, character or vigour needed for success, they felt compelled to leave them at home or send Indian-born offspring to be reared and educated in Britain. Emily Eden, the unmarried sister and companion of Governor-General Lord Auckland in the 1830s, felt sorry for the mothers of her acquaintance who 'are either parted from their children or feeling that they are doing wrong by keeping them here'; and she noted that young Anglo-Indians grew up strangers to their parents.[3] Thus parents jeopardized the emotional security of their children for the sake of their material prospects.

The difficulty was compounded by the fact that the children's future depended on their fathers' own safety, which was often at hazard in the service of 'John Company'. As Hunter's cousin Charles Stuart explained, he and other 'Bengal adventurers' risked all in 'this country, for it is a favourer of the Churchyard'.[4] Sailing ships making the long voyage around the Cape of Good Hope faced dangers from inadequate charts, hostile navies, pirates and hurricanes. On six journeys to and from India between 1768 and 1783 William Hickey narrowly survived storms and typhoons, outbreaks of scurvy, faulty Portuguese navigation and capture by the French – though he managed to avoid the alternative peril of deadly boredom by shooting sharks, albatrosses and any other wildlife in the vicinity.[5] Once in India young men could be felled at any moment by tropical diseases, the effects of excessive eating, drinking and fornicating, or wars against European and Indian rivals for power. Their wealth was as chancy as their health, vulnerable to bank collapses, business disasters and new Company regulations – such as the curbs placed on private trading and accepting gifts from Indian princes. Despite these perils the East India Company had no shortage of recruits and by the early nineteenth century 40,000 Britons lived in India. How did the nabobs cope with the problems of family life during the uncertain times of the American and French Revolutions and the Napoleonic Wars?

Older men going out for a limited term of office frequently left all the members of their family at home; but this solution could bring its own heartaches, as it did initially for Sir John Shore. The domestic fate of his successor as Governor-General, Lord Wellesley, was even less happy. His French wife, Hyacinthe, would not travel to India with him in 1798. Wellesley hoped that she, like Lady Shore, would change her mind. But she refused to alter her decision 'not to abandon my three sons in England, and risk the health and education of my two little daughters, by taking them to India with me'.[6] Wellesley soon began to find comfort in mistresses and prostitutes. These were not his only conquests. When his term of office ended in 1805 this ardent imperialist had fought, bullied or cajoled so many Indian princes into submission that Britain now controlled two-thirds of India. But he had lost his wife's affections and their marriage ended in 1810.

Younger men tended to delay marriage – though this did not necessarily mean a postponement of paternity. Like many of their contemporaries in Britain, Andrew Hunter and Charles Stuart prudently put off marital bliss until they felt able to afford it. Their unpublished letters from India to a cousin back in Scotland focus obsessively on their hopes and ambitions. Stuart, who had gone to Calcutta as a 'writer' (clerk) in 1762, is last heard of in 1771 involved in a scheme for the purchase of lottery tickets, which sounds a lucrative venture. Hunter's final surviving letter was written in 1785, by which time he had served twenty-two years' 'banishment' as a Company surgeon. He was clearly living well, yet he was determined to stay on, pursuing various interesting concerns and helping out friends 'whose wishes may lead them to adventure in this part of the world'. Hunter was disappointed that he had not been promoted by the departing Governor-General, Warren Hastings, and was looking to his Scottish successor 'for favours'. We do not know whether he lived to succeed in this or in a more personal ambition expressed in a letter congratulating cousin James on his marriage. Hunter wrote that he himself was reserving 'that Joy' until such time as he had made enough money to support a family comfortably in his native country.[7]

There is no evidence that the cousins consoled themselves by indulging in the widespread eighteenth-century Anglo-Indian practice of keeping an Indian mistress – or even a whole *zenana*. The pious Shore himself, who had earlier spent fifteen lonely bachelor years in India, had just such a liaison, which produced three illegitimate children, John, Francis and Martha, baptised in 1777 and 1785.[8] Not surprisingly, the memoir composed by Charles, his son and heir, contains no mention of this. The fate of mixed-race offspring, which will be discussed in the next chapter, was frequently a sad one even though at that time no stigma automatically attached to being born on the wrong side of the blanket.

While the Scottish cousins in Calcutta apparently confined themselves to pursuing 'fair lady' Fortune,[9] Francis William Pemberton of Bombay managed to acquire both a handsome fortune and two broods of children. He was also a prolific writer of letters, which were carefully preserved by his father and then by his descendants. Sent out in 1771 to restore the family finances, the young Pemberton was initially so sick at heart and in body that he soon took a boat back to England. His father apparently stiffened his resolve through 'well-timed severity' and by January 1774 the 'idle fellow' (as he called himself) had returned to Bombay, determined now to be 'more diligent'. Then, as often happened, his ambitions grew as new opportunities for profit arose. He did particularly well as Commissary to the Army which was fighting Tipu Sultan in the south in 1791 and as Custom Master of Bombay after 1792. So he prolonged his stay in India, where he had built an 'elegant and commodious' new house, until such time as he had made 'a fortune, to enable me to live as I should wish, and to indulge myself with the delight of assisting my relations'. After all, he continued, 'India is now as healthy as any part of the world'.[10]

Pemberton was less optimistic about the salubrity of Bombay where his four sons were concerned. Born to his half-Armenian wife between 1778 and 1783, they were sent home to his father's care at the age of two or three on the grounds that 'this climate is rather unfavourable to children and the sooner they get out of it the better'.[11] The first to go was two-year-old Frank, 'the sweetest little rogue that ever was seen', consigned in 1781 to the care of Mr Scrocold and a 'slave' for a journey of over six months on board the *Prime*. The agony of such a separation is vividly conveyed in the letter Francis Pemberton wrote to his father just before Frank's departure:

> Convinced that you will love and dote upon my dearest child, I am almost ashamed to say, my dear Father, take care of him because I am sure you would do it without being asked, but you must excuse me; my foolish heart bleeds for him; poor little dear! He will suffer many inconveniences before he is received into your affectionate home; however I am determined and he must go.

Jerry, Harry and Tom followed him back to England, so that the old Cambridgeshire mansion rang with the cries of children again.

Pemberton hoped that his father's 'strict propriety' would be tempered by the motherly attentions of the family nurse, 'good old Waller'. But she died before the boys arrived, as did his mother.[12] The result was that his sons experienced little in the way of feminine tenderness, for his younger sisters would soon leave home to be married. Pemberton forbade his wife all access to the children because she had engaged in some misconduct, its nature undisclosed but sufficient to warrant his denouncing her as 'so infamous a monster'. And he would not allow the boys to live with his older sister Anne Ward, whose son he had sponsored in India. Evidently she lacked 'that steadiness and uniformity of conduct necessary to be observed towards children' and would not therefore mould their characters appropriately.[13] Pemberton expressed anxiety that the care of 'such little fellows' would prove troublesome to his father, by which he probably meant that their upbringing would be too stern. Yet despite his real concerns and his many laments at losing them, Pemberton does not seem to have written to the boys. Moreover he visited them only once, in 1790, when he brought his five-year-old daughter Charlotte to England. She was 'stout and hearty', even though he had kept her in India for longer than was normal, as he explained in 1786:

> I consider her an object of compassion for the misfortune she has experienced in the loss of a mother at so early a period – she is the image of my poor dear lost Jerry [who had died in 1784] and of course like Frank. The mention of my children overpowers me; I ardently long to see them; but prudence I am determined shall guide me.

He told his father that he would not 'encumber' him with this further charge but would leave the little girl with his brother Henry, who had known her as a baby when he himself was in India.[14]

As it happened, Henry Pemberton died in 1793 and Charlotte was sent to one of the married sisters, a temporary arrangement pending Pemberton's planned return to England. She was presumably still there when her father himself died in June 1794. Francis Pemberton succumbed to a liver complaint, which was an occupational hazard of nabob life and particularly common in Bombay.[15] Frank was by then at Eton and the two youngest boys were at school in Suffolk. From the family tree and from other family correspondence we learn that none of the sons followed their father into the East India Company's service as he had wished. Frank and Harry went into the Army and Tom ended up in prison for debt. Charlotte married a clergyman at the unusually late age of age of thirty.[16] But because the archive contains no correspondence to or from the children we can only guess at how they felt about their lack of parental care. What does emerge clearly is the fact that their emotional needs were less important than the Pemberton fortunes and good name. It was normal in this period for a family's welfare to take precedence over the individual interests of its members. Francis William guarded the Pemberton name so carefully that in his letters he never mentioned the existence of a second, illegitimate Bombay family. Its branches will be traced in the next chapter, thus filling a blank space in the 'Pemberton Pedigrees', as they called the family tree.

A still more revealing record of eighteenth-century parent-child relationships is a set of letters sent by Hew Stuart from distant Sumatra, where the East India Company controlled a trading post called Fort Marlborough. About once a year between 1775 and 1781 Stuart wrote to his young daughter Anny, who was initially at an Edinburgh board-ing establishment known as Mrs Fergus's House and later with Scottish relations among whom she could be 'introduced to a more general and genteel acquaintance'. Anny carefully preserved these letters. They must have been all the more precious to her since she was separated not only from her parents but also from her three siblings, Mary, Davie and Betsey, who were under the care of cousins in London. Stuart's letters frequently stress the need for academic and moral progress, a constant preoccupation in Anglo-Indian correspondence: 'I had great pleasure in receiving from all my friends such good accounts of your health and Mary's, and that you both improve so much in your edu-cation. . . . Continue, my Dear, in this line, to make me happy and yourself esteem'd by all your acquaintance.'[17] The tone was always one of affection, frequently confirmed by the exchange of presents; Anny made her father a fine waistcoat and he procured for her a small box of beautiful shells.

Stuart seemed to understand Anny's longing for her parents; for when telling her of his promotion to the Governorship of Fort Marlborough he tried to console her with the thought that by staying a little longer in India he would be adding to his fortune. At the same time he demonstrated a disregard for juvenile sensibilities remarkable even by eighteenth-century standards by failing to let Anny know at once of her mother's death. Mrs Stuart had died in 1778 and in his letter of 25 May 1779 he did not send the usual love from Mama. Only when he wrote on 20 September 1780 did he break the tragic news, attempting to justify his omission by his own anguish: 'This stroke affected me with a most tender grief and might perhaps have prevented me from mentioning it to you. Her care of you all was most exemplary, affectionate and proper which will ever make her memory dear to me.'[18] The loss was compounded in 1782. In that year Anny and her siblings heard that their father had died during his passage home from India. Governor Stuart left £12,500 to be shared between the three surviving children, not a very large fortune by nabob standards. To remind her of her lost parents Anny also had her mother's tortoiseshell box as well as the precious letters which have been passed down through the generations.

Most of the correspondence from this period is couched in the language of duty and propriety. Yet freer and franker expressions of feeling do occur, as in the letters written from Calcutta by Dr William Dick and his wife Charlotte to their dear friends, Allan and Eliza

Macpherson. Lieutenant-Colonel Macpherson had to leave India in 1787 after he was ruined in business dealings. Charlotte wrote chatty letters to Eliza about her babies, her miscarriages, her longing for a little girl and her enjoyment of the gay life of Calcutta – 'nothing but Balls every night all the cold season'.[19] William told Allan of his plans to build a 'madhouse' in Calcutta and complained of the heavy expense of maintaining both his immediate family, five sons and a daughter, and his twenty sisters and brothers back home 'without education or money'. Amid these concerns, eloquently expressed, both parents agonised over the perennial dilemma of what to do with their children.

In March 1792 Mrs Dick found it a severe trial to part with the three oldest boys, who would have 'nobody but strangers to take charge of them'. At the same time she was convinced that the delicate three-year-old Alexander could not live another year in India. Dr Dick voiced the regrets of all Anglo-Indian parents in a letter sent home on the same ship as his boys: 'I can neither have the pleasure of superintending their education, of rejoicing at their improvements, of watching over their health, or of securing their affection, but must trust the whole to Strangers and can be known to my own children only by name.' But he was determined not to let his longing for their company 'operate to their prejudice'.[20] By 1796 the Dicks were 'exceedingly distressed' about the fate of the next three children now that the French wars made the sea journey even more dangerous than usual. The doctor doubted whether his wife would part with their 'little Beauty' Eliza, 'as so many French frigates have appeared in India of late'. Reluctantly he decided that Eliza and her two younger brothers must go back and that Mrs Dick should accompany them, even though parting from her would be 'very disagreeable' for him.[21] At this point the letters peter out and it is not clear whether the painful separation was necessary, since the whole Dick family had returned to Britain by 1800.

The new century brought them fresh anxieties. Perhaps needing to recoup the family fortunes, William Dick went back to India in 1806 as doctor to the Dundas family. He took with him only his third son, Alexander, now a sixteen-year-old lad, who had belied his father's fear that he would be a stranger to his own offspring. However, a more terrible fate was at hand:

> His prospects were very great, being the senior writer on his Establishment, his talents very very good and his disposition the most amiable. ... His dutiful and affectionate attachment to me was

beyond anything I had any idea of. He was taken ill immediately after we left England [and] he breathed his last in my arms four days before our arrival here. ... He passed his short life in the most innocent and virtuous manner impressed always with the strongest sense of religion.

At the same time as he endured this bereavement, the doctor's mind was 'upon the rack' over his oldest son, Robert, who was fighting the French on the Continent. Six years later he despaired of ever seeing 'the poor boy' again, for Europe was 'a scene of perpetual fighting'.[22] In fact, Robert was wounded at the Battle of Waterloo but he survived and went on to become a major-general. Meanwhile the second son, William, had followed in his father's footsteps to Bengal, where he had his own family and relived some of his parents' experiences. Thus evolved one of many Anglo-Indian dynasties, whose ramifications were legion – for Anglo-Indians, like European royalty and the English Whigs, seemed to be 'all cousins'.

Related to the Dicks in various ways over the generations was the Macnabb family. Dr James Macnabb, another member of the Bengal Medical Service, married Charlotte Dick's sister Mary and in 1818 his daughter Eliza was to marry the Dicks' soldier son Robert. By the time of Eliza's birth in 1796, her older brother James Munro had already been sent to live with guardians in England and two of his childhood letters survive in the huge Macnabb archive housed in the India Office Library. The first, penned in a six-year-old's large copperplate writing, vividly evokes the childhood concerns and excitements of the age:

My dear Mama Reid says I must write to you but I am ashamed because I cannot write so well. I wish to hear my dear Papa and Mama that you are well. My Papa and Mama Reid are so very good to me I am very happy. They took me to *The Cure for the Heart-Ache* and they promise to take me to Astley's [Circus] and to the Top of St. Paul's. At the play I saw a Man made into a candle and the clown burnt it, and Harlequin conjured him into an apple tree and he jumped out alive. ... I hope dear Papa and Mama you will write to me and direct the letter to me, and I will try to make my next better. I am dear Papa and Mama your Dutiful son James Mac Nabb.[23]

The play, with its poignant title, was clearly a treat provided by his kind guardians to cheer up the little boy. He seems to have enjoyed the outing but he must have been disappointed that so few of the parental letters he longed for ever came. In 1800 James thanked his grandmother for passing on news of his parents' good health – as well as describing further treats with the Reids, including an exciting popular play about the death of Tipu Sultan.

There is no evidence that James saw his parents before he himself joined the East India Company after leaving Rugby School at the age of sixteen. He describes here the family reunion in Patna (up the Ganges from Calcutta):

> I found my father looking out for me at the riverside at eight-o-clock at night. Our meeting was as you may suppose very joyful, but then I had the worst to brave, on approaching the house I found my poor dear Mother fainting away on the terrace and . . . she really would not believe that it was her James for a long while. However here I am as happy as a prince.[24]

The loyal James did not repay his uncommunicative parents in kind; while attending the East India Company's college at Fort William in Calcutta he wrote to them frequently, as he did while on an official tour of north India with the Governor-General, Lord Hastings, in 1814–15. Despite his initial feeling (expressed in the letter to the Reids) that Calcutta women were 'a set of cats that have been withering away for these last ten years', he found a wife there in 1820. She was Jane Campbell, who had come out to India in 1818 with her cousin, Flora, wife of the Governor-General.

The history of their early married years (living in the Macnabb parents' old house in Calcutta) illustrates vividly the continuing perils of Anglo-Indian life. Jane's correspondence reveals how much she longed for home despite the help and comfort she received from the fatherly 'old peer' (Lord Hastings) and from Lady Hastings, who was present at the birth of her first child. In a moving letter to his parents James reports the death of that child, also named Flora, at the age of six months:

> She was the companion and delight of our days and she smiled and slept by our side at night. . . . Under the tamarind trees nearest to the garden I dug her grave. It was not what the world may call consecrated ground but in my heart every spot that surrounds this house is consecrated by recollections of parental love, and in this

foreign clime I have a melancholy pleasure in the thought that my child was permitted to breathe its last in the house which my father had built and so long had inhabited.

By 1828 they had lost another baby; but they also had two healthy girls. In the meantime they had heard sad news of James's cousin, 'poor dear William Dick' (Dr Dick's second son), whose first two children had died. James expressed the hope that if the Dicks were blessed with a further family 'they will not hesitate to send their children at once to England'. The Macnabbs, however, did not have to face this dilemma. In 1831 they were obliged to return to Britain when James lost, in a Calcutta bank collapse, the huge fortune of over £60,000 he had made during a successful career ending in his appointment as Commissioner of Revenue. Their greatest consolation in all these severe trials was the enduring familial love so often expressed in their letters. Three of their seven surviving children went out to India and demonstrated in their turn the truth of their mother's assertion that people cannot easily 'divest themselves of associations and impressions received in childhood'.[25] Their story amply bears out a historian's claim that 'distance did not dissolve kinship ties'.[26]

However, this rule had its exceptions. The eventful saga of George Hilaro Barlow and his family shows that family bonds did not always withstand the severe stresses of an Anglo-Indian career. Barlow joined the Bengal Civil Service in 1778 and rose to become Chief Secretary to the Government in 1796 and a member of the Governing Council in 1801. Sir George, as he had now become, was well placed to step into the shoes of the Governor-General, Lord Cornwallis, who died soon after arriving in India in 1805. But the Whig Government which took over in London after the death of Barlow's patron, Prime Minister William Pitt, refused to ratify his appointment and he was replaced in 1807. His consolation prize was the Governorship of Madras but he lost this position too after a dispute with the Army, culminating in the 'white mutiny' of 1809. On his return to Britain after thirty-three years, during which 'his official labours have scarcely known the intermission of a day', Barlow had not made the fortune normally expected by East-India men of his time.[27]

According to his contemporary William Hickey, this 'cold, distant and formal' man also lacked 'a single friend in the world' – though this opinion may have been influenced by snobbish Calcutta gossip that Barlow was the son of a silk mercer and that he really belonged behind a counter. Hickey's memoir also gloats over his evident incompetence. In 1801 thousands of undelivered letters were discovered in Chief Secretary Barlow's office. Some were addressed to, and some had been sent from, England, but they had been opened, presumably by corrupt clerks on Barlow's staff, and then just left to gather dust in cupboards. 'The whole settlement were delighted at hearing that there were a great many of Mr George Barlow's letters among them,' recorded Hickey.[28] It is difficult to share in the diarist's malicious pleasure, though, when one realises that some of Barlow's many children were in England awaiting replies to their laboriously written missives. Nor does it quite fit in with Hickey's judgement of the man that Barlow carefully preserved all his children's letters, which now form the basis of a large collection in the India Office Library. They reveal much about the contemporary problems of Anglo-Indian life for parents, children and guardians.

During the course of his Indian career Barlow and his wife Elizabeth produced fifteen children and by 1801 the three oldest had been sent home. Eliza was living with a sickly great-aunt in London and her brothers George and William were at a school run by Mr Roberts, spending their holidays with Barlow's brother, their Uncle William. The most frequent correspondent among these offspring was Eliza, and to judge from her letters she was unhappy. She took pleasure in learning music only because she fancied that her mama was playing beside her. She felt that she had to thank her parents for wanting to have a picture of her. She anxiously promised to strive to do her best in everything and hoped that 'I shall deserve your kindness'.[29] However, Eliza cheered up in 1803 when another of Barlow's older brothers, the Revd Thomas, rescued her from this 'gloomy situation'. He reported that she 'did not manifest the most trifling symptoms of regret at leaving her aunt. . . . Eliza's great improvement, apparent to everyone who knew her before, is convincing proof that her former treatment must have been radically bad.' It probably helped that she had been joined by her sister Charlotte with whom she now attended a school in Twickenham run by the Misses Warwick and Dutton. Nevertheless her uncle's letters suggest that Eliza was still in rather a disturbed state: 'Eliza does not like school quite so much as her sister, as she cannot patiently submit to restraint and the constant but proper attention that is paid to her manners and disposition by the ladies who have the care of her education.'

Eliza grew to love and respect Uncle and Aunt Thomas, who found

her 'very much improved' over the years. But they were clearly perplexed about how best to bring her up for 'few people agree in opinion
as to the management of young ladies in the plan that ought to be
adopted in their education'.[30] By the time she was sixteen Eliza herself
reckoned she had had enough education and begged to be allowed to
return to India. Looking forward to her mother's long-promised
arrival, she expresses her confused feelings to her father with a
frankness unusual at the time:

> Though for these nine or ten years past I have not had the happiness
> of being under maternal care, and neither recollect you or her, my
> affection, instead of being diminished, is redoubled by your long
> absence. ... Though I shall now be under the care of my dearest
> mother I cannot help regretting my parting with Aunt Thomas, on
> account of her very great attention to us.

Her uncle's feelings on the matter were more straightforward. The
experience of looking after Eliza had convinced him that 'no care or
attention on the part of any other person can supply the place of a
parent'. Thus, in 1806, the kindly parson anticipated the theme of this
book.[31]

Meanwhile Eliza's brothers had also been receiving avuncular, in
lieu of parental, care. Finding his eleven-year-old nephew William
'idle' and unable 'to encounter the least difficulty', William Barlow
had passed him on to another uncle, Admiral Sir Robert Barlow.[32] The
Admiral found the boy a place in the Royal Navy and sent him to sea.
Two years later he sent him to the Naval Academy at Gosport but had
to report, rather despairingly, that the lad disliked 'the restraints of
school' and 'is not over given to *application*'.[33] In his short, poorly
spelt letters to his parents the young William expressed gratitude for
his uncle's attentions but longed for 'the time when I shall behold you
after such a long absence'.[34] George, a much more academic boy, went
to Eton at the age of fourteen. From there he wrote his father extremely
long, formal and over-elaborate letters assuring him that he would
exert himself to the best of his powers and disapproving of school-
fellows who wasted their time keeping dogs and playing football, a
game which he considered 'childish and productive of quarrels'.[35]
Another view of George is provided by Uncle William, who seems to
have cared deeply for the lad. He worried that George's 'strength is
not equal to his spirits and his exertions' and that he often came home

for the holidays 'with a cough, much fatigued and very thin'.

Meanwhile more young Barlows continued to arrive in England. In 1803 Henry and Robert followed their older brothers into the care of Mr Roberts. Uncle William assumed responsibility for them and formed a particular 'affection and attachment' for Robert. As the years went on, however, William Barlow complained to his brother of the weighty financial and pastoral burden of his nephews, all of whom 'give way to most violent passion'. It is not difficult to imagine the problems he was having with Henry and Robert in 1805, when they had reached 'the most troublesome age [ten and eight], too old for the nursery and too young for the parlour'. The next batch of three children (Louisa, Charles and Fanny) were 'delivered' in 1805 after a difficult voyage during which the ship's captain had dismissed the people in charge of them and taken over their care himself. It was a miracle, thought William Barlow, that so many of his brother's children had arrived home safely in time of war. He could not help adding, while congratulating the couple on the birth of another little girl, 'I think you have now almost children enough.'[36]

Eventually, in 1807, Lady Barlow set off for England in 'an elegant little vessel [engaged] for the purpose'.[37] She was accompanied by Harriet, Richard and Anne, as well as by Captain George Pratt Barlow, her husband's young cousin and aide-de-camp. The twelve children were reunited in Wood Lodge at Streatham, which William Barlow had acquired and set up at great expense as a family home. It was complete with 'two footmen, a coachman and a helper in the stable, a gardener and how many woman servants I know not'. A governess, Miss Page, was hired for the girls and Lady Barlow gave birth to another son, Edward. Yet instead of staying to look after her children, so that they 'should not be brought up strangers to both their parents', she decided to return to India after less than a year. Had she (as William Barlow hinted) found it to hard to cope with her 'boys at their riotous age'?[38] Did she feel it her duty to be at her husband's side after his loss of the Governor-Generalship? Or were there, as later events suggest, other attractions to life in India? In any case, 'dearest Mama' departed in spring 1808, taking with her, on the strong advice of her brothers-in-law, her two oldest daughters. The baby and toddler were left with Elizabeth's mother in Bath. All the others remained in the Streatham house, which was now taken over by William Barlow and his motherly but delicate wife – who had no children of their own.

It is clear that William Barlow had mixed feelings about assuming this task. After the birth of two more Barlow infants in Madras his heart sank. 'When I look at my list and see how many there are to be thought of it calls forth all my exertion.' He was spending so much time and attention on his brother's family that his own business was 'a secondary task'. Often he found the assembled young Barlows with their 'high and restless spirits' hard to manage, particularly when there were quarrels among them or outbreaks of illnesses like whooping cough.[39] Sometimes he had to mediate between the boys and their stern though absent father, as when George pleaded to be allowed to enter the Army. His counsel was particularly valuable when Henry was involved in a riot at Haileybury (the East India Company's training college), though he was 'very sensible of his error' and anxious to 'wipe off the stains' from his character.[40]

What principally drove William Barlow on was Duty. He often expressed the thought that he was serving both his country and his family by assisting that 'great and good man', his brother. But something gentler, more affectionate and more beneficial to the children also comes through the correspondence – he cared about them and he often enjoyed their company. He was touched that George 'looks up to me as his sincere friend', amused that 'my little Richard can do nothing less than be a Lord Chancellor' and proud of Henry, whom he saw off from Portsmouth when he went out to India as a Company writer.[41] The younger children's letters suggest a happy household at Streatham. The boys wrote of enjoying their Christmas and summer holidays there and the girls, who were taught at home by Miss Page, flourished. Louisa catches the scene at the beginning of the Regency period: 'Our evenings are always very pleasant; we go down to Aunt and Uncle every day after dinner and Uncle dances with us: indeed they are both very kind to us. . . . I wish you could take a peep at us sometimes when we are dancing for we are so happy and merry.'[42] The Revd Thomas Barlow confirmed this impression after a visit to Streatham, where he found a 'most happy and cheerful party'.[43] It seems that once the family situation became established after 1808, the remaining children were more secure and settled than their three older siblings had been in the early years. As there are no surviving letters from the parents it is hard to establish their involvement in the children's upbringing. The main clue is the children's frequently expressed anxiety to impress on their father that they are as diligent and as studious as he would wish. I can find no evidence that Elizabeth Barlow wrote to her children after her return to India in 1808.

By 1813 Sir George's Indian career had come to an end and both parents set off for home. They were accompanied by Emma and Frederick (the two youngest children) and Major Barlow (the promoted aide-de-camp), and they spent three months at St Helena en route. Once they took over the Streatham household it soon became apparent that family bonds had been damaged over the years. According to William Barlow, Lady Barlow 'behaved with great unkindness towards Sir George and to all her children excepting Frederick the youngest son'. Miss Page observed that 'in any of our little excursions she never will be persuaded to join us'. Lady Barlow would not visit the children in their schoolroom but preferred to stay in her own little drawing room, to which Major Barlow was a frequent visitor. It was not long before Miss Page surprised Lady Barlow in this room with 'one hand placed upon [the Major's] thigh and apparently engaged with the other in buttoning the lower part of his pantaloons which were military ones and made in the usual way with buttons and chains'. Later the governess intercepted love letters and, confronted with this evidence, Elizabeth Barlow admitted that 'she had been in the habit of criminality' with Major Barlow for the last six years and that Frederick was his child. She then departed to her mother's house in Bath (with or without Frederick – we do not know) and Sir George sued for a divorce, which was granted in 1816.

There is no evidence to explain what drove Elizabeth Barlow to risk losing her children, the inevitable fate of a divorced woman in those days. Early and prolonged separation may well have deadened her love for them – or perhaps her husband really was the monster depicted by Hickey. In any case, the young Barlows had lost the Mama for whom they had yearned over so many years. Sir George, on the other hand, seems to have established good relations with them; the divorce papers recount that in the evening he 'usually sat in the School Room with his daughters'.[44] The archive also contains much correspondence from his children as they grew up and from his grandchildren. His son Charles, for instance, wrote frequently to convey the joys and miseries of life in the Royal Navy which he joined as a midshipman in 1813 at the age of thirteen.

It is not, of course, possible to calculate accurately the effects on the children of their fractured family life; nevertheless the tragic fates suffered by the three oldest Barlows may be partly attributed to their difficult early years. The refractory William did not settle down at naval college and was sent instead to Haileybury, from which he was expelled for bad behaviour in 1809. Admiral Barlow then helped him to get back into the Navy, exhorting him to 'do all in his power to redeem the past time'.[45] Nothing more is heard of him until a letter from George attempting to console his father after his 'poor brother finally had left this for a better world'.[46] It seems that William had died in a shipboard accident in 1811. George himself, who had never been very strong, had tried all too hard to do his duty to family and country. He was frequently ill and twice wounded during the Peninsular War, returning to action after being nursed back to health under Uncle William's devoted care. He fought in the Battle of Waterloo in 1815 and then went to serve in India. Here he died in 1824 soon after marrying his cousin Hilaire, one of Admiral Robert Barlow's daughters.

Eliza's story is the most surprising. Soon after returning to India in 1808 with her mother (whose love affair may well have been apparent to her) she married Captain Pownoll Bastard Pellew and came back to England with him. Her brothers and sisters in Streatham mention the pleasure of seeing Eliza, the Captain and 'our little nephew' in 1812.[47] Two more children were born but then everything went wrong. By 1816 her father was upbraiding her for her 'revolting and insupportable behaviour' towards her husband and for 'throwing away all the good fortune and all the blessings which have been showered upon you'. Neither Eliza's letters (written in an increasingly illegible hand) nor Sir George's reveal exactly what happened. But the marital crisis ended with a legal separation in 1819. According to the laws of the day Eliza lost her 'three darlings' and she seems also to have been spurned by her own family: 'I consider their behaviour to me altogether as the height of unkindness but this is forgiven most cordially.'[48] She died in 1833 at the age of forty-four.

The fate of her sisters is more usual for their time: Charlotte married an Indian Army officer and had several children; Emma and Louisa died young; Fanny, Anne and Harriet lived long lives as spinsters. All the remaining boys went into the Bengal Civil Service, Richard and Robert surviving long enough to have their own children, who were duly sent from India into the care of their grandfather and one of their maiden aunts. In 1846, for instance, Fanny gave her father detailed reports from Hastings of teaching Robert and Richard's boys to swim and to shoot: they were 'getting on famously'.[49] After Sir George's death later that year Fanny seems to have shouldered the responsibility alone.

It was normal during Georgian and Regency times for family members to take on the care of 'Indian children', even when this proved an almost overwhelming burden. Nevertheless, as the number of potential charges increased the practice of private fostering grew, as a further case study indicates. In 1817 William Prinsep went to work for a shipping business in Calcutta, where his brother Henry was already employed and where he was in due course joined by four more siblings. William had sent four sons to his sister Emily in England by 1834, when he and his wife made the homeward journey with another son and a daughter. As he wrote in an unpublished memoir:

> The principal object of our coming home was how best to relieve my sister of her responsible charge of my boys who were now fast growing to an age beyond her power of control. I had therefore to advertise and to read answers of men desirous of such means of occupying themselves ... and then it was difficult to select the best man for the purpose. ... I think it was the most unsatisfactory and harassing job I ever had in my life.

Eventually the Prinseps found 'an excellent clergyman' in Richmond and were able to leave their children (including four-year-old Harry) 'with heavy hearts indeed in their new home, each with some present to remind them of their parents, who were unable to tell them when they would meet again'. In 1837, however, the arrangement broke down when the clergyman accepted a living in Kent and it was Emily Prinsep's task to find her nephews 'a fresh home with Mr Furlong in Berkshire, but it was only a school and not a very successful one'. It is not clear what happened to the boys after 1839, when the school burnt down and young Harry Prinsep was the last boy to be saved as the ladder broke when Furlong was bringing him down from the window of his room.[50] Their aunt seems still to have been involved in their upbringing in 1840 when William sent back their 'impulsive, high-spirited' daughter Amelia 'to add to dear Emily's other cares'. Later in the same year the oldest son, William, became a further burden. He had gone to join his parents in India, developed a diseased liver (as a result of being 'too great a favourite in our social circle') and had to return to England, 'a terrible addition to the labour and anxieties of my dear good sister Emily'.

Prinsep was conscious that fortune had played a role in the survival of his children. When he finally left India in 1842 (with two more children) he thanked his Creator 'for thus finally bringing us back with so much health to the arms of our dear ones ... [although] still there remained the heavy anxiety about the life of our first born'. Luckily young William recovered when fed with lamb chops, leading Prinsep to conclude that his ailment stemmed from malnutrition and 'that he was saved from being starved to death'. The fond father did not recognise Amelia when he passed her in the hall and his 'big boys [had] grown into young men'.[51] As is natural in a memoir, Prinsep concentrates throughout on his own feelings, assuming that he and his wife felt the partings more keenly than his children. With no other evidence to go by, we can only guess at the reactions of his offspring to their long absence from their parents.

No doubt the youngsters who feature in these stories enjoyed the adventurous journeys, exotic presents from the East, news of their parents' activities and the attentions of kind guardians. But the sudden partings from familiar surroundings and beloved ayahs, the lack of a settled home, the long separations and the infrequency of communication must have taken a psychological toll. The childhood letters of William Makepeace Thackeray to the 'dearest of all dear Mamas' may betray little emotion:

> Your old acquaintances are very kind to me and give me a great many Cakes, and great many Kisses but I do not let Charles Becher kiss me. I only take those from the Ladies. . . . I am grown a great Boy I am three feet 11 inches and a quarter high. I have got a nice boat. . . . I am very glad I am not to go to Mrs Arthur's [the school where he had been unhappy]. I have lost my Cough and am quite well, strong, saucy, and hearty; and can eat Granmamas Goosberry pyes famously after which I drink to yours and my Papa's Good health and a speedy return.[52]

Yet when the little boy met his mother on her return from India in 1819 he was so overcome that he could not speak. The adult Thackeray never forgot the early parting from his mother. In an essay written towards the end of his life describing the sight of a farewell between a mother and two little boys in black, he admitted: 'I smart the cruel smart again: and boy and man, have never been able to bear the sight of people parting from their children'.[53] Thus we must still ask the question which nabob parents did not seem to ask themselves: did the heartache of being sent home outweigh any benefits it might have brought?

*

The benefit most often cited both then and now is better health. Visitors to Indian graveyards are always struck by the tragic head-stones commemorating children's deaths. Among about 1,500 British graves in Calcutta's South Park Cemetery one carries a typical inscription:

> *To the memory of a Child*
> *Who died AD 1787*
> *His Father's pleasure and his Mother's pride*
> *Belov'd he lived and lamented died*

It may well be true that at this time 'Europeans abroad were more likely to die from disease than those at home.'[54] In addition to the illnesses which killed thousands in England (typhoid, diphtheria, whooping cough, tuberculosis, scarlet fever and simple diarrhoea), diseases like tropical malaria and cholera could also prove fatal. Small-pox was a diminishing scourge thanks to the practice of inoculation, which was widespread in both Asia and Europe well before Edward Jenner pioneered his famous vaccination in 1796.[55] Dr Dick wrote from Calcutta about having one of his sons inoculated in 1787 and Mrs Sophie Plowden's diary refers to having eighteen-month-old William inoculated in 1789 'without any problem', except that he suffered a mild 'dose of smallpox' a few days later.[56] In other respects conditions seem to have become more dangerous in India in the late eighteenth century with the settlement of the unhealthy Bengal delta and the increasing incidence of cholera. There were not yet any cool hill stations to escape to in the hot weather, during which medical men advised Anglo-Indians to don flannel underwear, a measure which cannot have helped children to avoid the 'prickly heat' to which letters and journals often refer.

And, of course, outlandish dangers lurked in every Indian garden, as is illustrated in a letter by Charles Grant of the East India Company. He and his wife had already lost two 'sweet little daughters' to smallpox within nine days of each other in 1776. Their 'desolated home' was soon brightened by the arrival of more children, one of whom had a 'remarkable escape' in 1784:

> Running into a grassy part of the garden, where a little summer-house stands, [Charles] trod upon a large cobra, which reared its head upon him; but the rapidity of his motion had, in the same

moment, carried him into the summer-house. Had not a gracious God prevented, how easily might this accident have spread desolation among us! The child felt the snake soft under his foot, which was bare. May God bless and sanctify the life which he had preserved.

In fact, Charles survived his remaining time in India, as did Maria, Robert, Charity Emilia (known as Charemile) and a baby born shortly before the family's departure for England in 1790. Grant's biographer commented that the children were 'remarkably well and carefully raised', although 'rather old for residence in India'. There is no evidence to show whether their survival was due to the fact that their father had become 'a sincere and consistent Christian' after the loss of his first two infants.[57] Nor are there specific death-rate statistics for British children in India at this time. But archives as well as gravestones indicate that early death was common.

On the other hand, infant mortality was high in Britain too and parents were not necessarily protecting their children by sending them away. Of those who feature in this chapter Jerry Pemberton, Betsey Stuart, Alexander Dick and Emma Barlow died in childhood after arriving in Britain. Warren Hastings, India's first Governor-General between 1774 and 1784, suffered a similar bereavement. In 1761 (when he was already a widower) Hastings sent his only surviving child, George, to be educated by the Revd George Austen (the future father of Jane Austen). Three years later Austen married Cassandra Leigh, who became so devoted to the child that, when he died of diphtheria in 1764, 'she declared that his death had been as great a grief to her as if he had been a child of her own.'[58] Hastings did not hear of George's death until he landed in England in 1765. It is said that the news left a shadow on his face for years and (unlike the Austens) he never had any more children, even after his second marriage.

In addition to illness in Britain the young exiles risked shipwreck on the way there. Francis Pemberton did not learn until 1783 the story of his son Frank's escape from death when the *Prime* sprang a leak at St Helena in 1781. Mr Scrocold had saved his life 'by risking his own in a small boat in a gale of wind. . . . He took the dear child out of her and carried him safe on board the *Jason*.'[59] The seven-year-old son of the eminent Bengal judge, Sir Robert Chambers, was not so lucky; he lost his life after the *Grosvenor* was wrecked off the east coast of Africa in August 1782. Tom Chambers had been sent off with family friends while four other youngsters had been entrusted to the care of the captain for the same voyage. News of the wreck did not reach Calcutta until August 1783, when rumours were spread by gossips like William Hickey that the passengers had been 'murdered or carried prisoners into the interior of the country by the natives' after being cast ashore.[60] But no one dared to tell Sir Robert and his wife until February 1784, after which Lady Chambers recorded in her diary: 'Went into mourning for my dear unhappy Thomas'.[61] Elsewhere she wrote down a consoling quotation from the Bible: 'The deep shall give up her dead and the pure in spirit shall see their God.' A recent historical investigation reveals no evidence of African brutality towards the passengers and concludes that most (including young Tom) simply died 'of starvation, exhaustion or despair, somewhere along that shore'.

Something is known of the fate of one of the other children on board. A survivor told an inquiry in 1783 the story of Thomas Law, the Eurasian son of a wealthy East India Company man, who was en route to Britain for his education. This homesick child had formed an attachment to the ship's steward, Henry Lillburne, who declared after the wreck that 'he would save the boy's life or lose his own'. Apparently the steward and other crew members took turns in carrying the lad when he grew weary but their efforts were unavailing. Young Thomas died on 3 November 1782 and Lillburne survived him for just three days. They were only about forty miles from the Dutch farm where six castaways reached safety.[62]

Another danger on board these wooden sailing vessels was fire. Lady Nugent's journal tells of the plight of 'a great number of wretched little Indian children and their ayahs' who had to be taken on board the *Astell* in 1811 after losing everything in a fire on their own ship. Maria Nugent, who was sorely missing her own children from whom she had been separated for four years, took the young passengers under her wing. At the Cape she bought frocks and bonnets for three of the little girls so that they would 'make a more decent and comfortable appearance when they see their friends in England'.[63] These children were lucky to find a protector, for unaccompanied minors did not always fare so well. A major's widow, Mrs Doherty, travelling home in 1820 with her two little boys was too preoccupied with her own troubles to help a couple of youngsters who had no parents or servants with them. Four-year-old Billy was constantly teased by the

'Gentlemen' on board while his 'delicate, elegant' seven-year-old sister, Amelia, became 'the color of Mahogany more from *dirt* than sun-burn' and 'as rude and ill-bred as possible'.[64] Even naval officers' children got out of control during sea voyages: Mrs Mansfield, the wife of a ship's captain who went to sea with her husband during the Napoleonic Wars, wore a dress with epaulettes to match the captain's uniform but 'her shipmates remarked that her powers of command did not extend' to her two daughters.[65]

It is easy to forget that children had as much reason to fear the death of their parents as vice versa; a tally of burials in Park Street Cemetery, Calcutta between 1814 and 1833 shows very high numbers in the twenty-one to thirty age group.[66] The Doherty family's story is not unusual. Mrs Doherty had wanted to leave her toddler and baby with her sister when her husband was posted to India but 'their father would not consent to it'. As it happened, Mrs Doherty herself nearly died soon after their arrival in cholera-ridden Arcot in 1819, giving one-year-old Henry cause to 'fret himself'. The family moved to the healthier climate of Bangalore, where the children 'grew strong and rosy'. They certainly appear healthy and happy in their mother's drawings. But it was not long before Major Doherty, a man 'particularly formed for domestic life', died of 'violent brain fever', leaving her to make the sad journey home with her 'poor Babes'.[67]

Even more distressing is the case of Fanny West. On 30 March 1827 her mother Lady West (wife of the Chief Justice of Bombay) wrote in her diary: 'Our dear Fanny Anna's [first] birthday, thank God, she is well, good, interesting and everything we can wish. May God spare her to us in health and goodness.' But God did not spare her parents to Fanny. By August of the next year Sir Edward had perished in a cholera outbreak, Lady West had died in childbirth and Fanny was on a boat to England with an ayah.[68] In 1839 Julia Maitland was just about to take her daughter Henrietta back to England from Madras (mainly because she disapproved of 'the "native" system of managing a child') when her husband died of a liver complaint. Like Mrs Doherty she had to leave India bereft of her husband but with her two children who were 'well and intelligent'.[69] Another tragic tale is told by Mrs Elizabeth Smith (née Cruikshank) about her grandfather and his siblings; all these small children were put on a homebound boat after both their parents died of cholera on the same night.[70] Other children, like the Stuarts and Pembertons, were bereaved after they came to Britain. The point is that adults were as subject as children to tropical illness. In addition they faced risks to which children were not exposed – venereal disease, alcohol abuse, combat and childbirth. There are no statistics to show the respective levels of risk in the early nineteenth century. But contemporaries certainly reckoned that living in India was more likely to cause death or physical degeneration to children.

Thus a handbook published for Anglo-Indian parents in 1810 was correct in asserting that 'few children, born of European parents, are retained beyond their third or fourth year in the country.' But the author adds an explanation which goes beyond the physical: 'The generality of those remaining, even for that term, under the care of ayahs, become crafty, proud and unmannerly; . . . ayahs will initiate their young charges in many practices and especially in language, such as must require infinite assiduity to subdue.'[71] Similar admonitions were conveyed in the influential writings of Mary Sherwood, the ardently Evangelical wife of an army paymaster posted to India in 1805. The Sherwoods left their baby daughter behind to be brought up by Mary's mother 'amongst the lambs and flowers . . . and educated in the fear of God'. After the early death of their second and third babies in the notoriously unhealthy environment of Indian Army cantonments, she nearly decided to 'make a shipwreck' of their domestic happiness by going back to England with the next baby. But two medical men advised her to keep the child in the country for some years at least and she struggled on. Altogether four children – Lucy, Henry Martyn (baptised with the same names as their friend, the well-known missionary), Emily and Sophia – survived in India. In her autobiography Mrs Sherwood attributes this to the advice of an old ayah that she should procure a *dhye* (Indian wet-nurse) for Lucy, whom she had already weaned, and keep her on milk for as long as possible, a practice she adopted with the other children. Mrs Sherwood wrote warmly of the sight of 'the European babe hanging on the breast of the black woman', admitted to feeling guilt about the death of the dhye's own child and described a tender reunion between nurse and nursling just before the family's departure for England in 1816. She also expressed her gratitude to their devoted bearer who helped to save Sophia from dying of jungle fever by sitting up with her all night. Despite all this, in other parts of the book she bitterly accused Indian servants of encouraging their charges to worship Hindu idols and giving them copious doses of opium.[72]

In the popular children's novels Mrs Sherwood wrote after her return to England the hostile view predominates. In *Lucy and her Dhye* (1825) a motherless child, brought up entirely by Indian servants, adopts their 'lounging and indolent customs', cannot speak English and at the age of seven is 'wholly unacquainted with the use of a book'. Transplanted with her wealthy father to the more bracing moral atmosphere of England, she grieves for her beloved dhye. But she consoles herself (before a romantic early death) by praying for, and contributing to, missionary work in India which will serve the dhye's 'spiritual good'.[73] Such earnest Evangelical tracts were 'an important weapon in the armoury of education' in the late Georgian period; the moral tales of Hannah More, for example, sold two million copies in 1795.[74] Their influence doubtless encouraged the early removal of many Anglo-Indian children from the 'heathen' land of their birth.

As well as bringing up her own children in India, the energetic Mrs Sherwood adopted destitute orphans and set up schools in the military cantonments at Dinapore and Cawnpore. Her first school soon had forty or fifty pupils, the offspring of ordinary soldiers and of local merchants down on their luck. She prided herself on turning none away, 'not even when the children were coloured'.[75] It was a valuable service. European schools were scarce in India at this time since the East India Company did not much concern itself with poor children and encouraged prosperous employees to send their sons and daughters to England to be educated. However there was no guarantee that this option would be wholly beneficial since the quality of English schools varied enormously. They certainly showed little influence of the new doctrine of education contained in Jean Jacques Rousseau's *Émile*. Evangelical writers like Hannah More condemned the French philosopher's emphasis on 'a free and natural education' and his advice that parents and teachers should 'love childhood, indulge its sports, its pleasures, its delightful instincts'.[76] As she exclaimed when she heard of Mary Wollstonecraft's *Vindication of the Rights of Woman* (1792), 'We will be hearing of the Rights of Children next!'[77] It was to be at least a century and a half before her fears were realised. For the time being schools were 'committed to ancient rituals and established forms'.[78]

The expensive public schools, often costing parents over £100 a year, gave boys the classical education which conferred gentlemanly status. But even here the quality of instruction doled out by ill-paid schoolmasters was often low and the curriculum was unappealing to all but the most assiduous scholars. One of the Revd Sydney Smith's witty letters poured scorn on these schools' obsession with the classics, which involved pursuing 'needless [linguistic] perfection' and becoming 'perfectly acquainted with the intrigues of Heathen gods'.[79] It could be a debilitating regime, as George Barlow junior found to his cost at Eton, and it would not bear decent fruit, in his opinion, unless the boy was 'thoroughly grounded' in the classics beforehand. This may explain why many Raj parents (like Francis Pemberton) were disappointed with their sons' progress at these famous schools. George Barlow's final verdict on Eton was pious and perceptive: 'No where does Idleness, Luxury, and Vice of every description meet with more frequent or better opportunities for exercise, greater success and encouragement and less restraint. ... It is the best, or the worst of places.'[80] His clever brother Henry was clearly more susceptible to Etonian vices, as his uncle reports:

> The bustle or rather the dissipation of Eton seems to have totally changed his disposition. Before he went to Eton he was never without a book in his hand, now he seldom looks at one, he is idle, negligent in every way, and is so often flog'd that Mr Goodall says he fears he has lost all sense of shame.[81]

Public schoolboys often rebelled against such cruel and authoritarian regimes – and in doing so they had the sympathy of Sir John Shore, who thought flagellation of youths 'intolerably blackguard'.[82] In 1770 boys used pistols at Winchester. At Westminster in 1793 they imitated French revolutionaries by tearing up paving stones and planting the red cap of liberty on the Founders' Tower. In 1797 Rugby boys rose against a headmaster known as the 'black tiger'.[83] Eton, Harrow, Charterhouse and Shrewsbury had similar troubles. So did Haileybury, where both William and Henry Barlow took part in 'unhappy disturbances' involving drunkenness and firearms. George Udny Yule, the son of an Indian Army officer, found that, as well as 'long lessons in languages we know scarcely anything of', there were drunken rows, with 'plenty of windows broken and more doors kicked through'.[84] Nevertheless, most Haileybury pupils acquired sufficient administrative and linguistic knowledge to be able to serve in India.

Parents often preferred to send their children to one of the many small private academies that proliferated at this time. These also had the advantage of being cheaper. Most catered for a dozen or so pupils, who paid £30 or £40 a year. It was hard for Anglo-Indian parents to judge their quality, which was variable and depended on the ability and disposition of the proprietor. Thackeray's 'deluded parents had heard a favourable report' of a school at Southampton but, the writer recalled, it was 'governed by a horrible little tyrant who made our lives a misery' with 'cold, chilblains, bad dinners, not enough victuals and caning awful!'[85] Henry Pemberton, Francis's brother, wanted his nephews removed from their Suffolk boarding school: 'I am attacked ... by all my brother's Suffolk acquaintance for continuing them there. Harry ... is irrevocably ruined in speech.'[86] But their father wished them to stay until they were fifteen, persevering with the classical education required for a career in the Indian Civil Service.

William Dick sent his two oldest sons to Doctor Bisset's academy so that they would 'have an opportunity of forming a friendship with young gentlemen'. But two years later he found, presumably on the evidence of their letters, that the boys were 'very backward indeed' and wished that he had had them educated near his relations and their younger brother in Perth.[87] Sir George Barlow initially chose Mr Roberts's school because the proprietor had a 'pleasing and sensible wife' who, having no children of her own, could 'devote her whole time to the care of the boys'. Later on, though, William Barlow lost confidence in Mr Roberts. As the fourteen-year-old George testified, the schoolmaster had a 'deficiency of patience', relied too heavily on 'a stick or a rod to inculcate knowledge' and could only 'instil the first rudiments of the dead languages'.[88] So the younger boys were sent to Mr Oakes's school at Linton – with varying degrees of success. Richard, aged seven, was grateful at least that he had not been severely punished 'and I hope to be such a good boy as not to deserve it'.[89]

By this time there were also some girls' private schools, which concentrated heavily on 'moral training and genteel accomplishments', designed as 'coaching for success in the game of matrimony'.[90] The Twickenham school attended by Eliza and Charlotte Barlow seems to have been typical. Fashionably situated near London, it was run by good spinster ladies who 'paid the strictest and most minute attention to [the girls'] improvement in every useful and virtuous accomplishment'.[91] It is difficult to establish exactly what the girls were taught. But they both had excellent handwriting and could write in French; they referred to music and drawing lessons and one of Eliza's letters sought to impress her father with a long account of a lecture she had attended on Electricity. However there is evidence that this school, like others of its kind, imposed an 'austere regime' and 'close confinement', leaving pupils with 'their constitutions undermined'.[92] Robert Barlow feared that his nieces' health was being impaired 'by the anxiety and fatigue inseparable from their situation'. His wife worried that Eliza 'grows rather too much *en bon point* [podgy]' and resolved to 'make her take more exercise'. In 1806 Charlotte needed sea air and the following year her health was 'most astonishingly improved by the kind care which has been taken of her for the three weeks she has been at home'.[93] Both girls did fulfil the object of their education by finding eligible husbands – though the early collapse of Eliza's marriage suggests that she chose hers too hastily.

It was more usual for well-off girls to be educated by tutors or governesses, as happened in the case of the younger Barlow daughters. They received such an excellent grounding from Miss Page that William Barlow found them 'infinitely better informed than the boys in everything except Latin'. The girls' letters from the schoolroom showed off their classical learning:

> I have read the Grecian history and I like it very much; the following are the characters I like the best, that is, Socrates, Leonidas, Miltiades, Aristides, Eponimondas, Pelopidas and Alexander. . . . I am sure you will smile at the idea of me reading Homer's Iliad; because you will think I do not understand it, but I assure you I do, with the assistance of Miss Page who is so kind as to explain every difficult passage. . . . I hope you will excuse all the mistakes I have made, as we always compose our letters ourselves.

The girls obviously enjoyed Miss Page's company too; Louisa liked their daily walks and was pleased that 'Miss Page is so kind as to read some of Cicero's and Lord Chesterfield's letters to us'. Miss Page herself showed an obvious concern for the 'delightful children' during the divorce case.[94] Not all governesses proved as satisfactory. Colonel William Kirkpatrick (Resident at Hyderabad 1793–7) found the letters of his daughters' governess 'very vulgar' and concluded that she 'was not qualified to give that sort of polish to the mind or deportment of the children which I could wish to distinguish them'. He instructed his father, who had care of the girls, to place them in a boarding school.[95]

Many of these children were lucky enough to have relations who visited them and had them to stay for the holidays. In fact, schoolmasters sometimes complained that frequent visits from parents' indulgent friends interfered with the discipline they were trying to maintain. Without such visits, however, children could be entirely at the mercy of their teachers, though some claimed that harsh treatment made men of them. Lieutenant-General Sir John Bennet Hearsey attributed his soldierly powers of endurance to the hardships he suffered at Manor House School in 1796–8 when he had no one to protect him and he was 'made into a regular household drudge'. His mother's return to England 'put an end to all this, and I was then treated like the other boys'.[96] The danger of maltreatment was increased if a child were left at a school for years without going home for the holidays, as was likely to happen in Anglo-Indian families. The percipient Dr Dick worried about this risk when he moved his boys to Westminster School: 'What care will be taken of them there, I cannot guess, but there they must now remain. ... The very business of vacations alone at the English schools is perplexing beyond measure and distressing to children whose parents are at a distance.'[97] There is no record of how the Dick boys fared at Westminster, 'the most fashionable school in England ... [but] notorious for its violence and lawlessness',[98] Perhaps their experience was happier than that of James Anthony Froude, who was bullied and starved there for an unbroken period of three and a half years. It left, he said, 'indelible marks on my memory and perhaps on my character'.[99]

Direct and apparently uncensored evidence of what such long periods at school felt like appears in the letters of George Yule and his brother Robert. Even though their father, Major William Yule, had retired from the Indian Army by the time he sent them to Dr Swete's school near Bristol, the boys seem not to have gone home for the holidays. Their letters tell of the long school day during which they got little play and 'scarcely any dinner', and of not daring to speak out loud in the schoolroom or to run about and climb when they went out walking. George was sorry 'to hear that the pony is ill and the cat dirty'; Robert was anxious that his mother should 'learn baby to say Georgy and Bobby'. They longed for more letters from home. Saddest of all are their accounts of the holidays when 'most of the boys are gone'. Robert begged Mama to let them come home: 'I cannot help crying when I think of it.'[100] The boys' pleas may have had an effect, for after a couple of years the Yule parents removed them from Dr Swete's care. But as the lads grew into adults the family separated once again. George entered the Bengal Civil Service and became Sir George Yule, while Robert went on to distinguish himself in the Indian Army before being killed in the Mutiny of 1857. Their younger brother,

Henry, incidentally, also went out to India and produced the famous glossary of Anglo-Indian words known as *Hobson-Jobson*.

Why, since English schools were so often unsatisfactory, did Anglo-Indian parents not make greater efforts to educate their children in India, where they could have kept a closer eye on their progress and welfare? They could, like the French residents of Chandernagore and Pondicherry, have hired tutors and governesses or set up small academies.[101] But such arrangements might not have produced the successful English (or Scottish, or Irish) gentlemen and ladies the nabobs wished their sons and daughters to become. In pursuit of gentility small children were dispatched on dangerous six-month journeys halfway round the world, to be received by relations and guardians they had never met, not knowing when (or whether) they would ever see their parents again. Coping with these physical and emotional hardships, their parents believed, would help to give them the character needed for success in a tough world of commercial competition, imperial adventure and naval conflict. Admiral Robert Barlow summed up this philosophy of child-rearing as he sent his eleven-year-old nephew off in severe weather on the *Triumph* in 1804: 'I almost wish I could take him with me to Bath but . . . you know nursing is not a good initiation into a life of enterprise and hard work'.[102] If they survived the rigours of their childhood, lonely young exiles of Empire would stand to gain from Britain's increase of power and wealth during the years when she became the mistress of the seas and the workshop of the world. In this respect, of course, they were luckier than their puny contemporaries labouring in mills and mines. They were also more privileged than their half-Indian brothers and sisters who, as the next chapter will show, could hardly ever share in the benefits of an age of enterprise.

TWO

'A Forlorn Race of Beings'

Eurasian Offspring

'If England is the land of our Fathers, India is the land of our Mothers.'[1] Raj children often thought of India as their mother, but for the historian who made this observation, it had a literal meaning. Herbert Stark was referring to the offspring of British men who married, lived with or simply had sexual encounters with Indian women. Such liaisons were common in the eighteenth century not only among the British but also among the Portuguese, Dutch and French residents of India. Their children were thus accurately described as Eurasian since they had mixed European and Asian parentage. In the British community, however, the term 'came to have a derogatory implication, which the Eurasians sought to elude by appropriating [in 1911] the label Anglo-Indian from the resident Britishers who had invented it for themselves'.[2] A current website on 'Anglo-Indians' illustrates the importance of employing the term precisely. It includes under that heading such diverse characters as Lord Salisbury (who never set foot in the subcontinent but served for a time as British Secretary of State for India), Sir George Barlow (the nabob of exclusively English origins encountered in Chapter One) and Herbert Stark (the writer of mixed race whose words open this chapter).

Terminology is not the only hazard in this delicate area of study. Another is the obfuscation practised by families and biographers over the past couple of centuries. Family trees such as the Pemberton Pedigree tend to omit those who were born outside marriage, especially if they were of mixed race. Indeed such black sheep were often disguised under another name. Victorian and Edwardian biographies were also economical with the truth. J. W. Kaye's *Life and Correspondence of Charles Metcalfe*, written in 1858, does not mention that the eminent administrator had three half-Indian sons. In his book about the Hearsey family, written in 1905, Hugh Pearse refers to Hyder Hearsey as a 'near relation' of Lieutenant-Colonel Andrew Hearsey, when he must have been his Eurasian son.[3] In these days of greater biographical honesty and diminished racial prejudice more truthful family histories are emerging. The new *Dictionary of National Biography* is more inclined than its predecessor to mention the Indian blood of those whose ancestors had 'Blundered', as the novelist John Masters said of his own great-great-grandfather.[4] The emphatic capital letter was his.

It is not always easy, though, to distinguish European from Asian antecedents. Historians often state, for instance, that the early-nineteenth-century Prime Minister, Lord Liverpool, had mixed Indian and English blood.[5] It is true that his maternal grandmother was a Calcutta-born woman, Frances Croke (1728–1812), who lived in India all her life and became known in her fourth widowhood as 'Begum Johnson'. The title, which is normally given to high-ranking Muslim women, was apparently applied to her because of her constant reminiscences about her friendship with the Begum, mother of the Nawab of Bengal. Mrs Croke's father was an English civil servant and there is no evidence that her half-Portuguese mother, Isabella Beizor, was Eurasian. Frances Croke's third husband (Lord Liverpool's grandfather) was English, as was their daughter Amelia's husband, Sir Charles Jenkinson.[6] Mystery also surrounds the question of whether the dark good looks of Cliff Richard (né Harry Webb) can be attributed to Eurasian origins. The most that Steve Turner's careful research into Richard's Indian background reveals is that one of his grandmothers may have had Burmese connections and that the other was a half-Spanish woman whose second husband was a Eurasian railway inspector. The fact that the Webbs lived with this grandmother's second family after coming to England in 1948, as well as young Harry's sunburned skin, prompted persistent playground taunts of 'Red Indibum'. A teacher added to the child's miseries by telling him that he couldn't run off to his wigwam any more.[7]

It was doubtless British attitudes like these that led some Eurasian families to disguise their racial heritage. Margaret Whittaker (née Thompson) told me that her cousins were forbidden to talk to their father in the street in Calcutta lest their slightly dark skin should betray his marriage to a Eurasian and put his job at risk.[8] Patti Rundall (née D'Souza) of Baby Milk Action, one of the fourteen children of an Indian doctor and his Welsh wife, remembers pretending that she was Portuguese. Another woman told me that her husband revealed the evening before their wedding that his parents, who had always claimed to be Maltese, were Eurasians from Bangalore. Such distortions and omissions may make it difficult to trace some Eurasian children. But they also provide a valuable clue to the shame, fear and confusion which many must have suffered in the past over that most odious of taints and taunts – 'a touch of the tar-brush'.

If the evidence of family letters and memoirs is not always reliable, baptismal registers and wills provide more trustworthy data. At St John's Church in Calcutta fifty-four per cent of the children baptised between 1767 and 1782 were Eurasian and illegitimate. And one in three wills made in Bengal from 1778 to 1785 contain bequests to Indian mistresses and their progeny.[9] Apart from these children, publicly acknowledged by their fathers, there were probably far more who were neither baptised nor bequeathed money. Historians estimate that about ninety per cent of the British men in India by the mid eighteenth century had married (officially or unofficially) Indian or Eurasian women.[10] The East India Company even encouraged the practice by giving a christening present of five rupees to the babies of soldiers married to Indian women. But as the Eurasian community grew and began to outnumber the British civilian population in India, official policy changed. In the 1790s Eurasians were barred by law from the covenanted (higher) ranks of the Indian Civil Service and disqualified from joining the Army except as bandsmen or farriers. The explanation usually given for these measures against the Eurasians is that the British authorities feared they might be a rebellious element in Indian society at a time of American and French revolutions and slave uprisings in the West Indies. The discrimination could well have had the effect of alienating Eurasians, who had never shown anything but respect for their fathers and their fathers' homeland. Luckily for the British Government, their loyalty was constant. But it was, say historians who think they were too subservient, 'misguided'.[11]

Another reason for the new disapproval of miscegenation was that increasing numbers of Evangelical missionaries came to India after 1790. But while hardening moral attitudes, they also helped the poorer children of mixed marriages and unions (who had often been abandoned) by setting up schools. Mary Sherwood was typical in condemning sin but alleviating its consequences. She took pity on 'the daughters of Englishmen – of men who have known what it is to have had a tender, well-educated Christian mother and honourable and amiable sisters [and yet] neglect the good of their own offspring'.[12] And she set up an asylum for orphan girls in Cawnpore – a location of extreme peril during the Indian Mutiny. From the mid eighteenth century the Society for Promoting Christian Knowledge (SPCK) in the Madras Presidency was busy educating children of 'soldiers and the lower order of people [who] neglect their offspring and suffer them to follow the caste of their mothers'.[13] The schools taught reading (in English), writing, arithmetic and the elementary principles of Christianity to 'this forlorn race of beings'. In consequence, it was hoped, they would not be 'left to the destroying influence of ignorance, beggary and idleness'. The Society's annual reports lament that in some districts they had no such schools for 'children of half-European extraction'. What better object for Christian benevolence could there be than 'to remember these destitute youth and provide a school for their Christian education'?[14]

Meanwhile the East India Company had recognised the need to provide for army orphans, European and Eurasian, whose distressed state might otherwise bring the ruling race into disrepute. In 1783 it launched an Orphan Society financed by government grants as well as by charitable donations. With typical Anglo-Indian respect for hierarchy, it established in Calcutta an Upper Orphanage for officers' children and a Lower Orphanage for those of other ranks. Further institutions followed in their wake so that by 1820 at least 1,200 children were accommodated. In fact not all of them were true orphans; the fathers of some had simply gone home after being discharged from the Army. In many cases, though, the fathers had fallen victim to disease or battle. Frequently the children were taken from their 'native' mothers after 'a painful struggle between duty and nature'. Captain Williamson (author of the *East India Vade-Mecum*) says that he 'repeatedly witnessed the distress of mothers, on such occasions' but he was convinced that it was good policy to make provision 'for the children of the soldiery'. Williamson approved of the system whereby the orphans were trained to do useful work in India as apprentices 'to some good business' or as drummers and fifers in the Army. In any event, they should not be sent to Europe lest 'a very extensive importation of persons of colour take place among us'.[15]

Since there were fewer opportunities for female employment,

orphan girls had to be prepared for marriage. 'When a tradesman or a non-commissioned officer wants a wife,' remarked Emily Eden after a visit to the Society's establishment for officers' daughters in the Kidderpore district of Calcutta, 'he goes there and chooses one.'[16] A British captain's memoir provides a glimpse of the possible humiliations of the marriage market. In the early nineteenth century Captain Bellew attended a dance at Kidderpore. He was presented to a Miss Rose Mussaleh, with 'a complexion tending to a delicate saffron, bespeaking plainly her Asiatic maternity'. In the lilting 'chi chi' accent characteristic of Eurasians Rose assured the Captain that 'no native comes to these balls', at which he 'could not suppress an emphatic *humph*!' Obviously his racial prejudice overcame his physical attraction for Rose's 'dark languishing eyes'[17] – she would have to try flashing them at another hop. Doubtless the 'orphanages' did good work. But one historian goes so far as to compare their treatment of Eurasian children to the recycling of waste. 'The orphans of one generation of soldiers ... and their wives were re-cast as the soldiers ... and wives of the next.'[18] No wonder Kipling's Kim 'learned to avoid missionaries and white men of serious aspect who asked him who he was and what he did'.[19]

Not all Eurasians had such a bleak childhood. More secure and happy were those whose fathers prospered and settled in India with their families. This was still quite common in the late eighteenth and early nineteenth centuries, when racial intolerance had not yet reached its Victorian heights. At this time, too, there were still plenty of Indian princely states, such as Oudh, Hyderabad and Jaipur, in which Indophiles and their Eurasian children could pursue military, civil or commercial careers independently of the Raj. Such parents possessed the wealth to help their children and had contacts with potential European as well as Indian patrons. Above all they took pride in their offspring and in the strong links they had forged with India. The French soldier-of-fortune who served the independent Maratha confederacy, General Benoit de Boigne, observed how difficult life was for young people without such paternal support. He could help only a fraction of the 'country-born young men' who applied to join his regiments. For few had been left anything by their fathers and 'some had no friends to recommend them or means to go up'.[20]

The sons of General William Linnaeus Gardner suffered no such disadvantages. Gardner himself came from an aristocratic English background but was born in America, where his father served in the British Army. The family had to leave when the thirteen colonies won their independence and in 1789 the young William went to India as an ensign. His movements over the next few years are difficult to trace, but in 1815 he explained why he had become 'fixed to this country and changed the ... course of pursuits in His Majesty's service'. A letter to his aunt tells a romantic story dating from 1798. While engaged in protecting and negotiating the release of the kidnapped wife and daughter of the Nawab of Cambay, he caught a glimpse of the fourteen-year-old girl's beautiful dark eyes behind the *purdah* curtain. 'What originated in humanity and pity,' he records, 'gave way to other sentiments, and I was soon united to the lady with all the ceremonies which by their [Muslim] religion were considered binding.' Gardner left the British Army, served for a time in the army of a Maratha ruler and by 1815 commanded an irregular cavalry regiment. His marriage had produced four children, of whom two sons survived. In 1818 he told his aunt that he had been able to help his sixteen-year-old son, James Valentine, to gain appointment as a lieutenant in his regiment; he was grateful for 'a larger share of happiness than usually falls to the lot of man. My wife never heard of Baker Street and my children and grandchildren are all under the same roof. ... Here I propose to live and die.'[21]

Gardner's domestic happiness increased as his sons' Indian wives provided him with more grandchildren to populate his estate near Agra. In letters to his cousin Edward (who was the British Resident in Nepal) he often recommended marriage and family life: 'I would rather sprawl upon the floor with half a dozen of my dingy progeny tumbling and romping over me than sit upon the Governor-General's throne. It is so delightful to be surrounded by those who love you and can be made happy by a kind word or look.'[22] There were no chilly English boarding schools for the Gardner offspring. In fact, as the Colonel later explained to the diarist Fanny Parkes with reference to his son James, 'his mother would never hear of her son's going to England for education – and to induce a native woman to give way to any reasons that are contrary to her own wishes is quite out of the power of mortal man'. Fanny, who recorded all these conversations in her journal (published in 1850), observed that James had turned out 'a remarkably shrewd, clever, quick man ... most perfectly suited to the life he leads'. She was impressed by the zenana system of education where boys and girls got the same instruction. Indeed, she compared it, perhaps rather too favourably, with the practice in Europe where men received 'a superior education and . . . the women are kept under and have not fair play'.[23]

Fanny got on so well with Colonel Gardner, a 'kind, mild, gentlemanly, polished, interesting companion', that she was invited to his household in 1835 for the wedding of Susan, one of his granddaughters. While she was there Fanny went several times into the zenana, where she met the old begum, her daughters-in-law and the grandchildren. In her journal she does not criticise the strictly secluded life which she observed there. But nor does she sound enthusiastic about the confinement of girls from the age of six, after which they could no longer 'run about, play with boys and enjoy their freedom'. 'They never ride on horseback, or go on the water,' remarked Fanny who was herself devoted to riding, sailing and 'vagabondising over India'. She noticed that James's wife routinely put small pieces of opium into the mouths of her young brood. Nevertheless, she found them 'remarkably handsome, intelligent children [who] appeared as gay and happy as possible'.[24]

Fanny's account of Susan's marriage to a young prince of Delhi suggests the problems that could arise for girls who had grown up in a mixed-race household. She seems to pity the passive painted bride 'looking like a lump of gold' as she waits for her husband to carry her off. When Gardner embraces his granddaughter he looks 'pale and miserable', trembles 'in every limb', and voices his worries about 'this poor girl'. 'Who may prophesy her fate?' he exclaims. 'However, she wished it; her mother and the begum had set their hearts on it and . . . women will have their own way.' He had been much happier when he gave away Susan's sister Hirmooza to her second cousin, Stewart Gardner. The old Colonel did not know what to do with James's daughters by his first marriage, two pretty and lively girls of fifteen and fourteen called Morning Star and Evening Star – or with the various other granddaughters, distressed relations and orphan girls for whom he was responsible. At one point he even told Fanny that he 'would not advise a European gentleman to marry a native lady', although he had been so happy in his own marriage.[25]

Colonel Gardner was feeling unusually morose during this conversation – he died later in 1835, closely followed to the grave by the Begum. But he identified a real problem. It was exceedingly hard to decide on the best upbringing for girls in European/Indian families. Another father facing this dilemma was the distinguished soldier of

Scottish descent, Sir David Ochterlony. While holding the post of British Resident of Delhi and defending that city against Maratha attacks in the early years of the nineteenth century, he acquired thirteen wives. It was their celebrated habit to promenade around the city after him in the cool of the evening, each one riding her own elephant. Sadly, there is little evidence about his family life and the 152-foot column that still dominates the Eden Gardens in Calcutta is a tribute to his prowess at making war not love. Even the story about the elephant procession may be apocryphal. But one extant letter does reveal some of his heart-searching. In it Ochterlony tells his friend Major Robert Sutherland that he was tempted to bring up his young daughters according to Gardner's 'Agra system' (adopted by Sutherland himself in his own mixed family) since it avoided 'the cruelty of departing from them and teaching them to despise their tenderest parent'. But this instinct was tempered by his fear that he would thereby fit the girls for marriage only 'with officers in the Maratha Service accustomed to the manners of Hindustan', who might want to put them in a harem.[26] If, on the other hand, he brought them up as Europeans they might still be rejected in illiberal Anglo-Indian society, despite their fair skin. In either case he worried about the girls' future. However, they were at least secure financially for in 1816 Sir David established a trust to provide annuities for any daughters remaining unmarried at his death.[27] Since he set this up in India and never himself returned to Britain, where he had neither friends nor relations, it is likely that his daughters remained in the land of their mothers.

Some fathers faced both emotional and financial problems in providing for their Eurasian offspring. When Captain Hercules Skinner sent his daughters to school in 1790 his Indian wife killed herself, 'thinking that the Rajput honour of the Purdah was broken by her daughters being separated from the protection and care of their mother'.[28] In the end all three girls made successful marriages to 'gentlemen in the East India Company's service'. Meanwhile the Captain himself fell on hard times and he had to send his sons James and Robert to a charity school. Aged eighteen, in 1796, James was apprenticed to a printer but hated the work so much that he ran away to seek his fortune as a soldier or sailor. At this point, fortunately for him, his English godfather Colonel Burn came to the rescue. He could not get James into the British Army because of the new laws but he did give him a letter of recommendation to General de Boigne, who accepted him into a Maratha regiment.

James Skinner's career illustrates both the opportunities and the obstacles facing an ambitious young Eurasian in India at this time. When war broke out between the British Raj and the Indian Maratha states in the early nineteenth century he had to leave the Marathas' service because mixed-race officers were thought to be potential traitors. Eventually this tough and daring soldier formed the famous irregular regiment known as 'Skinner's Horse' and placed it at the service of the British. He also made a fortune out of extensive land-holdings which he acquired and, as a Eurasian rather than a British citizen, was allowed to own. Despite the campaigns he fought on behalf of the Raj, the British Army refused at this point to award him any military rank. In his memoir he describes the bitterness he felt: 'I thought I had now served a nation that had no prejudice against caste or colour, but Alas! I was mistaken.'[29] In the end his personal charm, lavish generosity and military renown overcame the disqualification of his dark skin. His British patrons ensured that he was given the honorary rank of lieutenant-colonel and the Order of the Bath. Apparently, though, while living in Mughal magnificence in Delhi, he 'had an old spoon placed on his breakfast-table every day, to remind him, as he said, of his origins'.[30] It turns out that the Colonel's bitterness was posthumously justified. In 1944 a young British couple were invited to meet his descendants in Skinner's grand Delhi house. They were shocked to find that they 'were all of the wrong complexion'. Afterwards the husband forbade his wife, who had been brought up largely in India, 'to hob-nob with Indians' or to reveal that she spoke their language since whites would think she was Eurasian.[31]

Little is known of Colonel Skinner's private life. He certainly had a series of Indian mistresses and after he died in 1841 about eighty people claimed that they had a right to inherit some of his great wealth. He recognised seven children as his own, educating them and providing for them in marriage settlements or in his will. One son, Hercules, was sent to Edinburgh Academy to receive 'the education of an English gentleman'. This enabled him to join the entourage of the liberal-minded Governor-General, Lord William Bentinck, but despite his 'unexceptionable conduct and character' he was denied a commission in the British Army. In 1832 Lord William's recommendation gained him a position in the army of the Nizam of Hyderabad.[32] Hercules married an English woman while both his sisters married captains in the British Army, thus extending close ties of blood and affection between the European and Indian communities.

No one depicts these bonds more movingly than Johann Zoffany – in his famous portrait of the Palmer family in 1785. General William Palmer, a renowned soldier who had become British Resident at Lucknow, poses with his lovely Indian wife, Fyze Nissa Begum, their three children, his wife's two sisters and two ayahs. It is not an idealised scene for Palmer was a true Indophile, deeply attached both to his family and to the country itself. It is true that he sent his children to be educated in England – but it was always understood that they would come back to the parental home in India. When William Palmer junior (the oldest child in the portrait) did return from the Royal Military Academy at Woolwich his father helped him to gain a commission in the Hyderabadi Army, where he acquitted himself well. The Palmer family history recounts that he 'lived as a Mohammedan and observed all their habits more especially in his private and domestic life. His wives were Mohammedan.'[33] In addition to his military duties William junior also ran a hugely profitable banking and trading business in Hyderabad. Its fortunes demonstrate the ambiguous position of Eurasians in India at this time. As a native of India working in a princely state, William was exempt from the law forbidding British citizens to lend money to Indian rulers. But after he brought an Englishman into the business he had to apply for a licence from the Governor-General, which was granted. In 1820, however, it was suddenly withdrawn and the business began to fail. Apparently the House of Palmer had to go once it 'stood in the way of the exercise of official British influence'.[34] Nevertheless, the Palmers continued to find opportunities in the subcontinent. After the General's death, William took his mother into his household and his seven children pursued careers or married in India. Several of his sons followed him into the Nizam of Hyderabad's army but the two youngest, James and Hastings, entered the East India Company's covenanted service, on the nomination of Sir Charles Hopkinson, one of the Directors. This was made possible by the removal of the colour bar in 1833.

A Eurasian near-contemporary of William Palmer junior, who would have been just below him at the Woolwich Military Academy, was Hyder Hearsey. Born in 1782, he suffered from multiple disadvantages. He was illegitimate and he bore the name of one of Britain's archenemies on the subcontinent. In fact his father, Lieutenant-Colonel Andrew Hearsey, who is referred to as his 'guardian' in Pearse's history and may himself have been Eurasian,[35] had led British troops against Hyder Ali and his son Tipu Sultan in Mysore. Doubtless Hearsey senior chose the name Hyder as a tribute to the 'Tiger of Mysore'. At any rate Hyder was given a better education than his legitimate younger half-brother (known as his 'cousin'), John Bennet Hearsey, whose English mother was left penniless after Andrew Hearsey's sudden death in 1798. Shortly before that the Lieutenant-Colonel had used his influence to gain the sixteen-year-old Hyder an appointment as aide-de-camp to the Nawab of Oudh. After some years of hard fighting in princely armies, Hearsey (like Skinner) threw in his lot with the British in 1803 during the Maratha wars. Lord Wellesley subsequently gave him a pension and he married Knanum Zuhur-ul-Nissa, the sister of Colonel Gardner's wife. Hearsey acquired a considerable estate, gaining advantages from both the British and the Indian side of his heritage. He continued to pursue an adventurous career, surveying the shifting course of the Ganges, fighting alongside Gardner and Ochterlony against the Gurkhas, and purchasing the Himalayan town of Dehra Dun (now the home of India's best public schools). He was eventually given the rank of major in the Company's army and lived 'in great state and happiness' until 1840.[36] All three of his sons entered the Nawab of Oudh's service and his daughter Harriet united the two sides of the family by marrying his half-brother, Captain (later Lieutenant-General) John Hearsey. Thus was established an Indian dynasty, which was cemented by further intermarriage. General Hearsey's son Andrew married one of Hyder Hearsey's granddaughters and his daughter Amelia married a grandson.

Friendship and patronage as well as almost incestuous inter-marriage linked this group of ambitious families in and to their Indian motherland. The younger William Palmer was helped on his way in Hyderabad by his father's friend James Kirkpatrick, who was the British Resident there. Kirkpatrick had fallen in love with and married Khair un-Nissa, a Hyderabadi aristocrat – a story vividly recounted by William Dalrymple. But Kirkpatrick's family did not follow the same Indian path as that of other 'White Mughals'. Before his marriage, as the result of a casual liaison, he had acquired an illegitimate Eurasian son who was sent back to his father, Colonel Kirkpatrick, in England. This 'Hindustani boy' is never mentioned in letters until his death, aged thirteen, in 1804. Khair's children, Sahib Allum and Sahib Begum, were obviously much dearer to Kirkpatrick. Nevertheless he dispatched them too to England, at the ages of three and five, to be brought up by his father. They were given new English names, William George and Katherine Aurora. It is not clear whether Kirkpatrick intended the children ever to return to India, which he regarded as home, for he died soon after they set sail from Madras in 1805. They lost their mother as well as their father because, once in England, they were denied any communication with her and they never saw her again. Forty years later Katherine (Kitty) wrote that she passed no day of her life without thinking of her mother. 'When I dream of my mother I am in such joy to have found her again that I awake, or else am pained in finding that she cannot understand the English I speak.'[37] George Chinnery's famous portrait of the children, painted shortly before their departure, certainly conveys 'the intense sadness of separation'.[38] It also powerfully suggests the loss of that part of their nationality symbolised by the glittering Indian clothes they wear.

Until the death of old Colonel Kirkpatrick in 1818 the children lived at his house in Kent. He seems to have looked after them kindly but when William was eleven he fell into a copper of boiling water and was disabled for life. At least he had his deceased father's money behind him and could afford to marry and live as a poet until he died at the age of twenty-seven. His sister Kitty had the advantage of great beauty as well as a fortune of £50,000. Her 'soft brown eyes and floods of bronze-red hair' so captivated the writer Thomas Carlyle that he based on her the character Blumine in *Sartor Resartus* – 'the fairest of Orient light-bringers'.[39] Even so, it was not until she was in her early thirties that Kitty found happiness. She then married Captain James Phillipps and had seven children, of whom four survived. She described them fondly to her Indian grandmother in 1841, concluding that 'they have a good intellect and are blest with fair skin'.[40]

In sending his Eurasian offspring to England, Kirkpatrick was following the normal practice of high-ranking East India Company fathers during the Georgian period. The assumption was that their children's prospects would be served better there than in India. In practice this was not always the case, as the French naturalist, Victor Jacquemont, discovered during his tour of India between 1829 and 1832. At Agra he met 'several young women of mixed race, whose colour clearly indicated their origins'. They had been educated in England but found themselves ineligible for marriage there 'in the class to which their fathers belonged'. Back in India, however, they were likely to tempt a young officer as long as they possessed beauty or (preferably) a decent marriage portion.[41]

The two illegitimate daughters of Francis Pemberton, the Bombay nabob encountered in Chapter One, enjoyed at least the latter advantage. They make no appearance in the family papers until they are named in his will of March 1794. In it he bequeathed 20,000 rupees (£2,000) as well as plate and household furniture to his 'natural daughter christened Sophia'.[42] She must have been born before his marriage, probably to an Indian or Eurasian mistress, and would have been about eighteen. The will states that she had been brought up in England by Pemberton's sister Mrs Jefferson but was now living with him in Bombay. She was to come into this money when she reached the age of twenty-one or on the day of her marriage. In August Pemberton died and that very same month Sophia got married – to Roger Fildes, one of the witnesses to the will. We do not know whether Sophia was beautiful or fair-skinned. But no doubt her English upbringing and her inheritance, which Fildes was in such a good position to appreciate, helped to win her a white husband.

Sophia's sister, who was still a child and had probably been born after the breakdown of Pemberton's marriage, was named as Nancy Stevens. She was still in the care of Mrs Jefferson, who was to receive the interest on the £2,000 left to Nancy. This would pay for her maintenance and education until she was twenty-one or married with her guardian's consent. If she were to go 'to her native country' she was to be given enough money from the legacy 'to provide for her genteel establishment and the other expenses of her passage to India'.[43] No further mention is made of 'Nancy Stevens' in the Pemberton Papers but the 'Nancy Pemberton' to whom letters are addressed in 1810 must be the same girl, now a young woman in her twenties. The affectionate and solicitous tone of the first letter suggests that the 'PJ' who signs it is Mr Jefferson:

> You are very soon my dearest girl to be left to the sole guidance of your own principles and of a virtuous heart, hitherto not estranged from the happy influences of religion, for your future conduct, and these properly consulted will I am sure, on all occasions lead you to a just decision. Be cautious then my dearest girl what acquaintances you form on your arrival in India and let your friendships, if you form them with the other sex, be most circumspect. ... There is, I fear, a great laxity, both of moral and religious principle in the East and I have so good an opinion of your disposition, as to believe that you can never be happy with a libertine.[44]

As Nancy departed for unknown perils in India two further letters from Christopher Pemberton (her father's brother and trustee of her legacy) settled the stock and interest which she was to receive while in India.

A final letter of 1821 addressed to 'Nancy Keighley, care of Lieut. Keighley, Cantonment Adjutant, Arcot' indicates that Nancy had found a husband in India. The correspondent, Richard Eaton, tells her that he has recommended Lieutenant Keighley to Sir Alexander Campbell, the husband of Francis Pemberton's niece, who was just about to take up an important post in India. He hopes that Keighley's 'duty will take him soon into the august presence of Sir Alec and that he will be favourably received and acknowledged'.[45] Fragmentary though they are, these letters show that after Francis Pemberton's death the family did not abandon his natural daughter, even when she returned to her mother country. On the contrary, her moral, social and financial welfare were seen as their concern.

Not all Eurasian girls were so lucky, as the Thackeray family story illustrates. Richmond Thackeray (a civil servant and a 'considerable personage' in Bengal)[46] had an illegitimate daughter called Sarah before his marriage to Anne Becher. He bequeathed the girl a small annuity of £500 in his will and she must have received the interest on this when he died in 1815. The bulk of his fortune, £18,000, was left in trust for his only son, William Makepeace Thackeray. In 1820 Sarah married James, one of the illegitimate Eurasian sons of Richard Blechynden, an English architect working in Calcutta. But James died young and Mrs Blechynden fell on hard times.[47] In 1832, when William came of age in England, he frequently expressed guilt about the difference between the size of his fortune and that of his half-sister. On 10 June, for instance, he dined off turtle and cold beef but then wished that 'the turtle had choked me – there is poor Mrs Blechynden starving in India, whilst I am gorging in this unconscionable way here'. Just before coming into his inheritance he told his mother that he was resolved to pay her £60 per annum out of his 'vast fortune'.[48] The evidence suggests that he never acted on this good intention.

The next reference to Mrs Blechynden in Thackeray's correspondence is to her death in 1841, when he was full of remorse: 'It is the sorest point I have on my conscience never to have taken notice of her.' When his uncle wrote from Calcutta begging him to continue his father's annuity on behalf of Mrs Blechynden's young daughter, Thackeray (who had lost most of his inheritance in gambling and in the Indian bank crash of 1833) replied that he did not think 'the daughter should have as much as was allotted for the support of daughter and mother'. Seven years later Miss Blechynden visited Thackeray in London, perhaps hoping to prompt him to greater generosity. Her arrival embarrassed him, as he explained to a friend: 'I have got a black niece staying with me. . . . She was never in Europe before and wrote to my mother the other day as her "dear Grand-mamma". Fancy the astonishment of that dear majestic old woman!' A month or so later he expressed his relief at having got rid of his niece, whom he never names. Poor Miss Blechynden was obviously too dark for polite English society.[49]

As Maria Graham wrote in her *Journal of a Residence in India* (1812), it was 'a cruelty to send children of colour to Europe, where their complexion must subject them to perpetual mortification'.[50] Because of this prejudice some dark-skinned children were never sent to England, even when money was available for their fares and education. James Blechynden had been educated in England but earlier on his father had clearly worried about how his oldest Eurasian son, Arthur, might be received: 'I really have a great mind to do it – when my pocket enables me – for surely my relations must have more liberality of sentiment than to refuse to notice him because he is illegitimate – that is not his fault but mine.'[51] Richard Blechynden was doubtless concerned about the child's colour as well as his illegitimacy but in the event it was the paucity of his pocket that prevented the child's dispatch; Arthur stayed in Calcutta, eventually becoming his father's business assistant.

The problem of the colour line is further illustrated in correspondence relating to William, Charles and John, the three natural sons of Julius Imhoff, Warren Hastings's stepson. Imhoff died in Calcutta in 1799, leaving his young children in the care of John Palmer, a wealthy banker (who was a son of General William Palmer by his first wife). The boys would in time possess 'handsome fortunes for a middling condition in life'. Worried about the 'declining state of public instruction' in Calcutta, Palmer consulted Hastings, who had long since retired as Governor-General, on how best to secure 'their permanent or ultimate happiness'. He explained that an English education would be suitable only for William and Charles, the two oldest boys, as John was too dark-skinned to benefit from this advantage. As it happened Charles was 'snatched away' in March 1802, under mysterious circumstances. Some accounts say that he and his ayah drowned in a well, but Palmer describes a distressing last illness 'apparently of an hereditary nature'. Later that year Palmer gave Hastings further particulars of William, who was about seven. 'He is fairer than the ordinary run of these children, but is still discernible in his complexion to be of a native mother.' He thought his capacity was probably good but found it difficult to judge as he had not been well taught. As for John, who was 'dull and idle' as well as black, he concluded that 'it can never be advisable that this child should go home', recommending that he should be educated in 'our Mughal schools'. Thus, at the age of three or four, John's fate was sealed by his skin.[52]

In 1804 William, known by the surname Fitzjulius rather than Imhoff, entered the household of Mr and Mrs Warren Hastings at Daylesford House, where he was fitted out with a blue coat and pantaloons.[53] At first all went well. Hastings told his surviving stepson Charles Imhoff that 'Little Fitz . . . has made himself a great favourite at Over Norton [the Oxfordshire village where Daylesford was situated]'.[54] The boy was sent to a small school run by a clergyman. But he acquired there only 'a strong disinclination to every species of application and restraint'. In 1805 Hastings asked his friend David Anderson of Edinburgh to suggest a Scottish school which would apply more rigorous control. The terms in which he recommends William are significant:

> I have mentioned his complexion, as liable to objection, but I must qualify it by saying that I have seen children of English parentage to the full as dark. To counteract this defect, the boy is handsome, lively, wonderfully active, and good-tempered; and before he went to school, showed as forward a disposition to learn, as he has now, or seems to have, an aversion to it.

It is sad to discover in subsequent Hastings correspondence that, as William got older, his defects were judged to outweigh his merits. Anderson recommended a school where he could be taught Latin and Greek — though there was a danger that he might also acquire 'the Scotch language'. But Marian Hastings, the boy's grandmother, apparently decided that this plan was not 'the most suitable to his disposition and propensities, which require . . . a strong control, and an unremitted application of it'.[55] So William was apparently sent back to the same clergyman, the Revd Perkins of Dawlish, who later refers to having known him since May 1804 and to his having 'been <u>so long</u> under my care and instruction'. Perkins's letters are a tissue of schoolmasterly complaint. He laments Fitzjulius's deficiency in learning, his failure to acquire any Latin, his partiality for drinking, his indebtedness and 'his unfortunate propensity to Falsehood'.[56] He agreed to keep the boy on, following a curriculum consisting largely of book-keeping and writing, for which he charged over £100 every half-year. These were unusually high fees but they probably had to cover the cost of William's extravagances, bills run up at the local public houses and riding stables. They also paid for William's keep throughout most of the vacations.

However, there was a further expense. When presenting his final account, Perkins explained that he had been able to take no other pupils while Fitzjulius was with him, and he now asked Hastings to recommend him to any of his friends who might have young gentlemen in need of 'classical and general education'.[57] Of course, the boy's bad behaviour might have been a deterrent to other parents but it was hardly unusual at that time. It is difficult to escape the conclusion that racial prejudice in Britain was more common than is sometimes claimed.[58] Frederic North, son of George III's Prime Minister and Governor of Ceylon at the turn of the century, reflects the attitudes of polite society in a letter to his sister in 1801. Repeating current malicious gossip, he recounts the story of what happened when General Fullerton, 'an old twaddler from Bengal' who walked about 'with a round straw hat and green gauze veil, on account of his eyes,' took his 'Hindoo wife' to Scotland. Allegedly 'she shocked the neighbours by plastering the walls of her drawing-room with cow-dung'.[59]

It is not clear why Warren and Marian Hastings refused to have William home to Daylesford during the holidays. Hastings was in general very fond of children (having lost his own long ago) and welcomed many of his friends' offspring to his house. In 1810, for instance, he invited young John D'Oyly 'to pass as much of the next vacation as you can at Daylesford'.[60] Later he helped to prevent John's expulsion from Haileybury when he was implicated in a riot there — probably the same one in which young Henry Barlow was involved. And while in India Hastings had shown more respect for Indians than had most of his countrymen. Yet he clearly found Fitzjulius an 'embarrassment' and admitted to his stepson that to have the lad to stay in 1809 before his departure for India 'would prove a torment and discredit to us and this would be the more unfortunate, as we expect much company during all the time that he would be with us'. Charles

Imhoff was also unwilling to receive his nephew, who probably remained at Dawlish until it was time for him to leave. It seems evident that William felt unwanted. There is a letter in his best copperplate handwriting, saying how happy he was to hear that he was going back to his 'native country' and only wished 'that the time was <u>come</u>'. Nevertheless, he hoped to have the pleasure of seeing his grandparents and uncle before leaving England.

The cruellest episode in this sorry tale is the East India Company's rejection of Fitzjulius. Hastings's friend Colonel Toone applied on his behalf for a post as a writer at Bencoolen, a remote Sumatran outpost run by the Company. But the Board of Control turned him down on the grounds of the Standing Order banning 'native Indians' from the service. Exceptions could not be made, the 'mortified' Colonel explained, even though 'all possible respect was paid to [Hastings's] name'.[61] Another ex-Governor-General, Sir John Shore, was similarly disappointed when he applied for a post for one of the Eurasian sons mentioned in Chapter One.[62] Meanwhile a white nephew of Marian Hastings had been given a cadetship with the Company – only to be sent home shortly afterwards for embezzlement and desertion.

Denied the gentlemanly status promised by an English upbringing, Fitzjulius had only one recourse: 'to apply and to qualify himself for being useful'.[63] Once he was back in Bengal, John Palmer found him a job 'in the indigo line' at Semalbarree, described by the boy as 'nothing but a jungly place, where we see nothing but Tigers and other whild [*sic*] animals'. For over a year he endured this lonely existence out of temptation's way, receiving few letters from his Hastings and Imhoff families and (by his own account) spending 'almost all day out in the sun' and contracting fevers.[64] He then took himself back to Calcutta where, on returning from a sea voyage, Palmer found him. The lad had not apparently been 'seduced into any extravagant or vicious habits' but he showed every sign of 'natural indolence' as well as 'diffidence and timidity'. Fitzjulius himself wrote that he was 'in much want of friends'.[65]

Late in 1813, Palmer had still not been able to place his ward in another job but he assured Hastings that he would not neglect him. Fitzjulius seems to have stopped writing to Hastings at this point, so it is difficult to establish whether he ever did find useful employment. Legal records show that he and his brother successfully challenged their father's will to establish their legitimate rights.[66] But Fitzjulius did not enjoy any benefits this might have given him, for he died in

1824 aged twenty-nine. Plainly he was a feckless young man, who could not cope with the normal hardships facing new recruits in India. But as William Wordsworth famously wrote, in the year that Fitzjulius arrived in England, 'The Child is father of the Man.' The poet further said, in *The Prelude*, that only a child who is loved – as Fitzjulius never was – can develop a strong moral character, capable of overcoming adversity:

> No outcast he, bewildered and depressed:
> Along his infant veins are interfused
> The gravitation and the filial bond
> Of nature that connect him with the world.[67]

Incidentally, Wordsworth himself had need of such strength in 1805. His beloved brother John drowned when the ship he captained (the *Earl of Abergavenny*) sank as it set out to take a large contingent of recruits to India.

The story of Fitzjulius, which demonstrates how hard it was for Eurasian boys to find their place in the world, was far from being unique. Other sons of successful John Company men had similar experiences. Neil Edmonstone and Charles Metcalfe were well-known and respected public servants, whose duties kept them in India for uninterrupted periods of over thirty years. Both put their duties above the claims of family life, and Edmonstone boasted that he was never 'one day absent from duty' during his time in India.[68] Metcalfe told his sister: 'I have no present thought of quitting India. The Happiness of millions is affected and ... promoted by my individual conduct. I have had a hard struggle against Vice and Corruption. I have now a glimpse of victory, and I must perform the work I have commenced.'[69] Metcalfe never married and Edmonstone delayed marriage for twenty years – but both fathered three illegitimate sons whom they sent back to England to be brought up by dutiful women.

To avoid sullying the family reputation, Edmonstone gave his boys the surname Elmore, though he had apparently not disowned their Indian mother since the children regularly sent her their love through him. In 1802 he dispatched the two oldest, John and Alick, to live with the sister of his Scottish friend Colonel John Baillie. The youngest Elmore brother, Frederick, was born the following year and in 1811 he was sent to England and placed in a school near London. Frederick's story is tragically brief. Two neatly written letters tell his father of his 'pleasant passage from India' with Mr Mercer, of his school, where there were 'several other East India boys', of Mr Mercer's departure for Scotland and of a swelling in his neck, which did not prevent him 'from attending school, or from play'.[70] In 1813 the headmaster reported that his 'good-tempered, orderly, obliging and grateful' pupil was 'making good progress in his education'. But the growth had spread to his spine and Frederick had been 'reduced to a state of great debility'. He was 'brought down every day and drawn about in a little chaise for the benefit of the fresh air'. In a subsequent letter the headmaster explained that, despite the 'unabated care' he was given and the 'great expense incurred', the boy died at the school in 1815.[71]

Frederick probably never met his two brothers who were growing up in Inverness, whence Margaret Baillie sent progress reports to Neil Edmonstone and to his brother Charles in London. She found the care of these 'docile and tractable' children 'an easy and pleasant charge'. Indeed, she clearly grew to love the 'very affectionate' boys, defending them fiercely and taking a great interest in their success. She insisted on sending John to college, even though his father feared that this 'might give the boy ideas inconsistent with [his] views for him'. What his future would then be was not clear and uncertainty on this score, she explained, sometimes caused John to give insufficient attention to his studies. It was his ambition to go to India so that he could 'be near and under the immediate protection of a father he so much respects and loves'. But Edmonstone prohibited this. In fact he allowed neither of the boys to come to the subcontinent because of 'the difficulties attending their position there'. In 1813 John was a proud young man of seventeen (though neither he nor Alick knew his exact date of birth) with 'a great desire to be considered a Gentleman'. As Margaret Baillie said, 'Feeling the misfortune of his birth he eagerly grasps at what affords the quickest prospect of getting over it.'[72] John decided on an army career and his uncle (urged on by Miss Baillie) helped him to get a commission in a Scottish regiment. He joined the regiment in Ireland but he was soon put on half-pay. Whether this was due to his rather dark complexion history does not relate.

Alick was much lighter-skinned and could even be supposed a native of Britain 'by people unacquainted with his birth'. He had less academic ability than his brother but he was, wrote his devoted guardian, 'a boy of uncommon kind disposition' who deserved to do well. When he reached the age of seventeen he told his father that he wanted to try his fortune 'in the commercial line', expressing the hope that his uncle would help him to find a situation. The letter was taken to India by his 'dear companion', Colonel John Baillie's son, who must also have been brought up by Miss Baillie (his aunt) and who had obtained a Company post. Alick hoped for an early reply, having been 'greatly disappointed at not having the happiness to hear from [his father] for a very long period'.[73]

In 1817 Colonel Baillie returned to Britain and saw both the Elmore lads. He was disappointed to find John still not restored to full pay and Alick merely working for a manufacturer in Glasgow. His report to their father frankly states his opinion of how his friend had treated the boys: 'The two lads who were brought up by my sister ... are entitled to your name and the countenance of your family though unfortunately for them they are deprived of the one and enjoying but a little of the other.'[74] In fact Edmonstone, who by this time had five or six legitimate children, never did recognise John and Alick as his sons or heirs, and nothing more is known of them. Clearly their prospects were poor, although they had enjoyed the inestimable advantage of a secure and loving home for nearly fifteen years. Margaret Baillie had done her best to give a good start in life to these forgotten children of the Raj.

Charles Metcalfe also had cause to be grateful to a good woman for the care of his three sons who, he acknowledged, bore 'a Stigma inflicted by the fault of their father'. By 1819 he had entrusted Henry (always known by his second name, Studholme), Frank and James to his unmarried sister Georgiana. She was to choose guardians, tutors and schools and to 'let no expense be spared'. From the patchy remnants of Metcalfe's correspondence (consisting of letters transcribed by Mary Clive Bayley, a great-niece of Georgiana's) it is clear that he took a close interest in the boys' progress, even requesting sketches of them to be sent to him in India. They seem to have been well tended under their aunt's watchful eye. Metcalfe was pleased to hear, for instance, of 'Mrs Courtis's kind care of little James, [which] could not have been more tender if she had been a near relative'.[75] Georgiana was fond enough of her nephews to continue her charge of them after she married in 1823, even though she now had three stepchildren under her wing. Two years later, when she had a son of her own, Metcalfe decided that he was taking 'an unfair advantage' of her kindness and released her 'from the trouble which you have so generously and affectionately encountered for so many years'. In any case, he thought that the adolescent Studholme now needed 'a Man's tutelage', which came in the shape of his agent Mr Brownrigg.[76]

Like many Eurasian boys, Studholme faced a difficult future, though his fate was to be more tragic than most. In 1823, when he was fourteen, his father was at a loss. He wanted the boy to continue his education but didn't know of a suitable college; he could not recommend his going to India where there was 'no chance of an appointment' but could devise no better prospects for him. The problem was compounded by the fact that the boy did not seem to have the qualities required for success.

> I perceive ... that timidity stands in his way for all the bustling professions, and that he does not make up for this by an extraordinary Talent or Taste for Application. So there is no promise of eminence in any Line. He has got a promise from me that his inclination shall be consulted in the choice of his destiny, and as far as my means will admit, that promise shall be adhered to.[77]

In 1826 Studholme was still at school for, as his father wrote to Georgiana, 'his want of energy is against his undertaking any profession'. Metcalfe hoped that further instruction would 'give a better stamp to his character'.[78] But things did not improve. In 1830 Studholme suffered some kind of a breakdown and was nursed back to health by his devoted aunt. After that, despite his father's misgivings and probably because there was no alternative, he did go out to India. He went into business in Calcutta, where his father was based, but he did not make a success of it. Nor did he establish a position in European society – he does not seem, for example, to have met his smart Delhi cousins, Theo, Emily and Georgiana Metcalfe, even though they sometimes went to Calcutta. In 1838 Charles Metcalfe returned home, leaving his son behind. Two years later, in obscure circumstances, Studholme shot himself. Relying on secondhand reports, Metcalfe tried to explain his son's death – and perhaps to absolve himself from any blame for it.

> He fell a victim, I grieve to say, to bad habits, which he had not energy of character enough to shake off, after they had once fastened on him. He was in other respects I believe harmless, and only his own Enemy. A merciful God will I humbly hope pardon his offences and grant him greater happiness in the World to come, than he could ever with such habits have obtained in this.[79]

It was not unusual for a father to feel ashamed of a son's behaviour. As we have seen, William Barlow and William Prinsep caused paternal distress. Their contemporary William Hickey was packed off to India after he had repeatedly 'deceived and disappointed' his indulgent father; his habits did not improve when he got to Calcutta but he prospered all the same.[80] The oldest son of the new young Queen was to provide a notorious example of filial misdeeds. But young men like Studholme and Fitzjulius had to endure something more serious than stern lectures from parents and guardians. For without a good school record, a strong will to succeed and parents committed to them as to legitimate offspring, they faced banishment from polite British or Anglo-Indian society. Their experiences, and those of other young Eurasians sent to Britain in the late eighteenth and early nineteenth centuries, confirm the conclusion of a recent history of Asians in Britain by Rosina Vizram. Only the 'combination of fair skin, the wealth of a nabob father and a claim to descent from Indian aristocracy' allowed the offspring of cross-cultural marriages 'to win a place in English high society'.[81]

The youngest of Charles Metcalfe's sons, James, had both better luck and greater ability than his brother. After doing well at Addiscombe Military College, he came to maturity at a fortunate time, in 1835–6. The East India Company had just removed the race bar on recruitment and his father was acting Governor-General, so James was able to gain a commission in a Bengal regiment. He rose to become a colonel and aide-de-camp to Governor-General Lord Dalhousie between 1848 and 1853. By that time James was a wealthy man, for when his father died in 1846 he was the only surviving son, Frank having died in 1842. James inherited £50,000 as well as books, plate, engravings, court dresses and jewels. Even so, he could not escape all the consequences of his genetic inheritance. As an illegitimate, half-Indian son he could not inherit the barony which Metcalfe had been granted in 1845 in recognition for his services to the Empire. James would have been proud, however, if he had known that his entry was to appear on the same page of the original *Dictionary of National Biography* as that of his white cousin Theo, who became Sir Theophilus Metcalfe. Both won the Order of the Bath for gallantry during the Indian Mutiny – but only James appears in the new *Oxford DNB*.

The legislation which enabled the youngest offspring of William Palmer and Charles Metcalfe to enter the higher ranks of the East India

Company's service was passed partly in response to a petition from 700 Eurasians to the English Parliament. It was taken to London in 1830 by John Ricketts, the half-Indian son of a British lieutenant, who had been brought up in the Upper Military Orphanage. In his address to the House of Lords Ricketts argued that the Eurasian community had received from the East India Company 'nothing but studied insult, contemptuous indifference, or at best empty profession'.[82] And in his evidence to a House of Commons committee he compared this treatment to 'the more liberal policy adopted towards the descendants of European fathers by native mothers by the Dutch, French, Spaniards and Portuguese in all their settlements'.[83] There were no immediate concessions but when the Company's Charter came up for renewal in 1833 Governor-General Bentinck insisted that entry to its civil and military services should not be denied on the grounds of religion, birthplace, descent or colour.

In practice not many Eurasians had the education or the connections to benefit from this ruling in the way that James and Hastings Palmer and James Metcalfe did. Also, in applying for covenanted posts they faced increasing competition from greater numbers of Britons and from educated Indians. To an official inquiry into the Company's affairs before the next renewal of its Charter in 1853, Eurasians complained that little had changed. Most of them were still *crannies* (junior clerks). Between them and British gentlemen, wrote Frederick Shore, one of Sir John's legitimate and luckier sons, the distinction was 'almost as great as that of Brahmin and Pariah'.[84] In the late nineteenth and early twentieth centuries, however, more schools for Eurasians were opened by missions and by benefactors like Dr John Graham. Their pupils sometimes found these institutions grim and patronising. Edward Lamb, the illegitimate son of an English engineer and his Bengali mistress, says that he gained an inferiority complex from his years at Dr Graham's Kalimpong Homes. But Lamb, like other Eurasian objects of charity, admits that the education was rigorous and opened up opportunities for advance.[85]

From these schools girls often went into teaching and boys found jobs in the new telegraph and railway systems. These fields (as well as the junior ranks of the Civil Service) continued to be their traditional and proud preserve in the twentieth century. An English 'Chief Inspectress' of schools found in 1908 that her junior colleagues were all Eurasians. They were 'quite well educated,' she noticed with some surprise, 'and really very capable women'. She compared them favourably with Eurasians in general, whom she regarded as an 'unreliable and effectless lot'.[86] Talking to a group of impoverished elderly Eurasians in 1974, an English interviewer discovered that 'Most of you gentlemen have been skilled mechanics.' He had always heard that Eurasians (known as Anglo-Indians by that time) were 'very good at games but not very good at studies'. That was 'fair enough,' the interviewer added patronisingly, since 'we can't all be brilliant people with our brains'.[87]

Despite the advances, Eurasians found that the British continued to treat them with the lofty reserve that Jacquemont noticed in 1829. The Frenchman concluded, naturally, that the affectionate mixed-race French families of Chandernagore were 'nicer people' than the aloof rulers of greater India.[88] Be that as it may, British condescension is certainly illustrated in the *East India Vade-Mecum*'s view that 'the issue of a European father by a native woman is usually of an effeminate, weakly constitution and of a disposition by no means entitled to commendation'.[89] With more insight, Captain Bellew attempted to explain the social gulf which separated him from the dark-eyed young woman he met at the orphanage dance:

> Society full oft, by its folly, oppression and prejudice, begets the faults which it affects to hate and despise; and the fact of any classes being looked down upon, which is more or less the case as regards the half-caste or Eurasians throughout India ... has a depressing tendency, which naturally places individuals of that description in a highly disadvantageous position, deadening the energies and preventing that free and natural play and expansion of the mind and feelings which are ever the results of knowing that we stand well with the world.[90]

It was a shrewd analysis of the malign effect of low self-esteem. The prejudice it mentions never died and Eurasians rarely gained admission to British clubs. In the 1880s Stephen Turner, son of a British father and an Indian mother, who had been to an English public school and got into the Political Department in Baluchistan, was classed as a 'native of India' and told that 'socially he would never qualify as a member of the Quetta Club'.[91] As late as 1946 the Eurasian girlfriend of a British captain in a Gurkha regiment (a 'well-educated convent girl') was asked to leave a dance at the Secunderabad Officers' Club.[92]

Racial disdain often went hand in hand with physical distaste. It pervades *Curry and Rice*, an early-nineteenth-century book which continued to be astonishingly popular in the British community in India. One of the characters in this facetious survey of life on 'Our Station' is Major Garlic, who has 'married a darkie' and produced 'a piebald progeny with ... tawny complexions, black eyes and still blacker locks'. The author cautions against a visit to the Major's bungalow, 'that land of darkness', where 'the floor is infested with the brats that lie dormant in every direction, with vestments of an abridged, if not of an entirely abrogated nature'.[93] Emily Metcalfe was also upset by garments that revealed too much coffee-coloured flesh. When dutifully calling in 1847 on a family of her father's acquaintance who had 'a great deal of native blood in their veins', she remarked on the five daughters' 'utter ignorance of English customs as regards dress', deploring their 'white cotton dresses with low necks and short sleeves'.[94] An Anglo-Indian novel of about the same time describes a similar garment revealing the 'fat black arms' of a Dutch Eurasian woman whose marriage to an ICS officer had caused him to fall 'out of European society'.[95]

In a story written in the 1960s, Eric Linklater, who had once worked for *The Times of India*, expresses the disgust of his protagonist at the Eurasian relations arriving at the deathbed of a friend hitherto thought to be a pure European. The mother is 'a fat ungainly woman'; the aunt's 'exuberant breast strained the shiny fabric of her blouse'; the sister has 'the helpless allure of her kind'; and the brother is simply a 'disgusting small boy' who picks his nose. For Eurasian children the experience of being spurned in this way could be very painful. At Auckland House School in Simla one Eurasian pupil was presumably judging from her own experience when she assumed that her fair-haired English friend must be more cherished by her mother than her darker sister.[96] As a result of British 'racial fastidiousness' (Linklater's phrase) and Indian exclusiveness (on the grounds that they did not fit into the caste system), Eurasians developed their own distinctive communities and way of life.[97]

Yet, throughout the entire history of the Raj 'there was no question as to the unswerving loyalty of these people to the Europeans who had sired them'.[98] During the Maratha wars of the late eighteenth century most Eurasian officers obeyed John Company's call to leave their Maratha regiments and fight with its army – only to be discharged when the conflict ended in 1808. When mutinous Indian *sepoys* (troops) massacred white officers and their families in 1857 many Eurasians put their dark skin and knowledge of Indian languages at the disposal of the British Army by acting as spies and interpreters. Among them were members of families which feature in this chapter. Two of Hyder Hearsey's sons joined the British Intelligence Service. James Palmer took part in the march to relieve Cawnpore, losing his life en route. James Metcalfe acted as interpreter to the Commander-in-Chief, Sir Colin Campbell, 'whose side he never quitted'.[99] Hundreds of Eurasians died beside Europeans in the Mutiny. Among the victims were probably the current pupils of the school set up by Mrs Sherwood in Cawnpore. Captain Mowbray Thomson records that there were 'three hundred half-caste children belonging to the Cawnpore school' in the entrenchment at the beginning of the siege in June 1857.[100] He does not say what happened to these youngsters, whose number he probably exaggerates. But, as will be seen in the next chapter, it is most unlikely that they survived the ensuing privations, epidemics and massacres.

Eurasians also sided with the British during the struggle for Indian independence in the twentieth century. This was their natural instinct. But they knew, too, that under Indian rule Eurasians would lose the preference they had been given in certain government jobs under the Raj. Bill Newman, the son of a Bombay railway engineer, told me that when Independence came in 1947 'our people were up the creek. Indianisation meant your job was gone.' Deprived of fatherly protection, thousands of other Eurasians had to leave their motherland, Newman explained, 'to start again without a bias against us'.[101] He decided to stay on in Britain, where he had gone to university, and later pursued a successful engineering career with Ransome/Rapier Engineering. Many Eurasian families went to Australia, Canada and New Zealand where their education, Christian faith and proficiency in English enabled them to integrate into new societies.

'The British left us like crying orphans [with] no father, no mother,' concluded an emigrant living in Sydney.[102] The stories of Eurasian children over two centuries, as told in this chapter, often reveal them as abandoned, excluded, patronised, ostracised and stigmatised. Yet they were not all forlorn. Some were cherished, encouraged and protected while others won through against the odds. As Bill Newman concluded, on looking back over a life divided between his Indian motherland and his British fatherland, 'We are not easily submerged.'

THREE

'Alarming News'

The Mutiny and Other Perils

On 16 March 1859 Dr Joseph Fayrer bade farewell to his small son before leaving to take up a medical post in Calcutta. 'Little Bob was asleep in his cot and I would not wake him. I did not see him again till he was in the fifth form at Rugby.'[1] Shortly before his reunion with the teenage Rugbeian in 1873 the doctor gave a lecture on 'European Child-Life in Bengal'. In it he provided a scientific defence for such drastic periods of separation between parents and their children. While admitting that there had been 'improvements . . . of a sanitary nature' in India, he gave a strong warning to European parents living there. The dangers of physical and moral deterioration could only be avoided by sending children 'to the more bracing and healthy . . . atmosphere of Europe', even if this involved 'separation for years'.[2]

After twenty years' service in the Indian Medical Service, Dr Fayrer was seen as an authority on the perils of life in the subcontinent. He had lived with his wife and baby Bob through the siege of Lucknow in 1857, when he had amputated limbs, treated victims of fever, boils and diarrhoea, delivered babies and tended the dying. After a brief period of leave he had worked as Professor of Surgery in Calcutta, where he built up a profitable private practice. During this time he and his wife (whom he never names in his *Recollections*) sent three more sons to England. It was not until 1873 that the Fayrer children (now numbering seven) 'all met in the presence of their father and mother for the first time'.[3] Fayrer then embarked on a series of public lectures about such topics as the fevers of India, tropical dysentery and chronic diarrhoea, the poison of venomous snakes and the epidemiology of cholera – to say nothing of his disquisition on the life and death of 'the royal tiger'. Such was his renown that Queen Victoria asked him to accompany the Prince of Wales on his Indian tour in 1875–6. Fayrer safeguarded His Royal Highness's health, though the royal tigers fared less well since their dispatch was the principal purpose of the Prince's visit. Victorians accepted the validity of the good doctor's warnings about India. But does the evidence bear him out? Do investigators such as Florence Nightingale and the eye-witnesses of two famous mid-century Indian disasters tell the same tale?

In the first of these disasters, the bloody retreat from Kabul, children were placed in peril as a result of deliberate government policy. In 1839 the Governor-General, Lord Auckland, decided that the best way to forestall any Russian designs on the north-west frontier of India was to establish British control over neighbouring Afghanistan. He sent an army to dethrone Dost Mohammed, the popular king who had made friendly overtures to Russia, and replace him with a ruler controlled by a British Agent, Sir William Macnaghten. It was soon obvious, at least to Lieutenant Christopher Codrington, that the puppet monarch Shah Shuja was hated and that the British would for a long time be obliged to maintain 'a large force in this country to keep the king on his throne'. Codrington had sensibly told his wife not to come and join him in Afghanistan, which was 'not a place for officers to take their families [for] with wild countries like this there is no knowing what might happen'.[4] However Lord Auckland, a bachelor accompanied in India by two unmarried sisters, took a different view. He encouraged officers to send for their wives and children, 'it being supposed that they would have no wish to quit the country with their families settled along with them'.[5] Sepoys and the officers' Indian servants already had dependants with them but these were usually referred to, rather disparagingly, as camp-followers. Ordinary British soldiers were expected to leave their families behind. Thus Corporal Dunn, who kept a careful record of his 2,312-mile march from Agra to Kabul, made do with simple pleasures like picking wild mountain blackberries.[6]

Fruits of many varieties were some compensation to the officers' ladies gathered in the overcrowded Kabul cantonment. As even the lonely Codrington had to admit, the country had a 'delightful climate' which produced an abundance of peaches, apricots, greengages, cherries, plums, mulberries and grapes. But while the British residents cultivated their gardens and shot the local wildlife, the Afghans bore their presence 'very impatiently' and plotted vengeance.[7] They resorted to arms in the autumn of 1841. A brigade led by General Sir Robert Sale failed to quell the rebellion (during which Codrington lost his life) and had to retreat to Jalalabad near the border. As Christmas approached, Dost Mohammed's son, Akbar Khan, brought the revolt to the capital. It culminated in the murder of Macnaghten and several army officers, including Captain Trevor who had a pregnant wife and seven children with him in the city. Lacking supplies and effective leadership, the British agreed to leave Kabul on 6 January 1842, with a promise of safe conduct to the border. From the start the long line of soldiers, families and camp-followers, slowed down by immense amounts of baggage and by 'the dreadful effects of severe frost', became the target of Afghan tribesmen. As the column struggled through the first mountain pass on 8 January it 'presented the appearance of a rout', recorded Captain William Anderson in a pencil-written journal now preserved by the India Office Library. 'Women and children even were left to the mercy of the Afghans.'[8] Such was the confusion that Anderson's three-year-old daughter Mary (nicknamed Tootsey) and the youngest boy of Captain and Mrs Boyd were carried off.

It was in these desperate circumstances, after a night lying on the snow with no food or fuel, that the British received an overture from Akbar Khan. He offered to take all the European wives and children (with their husbands) under his protection – in other words, to make them prisoners. Most of the families were 'overwhelmed with domestic affliction'.[9] Anderson himself was responsible for a wife who had just given birth and a small child, to say nothing of the kidnapped Tootsey. Lady Sale and her twenty-year-old pregnant daughter Alexandrina were mourning the recent death of Alexandrina's husband, Lieutenant Sturt. Mrs Trevor had to cope on her own with seven children. Lieutenant Vincent Eyre had been wounded and could not adequately protect his wife and infant. As he wrote in his journal, none felt that they could refuse the offer even though 'it was a matter of serious doubt whether the whole were not rushing into the very jaws of death, by placing themselves at the mercy of a man, who had so lately imbrued his hands in the blood of a British Envoy.'[10]

Ten women and twenty children were taken captive, together with their surviving husbands and three other officers. They left behind an army of 4,000 together with 12,000 camp-followers, among them hundreds of Indian women and children for whom no refuge was proffered. Captain Colin Mackenzie, one of the hostage officers, whose own three daughters were in England, remembered as 'one of the heartrending sights of that humiliating day . . . a little Hindustani child, perfectly naked, sitting in the snow, with no father or mother near it'. Instead of being able to take up 'this poor little native of a tropical climate and cuddle it in his arms, and give it some warmth from his own body,' wrote Mackenzie's biographer, 'he was obliged to leave it there to die'.[11] The rest of the column met a similar fate. They succumbed to continued Afghan attacks, bitter cold and extreme hunger. Only one man survived. On 13 January 1842 Surgeon William Brydon, riding a dying horse, entered the British fortress at Jalalabad.

The white women and children fared better under the wing of Akbar Khan. In the first place of their captivity the Boyds, to their 'inexpressible joy', found their little son safe and sound.[12] The Andersons had to wait until May for Tootsey (whose name punctuates her father's diary) to be restored to them. All the surviving journals and memoirs record that she had apparently been treated 'with the greatest possible kindness'. According to Eyre's account she could speak only Persian, in which language she repeated the sentence: 'My father and mother are infidels but I am a Mussulman [Muslim].'[13] Her father wrote nothing of this but expressed concern for her health, which had been weakened by her four-month ordeal. When the party had to move on, two weeks after Tootsey's return, he made a litter to carry her in and he reports that 'the trip . . . appears to have done the child good'.[14] All the other children survived apart from a boy referred to as 'little Stoker', whose mother had died in the initial retreat. He had no one to care for him since the sergeant's wife, who was given that task, went off with an 'Afghan paramour'.[15]

Even the two babies born just before the retreat and the five born in captivity (among them Mrs Sturt's daughter) came to no harm. The infant son of Lady Sale's friend, Mrs Mainwaring, became a general favourite and was nicknamed *Jung-i-Bahadur* (Hero in Battle). In the one surviving letter written to her husband in Jalalabad, Lady Sale asked him to tell Mainwaring (an officer in General Sale's brigade) that the boy was in good health and 'busy sucking one of the barley-sugar lolly pops' brought to them by a man from Kabul.[16] There were other occasional treats. On 24 January Dost Mohammed 'took Mrs Trevor's boys and some gentlemen out walking in the sugar-cane fields near the fort, which they enjoyed very much'. On the same day Akbar Khan sent some chintz so that the women could make clothes for themselves and the children. When spring came their tents were pitched 'on a pretty and green spot' where Lady Sale and the rest of the party enjoyed a profusion of wild flowers: 'The field pea was in blossom [and] several sorts of cranesbill, gentian, forget-me-not, campions etc.'[17] Sometimes she received boxes of useful things sent by her husband – but apparently she would not share so much as a sewing needle with the other women.[18]

On the other hand, the party endured many discomforts as it moved from one fort or cave to another. There were no spoons or forks, the food was greasy, the fires constantly smoked and beds were notable by their absence. Lady Sale complained that constant exposure to the sun made them as 'black as Afghans'. And most of them were infested with lice, 'denominated infantry', and fleas, known as 'light infantry'.[19] However, Eyre concluded, these 'inconveniences were indeed of small moment, when weighed in the balance against the combination of horrors we had escaped'.[20] The party was protected from attack by tribesmen and the greatest threat to their safety came from earthquakes. Lady Sale's verdict on Akbar Khan's treatment of the families was that 'honour has been respected'.[21] Some of the children may even have enjoyed the adventure, although it would have been heresy to suggest this at the time.

The prisoners ended up in a mountain fortress near Kabul, from which they were rescued by General Sale in September 1842. On its march through Afghanistan the British 'Army of Retribution' had avenged the deaths of their comrades by burning crops, destroying villages and driving the inhabitants into the hills to perish. None of this was much use to the widows and orphans of the Afghan campaign, who received little other compensation. The East India Company did provide some help for officers' bereaved families but it gave nothing to those of common soldiers; their widows simply had to try to find new husbands. For the 'Widows and Orphans of Camp Followers and Other Sufferers' a charitable find was established. Back in England Julia Codrington collected her late husband's letters to form a record of 'what appeared to her from the first a wild undertaking'. 'The heart of a Wife and Mother sadly foreboded that no good could come of it.'[22] Charles Augustus Moyle, an officer stationed at that time near the north-west frontier, shared her opinion. In his memoir he compared the British Army in Afghanistan to 'Dog Toby who left the room when he saw he was to be kicked out'. (By that analogy Akbar Khan would equate with Mr Punch, who lashed out at Toby after being bitten on the nose.) Moyle went on to lament: 'Oh John Company, what a sad mess you made here.'[23]

Only twelve years separated the First Afghan War from the Indian Mutiny, and some military families were caught up in both. The most remarkable instance is that of Dr Brydon, sole survivor of the march from Kabul, who also lived through the siege of Lucknow with his wife and two infants. Colina Brydon's diary for 1857 reveals constant anxieties about her husband, who was wounded in what she politely referred to as the loins. She also worried about her five older children in England whom she might never see again and the two babies with her in Lucknow, who were often ailing. In fact, the only death in her household was that of the old Indian ayah, who ran away and was found lying dead outside the entrenchments. Mrs Brydon had scant sympathy, though, since the ayah had lost her life 'by her own wilfulness'. When the Brydons themselves got away from Lucknow in November they were allocated two camels to carry their property but there was no room for Colina's precious harp. After a few days, however, more transport was available and she sent 'four coolies' back 'through a good deal of firing' to bring out the harp. 'A round shot passed closely over the case but no one was hit.'[24] Mrs Brydon did not neglect to thank God that all her family had been spared.

Most collections of letters relating to both the mid-century disasters tell of some bereavement. Those of the Nicholl family are typical. Captain Thomas Nicholl was in charge of a troop of horse artillery during the occupation of Afghanistan while his wife and children stayed in Calcutta. He clearly missed them and wrote frequently to his 'very dear boy' Thomas, who with his sister Jane was waiting to be put on to a ship for England. Nicholl told the child where to leave his gun and assured him that there would be 'nice dogs in England' – thus indicating that young Thomas was already immersed in the traditional pursuits of Anglo-Indian males. He obviously preferred them to his studies for, at the age of nine, he was still unable to read his father's letters or to write back. In December 1840 Nicholl fondly attempted to instil a little discipline into his idle son:

I hope you are a good Boy and read your Book. I hope you are able to read this letter; if you can, then I shall know you are learning to improve yourself; you must mind what your dear Mamma says to

you, a little bird tells me that you do not mind what she says. . . .
You must always think of me my dear Boy, and write to me when
you can do so on board ship, you can write a few lines in Jane's
letter. . . . You will be very happy with Richard Glyn [his guardian
for the journey] but mind you do not fall into the sea.

In April Nicholl wrote of his hopes for the future. In three years' time
he would become a major and would take the rest of the family to join
Thomas and Jane in England: 'How happy you will both be to see us
all after being away so long a time.' But nine months later he was killed
in the retreat from Kabul.[25]

The younger Thomas clearly managed to imbibe enough learning to
be able in his turn to gain a commission in the Army. By 1857 Lieutenant Nicholl was stationed at Sagar in central India, where he helped
to maintain peace even though the district was 'entirely at the hands
of marauders and cut throats'. He wrote to his mother about the birth
of his own first son (another Thomas), who could not be christened
because 'the Padre's wife and child have had smallpox and . . . it is not
safe yet to allow the child into the clergyman's arms'. However, the
family survived these hazards and the Lieutenant escorted European
inhabitants out of Sagar in February 1858.[26] They were more fortunate
than Lady Sale's daughter. She and her second husband, Major Holmes,
were among the first victims of the Mutiny – they were caught riding
in their carriage at Sigauli and beheaded. Alexandrina's daughter, the
fatherless Afghan captive, must have been about twelve by this time
and she was probably in England when the news came that she had
lost both her mother and her stepfather. There is no record of how she
bore this further bereavement.

What none of these family stories reveals is the feature which dis-
tinguishes the Indian Mutiny from all other episodes in Anglo-Indian
history: deliberate and wholesale violence towards British children.
During the hot months and monsoon period of 1857 rebellious sepoys
killed hundreds of children and allowed many more to die after great
suffering. Such uncharacteristic ferocity was the product of quite
exceptional circumstances. For normally the *baba log* (little people)
grew up with the justifiable conviction that they could never 'be killed
or be in any danger from an Indian'.[27]

For some years before the eruption of 1857 a number of grievances
had been seething beneath the surface of Indian life. Georgian nabobs
had given way to Victorian sahibs, a new breed of imperialists as

much bent on moral improvement as on making money. Measures such as the abolition of *suttee* (widow-burning) and *thugee* (the ritual killing of travellers), the introduction of Western-style education and reforms in land ownership provoked fears that the British planned to destroy India's ancient customs and religions. Inspired by such liberals as Governor-General Bentinck and his legal minister T. B. Macaulay, these changes were benevolent in intent. But the conquest of further territory – Sind in 1843, the Punjab in 1849 and Oudh in 1857 – suggested that the British motive was not so much altruism as lust for power. Indians were also worried by the increasing activity of Evangelical missionaries, who condemned the caste system and fulminated against heathens in their blindness bowing down to wood and stone. One Baptist missionary at Serampore admitted in a letter to his parents that 'one of the chief causes [of the Mutiny] has been the hatred of the sepoys and Musoulmen against Christianity'[28] Racial arrogance often accompanied religious intolerance – both on the increase in Victorian India. The American historian Andrew Ward finds that the Europeans of Fatehgarh (whom he describes as 'over-extended merchants and disappointed officers') were especially 'notorious for their nastiness toward Indians'. He singles out Magistrate Robert Thornhill, son of an East India Company director, who used to recite in court doggerel about the hookah smoking habits of 'the stinking nigger'. Ward is not surprised that the *burra sahibs* (important Europeans) and American missionaries fled from the station in June 1857 fearing that the 'disgruntled populace' would rise against them.[29]

It was in this atmosphere of antipathy, distrust, fear and misunderstanding that the British Army introduced a new rifle early in 1857, the centenary of the Battle of Plassey and the year 'fixed by native prophecy for the *ferringhies* [foreigners] to be driven out of India'.[30] The cartridges for the Enfield, which had to be bitten off, were lubricated with tallow made from animal fats and no one could be sure what animals had been used. Since beef fat would defile a Hindu and pork fat a Muslim, the imposition of the new cartridges seemed like a deliberate attack on Indian religious beliefs. Some older officers were able to forestall trouble. At Barrackpore, near Calcutta, sixty-four-year-old General John Hearsey (whose close family links with India appeared in Chapter Two) nipped mutiny in the bud by enforcing firm but fair discipline and making a tactful appeal to the sepoys in his fluent Hindustani. But by this time (May) the seeds of rebellion had already been distributed to other regiments, whose commanders did not always show the same wisdom.

Among the first victims of the sepoys' fury was the youngest son of James Munro Macnabb, eighteen-year-old Cornet John Macnabb, who had only just arrived at the Meerut station. Inexperienced though he was, he could see that the punishments inflicted by Colonel George Carmichael-Smyth on sepoys refusing to use the new cartridges were 'injudicious'. Eighty-five men were shackled and paraded in their irons before being taken off to serve long terms of imprisonment. John was trying to explain all this to his mother but he did not live to finish his letter. Instead she heard from his brother James, who was also in India and wrote, on 23 May, incoherent with grief: 'I have wretched news from Meerut where the 3rd Cavalry mutinied and killed several of the officers [on 10 May] and the list today tells me that dear John is among them. . . . What a comfort it is knowing from all the dear boy's letters that he was still living close to God.'[31] On the same day the sepoys murdered about twenty civilians living in the cantonment, including at least eight children. There would have been more young victims had some not been rescued by faithful servants after the death of their parents.[32]

The mutineers moved on to Delhi and quickly gained control of the city, killing most of the Europeans living there. Again many children were among the victims, deliberately hacked to pieces with swords and spears. A plaque in St James's Church exemplifies the great loss suffered by some families. It commemorates Deputy Collector Thomas Collins who was 'barbarously murdered on or about the 11th of May 1857', together with his wife, mother-in-law, three brothers-in-law, four sisters-in-law, seven nephews, three nieces and three grand-children. The tablet was erected by 'the three surviving orphans', who were presumably in England at the time of the massacre. Among the few who escaped death in Delhi were members of some families who appear in other chapters.

Mrs Elizabeth Wagentreiber, one of Colonel Skinner's daughters, was able to save herself and her family thanks to her Eurasian origins. She was as dark-skinned as her father, whose memory was still revered in the Delhi region, and she naturally had a much better understanding of Indians than her English husband George, who 'had not long been out in India . . . and would have either abused them or struck them'. The Wagentreibers' youngest daughter Florence tells the story of the family's hazardous escape from Delhi, during which they were attacked or threatened by *dacoits* (robbers) as well as by sepoys. They were eventually saved by meeting an old man who had been a servant of Colonel Skinner and declared that he would give his life 'for any of his children'. Florence tells how he escorted them in the final stage of their journey, through 'my grandfather's villages ... where the village people made low obeisance, my mother raising her hand to her forehead in acknowledgement of their salute'.[33] In general, though, half-Indian blood was almost as likely to flow as British. All the Eurasians whom Emily Metcalfe had met in Delhi in 1847 lost their lives during the occupation of the city.

Only tough and lucky Europeans escaped, among them Emily's brother, Sir Theophilus Metcalfe. He was 'a powerful as well as a decisive man',[34] and he did well to get away from the elegant Metcalfe House, which was a natural target for the rebels. With the help of a good horse, a gun, a sword and some native clothes, he managed to make his way out of the city. He soon returned, however, to join the other volunteers and soldiers massing on the Ridge above Delhi in order to besiege and recapture the city. One of the officers who fore-gathered at the camp was Sir Edward Campbell, who was married to Metcalfe's sister Georgiana.

The surviving correspondence between Sir Edward and Lady Campbell (who was in Simla) reveals the strains that the Mutiny inflicted on family life. She wrote almost every day, on mourning paper sent in tiny black-edged envelopes, presumably in memory of those who had already been killed. Her faint and almost indecipherable handwriting betrays the agitation of a young woman terrified about the dangers her husband and brother were facing 'at that horrid picket' and finding it hard to cope with the responsibility of the children they had left with her.[35] In addition to the Campbells' two-year-old Guy and infant twins there was her brother's toddler Charlie, whose mother had died soon after his birth. Guy, who clearly missed his father, was sometimes 'troublesome and naughty' and followed her round like a shadow. Nevertheless Lady Campbell found in her little son her 'greatest earthly comfort'. But the obviously insecure Charlie drove her to despair. He would go into 'frightful passions' accompanied by nosebleeds and dreadful screaming. When she told him how naughty he was, he would 'throw himself to the floor again and scream worse than ever'. She wanted her husband to 'speak to Theo', telling him that it was 'not *his* duty to go to the scene of action ... into danger' and that it was wrong for him to do so 'while he has poor little Charlie entirely dependent on him alone'.[36] But Sir Edward and Sir Theophilus continued to do their duty as they saw it. They were lucky enough not to be among the hundreds killed during the assault on Delhi which began in July. They also survived the outbreak of cholera in the city.

During these hot summer months, always so hard on Europeans, mutiny had also broken out at many military stations throughout north-west India, especially in the newly annexed province of Oudh. Well aware of the massacres at Meerut and Delhi, some British families fled into the *mofussil* (countryside). Others looked to the Army for protection in military encampments or cantonment towns. Generally speaking, though, uprisings were quickly contained and in most parts of the subcontinent calm prevailed. After early alarms Calcutta remained quiet and for children there the Mutiny was a source of excitement rather than terror. William Ritchie, Thackeray's cousin, lived through it with his wife and younger children. In July he told his older children, who were living in Paris with his mother and sisters, about the miniature volunteer uniforms which had been made for Gerald and Richmond: 'They have jack-boots and breeches tucked into them, dark blue coats all braided and turned up with red little pouches with a belt over their shoulders and sabretaches with CVG for Calcutta Volunteer Guards on them in silver, and no end of silver buckles and mountings. I call Richmond General Tom Thumb.' As an adult Gerald remembered that a picture had been painted of them 'going up to a gigantic sepoy at Barrackpore and asking him where his gun was: *Tumhara banduk kahan hai?*'[37] In fact Hearsey had disarmed Indian troops at the beginning of the crisis. Meanwhile, at an army base in central India Major Walter Erskine was equally untroubled. He devoted less space in his diary to the Mutiny than to the weather. On 31 December he was able to record: 'I have indeed reason and so have all the residents of Jubbulpore, to thank God Almighty for preserving us to see the end of this year.' But others had more traumatic tales to tell and, as Erskine noted in May 1857, from other cantonments there came a constant stream of 'alarming news'.[38]

Captain Alfred Simons was stationed at Lucknow, the capital city of Oudh and an important army base. He had arrived in India at the end of 1854 with his wife Catherine (née Stock) and baby daughter Lucy Amelia Collingwood, whose third Christian name commemorates the ship on which she was born. From Lucknow in May 1857 the Captain wrote to his brother-in-law: 'Some horrible scenes have occurred lately at Meerut and Delhi, ladies and children, officers and civilians butchered without mercy. ... There is every disposition to try the same game here, but we are too well prepared, I fancy, for our ruffians to try it.'[39] However, the garrison took precautions. Europeans crowded into a fortified area around the Residency and Simons himself quickly sent Catherine, three-year-old Lucy, baby Ernest and the ayah off to the hills. He was just in time. On 30 May the Lucknow regiments mutinied and within a month the Residency was under siege. At the hill station of Naini Tal Catherine lived in a constant state of fear about the safety of 'dear Alfred' in Lucknow, from where she received no news. The fat 'affectionate little monkey' Ernest was some comfort for he bore such a close resemblance to his father that, as she told her mother, 'I do not need a portrait of my husband while I have him.' But in August, to her inconsolable grief, Lucy died. Catherine Simons was convinced that the cause of her death was an illness brought on by privations suffered during their flight from Lucknow. Though Ernest continued to be 'a merry little man' and she liked having the ayah with her, she felt Lucy's loss more every day. In October she remembered how 'she used to say "Gentle Jesus" to me every morning and when she had finished throw her arms around my neck and say "My Mama" so prettily in Hindustani.'[40]

Catherine's last letter from Naini Tal is undated but was written after the relief of Lucknow in November. She had received a list of survivors which did not include her husband. Like most Anglo-Indians in mid-Victorian days, she was a sincere Christian and now her greatest consolation was her faith: 'What was it that gave me such a dreadful presentiment, when I saw [Lucy's] dying smile, that she was going to join her father? I do not grieve for her now; not for worlds would I take her from him who loved her so dearly, and it is such an inexpressible comfort to me to think that they are not separated.' There is no written evidence about the final stage of the Simons' Mutiny story. But the Stock family (which preserved these letters) has handed down the tale that the ayah stained Catherine's and Ernest's faces and hands brown and helped them to reach the coast, through countryside which was still disturbed and dangerous. At any rate they did manage to get back to England. The Stock papers contain a photograph of a sad-eyed Catherine with baby Ernest on her lap, which was probably taken soon after she arrived home. On 10 June 1857, in the midst of her terrible ordeal, she told her mother to warn 'all girls to think twice before coming to India'.[41] Nevertheless Catherine herself returned to the subcontinent in 1866 with her second husband and another child. As none of her subsequent letters mention Ernest's presence it can only be assumed that she had left behind her affectionate little monkey, now a boy of ten, who would have to be sent to an English boarding school.

While Catherine Simons was preparing for her journey to the hills, Mrs Huxham, the wife of an officer stationed at Lucknow, obeyed the orders of Chief Commissioner Sir Henry Lawrence to take shelter in the fortified area of the Residency. It contained 1,700 men (including British and Indian troops and civilian volunteers), as well as 700 Indian camp-followers and servants and about 550 women and children. A list issued by the Governor-General at the end of the year named all the people in the garrison, showing that 270 of them were children.[42] When the siege was over Mrs Huxham (we do not know her Christian name) wrote a 'Personal Narrative'. It describes what happened to her own children (a 'sweet baby' and 'little Willie') and to other beleaguered youngsters. She writes of the intense heat, which Willie felt particularly; the plague of flies which 'swarmed on the children as they slept'; the appearance of cholera from which 'two dear little children of three years old died in great suffering, their little forms writhing in agony'; the diet of tough stewed meat which 'Willie could never be induced to touch'; and the constant 'showers of bullets' among which the children played war games. Sometimes Willie brought her spent bullets, 'having picked them up while still hot from the gun'. By July 'many little ones [had] succumbed for want of proper food and fresh air' and Mrs Huxham now faced tragedy herself. Her baby girl contracted dysentery. 'The disease made rapid strides,' she recorded, and 'her pure spirit passed away to her Home in Paradise on the early morning of Sunday 9th August.'[43]

Mrs Huxham goes on to describe the advent of the first relief force in September which raised 'false hopes', the continuation of the siege until a second force arrived in November and the fierce fighting during which her husband was wounded. Finally, on 18 November, 'We left the place where we had been made prisoners so long with mingled feelings of joy and gratitude.' By the time the family reached Calcutta, to be welcomed by her sister and her husband in January 1858, 'poor little Willie was very thin and white, but soon picked up and flourished under these brighter surroundings'.[44] Other children showed a similar resilience – which rather contradicted Victorian stereotypes about juvenile frailty in India. For example, in July and August Dr Fayrer said that his one-year-old Bob was 'getting to look like a wizened little old man' and 'a little puling skeleton'. But Bob survived several attacks of diarrhoea and fever and was 'picking up' by October when the weather grew cooler.[45] However, like the Huxhams, the Fayrers did lose a baby. He was born on the roadside in December, as evacuees were marching from Lucknow, and died a few days later.

It is hard to know how many died altogether and in what proportions.[46] Undoubtedly the defence of the Residency and fighting during the first and second reliefs of Lucknow cost the lives of a large number of men. The most reliable estimates cite losses of nearly 500 British and Indian soldiers and volunteers, getting on for a third of the total. This does not include the 230 Indian troops who deserted.[47] The fatalities included Sir Henry Lawrence, whose death early on in the siege orphaned his three children. The Governor-General's list shows that fifty-four children (or a fifth of the original number) perished.[48] So it seems that, vulnerable though they were, young Britons were not as much at risk in this crisis as their fathers, uncles and older brothers.

Most of the besieged children were infants under five since, by the nature of Anglo-Indian life, the older ones were at school in England. (Among their number were Alick and Harry Lawrence, whose careers will be discussed in Chapter Four.) But an older group of youngsters did take refuge in the Residency: fifty-seven European and Eurasian boys from Lucknow's famous La Martinière School along with eight of their masters. The pupils were aged between ten and sixteen, although the roll includes one who was only five – unlike the other lads, he was not awarded the Mutiny medal. The adolescents participated in the defence of the Residency, the more daring ones taking up their position on the roof so as to get a better aim. Younger lads first acted as servants to some of the families but later they were needed to grind corn for the garrison. Some also worked in the hospital, carried water and helped with the cooking. Mrs Brydon noticed that they 'sang very nicely' at evening service.[49] The boys obviously made themselves useful. But theirs was dangerous work, especially when compounded by 'constant exposure, bad food and the unhealthy atmosphere', and they often landed up in hospital. The edition of the school magazine marking the seventieth anniversary of the Mutiny (and produced when some of the boy defenders must still have been alive) records that 'under the careful nursing of their masters almost all of them recovered'.[50] Whether or not the teachers' ministrations were the main factor, the fact is that only two of the boys died during the siege. To this day La Martinière prides itself on the badge of honour won by its boys at Lucknow.

There is no evidence that the mutineers at Lucknow deliberately targeted children, who died as a result of daily bombardment and squalid siege conditions. At Cawnpore, however, events took a more terrible turn. As late as the end of May the commander of the garrison, Major-General Hugh Wheeler, was convinced that he could prevent any rebel attack there. Like General Hearsey, he was 'an old-style Company officer, the father of half-caste children, fluent in the vernacular, loved by his men, proven in battle'.[51] But on 6 June the mutineers from Delhi, who were now led by an embittered local prince, Nana Sahib, mounted a powerful attack on the city and the Europeans and Eurasians hastily crowded into the army barracks. From the start juvenile deaths occurred both at random and by design.

Throughout the siege the death rate was higher than it was ever to be at Lucknow, partly because the over-confident Wheeler had not prepared as carefully as did Sir Henry Lawrence. Jonah Shepherd, who as the Eurasian Head of the Commissariat Office was expert at keeping lists, estimated that there were originally 455 men, 225 women and 320 children with him in the entrenched position.[52] Included among the children were fifty pupils of the Cawnpore Free School. The mutineers reduced these numbers rapidly and after two weeks the barracks contained no more than 'a few hundred half-starved and wounded wrecks'.[53] One of the first fatal casualties was Lieutenant Godfrey Wheeler, the General's favourite son. After the bereavement he himself aged quickly and kept to the small room he shared with his wife and two teenage daughters. Shepherd's careful records show that most of the deaths in this period were due either to sunstroke, caused by lack of shelter and water, or to gunshot, the result of Nana Sahib's relentless bombardment. Major Vibart, who took over effective command from Wheeler, saw two of his four young children die in just these ways – baby Louisa of sunstroke and Johnny shot as he ran out to greet his father returning from his post on the walls. Shepherd himself lost an infant to a sniper's bullet. His five-year-old daughter Polly survived those first weeks, though it made her father's heart bleed to see her sitting in the corner, 'the very picture of patience', trying not to upset her parents by complaining of hunger and thirst.[54] More energetic youngsters, according to Captain Mowbray Thomson, 'would run away from their mothers and play about under the barrack walls . . . and not a few were slain and wounded thus'.[55]

Some parents did not have their children with them. Major William Lindsay and his wife Lily had dispatched their three to England even though the parents' earlier letters from Cawnpore show the children to have been generally sturdy and cheerful. The main reason for sending them home was clearly educational. 'The intelligent and interesting' Willie had become 'a little wild' by the age of five and Mrs Lindsay felt that he was 'already beyond her'. His father wrote that Willie was 'very sharp and would soon learn to read had he anyone to teach him regularly for an hour a day'. But the Major had not the time 'and sometimes not the inclination' to give him regular instruction. Charlie, aged three, was said to be 'very backward . . . both in his speaking and activity'.[56] So he was thought to be even more in need of English schooling. Mary Anne was still just a baby and did not merit progress reports; but of course she would have to be brought up to be a lady. It would have been unthinkable to send an officer's children to the Cawnpore Free School, established in 1822 for 'the second circle' of British residents – including coach-makers, tailors and bakers.[57] So about two years before the Mutiny Lily had taken them to live with her husband's sister, Mary Drage, in Rochester, and both parents were longing for the time when they would 'be free to go to them'. In December 1856 they could hardly recognise the children in a 'stereoscope likeness' sent by Aunt Mary. Lindsay's last letter, dated 19 May 1857, told Mary of the massacre at Delhi but expressed the opinion that 'the crisis is past and matters are now all improving for Christians in all parts of the country'.[58] A month later he was killed by a shot in the face and, according to Thomson, 'his disconsolate widow followed him a day or two afterwards, slain by grief.[59] So three more orphans were added to a lengthening list.

After nearly three weeks of accumulating agony the survivors in the Cawnpore barracks accepted a truce offered by Nana Sahib, with whom Shepherd (disguised as a cook) had been sent to parley. Amid singing and dancing, arrangements were made to give all the besieged a safe passage to Allahabad. But on 27 June, as the men, women and children began to move off in boats from the Satichaura Ghat, sepoys hidden on both banks of the river opened fire. Meanwhile the boatmen ignited the straw roofs of the vessels. The men who survived the initial attack were shot and some 150 women and children were taken prisoner. Among those who died in the massacre were General Wheeler, his wife and one of his daughters. Mrs Vibart, Mrs Shepherd and the rest of their children were killed. According to eyewitnesses, the schoolmistress and twenty-two 'missies' from the Free School were 'burnt to death'.[60] The Lindsays' teenage nephew George, who had come to visit Cawnpore with his widowed mother Kate (the Major's sister-in-law) and his three 'fishing fleet' sisters, also met his death.

A few escaped the carnage. Captain Thomson, Major Vibart and several other men got away in a boat and evaded their pursuers. Sepoys apparently helped some Eurasian wives and children of army bandsmen to flee and abducted two eighteen-year-old Eurasian girls, Amelia Horne and one of General Wheeler's daughters. Amelia survived to tell the famous tale of her captivity and flight while Miss Wheeler was discovered as an old lady still living in Cawnpore where she had married the sepoy who carried her off.[61] The story of the massacre was pieced together from depositions given on oath by the bandsmen's widows and from Captain Thomson's memoir of 1859. But much remains obscure. Jonah Shepherd, who was in captivity at the time, never knew exactly how his wife, daughter and other relations died that day.

There is even less direct evidence about the further killings which occurred in the middle of July, as the British relief force approached Cawnpore. By that time some of the women and children held in the overcrowded Bibighar (Ladies' House) had died of cholera or dysentery. A pencilled list made by one of the surviving Lindsay girls, and found at the Bibighar, records that 'Alice died, 9th July' and 'Mama died, 12th July'.[62] Only Caroline and Frances remained alive on 15 July. Then Nana Sahib ordered the slaughter of all the women and children as well as the last fugitives from Fatehgarh, among whom were Robert Thornhill, his wife Mary and their two infant children. (The Thornhills' three oldest children, George, Henrietta and Edward aged fifteen, ten and nine respectively, were under the care of their grandmother in Essex.) The bodies of the victims were thrown into a well, to be discovered by troops who arrived two days later. Although in Victorian legend this came to be known as the 'Massacre of the Women', in plain truth about twice as many children were killed. One deposition tells a gruesome last tale. John Fitchett, a Eurasian drummer who had been saved early on by the sepoys of his own company, swore that he saw a child thrown alive into the well on the morning after the massacre: 'They were fair children, the eldest I think must have been six or seven, and the youngest five years; it was the youngest who was thrown in by one of the sweepers. The children were running round

84

the well, where else could they go to? And there was none to save them. No, none said a word to save them.'[63] Fitchett did not know what happened to the other children but there is no evidence to suggest that any of them survived.

Yet, at the same time and in the same district, Indian villagers risked their lives to help a lone English woman escaping from Faizabad with her three children. In a vivid unpublished memoir Mrs Maria Mill, a major's wife, tells the story of her terrifying journey to Calcutta between June and November 1857. In the course of it she, Alice, Johnny and unweaned baby Charlie faced dangers from mutineers, wolves, rainstorms, fever and cholera. They also suffered intense thirst, hunger and exhaustion, which caused Mrs Mill's milk to dry up. She survived only through the aid of Indians. A boatman defied the sepoys by taking her to Dinapore. Villagers gave her chapattis, buttermilk, water and *charpoys* (beds) even when there was firing in the neighbourhood. Nursing women offered their breast milk to Charlie, 'who was quite refreshed by it'. And a local rajah gave protection to Europeans passing through the area of his fort. There Mrs Mill took shelter in a shed with three sergeants' wives, who lent her clothes and shared with her 'old goat meat made into curry'. Even at such a time she worried that her children should hear the women's 'dreadful language'. She was also shocked when one of them, 'a half-caste' called Mrs Edwards, muttered 'native incantations' over a child dying of cholera.

At Gorruckpore Mrs Mill was relieved to be taken in by more *pukka* (respectable) Europeans, but her relief was short-lived. For here her own baby died and she herself fell ill. To her horror Mrs Edwards was summoned to nurse her but luckily another European woman, 'a very respectable person', also came and sat with her. Because this was still a dangerous area the depleted Mill family had to move on, accompanied now by loyal Gurkha troops who fought off attacks. Eventually they boarded a riverboat bound for Calcutta. The voyage took two months, during which Mrs Mill's remaining children contracted cholera. They survived but two further tragedies befell her at Calcutta. She gave birth to a stillborn daughter and she heard that her husband had been killed at Faizabad. Thus, she concludes, 'the terrible Mutiny of 1857 cost me the loss of three of the precious lives of my family, all my worldly goods and possessions, and many many hours of the most unspeakable anguish'.[64] All this was true. But, like many other white people during this great cataclysm, she also received kindness and succour, often from those whose race and class she despised.

Some of the Oudh villages where Mrs Mill received help might have been destroyed during the savage British reprisals which followed in the wake of the Mutiny. At Cawnpore rebels were made to eat pork and beef and to lick the bloody floor of the Bibighar before they were hanged. Theophilus Metcalfe watched men strung up from the burnt rafters of his house in Delhi. At other centres of revolt sepoys were bayoneted or shot from cannon. And as British troops marched from one place to another, often the worse for looted liquor, they randomly set fire to villages along the way. Among these implacable soldiers was Francis Pemberton's great-grandson, Major Francis Pemberton Campbell, who thought it 'very desirable to burn all the roofs and thatches as that will leave the villains without shelter from the rains, which they won't like a bit better than we should'.[65] 'No one can say', concludes Andrew Ward, 'how many thousands of Indians – including women and children – died during the suppression of the Indian rebellion, but many times more ... than the Europeans who died at Cawnpore.'[66]

As well as the satisfaction of revenge, soldiers also gained rewards in the form of medals, prize money and loot. Sir Edward Campbell, for instance, got £5,000 after acting as Prize Agent at Delhi, as well as his share of the treasure dug up there – though he took no pleasure in the slaughter of mutineers. Dr Fayrer attained the brevet rank of surgeon, twelve months' prize money and a medal. Colina Brydon's Lucknow diary several times records that her husband acquired 'pretty bits of china' in prize property.[67] In due course many English households received Kashmir shawls, items of Indian silver and other exotic finds sent back from these sites of mayhem and mourning.

Other homes, however, received letters telling them that they must give up hope of their loved ones being found alive. Captain Thomson points out that some families experienced 'sorrow after sorrow'. 'By reason of intermarriages, long cemented friendships and family ties, the losses sustained were in many instances concentrated into small circles.'[68] Four Thornhills were killed in addition to those from Fatehgarh. Jonah Shepherd lost ten relations. The Lindsay family mourned for seven. But 'poor dear orphans' like the Lindsays' three children found it difficult to take in news received some weeks after the event about parents they had not seen for several years. Adults expected them to grieve in an appropriate fashion and were upset when they continued to behave like children. As William Lindsay's sister put it: 'Willie distressed me – after the first cry which he took when I told him – he never seemed to mind, and to me the sound of them laughing, whistling, singing and romping when they are all here . . . has been painful and mystifying.'[69] Who knows what Willie's true feelings were? He must at some point have needed to reconstruct the early years of his life with his lost parents. For the Lindsay Papers contain notes he made from his parents' letters about his own and his siblings' development. But they say nothing about the pain of loss.

Robert and Mary Thornhill's twelve-year-old daughter, Henrietta (known as Minnie), also upset her relations by boisterous behaviour when they thought she should still have been in mourning. Her grandmother came to hear from her aunt and uncle of some larking about with a locket – could this have been the gold locket containing her parents' hair which was preserved with the Thornhill Papers? Sternly she reminded her grandchild that 'all romping is unmaidenly'. And in a special birthday letter her grandmother warned the child that it was 'wicked to feel that you expect much happiness'.[70] Having been removed from physical danger, Minnie was now the object of Victorian moral training thought to be unavailable in India.

In the years to come orphans like the Lindsays and the Thornhills suffered financial as well as emotional hardship. For the wills of Mutiny victims were often either lost or disputed and their offspring were then dependent on the benevolence of relations and charitable funds. William Lindsay's sister received a letter saying that her nephews and niece would 'in due time receive the usual allowance made to the children of a Captain from the Bengal Orphans Military Fund' and she hoped thus to be able to give the boys an education to fit them 'for some employment'.[71] George and Edward Thornhill were allowed to finish their education at Radley but they then had to seek their fortune in New Zealand. After the death of her grandmother in 1866, Minnie was taken in by Aunt George, the wealthy widow of a great-uncle. Robert Thornhill's will was not settled until 1910, by which time most of the legacy had been eaten up in costs; each of his children received about £17.[72]

The events of 1857 clearly did grievous harm to hundreds of children. It brought them death, illness, fear, poverty and a sorrow they often could not express. But if the mutineers, or freedom fighters in what Indians now call the first War of Independence, hoped to get rid of their oppressors by attacking what was most precious to them, they miscalculated. The British aimed to conserve their way of life in India.

The Government made concessions. There would be no more annex-ations of Indian territory. All religions were to be tolerated. And the East India Company was abolished, so that the British could rule directly from London, with a Viceroy replacing the Governor-General and acting as the monarch's deputy in Calcutta. The Queen herself was keen to conciliate, pardoning all rebels who had not actually murdered Europeans. Although she understood as 'a Woman and above all a Wife and Mother' the 'agonies gone through of the massacres', she deplored the 'blood thirsting' response of British people.[73] She wanted her Indian subjects to know that 'there is no hatred to a brown skin – none; but the greatest wish on the Queen's part to see them happy, contented and flourishing'.[74]

Towards the end of 1858 Calcutta celebrated the advent of the new regime with illuminations. The Ritchie boys were delighted with 'lights tracing out the outline of the buildings and columns, and a great God Save the Queen, with VR and a crown above all'.[75] Protected by more British troops, Anglo-Indians resumed their daily routines. They were never again to be the object of wholesale violence, not even during 'the second War of Independence' in the 1940s. Nevertheless, as Dr Fayrer's lecture shows, they continued to regard the subcontinent as a dangerous environment for their children. What evidence is there to suggest that he was right?

Cemeteries, ironically, can bring the past to life. While researching this book I came across two tombstones, both of which recorded the deaths of three offspring in one family within a few days of each other. One was situated in Fairford, Gloucestershire (1846) and the other in Pussellawa, Ceylon (1866). The Fairford youngsters probably died in one of the cholera outbreaks which periodically swept Britain after its first appearance there in 1831. The memorial in Ceylon was erected by the children's father, a coffee planter, who wrote that his darlings had died of 'Asiatic cholera brought on by [eating] a poisonous plant'.[76] They too must have been victims of an epidemic of this disease, whose cause (as his explanation demonstrates) was still not understood. Such monuments conjure up tragic family stories in two continents, but they do not enable us adequately to compare the respective dangers of living at home and under the Raj.

Nor is anecdotal evidence always helpful, as emerges from a recent historical work. Its author, Mark Harrison, quotes Emily Bayley (née Metcalfe) as saying that every mother in India expected to lose 'at least three children out of every five she bore'.[77] In fact this statement was made not by Mrs Bayley but by M. M. Kaye, the editor of her memoir. Both she and Harrison cite Emily Bayley's experience as proof of the 'terrible toll' taken by India on young white lives and she did indeed lose four children, two at birth and two in their early years. But she bore thirteen. Moreover, one of them died (aged five) after having been left in London – his absent mother pictures him 'lying alone in his little narrow coffin'.[78] As this suggests, heavy child mortality was not confined to India. Annette Beveridge, a mother who will feature in the next chapter, came from a family in which five out of eleven died in Scotland when they were very young. Individual cases prove only that death in childhood was very common at this time, both in the home country and in the subcontinent. As another historian comments, 'A childish cold or cough was enough to send most parents into a paroxysm of panic.'[79]

Luckily, though, busy nineteenth-century investigators provided facts on this as on other topics. In 1859 the London Government, which was naturally anxious to improve the health of soldiers sent to India in post-Mutiny years, set up a Royal Commission to report on the 'Sanitary Condition of the British Army in India'. The driving force behind both the appointment and the work of the Commission was Florence Nightingale, whose 'hearty and true' offer to 'start at twenty four hours notice' for the mutinous areas in 1857 had been politely turned down by the Viceroy's wife, Lady Canning.[80] Although Florence Nightingale was not even a member of the Commission and was by 1860 a 'bed-ridden invalid of over forty, shattered in health and overwhelmed with other work', she sent out questionnaires to every military station in India.[81] The replies covered enough paper to fill a whole room in her house and it was on them (and not on any visits to the subcontinent) that the report of 1863 was based.

Its main point was that the death rate for soldiers in India was sixty-nine per thousand per annum, much higher than it was for soldiers based at home or for civilians in India. However, the report also included the first statistics about children living in India and compared them with figures for Britain. These were provided by one of the Commissioners, William Farr, who had for some years been producing annual *Abstracts of Causes of Death in England and Wales*. The surprising conclusion of the report was that the 'mortality of English children in India is lower than the general mortality of children at home': nearly sixty-six per thousand for the children of officers in

India compared to sixty-seven per thousand for children in England. These figures did not tell the whole story. The report pointed out that while children living in salubrious civilian bungalows died at a lower rate, the offspring of common soldiers in barracks were not so lucky – but it does not give a figure for either group. Also, of course, the mortality rate in England varied according to class and area; it could be as low as forty per thousand in 'healthy districts'.

In other words, child mortality in both countries depended on 'variable sanitary conditions'.[82] At the healthiest extreme were the thriving youngsters at the Sanawar Asylum in the hills who 'looked like lion's cubs'.[83] At the other end of the scale were the 554 wives and 770 children of Dumdum barracks, 'crowded together without care or supervision' when their menfolk went off to deal with the Mutiny. Here conditions quickly led to 'the destruction by dysentery of 64 wives and 166 children'.[84] A similar contrast could be made in Britain. While all Queen Victoria's nine children survived, being 'over-watched and over-doctored' in the seclusion of their nurseries at Windsor, Balmoral and Osborne House, 150 infants died during the cholera outbreak of 1848–9 at Mr Drouet's 'brutally conducted' paupers' baby farm in Tooting. Charles Dickens denounced it in *The Examiner* as 'a disgrace to a Christian community and a stain upon a civilised land'.[85]

So the picture was a complicated one. And it was rather less dramatic than that painted by Dr Fayrer in his lecture of 1872, by which time living conditions for the families of other ranks in the Indian Army were beginning to improve. In the lecture Fayrer claimed a death rate of 148 per thousand for European children under five in Bengal and nearly eighty-two per thousand for all white children in India. This is a higher child mortality rate than was cited by anyone else and very much higher than current rates in Britain. On the other hand, Fayrer asserted that in the Calcutta Asylum for Female Orphans, where there was 'careful and judicious management' of the charges, hardly any mortality or sickness occurred. It is difficult to believe that he was not exaggerating both sides of the argument. In any case, if he really believed his own evidence from the Asylum, he would surely have concluded, as the Commissioners did, that with 'proper care' children could thrive in India.[86]

Family stories show, however, that chance and constitution also played a part in children's survival in both countries. In the thirty years before the Mutiny Mrs Marion Battye 'was pregnant for a whole generation', giving birth safely in most unfavourable circumstances to one girl and ten boys. All survived childhood and the sons won renown as 'The Fighting Ten' – though the third, Quintin, lost his life in the Mutiny at the age of twenty-five.[87] Major Erskine survived the Mutiny, as we have seen, but his family had already had its share of tragedy during his thirty years of peripatetic service in India. Despite having good bungalows built, procuring the best medical advice and sending his family off to the hills, he lost six out of eight children, four to dysentery in India and two to whooping cough in Britain. For some time Erskine faced these deaths stoically: 'It is indeed hard to part with one of our beloved children,' he wrote in 1844, 'but we ought not to repine for our sweet departed babies; Amelia, Marian and Frank are now little Angels in Heaven.' In 1849 he worried about how his wife would bear up when John and Henry died within a fortnight of each other in England. But the final death, which occurred in 1854 while the family accompanied the Major on an exhausting series of marches, shook the Christian faith which had hitherto sustained him. As he sat through the last hours of his 'best beloved, handsome, sweet, engaging and most intelligent infant' Arthur, he asked himself in the privacy of his journal, 'Can I say Thy will be done?' He answered, in an almost illegible scrawl, 'No, I fear not.'[88]

Similarly, in the mother country, Charles Darwin was unable to find spiritual comfort when his 'dear good child' Annie died of tuberculosis in 1851. Indeed, the experience and memory of her lingering death was to strengthen his scientific theory that it was 'more satisfactory to attribute pain and suffering to the natural sequence of events' than to any divine will.[89] For both fathers, one an obscure soldier of the Crown and the other a scientist of genius, the death of an adored child heralded the long withdrawing roar of the Victorian sea of faith, which the poet Matthew Arnold was to hear on Dover beach in 1867.

In 1858 Major Erskine bade 'farewell to the Indian shore' and travelled home to join his two remaining sons, Walter and Gussy, in Scotland. At that point James Macnabb was just embarking on a successful career in the Indian Civil Service, which was not to end until 1886. He had to undertake almost as many tours as Erskine and he too was often accompanied by his family. He lost two wives, Amy in 1871 and Alice after their return to England in 1888, but all Amy's five children and four of Alice's five survived their early years in India. The parents' letters anxiously record frequent childhood illnesses (whooping cough, dysentery, bronchitis, abscesses, fever and the dreaded effects of teething). James wrote to his mother in 1863 about one-year-old Florence:

> Did I not know it was my Baby I would not believe the terrible change all this sickness has made in her. Thin and wan and pale, the poor little mouth and lips all swollen and sore, her voice croaking with the effects of the bronchitis and so wee and suffering. She has now six front and three back teeth the cause of all her troubles.

Both mothers looked after the children assiduously, taking them up to the hills, selecting 'respectable' English nurses or 'kind and careful' ayahs, dosing them with cod liver oil and having them vaccinated against smallpox. 'I would not I think be so fidgety at home,' explained Amy in 1864, 'but the climate here is so treacherous I think children require great care.'[90]

Amy and Alice Macnabb certainly did not confirm the view of an Indian historian that the Anglo-Indian mother's 'craze for socialising' kept her away from her children, who usually lacked 'proper care'.[91] In fact they seem to have worn themselves out with their 'thronging duties' and Alice sometimes yearned, in the words of a hymn she copied into her diary in 1885, for 'Peace, perfect peace'.[92] Amy's labours included an attentive watch over the children's moral development, healthy souls being even more important than healthy bodies. In 1864 she describes her regime for Florence when she reached the age of two:

> I always intend her to be very obedient. It will be much better for her to be able to give up her own will. It is the great lesson of life. . . . She will never need much punishment for she is very gentle and gives up her own way without a struggle and if I ever scold her she seems as if her very heart could break with scolding.

Later that year Amy's mother sent her a book on Moral Education which, she prayed, would help her to give the children 'loving gentle obedient dispositions [and] to put into their little hearts very early the love of his Holy name'.[93] Once the children had been sent home to Scotland their father was anxious to have 'good accounts' of them and hoped that they would not disturb their grandmother but 'be quiet when told'. Florence obviously remained dutiful; after her mother's death she wrote 'bright letters' to her father and later on she went out to India to help her stepmother with the new babies. Her younger brother James seems to have been a worry to his father, who doubted in 1872 whether he 'would turn out like other boys'.[94] The two youngest sons, Rawdon and Archie, were more predictable; both went out in their turn to form a fourth generation of Macnabbs in India.

The difference between the Erskines' and the Macnabbs' experience may be due partly to healthier conditions in the later nineteenth century – at any rate for Europeans. By moving troops into more spacious barracks in better locations and by providing purer water supplies, the Army reduced its death rate to fifteen per thousand. Families could travel more quickly and easily to hill stations like Simla and Darjeeling on the newly built railways. Quinine for the treatment of malaria became more widely available and cholera became less deadly. The supply of bottled soda water by firms such as Treachers of Bombay also made a difference.[95] As early as 1870 Florence Nightingale drew a startling conclusion: 'Bombay is at this time healthier than London. Calcutta, though not healthier than London, is healthier than Manchester or Liverpool.'[96] As she had insisted when the Sanitary Report was published, 'There is not a shadow of proof that India was created to be the grave of the British race.'[97]

None of this was enough to convince most Anglo-Indian parents that India could be a safe environment for their offspring. For, even in the midst of great physical peril, Anglo-Indian parents like Captain Nicholl, Mrs Mill, the Lindsays and the Macnabbs never lost sight of the other danger identified by Dr Fayrer and other authoritative voices: the danger of moral deterioration. In their own homes, 'left to the tuition of native servants', their sons and daughters would 'pass their time in listless inactivity ... playing with rude toys, listening to lascivious anecdotes of Hindu gods'.[98] They would learn to lie, cheat and steal. They might, like the children of Dutch, French and Portuguese colonials who stayed in India with their parents, become 'natives in their minds, if not in colour'.[99] When sending home children who had survived their vulnerable infant years in India, parents hoped that the bracing moral atmosphere of Europe would eliminate from their characters the effect identified by Fayrer of an Asian upbringing: 'a tendency to be deceitful and vain, indisposed to study'.[100] They believed that an upright, Christian, respectable and hardworking subject of Queen Victoria had to be home-grown.

FOUR

'A Horse Does Not Cry'

Young Exiles in Victorian Britain

O n a bleak Sunday evening at Mrs Pipchin's boarding school on
the south coast of England Master Bitherstone, whose relations
were all in India, asked Florence Dombey 'if she could give him
any idea of the way back to Bengal'. Twelve-year-old Florence knew
that India was 'a long distance off . . . many weeks' journey, night and
day'. But the little boy evidently remained uncertain about the time it
would take him to be reunited with his family. A week or so later,
after a day of being victimised by that irascible 'child-queller', Mrs
Pipchin, 'he began that very night to make arrangements for an overland return to India, by secreting from his supper a quarter of a round
of bread and a fragment of moist Dutch cheese, as the beginning of a
stock of provision to support him on the voyage'.[1] Master Bitherstone,
whose exile is so poignantly conveyed in Dickens's *Dombey and Son*
(1846), personifies the lonely plight of Anglo-Indian children in the
Victorian age.

At least he had chosen the quicker route to India, which was available to families by the 1840s and rendered their separation slightly less
drastic. Instead of going round the Cape of Good Hope, some travellers
voyaged by steamship to the port of Suez in the eastern Mediterranean,
went overland to the Red Sea and took another steam vessel across the
Indian Ocean. This journey could be done in six or seven weeks even
though ocean-going steamships were in their infancy and still carried
sails as an additional source of power. Sometimes there were political
as well as technical difficulties. In 1840 Emily Eden was worried about

'our dear Overland' as tension mounted between Britain and Egypt over the perennial Eastern Question. She pronounced it 'a bore' that her personal comfort should be put at risk by 'an uninteresting war' in this 'sandy, sphinxy and tiresome' country but trusted that 'if the Pasha is anything of a gentleman he will not interfere with our letters'.[2] This was a short-lived crisis but even so, many less grand passengers still had to use the sailing ships which plied the old route. On 5 March 1863, for instance, Mary Lugard set off from Madras in 'a dirty little troopship of only 1000 tons'. She had with her six children, including her five-year-old son Frederick, the future explorer of Africa. After suffering a series of trials – red ants, cockroaches, bugs, mosquitoes, food and water shortages, drunken officers, calms, storms and out-breaks of disease – the Lugard family reached England in early July. Young Frederick, at least, had enjoyed such excitements as the shooting of a shark, though his mother lamented that he was not 'nearly so good as when he came on board'.[3] Over the next three decades, however, the passage to India became much less of an ordeal. The opening of the Suez Canal in 1869, technical improvements in steamships and the linking of Indian cities by railway lessened the dangers as well as the inconveniences for Anglo-Indian travellers. By the end of the century the journey normally took three or four weeks and could be quite comfortable for families able to afford cabin accommodation deemed POSH – Port Out, Starboard Home.[4]

Like people, messages could also cross the seas more quickly. Victorian engineers had revolutionised international communication by means of the electric telegraph. British governments, nervous about security since the Indian Mutiny, invested heavily in a cable under the Red Sea. The first one failed but by 1870 telegraphic communication had been established between Britain and India, enabling messages to be received within six hours of transmission. Unreliable and expensive though the system was, it meant that families as well as government ministers could now convey urgent news quickly. No longer would a mother have to begin a letter to a child with the words: 'If you are alive now'.[5]

Thus Queen Victoria's reign, which lasted from 1837 to 1901, saw many changes which 'contributed to bring East and West together'.[6] The Queen herself, who was in many ways representative of the age which bears her name, played a part in some of them. For example, she made generous use of telegrams. Characteristically she sent electronic homilies to her eldest son when he visited India in 1875. But she did not employ the new means of intercontinental transport. Indeed, the Empress of India, to give her the title she acquired in 1876, never visited the subcontinent. She did, though, take a close interest in its affairs and she corresponded assiduously with her viceroys and vicereines. In 1886 she tried to familiarise herself with Indian people by proxy. She sent an Austrian artist, Rudolf Swoboda, to travel around making sketches of 'the various types of the different nationalities'. The forty-three paintings he brought back are not standard Victorian ethnographic studies but 'sure likenesses of real people ... men, women, children, Muslims, Sikhs, Hindus, tribals, military officers, villagers, princes'. The Queen was delighted with these 'beautiful things', which are still displayed in her special Indian Room at Osborne House.[7]

At about the same time the Empress, who like many of her subjects was fascinated by the romance of India and wished to have more than just a vicarious experience of it, engaged several Indian servants. Among them was Hafiz Abdul Karim who became her official Indian secretary, known as the *Munshi* (teacher) because he helped her to study Hindustani. As A. N. Wilson points out in *The Victorians*, Victoria was more enlightened in this respect than the present Queen, who (in 2002) had 'employed not one secretary, equerry or household servant of an Asian or Afro-Caribbean background'.[8] When members of the royal household turned on Karim after discovering that his father was a prison apothecary rather than a surgeon-general as he had claimed, Queen Victoria defended 'her good Munshi'. His detractors were prejudiced, she maintained. In any case, she herself had known 'two Archbishops who were respectively the sons of a Butcher and a Grocer' and there were baronets 'whose parents were very humble'.[9]

Towards children, as opposed to servants, the monarch was less forgiving and her attitudes in some way mirror those of her subjects. She thought babies 'rather disgusting' and refused to breastfeed her own, though she took an interest in her offspring when they reached the age of two or three. As they grew up she found most of them 'a bitter disappointment, their greatest object being to do precisely what their parents do not wish and have anxiously tried to prevent'.[10] Still, the royal champion of what became known as Balmorality was extolled in the middle years of her reign for her virtues as a wife and mother. A Leeds newspaper called her 'the brightest exemplar to the matrons of England'.[11] She and Prince Albert made great efforts to ensure that stiff doses of thrift, humility, respectability and industry were administered in the royal nursery. Maids were astonished by the frugality of the children's fare, typically boiled beef and carrots followed by semolina pudding. And tutors protested at the burden of study imposed on the reluctant Prince of Wales – he was made to work from eight in the morning until six at night. Punishments were freely meted out to children who broke the rules. Bertie (as his family called the Prince of Wales) was often beaten for his idleness and temper tantrums. When Vicky (Princess Victoria) lied about being given permission to wear a pink bonnet for an outing, she was 'imprisoned with tied hands'. The discipline induced fear as much as respect: the Queen's Private Secretary was once 'nearly carried away by a stampede' of young princes and princesses running to hide as Her Majesty approached.[12] But punitive pills were sugared with love. According to one historian, Prince Albert was 'an approachable, caring father, patient and kindly to all his children alike', with a special affection for his clever oldest daughter. The Queen, though usually so prone to slap down her children, could find little fault with her 'precious love', the placid Prince Arthur, or with Beatrice, the 'Baby' of the family.[13]

Just as the royal couple treated their nine children differently, so parents and guardians throughout the kingdom imparted Victorian values with varying degrees of rigour. Diversity reigned from palace to slum. The poor children interviewed by Henry Mayhew in the London streets in 1851 had hardly heard of God, let alone of Queen Victoria. Even so, when they spoke of their struggle for survival they often exhibited the virtue of Self-Help, classically recommended in the famous book of that name written by Samuel Smiles. An illegitimate flower girl aged fifteen proudly told Mayhew that ever since her mother's death she had got her brother and sister 'a bit of bread and never had any help but from the neighbours'.[14] If the siblings had turned to the parish they would probably have been sent to a workhouse, where families were treated harshly and separated by gender so that they would want to leave as soon as possible. One child left in the care of the parish was the illegitimate six-year-old John Rowlands, who became in later life the greatest of African explorers, James Morton Stanley. In 1847 he entered St Asaph's Union Workhouse, an establishment which had just been denounced by the inspectors as 'a nursery of female prostitution and male obscenity'.[15] In fact Rowlands seems to have derived love and comfort rather than sex from sleeping two to a bed and 'the other boys became his family' – which was not exactly what the Poor Law authorities had in mind when designing workhouses.[16]

By contrast, many middle-class households adhered to an even more stringent code of morality than Queen Victoria, who dared to treat the Sabbath as a day of recreation and amusement. Evangelicals' strong sense of sin and fear of eternal damnation made them especially earnest in training their children to 'habitual inner restraint, an early government of the affections and a course of self-control'.[17] Victorian imperialists, whose service in India had often been undertaken in response to a religious call, were particularly likely to be imbued with an Evangelical ethos. They believed with Sir John Lawrence, the 'saviour of the Punjab', who became Viceroy in 1864, that: 'We are here through our moral superiority . . . by the will of Providence. This alone constitutes our charter to govern India. In doing the best we can for the people, we are bound by our conscience.'[18]

By this time Anglo-Indian men had usually been joined by equally pious wives – many of whom had travelled out in the famous 'fishing fleet' for the express purpose of catching a husband. Such parents expected their offspring to aspire to their own high standards. Their letters contain constant references to the need for infants and even babies to be obedient and give up their own will. Once children reached the age of seven they had to be removed from the heathen environment in which their parents laboured. Relations and guardians were expected to impose Christian principles. Public schools were designed to produce 'responsible, honorable boys, willing to give their lives . . . to the preservation and expansion of the empire'. But in public schools as in workhouses, Victorian social engineering had its limitations; in their 'atmosphere of regimented manliness' the sexual molestation of younger boys was not unusual.[19] The humbler establishments designed for girls would give a less ambitious training. But their regime was still onerous.

As the case of Master Bitherstone shows, Victorians had only to turn to the works of Charles Dickens to understand what stern families, schools and institutions felt like to the children in their clutches. He saw them 'from a child's point of view – strange, odd, queer, puzzling'.[20] One critic goes so far as to say that Dickens 'wrote as a child, he understood as a child, he thought as a child and when he became a man he never put away childish things'.[21] One naturally feels for Pip as he sits through Christmas dinner soon after his terrifying churchyard encounter with the convict Magwitch and the theft of food from his sister's larder. He is surrounded by worthy adults like Uncle Pumblechook who 'wouldn't leave me alone'. Constantly they remind the guilt-ridden child that he should 'be grateful to them which brought you up by hand' and they castigate all young people as 'naterally wicious'. Pip's only comfort is his sister's husband Joe Gargery, who pours him more gravy as each stodgy lecture is doled out.[22] It is hard to forget episodes like this, or the flogging of Smike, or Oliver Twist's daring to ask for more, or the lonely death of Paul Dombey whose happiness has been sacrificed to the pursuit of wealth and power.

In his journalism, as well as in his novels, Dickens took the child's part. He would not rest, for instance, until Mr Drouet was found guilty of manslaughter for the maltreatment of pauper babies in Tooting mentioned in Chapter Three. 'No one doubts,' the novelist wrote triumphantly, 'that the child-farming system is effectually broken up by this trial.'[23] The climate of opinion was doubtless already beginning to change, but Dickens's touching descriptions almost certainly helped to create more sympathy for children. There is evidence that in the late-Victorian period parents and teachers were less rigid in their child-rearing and more sparing in their use of the rod. In 1884 the NSPCC was founded, sixty years after the RSPCA; at last the British were extending to children the same protection that they gave to animals. Many did not change, of course. Their priorities were still those of their Queen, who showed much more concern for the welfare of 'poor, confiding, faithful, kind things' like dogs than she did for children.[24]

None of the benefits of healthier conditions, improved communications or kindlier attitudes to children came in time to help the offspring of Anglo-Indian parents Edward and Clementina Benthall, as recorded in her copious unpublished diaries. After a four-month journey to India in 1841, during which Clementina endured severe seasickness and the difficult birth of her first child, they arrived in Calcutta to hear the dreadful reports from Afghanistan. Undaunted they travelled with their three-month-old son Clement to Jessore in the Ganges delta, where Edward took up his appointment as a district judge.[25] As the daughter of an Evangelical parson, Clementina did not complain but it was soon clear that this was not a healthy area. The Benthalls and their friends were often afflicted with fevers, dysentery, diarrhoea, prickly heat, coughs, headaches and liver disorders. There were also outbreaks of cholera, smallpox and even 'Egyptian plague' in the neighbourhood. But, Clementina noted, Europeans did not suffer as badly as Indians from these 'dreadful scourges'. Luckily the family had a good stock of modern medicines, including quinine, but they also relied on older treatments like leeches. Baby Clement thrived in his first year due, his mother felt, to his being 'properly vaccinated' against smallpox and successfully breastfed. A progress report for 3 October 1842 reads: 'He is very active, runs fast and is merry and good-natured, although rather quick in temper; we make him obey us, and he is generally a good child and easy to manage.'[26]

As Clementina's son got older and she had two more children, Ernest and Edith, her worries mounted. All were dangerously ill from time to time. In June 1846 Edith was so sick that her mother was almost tempted to challenge God's will by praying for her recovery. Only when Edith was better could her mother write in true religious spirit: 'Far rather would I lay my precious little girl in the dust even in this land of exile than rear her to be a lover of pleasure more than a lover of God or to be other than a faithful follower.'[27] This remote district harboured other perils. Venomous snakes fell from the nursery ceiling or were found in the compound; an Indian child was carried off by a jackal and another was eaten by an alligator. But moral dangers always loomed larger in Clementina's world-view than physical ones. When the children learned to talk she worried about their conversing with 'native servants who would be untruthful and in other ways objectionable as companions'. To overcome this hazard she hired girls from the European Orphan Asylum in Calcutta to act as nursery maids. Burdened as she was, Clementina sometimes suffered from 'depression of spirits'. On Easter Sunday 1845, for instance, she was in such a state that she could not even attend church and was thus denied spiritual solace.[28]

In 1847 the couple concluded that Ernest's recent severe illness was a 'warning from our Heavenly Father to send our boys to England'. They also decided that two-year-old Edith should go with them to save the extra expense of sending her separately. The children were to travel with a Mr and Mrs Fisher, acquaintances with whom they had spent only a single day. Clementina recorded that at the end of that day her son had said: 'I liked the Parrot and the Rabbits and an Owl and some soldier and tent toys I saw, and Mrs Fisher was very kind and I like Freddy and Florence but Mamma there's no place like Home Sweet Home.' Clementina opened a special diary for the months leading to the parting from her children, which took place in February 1848. Her account of their final moments together, which conveys both the parents' and the children's feelings, is almost unbearably sad: 'Edith held up her dear merry face to be kissed, little thinking that it was the signal of parting. I cannot describe the sorrow of the poor boys, Ernest's speechless look of anguish, and Clement's sobs and embraces and expressions of love.' The Benthalls felt at first as if their 'absent ones were all dead' but characteristically they 'blessed God for his mercies in surrounding us with so many alleviations to our afflictions'.[29] Among the blessings were three more children born between 1847 and 1856. All survived even though they too suffered spells of illness. Despite her other duties and distractions, Clementina herself tried to educate the older ones, Madeleine and Bertha. As is so often the case, the Benthall parents had a more relaxed attitude towards their younger offspring.

It is difficult to judge how the older trio fared in England for their letters have not survived, even though Clementina told Clement that she would keep them all and 'compare them frequently to see whether you improve'.[30] The children were sent to Edward's unmarried brother, Revd John Benthall, and two single sisters, who agreed to look after them for £250 in the first eighteen months and presumably for similar sums thereafter. That it was a commercial arrangement is clear from frequent references to their desire for Edward to find them more Anglo-Indian foster-children. Clementina's diary reveals, furthermore, that the Benthall family had been 'brought to the dust' in 1845 by the gambling and bankruptcy of a further brother.[31] Nevertheless, John's clerical household was deemed one in which the children could learn 'good principles and religious knowledge'. As an extra precaution, Clementina's parents monitored their moral progress, sometimes expressing dissatisfaction about their piety, as did an intimidating figure known as Aunt Thornton.[32]

Clementina's letters to the children urged them not to neglect their studies in favour of mere accomplishments like music, to sit still in church, to be obedient and kind and to do as the Catechism taught them. She often referred to the possibility that she or the children might die before they could be reunited, in which case they would all meet in Heaven. In lighter vein she gave them news of their little sisters and told them stories about the creatures they had liked so much in India. Perhaps they found some comfort in these moral lectures and jungle tales but they must have felt sadly let down in 1854. Their parents went on a recuperative cruise to the Cape and Clementina's letters promised that she would travel on to England with the two younger girls and a new baby born on board ship. But these plans did not materialise because she was reluctant to leave Edward, whose health was poor. She explained, too, that 'there are no ships going at this season of the year which carry passengers from the Cape to England'.[33] It was at least another year before the family was reunited.

The only clues to the effects of this long separation and strict upbringing come from letters written by and about Clement as an adolescent and young man. He was an anxious child with an earnest desire to please his parents but a tendency to lapses in conduct. In May 1850 he had to be rescued from drowning in a gravel pit to which he had been forbidden to go. His mother's letter to the eight-year-old child reads like a Victorian moral tale:

> We have felt most thankful to God for his mercy in sending the workmen to rescue you from the gravel pit and trust you will never forget how your life was saved – or what misery it would have been to us to hear that our poor boy was drowned owing to his going where he ought not to have gone. I hope and pray that whenever you die it may be so that all who love you know that you are happy with your Saviour.[34]

Later Clement sought to please his parents by telling them that he had not joined his friends in hunting and shooting expeditions. But not long after their return to England he upset them afresh by announcing that he wanted to join the Army rather than enter the Church as they desired. He got his way with the help of his Aunt Louisa, who explained to his parents that 'poor dear Clement feels very much the importance of the step he has to decide on'. He joined a cavalry regiment which was sent to India in 1859. He told his mother that on the journey out he had earned the nickname 'Dismal Jemmy' because he had refused to dance, smoke or play cards. Once in India he tried his hand at hunting, shooting and fishing and even at drinking beer. But he seems soon to have given up these traditional army pursuits. He would not go with other officers to watch the hangings of Indian mutineers because he was 'not fond of such sights'. His frequent letters home tell of his 'always meeting with some accident or other' and often being 'rather seedy'. He regretted that he had no accomplishments like music or drawing and urged his younger brothers to acquire them. His only pleasure was in cultivating his garden. For much of the time he could not even attend church because of being laid up by mishaps and ailments. It is clear that he had no 'special friendship with any officer of the regiment' and that he did not 'care to know any ladies'.

Clement's health and spirits continued to deteriorate and in 1873 he died in Allahabad at the age of thirty-two. His distraught parents, who clearly wanted to know more about the circumstances of his death, heard later from Louisa who was visiting India. She reported that she had not been able to find out anything about his last words or feelings for 'Clement was always reserved and would not have been likely to speak much'.[35] Among the possessions that were sent home were a Bible, a Book of Prayers and photograph albums containing pictures of the family with which he had spent so little of his life. The Benthall Papers also contain a photograph of Clement, a thin young man looking rather forlorn in his full dress captain's uniform. Like Ernest Pontifex, the hero of Samuel Butler's autobiographical novel *The Way of All Flesh*, 'he was not an ideal boy and he was not strong enough for his surroundings'.[36] It seems that he had not been able to cope with the moral pressures of his boyhood or the social pressures of army life. He was, perhaps, a victim of the early Victorian age.

Other youngsters were better-equipped for survival by having a stronger physique, a tougher character or kinder relations. John (Jacky) Fisher, who was to become First Sea Lord before and during the First World War, attributed his vitality to 'the imbibing of my mother's milk beyond the legal period of nine months'.[37] He was born in 1841 (the same year as Clement Benthall) to a struggling coffee planter and his wife in a remote part of Ceylon. At the age of six, Jacky was sent to England, an 'orphan of Empire' in Jan Morris's words, to be educated and to make his way in the world. He never saw his father again but remembered him as 'a handsome, brave and soldierly figure of the frontiers'.[38] He soon forgot his mother, however, and had no feeling for her when he met her twenty-five years later. He lived with his impoverished grandfather and did not see much of his six younger brothers and sisters who were also sent to England. None of this was an auspicious start in life but Jacky was a spirited, charming and handsome boy who attracted friends. The first was his godmother, Lady Horton, who often had him to stay on her Derbyshire estate and persuaded an influential neighbour to help him become a midshipman in the Royal Navy.

'I entered the Navy penniless, friendless and forlorn,' Fisher wrote in his memoirs. Like many new cadets the thirteen-year-old lad was treated badly on his first ship, HMS *Calcutta* (which was still powered only by sail). He stopped growing because he was given insufficient food: 'I had to keep either the first or middle watch every night and was always hungry. Devilled Pork Rind was a luxury and a Spanish Onion with a Sardine in the Middle Watch was paradise.'[39] He witnessed and experienced much brutality, fainting when he saw eight men flogged on his first day and being made by the captain to walk 'the break of the poop with a coil of rope round my neck, as he said I was born to be hung'. But hardship acted as a spur to the young Fisher, who explained: 'I have always had to fight like Hell and fighting like Hell has made me what I am. Hunger and Thirst are the way to Heaven.'[40]

Life got a little easier in 1856 when he joined a ship commanded by Lancelot Shadwell, 'the greatest saint on earth'. The Captain gave the midshipmen champagne and gingernuts when they were seasick. Fisher found further emotional comfort in 1859 when he was befriended in Shanghai by Mrs Warden, the wife of the head of the P&O shipping line. She became a substitute mother whom he addressed as Mams. In his frequent letters he tells her of the excitement and horror he felt when involved in hard fighting against the Chinese – 'a sad business, is it not, Mams?' He gives her a suggestive account of shipboard Christmas celebrations when all the men were dead drunk, 'hugging me and wanting me to take their grog'. He was tough enough to survive all these traumatic experiences and at nineteen he proudly told Mams of his promotion to lieutenant rank with a full dress coat – 'such a beauty!'[41] From then on Jacky Fisher prospered both in his private life, where he remained a great favourite with women, and in the Navy, which he dominated 'for close on a generation'.[42] But even his admirer, Jan Morris, has to admit that 'Ruthless, Relentless, Remorseless were the watchwords of his professional career.'[43] Perhaps these characteristics had developed in reaction to the adversities of his childhood.

Another case where hard circumstances were tempered by kindness was that of Emily and her sister Georgiana, daughters of the Resident in Delhi, Sir Thomas Metcalfe. In 1838, at the ages of nine and six, they were sent to Mrs Umphelby's school at Belstead, Suffolk. Mrs Umphelby was a disciple of Jacob Abbott, a well-known Evangelical educationist. He believed that 'childhood is the most fertile part of the vineyard of the Lord', a 'season of probation and trial' [44] The girls followed a demanding timetable:

> To rise at 7 o'clock. *Silence* in bedrooms. To be dressed by 7.30. To pray and read Bibles until afterwards prayers in the drawing room. Begin lessons at 9 o'clock. Classes lasting half an hour when we were small children, but afterwards lengthened. An interval of ten minutes' relaxation between classes when we might talk – otherwise perfect silence. Daily walk before dinner at 1 o'clock. An hour in the garden in afternoon. Tea at 5 o'clock. Prayers at 7.30. Supper of cake – then bed at 8 when we were small – afterwards 9 o'clock. [45]

Mrs Umphelby issued tickets of conduct to pupils who excelled in Truth, Obedience, Self-Control and Attention to Studies. All this sounds rather daunting for two young girls from India, placed under Mrs Umphelby's guardianship in the holidays as well as the terms. Yet Emily records happy memories of Belstead where she enjoyed birthday parties, trips to the seaside and the 'simple pleasures of country life'. Mrs Umphelby (known as Mamie) seems to have been a loving mother-substitute for the girls, whose own mother died in India in 1842.

Emily thought they were better-off than their brother, Theo, who was under the care of their Aunt Georgiana, 'a great disciplinarian'. Having already taken on the 'troublesome' orphaned daughter of her brother Theophilus and the three illegitimate sons of her brother Charles (who appeared in Chapter Two), this long-suffering aunt had had enough of Anglo-Indian wards. She must have been relieved to pack Thomas's girls off to Belstead. In Emily's opinion, moreover, she kept Theo 'too much at school as he was troublesome at home without companions, so he had not a happy childhood'. Theo's miseries culminated in the winter of 1845–6 while he was at Addiscombe Military Academy. He suffered (like Rudyard Kipling and several other Anglo-Indian exiles) 'great pain in his eyes'. In Theo's case, this 'ended in the terrible affliction of blindness in his right eye ... and the destruction of all his ardent hopes of a military career'. [46] (As we saw in Chapter Three, this disability did not prevent the adult Theo from fighting in the siege of Delhi.) While he was at Addiscombe, Emily had to leave her 'dear happy home at Belstead' for she was summoned to go and live with her father in Delhi. She kept up an affectionate correspondence with Mamie, whose influence must have helped to determine her choice of a husband. He was Edward Bayley, apparently the embodiment of Victorian virtue: 'He is everything he ought to be, courteous, learned, unselfish, gentlemanly, consistent, energetic, firm, tender, popular, but above all a truly godly Christian, a consistent humble Child of God.'[47]

These same merits have also been attributed to Brigadier-General Sir Henry and Lady Lawrence, that distinguished couple who 'gave their lives for India' and demanded a similar spirit of self-sacrifice from their sons. Through the dangers of the Afghan and Sikh wars of the 1840s, during her husband's tour of duty as Resident in the 'absolute seclusion' of Nepal, and in the course of her own protracted bouts of illness (compounded by the death of a baby girl), Honoria Lawrence struggled to bring up her first-born son Alexander in the true spirit of Christian imperialism.[48] She was determined that Alick, as he was called, should not be spoilt and 'animalised' as she observed some Anglo-Indian children to be.[49] From an early age he was slapped or whipped when he did not obey his parents — and even sometimes for not playing in a manly enough fashion. When urged to fire a little brass cannon he had been given at the age of four: 'Our boy hen'd [chickened out], and began to cry. I was very vexed. Much worse I was angry and gave him a slap. . . . I was determined not to yield to his cowardice. I took him on my lap and reasoned with him and assured him of punishment if he was so foolish. . . . At last he took courage and applied the match.' Twelve days later Alick enjoyed firing the cannon and his mother hoped that he would be 'a real son of a gun'. Honoria managed to teach the boy a little reading and arithmetic but he was slow to learn and worried about making mistakes. While she noted at the end of his seventh year that her son was 'painfully timid . . . with the hesitating timorous manner of a boy who had been accustomed to harshness', it did not occur to his mother that she and her husband had been too severe.[50]

When it was time for Alick to be taken to England in 1846 the couple had not only acquired another son, Harry, but two hundred British children 'rescued from . . . the heathenism of the barracks' for whom they had set up their famous school at Sanawar in the Simla hills, which will be described in the next chapter. There was plenty to absorb Honoria when she returned to her beloved husband, who was called to help his brother, Sir John Lawrence, bring law and order to the Punjab. Alick was left in Bristol under the rule of Honoria's sister and brother-in-law, Dr and Mrs Bernard, described by Harry's grandson John as a 'hard and cold' couple 'with a distorted piety'. In these circumstances Alick might well have been upset to receive rhapsodic letters from Honoria. She describes, for instance, an idyllic holiday in Kashmir, where Harry was 'in ecstasy pitching some tiny tents sent him by the king', and a school picnic at Sanawar where the children celebrated Sir Henry's birthday with a special anthem. None of Alick's letters survives in the huge Lawrence archive. But between the lines of the parents' letters which they sent to him (carefully preserving a copy themselves) one can discern an unhappy boy. Alick was 'listless and apathetic' in the holidays, uninvolved in 'athletic games' and uncommunicative about 'his inner mind'.

At the appropriate age he was sent to Rugby, having been taken to visit the house of Dr Thomas Arnold, 'the wonderful and good man' who had been its headmaster until dying in harness in 1842. Despite being given a copy of Arnold's sermons, Alick does not appear to have imbibed much of the school's famed 'godliness and good learning'. By 1853 it seemed likely that he would fail to get into Haileybury, thus causing his parents 'bitter mortification'. In one of her last letters before she herself died in harness, Lady Lawrence urged her son: 'Gird up your loins and strive, that is the word that includes all.'[51] After Honoria's death, Sir Henry continued the homilies, appealing constantly to the memory of 'dear Mama' and quoting her advice: 'Be pure, be honest, avoid evil women, avoid the harlot, avoid strong drink.' When the lad still made no progress and began to show signs of becoming 'girlish', he was withdrawn from Rugby.[52] Eventually, with the help of a tutor, Alick put his shoulder to the wheel and passed the entrance examination for Haileybury in September 1855.

By this time Harry had followed his brother to Bristol where, according to his grandson, he too spent a miserable childhood which 'seemed to break something within him'.[53] Still in India was their four-year-old sister Honoria, known as Honie, who did not receive the same rigorous upbringing. Her doting father described her as 'a very precious little thing, clever and self-willed; a sunbeam running in and out of my room all day; more intelligent than many children twice her age'. She often wrote to her exiled brothers even though she had never met them. They are delightful letters (dictated to Sir Henry) telling of her playmates, of her lessons with the children of a second Lawrence school at Mount Abu, and of going to see tigers in the wild. In 1856 she conveyed the exciting news that she was soon coming home with her father. But Sir Henry's insistence that he should stay on when the Mutiny broke out in 1857, 'to do some good and prevent more evil', deprived all three children of their remaining parent, as we saw in Chapter Three.[54] Honie came to England with Aunt Charlotte (Sir Henry's sister) and seems to have brought some sweetness and light into her brothers' lives. While Harry was receiving heavy and unheeded advice from his uncles that he should show himself 'a son of one of the best and ablest men who ever went to India' by going there in his turn, Honie told him how glad she would be when 'we two meet again . . . in thunder, lightning or in rain'.[55]

The two had great need of each other in October 1864 when they heard the shocking news of Alick's death in India at the age of twenty-six. The young man, bearing the rank of baronet in his father's honour, had joined the ICS and was at that time staying in Simla with Uncle John (now Viceroy), his own young wife and their 'sweet babe of six months'. According to an account by Lady Edwardes, who was also part of the viceregal party, 'he was welcomed by all as a legacy' from his parents.[56] 'One night there was a quarrel,' according to the only family account, and this may cast some light on Alick's state of mind at the beginning of this unexplained episode. The next morning he left the party to join his Uncle Richard on an expedition.[57] About ten days' march from Simla Alick rode ahead and fell from a precipitous mountain path into a deep ravine. The Lawrences' friend Sir Robert Napier lamented:

> Was all poor Lady Lawrence's teaching and good training of Alexander only to prepare him for such a sudden removal instead of, as she affectionately thought, a career emulating his father's? It is hard to carry one's mind away from that lone precipice – that dreadful crash – the poor form so shattered, without any hand stretched out to save.[58]

Honie consoled Harry with the 'delightful' thought that their brother had 'shown in his life that he was ready to be taken and to join our own beloved parents in Heaven'.[59] But would their stern mother have been satisfied? In 1845, when seven-year-old Alick spent his first night away from her, she had recorded in her journal a judgement which Sir Henry copied out for his son after she died: 'Your death would be a slight evil to your parents, compared to seeing you grow up selfish, cowardly, untrue, forgetful of your Maker, Redeemer, Sanctifier.'[60]

It was, as Ernest Pontifex found, difficult to emulate parents 'who had never done anything naughty since they had been children'.[61] The task was even more daunting if those parents were eminent Victorians. When Dr Arnold's son William visited Sir Henry and Lady Lawrence in the Punjab and saw for the first time the 'awesome vastness' of the Himalayas, he was irresistibly 'reminded of Papa'.[62] For Alick and Harry Lawrence, living up to their legendary parents and uncles must have been rather like climbing the Himalayas.

Later Victorian parents tended to be more flexible with their offspring than their flinty forebears. Anglo-Indian families, in particular, could modify their judgements now that separated members saw and communicated with each other more rapidly. Thus, when the wife of James Fitzjames Stephen hesitated over whether to travel with her baby daughter to join him in Calcutta as European war threatened in 1870, he sent the advice: 'Telegraph your decision to me as soon as you make it. "I shall come" or "I shall stay".' This was one of many telegrams exchanged between the couple while Stephen was on an important short-term assignment with the Government of India. The renowned barrister was engaged in codifying the laws of the Raj and delighted in the 'bracing and vigorous' moral atmosphere of Calcutta. He was generously paid for his efforts, managing to invest about £6,000 in two and a half years. But when he had the chance to stay on in India he refused on the grounds that it would mean prolonging the 'pain of separation' from his wife and six children.[63]

Among Stephen's zealous colleagues in Calcutta were the Strachey brothers. Sir John was a civil servant who toiled for years in the Finance Department and Sir Richard a soldier in the Bengal Engineers who did much to improve the railways, canals and roads of India. Members of a new breed of Indian administrators, both men were rationalists, openly agnostic in religion, as was Stephen. It was not uncommon in the later Victorian age for the clever offspring of devout Evangelicals to abandon the religion of their parents; famous examples of this trend are Samuel Butler, George Eliot and Leslie Stephen (brother of James Fitzjames and father of Virginia Woolf).[64] The poet Matthew Arnold was another sceptical son, as was his brother William who founded over a thousand vernacular schools in the Punjab in which the Bible was banned as a class-book. As William lay dying at the age of thirty-one, as he voyaged home in 1859, he was overpowered by 'awful Doubt of what lies beyond'.[65] When such agnostics became parents themselves, they tended to bring up their offspring more in the light of reason and common sense than by an unalterable code of conduct. This trend can be observed in the family life of Richard Strachey after his late marriage to Jane Grant in 1858.

The couple had ten children, of whom four were born before Sir Richard's retirement in 1872 and six spent their whole childhood in Britain. One of the last, born in 1880 when his father was sixty-three, was Lytton, whose famous essays *Eminent Victorians* were to deflate such towering figures as Thomas Arnold and Florence Nightingale. In his pioneering biography of Lytton Strachey, Michael Holroyd portrays the parents too as a 'staunchly Victorian' pair who never discussed 'the innermost feelings and ideas of the children' – although he admits that Jane enjoyed the company of young people and tried to be modern in order to retain the affections of her unconventional and homosexual son. Holroyd writes that in the late 1880s, 'Lytton first grew mesmerized by the riddle of the Victorian age being played out before his eyes.'[66] Yet this is not quite the impression given in the unpublished correspondence between the Stracheys as new parents and their absent Anglo-Indian offspring.

The first-born children, Elinor and Richard (Dick), were taken to Britain in 1867 when they were eight and six and left in the care of Jane's sister Elinor Colevile, known as Aunt Lell. They divided their time between the Coleviles' Scottish home, Craigflower, where they rode ponies and led a country life, and their house in London, where there were treats like the pantomime and Japanese jugglers. They were also taken on a trip to the French resort of Etretat, where they bathed in the sea and bought presents from a stall 'with many jolly things from India and China'.[67] The children clearly liked Aunt Lell, as in his turn did Lytton, who describes her as 'a demi-lunatic, harmless and wonderfully funny'.[68] A glimpse of her eccentric humour appears in one of Dick's letters to his mother: 'Aunt Lell said yesterday if you would not write she would stick a pin through your picture and we all laughed at her.' Dick does not seem to have been so fond of his cousin Andrew who got more coloured tickets than he did 'for doing our lessons nicely'. Reflecting the jealousy Anglo-Indian exiles often felt towards their guardians' own children, he wished that 'Andrew could be punished instead of me'.[69] Dick was probably relieved when Andrew was sent away to school in 1869.

While Elinor thrived at Craigflower, Dick's behaviour 'gave a good deal of trouble', writes a Strachey descendant.[70] This is apparent in his letters where he admits to getting into rages, being naughty and playing about in his lessons. Like other small boys, he also announced that he would like to be a blacksmith or a carpenter. The tone of Sir Richard's response was lighter and less earnest than that of the previous generation of fathers. He scolded 'master dummkopf' and hoped in jest that if he did not learn his lessons 'they will pull your ears and put you in a corner.' Sir Richard tried to arouse the boy's interest by sending him rice and cotton which he had picked on his travels around India, telling him all about how the plants grew. A conscientious and serious man himself, he attempted to convince his son that these were virtues worth acquiring for their own sake. In separate letters he wrote: 'It is not right to play when you ought to be doing lessons. ... You must begin to learn to have to do things which are not at first very pleasant. ... The only way to become wise is to be industrious.'[71]

Young Dick seemed to need his parents' advice. On one occasion Jane replied to a question from the seven-year-old about how he could stop himself once he got into a fit of crying. The mother's reply is full of practical common sense, although it does not inquire into the causes of the child's distress.

> When I was a little girl I used to do just like you and found it very difficult indeed to stop myself crying; now this is what I advise. Make yourself think of something else; if you can, go away and get a book or something to do ... or try to repeat a piece of poetry or a nursery rhyme to yourself, or see whether you can count backwards from ten to one, or how far you can hop on one leg; I think if at the time you are crying you really wish to stop and try my plan ... you may succeed.

The letters from Jane Strachey (whom her son often addressed in the modern way as Mum) are, like her husband's, consistently affectionate. She sometimes wrote him poems. In one she compares all the birds and reaches a conclusion that must have delighted her son:

> You may scream and claw for spite
> I don't care a bobbin;
> I know a bird that beats you quite
> You, crow, and master Robin.
> A bird that hops upon the ground,
> That sings and whistles gaily
> His saucy eye is black and round,
> He gobbles crumbs up daily.

So slim, so trim, so fair, so rare —
You're really quite absurd Sirs,
The first of birds beyond compare
Is my dear DICKY-BIRD, sirs![72]

By 1869 the Strachey parents felt able to congratulate Dick on turning over a new leaf, getting more tickets for his lessons and setting a good example to his distant baby brother Ralph.

In their treatment of Dick the Stracheys were, as a family biography puts it, 'relatively gentle by Victorian standards' — but they still did not consider the emotional dangers of long and distant separation. When they returned to Britain in 1871, Jane Strachey found Dick 'particularly hard to deal with' before he was dispatched to prep school in Worthing. There she sent him cakes, sweets and the heraldic crests which boys at that time were collecting. Although he liked this school Dick never became a great scholar. But his father's response when he did rather badly in his army exams was not that of a stern early-Victorian father: 'I do not think there is much appearance of the Strachey tendency being carried on into the future through my off-spring. Perhaps the world has had enough of it.'[73] In fact, he was mistaken. Two of his 'Indian children' followed in his footsteps — no doubt helped by his influence. Dick rose to the rank of Colonel in the Indian Army and Ralph became Chief Engineer of the East India Railway. The careers of the younger children followed less traditional paths. Pernel became Principal of Newnham College for women in Cambridge. Philippa got a CBE for her work in the feminist movement. James edited and translated the works of Sigmund Freud. And Lytton achieved fame as a writer and member of the Bloomsbury group, which of course included Virginia Stephen and her sister Vanessa. It was evidently possible to bring up children successfully without divine assistance.

The Stracheys and Stephens did possess good salaries and private means or comfortable pensions. They could afford some latitude in their careers and could travel and communicate by the most convenient methods. None of this applied to lesser Anglo-Indian employees such as William Wonnacott, an army schoolmaster. After losing a baby son and his wife Emily in 1871, he wanted to dispatch his remaining son and daughter to his wife's parents in England, believing 'in home associations, which can only be imbibed and impressed in young minds such as theirs in England'. With financial help from the Army he sent young Willie home 'in safe keeping with Sergeant Trump', who was unable to prevent all the boy's clothes being stolen on the journey. Later, in 1873, he sent Nellie too even though he would now 'be indeed lonely'. There was then a misunderstanding between Wonnacott and his parents-in-law over whether he should pay for the children's keep. He promised to contribute what he could afford, which was only £2 a month, and urged them 'to let this make no difference in your behaviour to the children for they, poor things, are not accountable'. He almost wished now that he had kept Willie and Nellie with him and could only hope that they would 'never forget their father who is now quite alone, fretting under an Indian sun'.[74] But a humble schoolmaster could not afford to change his mind.

Over the next five years Wonnacott took a close interest in the progress of his son and daughter. He advised his mother-in-law Mrs Short (who was widowed in 1873) to apply 'steady determination and strong will tempered with kindness' to Willie when he became wayward and played truant and to Nellie when she was too high-spirited with 'rude' associates at the local school. But his experience as a teacher told him that 'harsh measures too frequently defeat their own purpose' and that children's squabbles were 'safety valves for exuberance of animal spirits'. He would never, for instance, put pressure on the children to write to him more frequently because 'one must expect young folks to be thoughtless'. Nor did he ever mention punishment either in this world or the next. He encouraged both his children to learn drawing and music, which would be 'sources of amusement' to them – his own lonely exile was eased by painting (for which he won frequent prizes) and singing with a 'glee club'. Eventually both Willie and Nellie had to go to boarding school as they grew away from their grandmother's 'leading strings'. Their father explained to them that it was difficult for him to afford £60–70 a year since this was more than half his annual pay:

Again I have to ask you my dear boy to be a little careful of your clothes, for the reason that I spoke to you about before. You know my means are limited and I want you to help in keeping down as much as you can the expense of your schooling and boarding in this matter. I have nothing left for myself when I send home the money that has to keep you and Nellie at good schools.[75]

Wonnacott took his duties as a schoolmaster very seriously, priding himself on doing well in annual inspections and hoping to become an inspector one day. But such was his longing to see his children that he applied several times for compassionate home leave, even trying to take advantage of his mother-in-law's acquaintance with the Viceroy, Lord Ripon. He discovered a Royal Warrant of 1871 by which 'school-masters serving with the Colonial Corps are allowed eight months leave to England with pay and passage after seven years service.' But his applications were turned down. Bitterly he reflected that when he did return he would have spent thirteen unbroken years abroad: 'One more year would make it a favourite transportation term.' In January 1878 the regiment was sent to Aden as its 'last station on foreign service'. By this time, though, Wonnacott's health had broken down and he died in October on his homeward journey, during which he was herded in, as was usual for army schoolteachers, with the troops.

Among his effects were a collection of over a hundred books, a folio of his own paintings, sundry articles of clothing 'in bad condition', a cloak and scarf bought for Nellie and Willie in 1873 for which he had not been able to afford the postage and a bundle of letters from his 'dear lambs'. Wonnacott's brothers promised to be 'fathers to the fatherless'. But it seems that they did not preserve their letters, for the collection in the India Office Library contains only the father's side of the correspondence. That is enough in any case to show that the schoolmaster was a man with 'feelings as fine as those for whom so much trouble is taken' — his term for people at the top of the social heap. It is clear, too, that Wonnacott also had unusually liberal ideas on education and child-rearing. But he lacked much opportunity to put them into practice. It was 'all very well for the "bigwigs"', he wrote in 1877, but for him 'and others of similar standing' it was still extremely hard to preserve any relationship with their distant children.[76]

Even in a gentleman's family it was difficult to find a happy solution if the children's mother was dead. This problem faced Major Charles Augustus Munro, whose wife died in 1872 leaving him with three children under four. The family was in England at the time but the Major had to return to his regiment in Burma. His solution was to leave Edith, Charles and Hector with his widowed mother and two spinster sisters in a house he acquired for them in Barnstaple. On the face of it, there was nothing wrong with the Major's arrangements: the grand-mother was a 'gentle, dignified old lady', Broadgate was a commodious house and there were 'lovely fields and woods quite handy'. But he had reckoned without the nature of his sisters, Charlotte (Tom) and Augusta, as described in Edith's biography of her famous younger brother Hector, who in later life took on the pen-name Saki.

Edith remembers that her aunts 'entirely overruled' their mother, kept the house dark and fetid and would not take the children into the countryside because Aunt Augusta was afraid of cows. There were many other embargoes such as entering the lumber-room at the top of the house, going into the kitchen garden, playing with other children and eating the delicacies on offer at the village Christmas party. When they went away to school the pocket money their father had provided was not sent to them – so that Charlie at Charterhouse was one of only two boys who did not have a 'house bill' for tuck and treats. Edith sums up Aunt Tom as a 'reincarnation of Catherine of Russia [who] had no scruples [and] never saw when she was hurting people's feelings'. But she was benevolent compared to her younger sister: 'the autocrat of Broadgate a woman of ungovernable temper, of fierce likes and dislikes, imperious, a moral coward, possessing no brains worth speaking of, and a primitive disposition. Naturally she was the last person who should have been put in charge of children.'[77]

There were some mitigating circumstances. One was that the aunts were often too preoccupied with their own quarrels to focus on the children. A second boon for Edith (as a girl) and Hector (as a delicate child) was that they were not beaten, as poor Charlie was. Finally the three children had 'the refuge of their own company'. Hector, the youngest but most imaginative, was 'master of their revels' a distinction not appreciated at Bedford Grammar School, where reports said that he showed 'little application'. They raided the kitchen garden and the storeroom for forbidden treats, wrote a *Broadgate Paper*, acted their own plays, read the books sent to them by their father and invented endless practical jokes. When Munro came home every four years on leave or Uncle Wellesley visited from London there were picnics and excursions into the countryside, which the aunts had to allow in deference to their brothers. Even so it must have seemed a long exile before Colonel Munro (as he now was) took early retirement in 1886 'primarily to see at last to his motherless children'. Despite the oppressive discipline under which they had been reared for fourteen years, he found them in high spirits. Comfortably-off after his successful imperial career, he was able to set up a separate house for them and to take them on extended tours of Europe. This genial man also established a loving relationship with his offspring, though he must have been embarrassed by their mockery of guests at Continental hotels. 'We let ourselves go!' wrote Edith, who was by now nearly twenty. 'My father was soon nicknamed "the Hen that hatched out ducklings."'[78]

The main evidence for the Munros' childhood is Edith's biography of Hector, which was not written until the aunts were safely dead. Fiercely loyal to her younger brother, who grew up to a life of homosexual adventure as well as literary distinction before he was killed in the First World War, she destroyed all his letters. But, as Graham Greene pointed out in his essay *The Burden of Childhood*, Saki's best stories 'are all of childhood, its humour and its anarchy as well as its cruelty and unhappiness. . . . They cannot quite disguise, in spite of the glint and the sparkle, the loneliness of the Barnstaple years.'[79] It is no accident that the children in these stories are usually in the care of aunts or that the places and circumstances resemble those of Hector's childhood. Sometimes his bitterness shines through, as in the murderous revenge that takes place in *Sredni Vashtar*. But often the tales are in lighter vein.

In *The Lumber-Room* Nicholas evades the aunt's supervision to gain access to this forbidden territory after being left at home in disgrace while his brother and cousins go to the seaside. He spends an absorbing time in this 'storehouse of unimagined treasures', which includes Indian hangings, brass figures and carved sandalwood boxes. Nicholas then hears urgent calls from the distressed aunt who has fallen into a rainwater tank while looking for him in the gooseberry garden – also out of bounds. The boy refuses to rescue her on the grounds that only the Devil could be tempting him to be disobedient. 'Aunt often tells me that the Evil One tempts me and that I always yield. This time I'm not going to yield.' So the aunt spends a period of 'undignified and unmerited detention in a rain-water tank' while Nicholas feasts on his memories of a tapestry hunting picture he has seen in the lumber-room.[80]

In another story an aunt vainly attempts during a train journey to divert her three bored charges with a moral tale about a good little girl being saved from a mad bull. The children are much more amused by a story told by a bachelor in the same carriage. He relates that the extraordinarily good little Bertha is given permission to walk in a beautiful park from which children are usually banned. She is wearing her special medals for obedience, punctuality and good behaviour and it is the clinking of these which betrays her presence when she hides from a marauding wolf. She is then devoured by the wolf, an ending which the children consider 'beautiful'. 'A dissentient opinion came from the aunt. "A most improper story to tell young children! You have undermined the effect of years of careful teaching."'[81] With such witty tales Saki, an onlooker like the bachelor in the railway compartment, undermined the late Aunts Tom and Augusta and all that they stood for. Aunts were to suffer too when P. G. Wodehouse drew on his own 'infant world of aunts'[82] to portray the fictional Aunt Agatha who 'wore barbed wire next to the skin and conducted human sacrifices by the light of the full moon'. Was it mere coincidence, I wonder, that the old middle-class euphemism for lavatory was 'the aunt'?

'Aunt' was itself often a spurious title, which was assumed by many women who did not have that relationship with their wards. One of the sources of Nicholas's resentment in *The Lumber-Room* was that 'his cousins' aunt insisted, by an unwarranted stretch of the imagination, in styling herself his aunt also'.[83] And in Rudyard Kipling's well-known story *Baa Baa, Black Sheep*, when young Punch and Judy arrive at the house of a strange woman whom they are told to call Aunty Rosa, they have never heard of 'an animal called an aunt. Their whole world had been Papa and Mamma, who knew everything, permitted everything, and loved everybody.'[84] This story is largely autobiographical. Without any warning or explanation, Rudyard and his sister Trix were taken from India to England to be left with Captain and Mrs Holloway of Southsea, who had advertised in *The Times of India* for child boarders. Lockwood and Alice Kipling were probably rather worried, as were most Anglo-Indian parents, about the children being as spoilt as Punch is seen to be in the story. Trix said later that her brother was 'about as spoilt as he could be when he came home in 1871 ... and had never been taught to read'.[85] What remains unclear is why Alice did not choose to leave the children with her mother or with one of her three married sisters, all of whom had children of similar ages. For the 'circle of sisters' evoked in a recent book by Judith Flanders did not conform to the villainous type portrayed by Saki and Wodehouse. During the years at Southsea Rudyard enjoyed occasional visits to Aunt Louisa (Baldwin), where he got to know his cousin Stanley, and Aunt Georgie (Georgiana Burne-Jones) where there were cultured London diversions. But most of his time was spent with the Holloways.

Guardians varied as much as aunts and in this respect the young

Kipling was unlucky. A fearsome picture of Mrs Holloway emerges in this story (written in 1888) and in Kipling's memoir *Something of Myself*. She bestowed her favours on Trix, a welcome little girl, but victimised Rudyard, who may indeed have been a difficult child. He was branded, like Punch, as a 'black sheep', 'beaten when the occasion demanded', called a 'Child of the Devil' and threatened with 'the blinding horrors of Hell'. He was also left in the house with a servant while the Holloways took Trix on holiday.[86] Such methods of child-rearing were common in Victorian households. Even the happily united London family of the 1870s, classically evoked by Mollie Hughes, left the youngest boy at home with the servants for a period. As they returned his brother caught sight of him looking out of the window: 'His face was such a picture of misery that I have never been able to forget it.'[87] Pictures of misery were to be found as late as the 1920s, when there was at least one episode comparable to that in Kipling's story, when Punch has a placard inscribed with the word 'LIAR' stitched on to his clothes. Leslie Wenger, the son of a missionary, remembers that his strict Plymouth Brethren 'Aunt' Jessie made his five-year-old sister Marjorie 'carry a little imp round with her to remind her how naughty she was'.[88]

There is some doubt about the autobiographical accuracy of *Baa Baa, Black Sheep*. But the story is important because Kipling conveys with unprecedented power what it felt like to be an 'Indian child' thousands of miles away from his parents. His mother was more aware of her own feelings, which she recorded in a sentimental poem:

> He and she, o'er the sea
> Finding other pleasures,
> Scarcely miss, Mother's kiss
> Rich in childish treasures.[89]

Her son shows us the children crying when they 'lost all their world', Punch's yearning for a 'special place for him and his little affairs' and 'for a little affection'. Finally there is the revelation of his inexplicable clumsiness and inability to read even large print. 'So Black Sheep brooded in the shadows that fell about him and cut him off from the world.'[90] The explanation, both in the story and in real life, was that the boy had become half-blind. There are no letters from the young Rudyard to support most of this; even if they had survived they would probably not express the child's real feelings because, as Kipling himself said, 'children tell little more than animals, for what comes to them they accept as externally established'.[91]

Eventually, at Christmas 1876, Georgiana Burne-Jones realised that Rudyard was suffering 'some sort of breakdown' and conveyed this to her sister, who had not visited her children in the intervening five years. Lockwood Kipling, as a tutor in the Bombay School of Art, had been earning less than £500 a year, a salary which was adequate but left little to spare for travel. In 1875 he began to earn more as Principal of the Mayo School of Art in Lahore, but he contracted typhoid soon after the move and needed Alice as a nurse and helpmeet. Once she heard about her son's condition, however, Alice went to England, removed the children from Southsea and took them for a long holiday to Epping Forest. She did not return to India until the end of 1878, entrusting Trix again to Mrs Holloway and Rudyard to the United Services College, a minor public school run by a family friend at Westward Ho! in Devon. As a myopic and nervous twelve-year-old, Rudyard was not well suited to the military discipline of the school, where for a year he was homesick and the victim of bullying. But he became 'hardened enough', he wrote in 1882, to put up with separation and he made a few close friends, with whom he enjoyed japes and escapades such as those described in Stalky & Co. He was worried, though, about his sister now lodging in London, where she attended Notting Hill High School. Trix was lonely and had developed 'some morbid religious notions'.[92]

When Rudyard was sixteen he went to join his parents in Lahore where his father found him a job as a journalist. Trix followed a year later and for a few years the parents and children were together 'as a family square'. Biographers have detected in the adult Kipling the scars of his childhood trauma. Angus Wilson believes that the Southsea years made him 'a man forever exceptionally reticent except to children and his very few intimates'.[93] Kingsley Amis comes to a characteristically tough conclusion: he 'got what he needed' to make him 'a notably self-reliant man'. But Amis recognises in Kipling's writing 'a special tenderness' towards children which was 'partly derived from the memory of his own unhappiness'.[94] Amis might have been surprised to find his opinion shared by a psychotherapist, who cited the 'extraordinary love and understanding of children' as evidence of Kipling's 'ability to preserve the first six good years of his life'.[95] A supreme example of his empathy is Kipling's masterpiece, Kim (quoted in the Introduction), which draws also on the pristine knowledge of India garnered during the happy years of his early childhood and young manhood.

Such was Kipling's genius that memoirs and biographies often compare their subjects' years of exile with his. Thus José Harris writes that the childhood experiences of William Beveridge, whose 1942 Report became the blueprint for the Welfare State, were 'drearily reminiscent of the scenes described by Kipling'. However, the Beveridge parents were not typical Anglo-Indians. Henry was an irreligious district judge who believed that the main objective of British rule should be to prepare for its own extinction and before getting married Annette had lectured in a London working women's college and set up a girls' school in Calcutta. Admittedly, Annette Beveridge was indeed following Raj practice when she took her three children to England in 1883, although she did stay with them longer than was usual before leaving them at Bingfield, a Unitarian boarding school in Southport, Lancashire. For the next three years seven-year-old Laetitia Santamini (Letty) Beveridge – her Latin and Sanskrit names symbolising her parents' cultural duality – acted as a 'little mother' to Willie and Jeannette (Tutu) who had just turned five and four when they were left.[96] All three children were fond of their German governess, Emma Vogel, who stayed with them at Bingfield, and of the Turners, a Stockport couple with whom they spent some of their holidays. The school, chosen no doubt for its bracing air and its relatively unorthodox religious ethos, sounds satisfactory in the children's early letters. They write of roasting chestnuts and making bonfires in the winter of 1884, of a Christmas party with a conjuror, of growing bulbs in the springtime and of summer walks over the sandhills. As clever children, who took to books 'as ducks to water',[97] they received good reports on which their parents congratulated them.

Between the lines of their dutiful missives, though, the children sometimes betray feelings of loss.[98] Tutu's first letter (dictated to Emma Vogel) tells her mother: 'The man cut off all my curls. . . . I send you my love and kisses and I am sorry you will not come back so soon.' Two days later she wrote to her father with the same juvenile stoicism: 'We have your picture in the room and I often kiss it. . . . Mamma stays away a long time and I hope she comes back. . . . I played horse in the field and I tumbled but I did not cry. A horse does not cry.' As Christmas approached Tutu was pleased when Letty knitted her a 'very nice pair of mittens [for] my hands are very cold'. But she was sad that 'all the boys have gone home' and that her friend Ernest was not coming back because he was going to another school.[99] Willie's letters are less revealing. He writes, for instance, about having 'a cake with candles' on his sixth birthday, adding simply: 'I wish I could see you and show you my nice presents'. But in his memoir he recalls 'my bitter grief' when another little boy had a birthday to celebrate on the same day as I had, and I was made, in my mother's absence in India, to go to the other boy's party instead of having one of my own.'[100] Letty never complained. But some sentences in her letters suggest that she was missing India as well as family life: 'Please tell the old servants not to forget us.' 'I found a plant . . . that looked like a mother and her three children.' 'Yesterday we went to the museum [and] we saw a great many Indian things.'[101]

Such clues were not yet clear enough to arouse fears in Henry and Annette Beveridge. It was for medical rather than maternal reasons that Annette came to England in March 1886, leaving their baby Hermann with Henry 'to make him laugh and to keep him cheerful'. When she arrived, after a journey from Calcutta to Southport accomplished in exactly one month, she realised from conversations with the children, the Turners and Fräulein Vogel that she had been living in a 'fool's paradise'. Willie told her that 'he had been so frightened that he had told a lie'. Fräulein Vogel complained that the school fed her on bread and jam for supper four times a week. The Turners advised strongly against the children being sent back to Bingfield. And Letty 'could not speak or think of my going without tears'. It did not take Annette long to decide on a course of action that was radical in comparison to the measures taken by Alice Kipling. On 25 May she sent her husband a telegram: 'Operation well done. Children accompany me.' In the autumn she took Letty, Willie and Tutu to India, where they met their baby brother for the first time.[102]

Scholastically the older trio fared well. Annette rented a house up in the hills at Darjeeling, sent for the beloved Fräulein and arranged extra tuition with masters from the town's St Paul's School, sometimes known as the 'Eton of the East' (see Chapter Five). The children's cheerful and articulate letters to one or both of their parents in Calcutta tell about riding and picnics in the hills, putting on entertainments and plays, games and pets, and the Presbyterian Sunday school classes of which Henry Beveridge disapproved. They often wished that they could see more of their father – but at least they knew that he was only a train journey away. All was well in the family, apart from periodic attacks of violent fever for which 'treatment was as uncertain as diagnosis'. Hermann's was so bad that he suffered brain damage in 1886 and Willie nearly died in 1889. It was this that decided Annette again to remove all the children from India. This time she stayed in England with them, leaving Henry to his lonely labours in Bengal 'unless some misfortune happens to make my presence necessary to you more than to the children'.[103] It was a rational decision in which juvenile physical and emotional needs tipped the balance.

But parents can never know for certain what will damage or benefit their offspring. Annette Beveridge could not have expected that she would lose two children to influenza within three years of their return to England. The delicate, backward Hermann died in 1890. And the promising, affectionate Letty, who had rarely been ill in India, died three years later. Nor could Mrs Beveridge have thought that she was inhibiting her remaining children's emotional growth after Letty's death, as José Harris claims, by her 'increasing possessiveness and protectiveness'. It is true that William always idealised his mother and that his social life centred around her for as long as she lived. It is also true that her interference helped to prevent his getting married until he was sixty-three. Like Kipling, he found it easier to get on with children than with adults and simpler to love 'humanity in general' than his fellow-men.[104] It seems likely, though, that Beveridge would have been harmed more by his mother's prolonged absence during his childhood than by her domineering presence. He himself rejoiced that he and his siblings had 'argued their way out to India to join their parents'.[105]

Many other late-Victorian Anglo-Indian families remained sadly separated. It is true that letters now arrived within three weeks. But this did not stop ten-year-old Guendolen Talbot feeling that her parents seemed like 'locked up toys' whom she knew only as a name.[106] It is also true that journeys could be accomplished in three weeks. Nevertheless parents or children often died without a reunion being possible. A little girl dying of consumption at a Roman Catholic school in Hertfordshire edified the nuns by giving them a last message for her parents in India: 'Tell them I should like to have seen them, but it is not God's will, & I am quite resigned.'[107] It is true that more humane attitudes towards children were beginning to prevail. But young Archibald Campbell did not seem to feel the benefit of them at his boarding school in East Sheen. His drawing of a scrawny boy being held by the legs and beaten by a master bears the caption: 'I have not been done to what this illustration shows but I daresay I shall.'[108] The lonely, the dying and the frightened child could all spring from the pages of Dickens. His dream, and that of the old redeemed father at the end of *Dombey and Son*, was 'to see the child free and stirling'. The dream had yet to come entirely true. But at least eight-year-old Master Beveridge had been rescued from his child-quelling seaside boarding establishment and taken back to Bengal by the shortest route. His voice had been heard.

❦

FIVE

'Cold Showers and Porridge'

British Schools in India

'There are no nice schools for them to go to, and the people around them would be always teaching them to do very wicked things.' This is how an article in *The Juvenile Missionary Herald* for 1890 described the plight of missionaries' daughters in 'heathen lands'. The journal was successful in its appeal for funds to complete a new building in Sevenoaks for Walthamstow Hall, a school for 'little girls who are obliged to be away from their fathers and mothers ... in a far distant land'.[1] Actually there were by this time many British schools in India for the children of missionaries and other expatriates. The problem was that pukka Anglo-Indian parents did not usually consider these 'nice' enough for their daughters, let alone smart enough for their sons, whom they continued to send back to England.

Yet it was the missionary societies, both Protestant and Roman Catholic, which had set up the first European schools in India, during the eighteenth century. Designed for 'poor whites' or for the needy Eurasians encountered in Chapter Two, their aim was to rescue children from the 'demoralising scenes' they were likely to witness in the bazaars and barracks.[2] It was in the Madras Presidency that these free schools and orphanages first multiplied and where Doctor Andrew Bell pioneered his famous monitorial teaching system, which made it 'possible for a single schoolmaster and an assistant to attend the whole school'.[3] So, India led the way in providing cheap elementary education for deprived children. The Madras System became famous and was soon adopted by the new voluntary schools in Britain, where it enabled teachers like Dickens's Mr McChoakumchild to get large numbers of boys and girls simultaneously instructed in 'nothing but Facts'.[4]

The missionaries, though by no means rich, did not entrust their own children to these utilitarian schools. In the early nineteenth century Revd Henry Baker and his wife Amelia sent all their eleven children from Travancore to be educated in England at the expense of the Church Missionary Society (CMS), which eventually provoked a complaint from their pious oldest son that too much money was being spent for this purpose.[5] Mrs Pohle, a missionary's widow, went so far as to appeal for funds in the SPCK's Annual Report for 1822 to give her son Uriel an English education so that he could avoid an Indian charity school. Other SPCK records confirm the austerity of such schools, which Kipling's Kim viewed as one 'long grey vista'.[6] One boarding school issued the following regulations:

5 to 6	The children rise by gunfire, sing a hymn, wash & dress themselves.
6 to 7	Repeating lessons: reading and spelling lessons, and answers to written questions, and such papers are copied as may be ordered by the schoolmaster and superintendent.
7 to 8	Morning Prayer; take breakfast and go over to school to be there at a quarter before 8.
12 to 1	The morning school hours end and the children have their leisure hour; instruction in botany, natural history, astronomy or drawing for those who are desirous of these lessons.
1 to 2	Dinner.
2 to 3	Preparing the wanted copies for the different classes, or any easy employment.
5 to 6	Singing exercises.
6 to 6$\frac{1}{2}$	They take a walk in the garden, or gardening.
6$\frac{1}{2}$ to 8	Evening devotion in the Missionary Fulck's house & private instruction.
8 to 9	Take supper and go to bed.

This particular school met the requirements of the annual inspection in 1823 and certain children were recommended to receive prizes for their talent, industry, correct conduct and diligence. One little girl was rewarded for 'knitting stockings well'. All the leavers obtained a livelihood or got married – and 'two children only died'.[7]

All over India the churches and the army opened similar schools for deprived children. There were in addition private benefactors like Mary Sherwood, whose work was described in Chapter One, and John Low, the Resident at Lucknow, who set up a school in the Residency for the 'daughters and young sons of the poorer classes of Europeans in the City'.[8] Yet only one such school has made a significant mark on history: the Lawrence Military Asylum at Sanawar. It was essentially similar to its predecessors but it achieved fame and attracted unusually generous funding because of its new situation up among the pines and deodars of the Himalayan foothills and because of the celebrity gained by its founders, Henry and Honoria Lawrence.

In a Circular to Bengal regiments in 1845 Major Lawrence appealed to all gentlemen to 'come forward with subscriptions and donations' towards the building of an 'asylum in the North West Hills for the education of soldiers' children'.[9] He originally proposed that 'the children of European parents shall alone be admitted' but this restriction could not be rigidly imposed since the ratio of Eurasian to English wives was in some regiments as high as five to seven.[10] Preference was given to orphans, who (like all children admitted) had to have been born to married parents. This last ruling was strictly enforced, as I saw for myself in the old baptismal certificates collected by K. J. Parel, a chemistry master at the Lawrence School today. All showed two parents with the same name as the child. Neither orphans nor the offspring of living private soldiers were charged for their education but corporals and sergeants were expected to pay up to five rupees (about 50p) a month. Even though the establishment at Sanawar was 'run on the strictest economy', as promised in the 1845 Circular, the fees did not cover the school's costs. But Lawrence's appeals for charity were so effective that four million rupees had been raised by 1858. He himself was the principal donor, committing 5,000 rupees (about £500) from his annual salary in a spirit of true Evangelical philanthropy. This source of income came to an end, of course, when Lawrence (now knighted and promoted to the rank of brigadier-general) was killed at Lucknow in 1857, but such was the sympathy and publicity inspired by the Mutiny that charitable donations continued to flow. In any case, the Government of India took over the control and some of the financing of the school in 1858.

Still in use at the Lawrence School today is the printing press installed at its inception. This served two purposes. The boys were trained in the skill of operating it and it produced a stream of reports, rule books, lists, medical records, copies of letters, school magazines and minute books. Luckily Parel and his wife Manju Khan rescued much of this archive material 'just in time, before it could be sold off as *ruddee* [waste-paper]'. It provided valuable evidence for their admirable history of the school.[11] From such records emerges a vivid picture of boys and girls following their daily routine from 5 a.m. to 8 p.m. for all but four weeks of the year. We see them clothed in blue and red military uniforms or in 'jackets of drab edged with scarlet and white bonnets and tippets'. They are organised into companies under boy NCOs, corrected by caning and flogging, taught by juvenile monitors and fed a daily diet consisting of:

Meat	8 oz
Bread	16 oz
Rice and vegetables	8 oz
Milk	16 oz
Sugar	$\frac{1}{4}$ oz
Pudding extra	Twice a week

Despite the long school day, harsh discipline, lack of recreation and limited rations the children struck most visitors, such as Lord Dalhousie in 1851, as being of 'a strong healthy appearance', 'orderly demeanour and free cheerful bearing'.[12] Apart from epidemics of cholera, whooping cough and measles, one inspector reported, 'the health of the children has been wonderfully good'. The disease rate over eight years was 'less than the average of *ordinary* sickness in large Institutions at home'.[13]

The school (and its sister establishment at Mount Abu in central India) aimed to produce practical members of society: 'A boy may learn to work a telegraph, to survey a field . . . or make himself useful as a clerk.'[14] Sanawar also acted, according a report in *The Times*, as 'an unofficial marriage market [for] shy young sergeants with £5 in Post Office Savings and with matrimonial ambitions in their hearts'.[15] The marriage registers of Sanawar Church (also collected by Parel) do indeed show orphan girls being given away in marriage by the headmaster to suitable young men. On 10 April 1882, for example, fifteen-year-old Euphemia Wright was wedded to Sergeant Alfred Griffa.[16] Despite the schools' lowly aspirations, the children impressed

Sir Henry's son Alick when he visited Sanawar for the first time in 1861. He found the pupils 'well grounded in geography, arithmetic . . . and the Book of Euclid'. He came to a rueful conclusion: 'Indeed it quite shames me sometimes to think how well these boys get on at what at Home we should consider just a common village school. Their aptitude at figures is very great and they seem really to take a pleasure in learning.'[17]

Alick's reflection is interesting in the light of his own experience as an unhappy and reluctant scholar at Rugby. Perhaps it unwittingly bears out the feeling of Brian Hathaway, Secretary of the Lawrence Memorial Fund, that 'a young child cannot be sent many hundred miles'. He was voicing apprehension about a proposal, made in 1859, that the schools at Sanawar and Mount Abu should be amalgamated. No mother, he thought, would send her child to a school if 'the remote distance would put it out of her power to visit it'.[18] His advice was followed and the schools remained separate. Of course, Hathaway had not meant to imply criticism of families like the Lawrences for sending their own children thousands of miles away from their mothers. It was just assumed that burra sahibs were made of sterner stuff than common soldiers and that their children would develop a stiff upper lip in time to benefit from their expensive British education.

So when the Bishop of Calcutta, George Cotton, gave an address about European and Eurasian education on Christmas Eve 1860 he did not feel that he had to worry about the higher echelons of Anglo-Indian society:

> The wants of the richer residents in India, such as covenanted servants of Government, or officers in the army holding lucrative appointments, need not be considered at present. Such persons, being fully impressed with the value of a home education, will generally prefer, under all circumstances, to send their children to England.

The Bishop was concerned rather with 'what may be called the middle class in point of wealth', the growing caste of uncovenanted civil servants, many of whom were involved in organising the railway, telegraph and canal systems. Their presence in India was, he said, 'due entirely to our occupation of the country' and yet their salaries left 'a very small margin for education'. So their children were likely to 'grow up in ignorance and evil habits' as they ran wild 'among natives of the lowest order'.[19] Cotton claimed that at the moment their only chance of improvement lay with the 'Jesuits' and pleaded for the establishment of Protestant middle-class schools. It is true that Roman Catholic Loreto Sisters and Christian Brothers had established many moderately priced boarding schools beside their free schools and orphanages. But there already existed also some respectable non-Catholic academies like Calcutta Grammar School, Maddocks at Mussoorie, the Cathedral School at Bombay, La Martinière at Lucknow and the CMS St John's College at Agra – the buildings of which sometimes rivalled those of the greatest public schools in England. La Martinière is housed in the castle/mausoleum of its founder, Major-General Claude Martin, described as 'one of the most spectacular buildings erected by Europeans in India'[20] while St John's is an Indo-Saracenic edifice resembling Akbar the Great's palace at Fatehpur Sikri. Nevertheless, Bishop Cotton's plea gained the backing of the Governor General, Lord Canning, whose Minute of 1861 has become known as the 'Magna Carta of European education'.[21] He promised government grants for the worthy cause of sustaining a class which, rather than becoming 'dangerous to the State', would be 'a source of strength to British rule and of usefulness in India'.[22]

Both the Bishop and the Governor-General made a further distinction in planning these Anglican establishments. There should be two types of academy. Boarding schools in the hills, charging fifteen to thirty rupees a month, would cater for the more affluent middle class – and it was assumed that these would be pure Europeans, for whom the Himalayan climate was considered essential. Day schools in the plains would provide for parents 'of inferior means' and for those who 'shrink from the thought of separation from [their children] even for a time and do not desire at present any higher culture for them'.[23] Again there was a racial implication in the plans. It was assumed that the 'native blood' of Eurasians fitted them for the heat of the plains and that their large families required cheaper schools. Eurasians were also thought to be prone to that lily-livered tendency 'to keep their children with them'.[24] In practice, however, people were not as easily categorised as their British rulers wished. All the new schools enrolled pupils from both European and Eurasian families, not usually making any distinction in their records between the two groups.[25]

An example of this failure to discriminate can be found in the original Admissions Register of Simla Public School, opened in 1863 and renamed Bishop Cotton School to perpetuate the name of its founder (who was drowned in 1866 while touring Assam by river on the Governor's yacht). The Register shows fathers' occupations ranging from deputy collector and lieutenant of police down to brewer and bootmaker. But the only clue to racial origins lies in their names; Hero Anthony and Duncan and Edward Ricketts, for instance, bear surnames which were those of well-known Eurasian families. Whatever the case, a government inspector was satisfied in 1873 that the 'right class of children has found admittance'.[26] The Remarks column in the Register tells us a little more about the boys themselves. Most were boarders; quite a few were withdrawn because of 'inability to pay'; some died of pneumonia or were 'unable to stand a hill climate'; and some were expelled. Duncan Ricketts was dismissed for running away from the school five times, and Clarence Hoskins was expelled for 'insubordination'.[27] Perhaps these boys found it hard to take the old regime of 'cold showers and porridge' described by a recent headmaster, Kabir Mustafi. Mr Mustafi told me, however, that most lads were probably 'tough enough to handle it' and that they benefited from the British public school methods copied at Bishop Cotton.[28]

John Cotton himself had earlier taught at Rugby and had reorganised Marlborough School on Arnoldian lines when he became its headmaster in 1852. Naturally he insisted that the school at Simla should have a house system, organised games and prefects, whom he viewed as 'the governors of the school'.[29] The 1873 inspector was duly impressed by the cricket club and he also gave patronising approval to the school's academic efforts:

> Although the false quantities made by the boys in reading the Aeneid were so numerous and ingenious as to be absolutely wonderful, and the translation of a passage of English into Latin by every boy in the class neither more nor less than a single incredible solecism, their translation and retranslation of Hindustani was very good; . . . their mathematics fair, and their answering in English literature, in geography, and in history very creditable.

He congratulated Headmaster Samuel Slater and his assistants on the results they had produced with boys who were starting education late in life and often coming from 'home associations which are adverse rather than auxiliary to classical education'.[30]

By the time this report came out European schools had sprung up like mushrooms in India and the Government of India was spending 'considerably more *per capita* than it did on schools for Indian children'.[31] Nine and a half thousand boys attended eighty-nine schools and there were nearly four thousand girls at fifty similar establishments.[32] Among the latter was Auckland House, set up at Simla in 1866 on the initiative of Mrs Cotton. It too received a stamp of approval from the 1873 inspection, which found its clientele (largely the children of clerks, teachers and widows) 'just that which such a school is designed to assist'. Its standard of health was excellent and its education was said to be of 'a useful rather than an ornamental character'.[33] The new academies not only looked English in their gabled, timber-frame buildings complete with ivy-clad Gothic chapels and spacious playing fields; they were also run on traditional public-school lines, providing strict discipline, abundant sport, plain food, smart uniforms, traditional curriculum and a Christian atmosphere. Thus they supplied what was prized by European parents, if not always by their offspring, the complete 'single-sex institutionalized existence'.[34] The older schools also began to conform to the new model. Calcutta Grammar School moved up to fashionable Darjeeling, where it became known as St Paul's. La Martinière tended to favour 'the pure European against the dark-coloured boy'. Even the Lawrence Military Asylum was soon to introduce houses, prefects, Latin, compulsory games and fagging.[35] Schools competed to become known as the Eton or the Cheltenham Ladies' College of the East.

All except the city schools preferred to take pupils as full boarders. This was to avoid irregular attendance, time spent on journeys (often through monsoon rain) and unsuitable conditions for home study. Moreover, boarding was the English public school practice and therefore carried more prestige. But Indian hill boarding schools differed from their English models in that they had a nine-month term ending with a long winter vacation and broken by a short spring break, usually spent in school. There were practical reasons for this. It would have been difficult to keep the hill schools warm during the coldest months. The principal of Woodstock School at Landour (above Mussoorie at over 2,000 metres) complained in February 1913 that he had 'NO MEANS of heating the place, in such bitter weather as we have experienced in the last ten days'.[36] Furthermore, travel in India took so long that more frequent vacations were impractical. In the early days of Bishop Cotton School, before the narrow-gauge Simla Railway was opened in 1903, boys often walked the ninety-five kilometres from

Kalka, the nearest station, along a steep, winding road liable to be swept away by avalanches. Schools also regarded the lack of contact with home as a 'protection from outside infection'. For this reason the Panchgani Boys' School prospectus insisted that during the mid-year three-week holiday 'the boys will remain at the school'.[37] But there was another consideration. Teachers believed that the pupils' homes 'are not always the best place for them, and even boys of exemplary character often return in a strange state of unrest'.[38] Perhaps the behaviour which the masters observed was simply due to the homesickness which would be natural in children embarking on another nine-month stint at school. Limitations of transport and of financial means prevented most parents from visiting their offspring, whose only contact was therefore the weekly letter.

The 1873 inspectors showed a rare understanding of pupils' needs when they made a strong recommendation in their report: 'No school should be allowed to close its doors to day scholars. . . .The schools are founded for the benefit of boys rather than of masters, and the masters are not altogether the best judges of the general question.'[39] They were also conscious of families' financial circumstances, of course, when making this pronouncement. It did not have much effect; most schools continued to favour the practice of boarding. Hard though this was, Indian-educated pupils endured a less drastic separation from their families than their banished contemporaries. Going-Home Day, with its celebratory bonfires and picnics, was never more than nine months away.

The figures and reports which A. J. Lawrence gathered in 1873 suggest that the Indian public schools got off to a good start, attracting children from a range of backgrounds though rarely from the heights of Anglo-Indian society. But by the first decade of the twentieth century most of them were 'struggling against adversity', according to the 1904 *Report of a Committee inquiring into the Financial Condition of European Hill Schools*.[40] The Bishop of Lucknow lamented that 'all attempts to found an Indian Eton seem foredoomed to failure'.[41] It is difficult to compare numbers but the totals sound too low for the schools' comfort: in 1904 1,281 boys and 1,740 girls were attending hill schools. Yet Roman Catholic establishments, many of which were in the plains, seem to have been flourishing. Reverend Brother Fabian told the Committee that the Christian Brothers had seven schools in India, attended by 1,600 boys. Similarly, Mother Provincial Gonzaga reported that the Loreto Order ran twelve schools with a total of nearly

2,000 pupils. It might well have been easier for the many Roman Catholics in India to find a suitable school there than in Britain. And the nuns' and monks' reputation for rigorous teaching also attracted non-Catholic children, who were readily accepted. One of the 1873 inspectors had been surprised, for instance, 'to find Scotsmen in receipt of good pay' sending their girls to the convent at Mussoorie.[42] Convents were flexible too in their gender intake and Terence (better known as Spike) Milligan was not the only little boy to attend a predominantly female establishment.[43]

Many schools that were declining in numbers had to make drastic economies. St Paul's, Darjeeling actually restricted the diet of its seventy-three remaining pupils:

8.15   Breakfast – porridge or eggs, or dhal and rice
11.00   Bread and butter
2.00   Dinner – meat and pudding, with water
6.00   Tea, bread and butter with, occasionally, jam
The boys buy a good deal of food themselves at the school shop.

An inspector concluded that the new rector's reforms 'in the matter of school discipline, though no doubt necessary and salutary, did not commend themselves to the parents' and he noted that 'an agitation was got up in the press about the "atrocities" which were being committed at the school'. No detail is given but it sounds as though unduly severe punishment was being administered. At the same time Bishop Cotton School had run up large debts and it was reported that 'the class of boys . . . has considerably deteriorated since the early days of the school'.[44]

The causes of these problems were apparent to those giving evidence in 1904. The Archdeacon of Calcutta lamented, 'More and more boys go home every year.' The growing ease and cheapness of travel between Britain and India was symbolised by the opening of Thomas Cook offices in Bombay and Calcutta in the 1880s. At this time the price of a P&O ticket was £68 – still more than three years' worth of education at a school like Bishop Cotton. For a schoolmaster on a salary of '40 rupees [about £4] a month with everything found' the fare was prohibitive. But many parents could afford it quite easily. The principal of the Lawrence Military Asylum heard that 'the owner of a piggery is sending his nephew home'. Revd J. W. Papworth of Lahore pointed to another reason that children were sent to England and thus deprived of the family life which could act 'like a sacred influence to compel them in the path of right'. He said that 'the branches of service open to lads educated in this country are very few'.[45] There was a prejudice against 'domiciled' boys born in India, who were thought to be slack and lacking in initiative. Until 1919 the examinations for entry into the covenanted Civil Service were held only in England and twice as many marks were awarded for a knowledge of Latin and Greek rather than of Oriental languages. This was a source of great frustration to a boy like James Staines, who left St George's School, Mussoorie in 1924:

> We had had a good general education, as good as any provided by the public or grammar schools of Britain, taking the same examinations as they did. We were of British stock. . . . We had an intimate knowledge of the Indian people and their customs and could speak their languages well. And yet, by making England the venue for all higher education and therefore for all recruitment to the top jobs, we were, at a stroke, denied the chance to compete for them and hence were condemned to fill only lower positions.[46]

Staines's first job was as a railway ticket collector at Allahabad. Parents who wanted their sons to follow a more exalted career in India would either not send them to school there or would have them finished in England. The boys thus left at the very time when they would have been 'likely to reflect credit upon the schools from which they have been withdrawn'.

Parents were also more likely to choose schooling in the home country if they had their eye on British colleges and universities. For it was difficult to gain entry to them without the help of the 'old boy network' and teachers with the right 'know-how'. Peter Lloyd, an army officer's son who had set his heart on a career in the Royal Navy, believes that he would never have passed the Latin entrance papers for Dartmouth Royal Naval College in 1937 if his English prep school had not already given him the very same exercises which were set.[47] Some Indian schools, on the other hand, did not even offer Latin, which was an entrance requirement for all Oxford and Cambridge colleges. This 'form of discrimination' applied as late as 1954 when seventeen-year-old Haroon Ahmed came to Britain from St Patrick's School, Karachi for his higher education. Luckily there was no such hurdle to prevent him from taking a degree in Engineering at London University and a Cambridge Ph.D. Professor Ahmed is now Master of

Corpus Christi College, Cambridge.[48] These worries did not usually affect girls, who were still unlikely to have careers. As the figures indicate and as the headmistress of Auckland House observed, 'Parents send their sons home more than their daughters.'[49]

These were all hard economic or vocational factors militating against European schools in India. A more profound but less distinct explanation for their falling rolls was the inveterate snobbery of British India. This was classically enshrined in the complicated Warrant of Precedence, ranging from the Viceroy, Lord Chief Justice and Commander-in-Chief to Assistant Directors of Public Health, Income Tax Officers – and teachers. Not even included in the list were *box-wallahs*, those engaged in trade and commerce, the very activities that had brought the British to India in the first place. Thus when the 1904 report made an alphabetical list of the parentage of children sent to hill schools, it was implicitly explaining why top civil servants and military officers did not use them:

> Barristers, captains of river steamers, clerks in business, coal mine managers, college professors, deputy collectors, district engineers, district superintendents of police, engineers, forest service, government clerks, government pensioners, hotel managers, medical officers, missionaries, municipal service, opium department officers, pleaders, pilots, police inspectors, post office, railway subordinates, shopkeepers, station masters, superintendents accounts department, survey department, teachers, tea and indigo planters, telegraph department, traffic superintendents.[50]

Such company was good enough for the non-U 'country-born' but not for the ICS 'heaven-born'.

Parents' racial prejudice was an even stronger bar than social snobbery. It was conveyed unashamedly in the evidence of Lieutenant-Colonel Bomford of the Indian Medical Service. Finding his students at the Bengal Medical College 'childish, both mentally and physically', he attributed their failings largely to the fact that many of them had 'a very considerable admixture of native blood in their veins': 'No school, in the hills or elsewhere, can be expected to impart the character of the pure European to the sons of Madras ayahs, Goanese women, or indeed of any native woman, whatever the father may have been.'[51] M. M. Kaye (called Mollie as a child) and her sister Bets were taken away from Auckland House after just one term when their mother realised that the school 'included a very large proportion of what was then called Eurasians, the majority of whom spoke with a lilting sing-song accent that was very like a Welsh one and was known as chi-chi'. As this was during the First World War, when German U-boats made sea voyages hazardous, the girls could not join their brother who was already in England. 'We had no more proper schooling until the war ended', remembers M. M. Kaye, who had no regrets at the time.[52] Meanwhile the Godden sisters, whose father ran a shipping line on the Hooghly River, were being taught at home by a maiden aunt because 'English children of any family did not go to the hill boarding-schools where the children were chiefly Eurasian'.[53] 'Sallow-faced' youngsters such as Kim's 'self-reliant mates' at the fictional St Xavier's (based on La Martinière), who spoke with 'quaint reflections', were not considered fit company for the offspring of burra sahibs.[54]

Despite these adverse circumstances, not to mention out-and-out disasters like landslides and fires, most European schools in India survived and enjoyed better fortunes as the twentieth century progressed. Not all parents were as blinkered as the Kayes and some schools actually attracted pupils who were marooned in India during the First World War. Afterwards, when Civil Service examinations were held in India, some hill schools introduced special courses to enable their pupils to compete effectively with British-educated boys and also with Indians, whose numbers were increasing in the ICS. Some of the public schools in the subcontinent opened their doors to wealthy Indians. Between 1928 and 1947 Bishop Cotton had four Indian school captains, who were 'groomed for leadership of Indian affairs'.[55] Records at Auckland House show that the first Indian pupil was admitted in 1926 and that there were several Indian prefects during the 1930s.[56]

Other schools modernised in different ways. The renamed Lawrence Royal Military School brought in university-educated staff. It also introduced Senior Cambridge Certificate examinations for its pupils, most of whom were no longer orphans or children of 'the much despised, poor bloomin', eight-anna, dog-stealin' Tommy of Kipling's day'. Now it was beginning to resemble the English public schools, which had long since moved away from 'their original character as charitable institutions'.[57] Under a new principal, Eryk Evans (1934–41), it lost some of its military and muscular character. He cut down on beating, compulsory games and military uniform while bringing in better food (including a tuck shop), annual Shakespearean productions, an orchestra and mixed classrooms. Such liberal ideas upset many of the staff, as well as governors and Old Sanawarians. But, as Evans recorded in an unpublished memoir, 'examination results got steadily better, and Inspectors began to favour us with thin smiles of approval.'[58] Some of the changes were reversed after his departure but the school remained a more cultured and academic institution than ever before.

In fact, as Viola Bayley found with some surprise in the 1930s, 'there was a good education to be had' in India. She was probably thinking more of small private schools such as her own children had attended: Miss O'Brien's at Simla and Mary Grove's in Gulmarg. There were many such establishments for middle-class Anglo-Indians at this time. When Lorraine Gradidge went out as the wife of an Indian Army officer, she sent her son and daughter to the same 'dear little school run by two stalwart English sisters' at Mussoorie which she had attended as a young child. Penny Francis (née Elsden-Smith) went to three such schools between the ages of five and thirteen – at Takdah, Darjeeling and Kalimpong. These tiny academies, run by eccentric but kindly expatriates, provided Penny with 'proper lessons', daily walks on flower-strewn hillsides (complete with wild boar drill) and drama training from an ex-Tiller girl, all of which has stood her in good stead. Of course, their small scale prevented them from providing the more specialised secondary education which could be found at Indian public schools. But 'the tradition of sending children home for schooling' was so strong that most British parents spurned all educational establishments in India. 'And tradition dies hard,' said Viola Bayley, especially in the conservative Anglo-Indian community.[59] Iris Portal's decision to take her daughters home in 1939 seemed absolutely normal 'as I was the third generation of my family on my mother's side to do so'.[60]

The biggest boost to Indian public schools came not with any Anglo-Indian change of heart but with an influx of pupils during the Second World War. It is true that some Anglo-Indian parents decided to leave their children in England – in Mrs Portal's case, with her brother Rab Butler and his wife Sydney. But many others hastily brought them back to India for fear of German invasion or bombing. Hazel Craig (née Innes), who later wrote about her experiences, was among these early evacuees, returning with her twin brother. The Foss family, who were on leave in England, also tried to get back to India. But in 1940 their boat, the *City of Simla* which had sailed from Glasgow, was torpedoed.

They were all rescued and Captain Foss travelled alone to join his regiment, leaving his wife and two sons in Britain until 1944 when 'the Atlantic sea-routes were deemed safe enough for families to return to India'.[61] Chapter Eight will introduce other families who faced the dilemma of whether to go or not to go.

Fear of submarines, the Blitz and German jackboots on British soil deterred most Anglo-Indian parents from sending their children home in the traditional fashion. So the European schools in India were patronised as never before. Admissions to Bishop Cotton went up from 200 to 400 between 1940 and 1941. American mission schools like Woodstock and Mount Hermon in Darjeeling found themselves swamped by English entrants. And at the Lawrence Military School Eryk Evans reported in summer 1940: 'The school is full to bursting; with all passages home virtually cancelled and no-one retiring from the Service, India is full of children who would, normally, be going home to England. Consequently we have been unable to accept all those who would like to come to us.' By the winter he felt 'almost ashamed that the war has not disturbed us more' – for this time the school did not send contingents directly to the battlefield as it had in the 1914–18 war.'[62]

But even during the greatest conflict in history some parents would not consider the existing schools. Haunted by the old fears of class and race contamination, they preferred to send their offspring to smart new 'war schools' which quickly sprang up after 1939. Even though at first they were short of both staff and equipment, establishments like Sheikh Bagh at Srinagar, the New School at Darjeeling and Hallett War School at Naini Tal charged such high fees that they excluded both domiciled Europeans and Eurasians. But at least rich parents would not have to worry about their children acquiring the dreaded chi chi accent. The fact that they might fail their School Certificate (as ten out of twenty-six pupils at the New School did in its first year) was a secondary consideration. The pupils themselves did not concern themselves with such matters. Mark Tully simply remembers that 'Harrow on the Hooghly' or 'the snob school' (as the New School was variously nicknamed) was much nicer than the English public school he later attended. And what pleased Michael Thomas most about passing the Common Entrance exam was that Sheikh Bagh got a half-holiday.[63]

In 1941 Anglo-Indian parents had something new to worry about. For after Japan's entry into the war there was a real fear that India would be attacked and invaded. So, at this point some parents did send their offspring off to brave the seas, not knowing whether they would see them again. But most children stayed on in India. Often, like Hazel Innes, they considered themselves lucky to be spending their schooldays 'under the old school topee'.[64] In the event they remained secure since the Japanese threat to India never materialised. It was a different story for those whose homes happened to be in Burma. By 1942 north Indian hill stations like Mussoorie were 'over-flowing with refugees' from 'the Golden Land'. Woodstock took in 'as many children as books and seats would permit'[65] and other schools also made room for traumatised pupils who had had rather more to worry about than their maths homework.

Once the war was over the new schools closed their doors, having done their job of providing a safe, exclusively English haven for war-stranded children. On the whole their memories were happy ones. But one master at the New School in Darjeeling felt that their moral fibre had suffered as a result of their cocooned existence:

Their attitude to this country and to Indians – on whom rest, of course, part of the task of keeping them so well fed and provided for – has often been far from perfect. . . . They assume that the world is organised to maintain them in a state of luxury, and I am sure that our percentage of greed, absent-mindedness, destruction and untidiness would take the world record.[66]

The older Indian public schools carried on but were badly affected two years later by Independence and Partition. Most of their British staff and pupils left in 1947 and they were followed by Muslims whose homes were in what was now Pakistan. The fate of two friends at Bishop Cotton School illustrates the unsettled tenor of the times. Ruskin Bond, the son of an English RAF officer, would have gone to England at Independence had his father not died in 1944. Since his only home was now with his Eurasian mother and Indian stepfather in Dehra Dun, Ruskin stayed on at Bishop Cotton School. He had not found it easy to find a friend 'among the horde of rowdy, pea-shooting fourth-formers' but he had eventually hit it off with a quiet boy called Omar. One morning the headmaster announced that fifty or so Muslim boys whose parents lived in the new Pakistan would be leaving in an armed convoy. Omar was one of this party. 'The rest of us – Hindus, Christians, Parsis – helped them load their luggage into the waiting trucks. A couple of boys broke down and wept.' Some years later Ruskin heard that Omar had been killed while taking part in a bombing raid over Ambala during the war between India and Pakistan. 'Did he, I wonder, get a glimpse of the playing fields we knew so well as boys?'[67]

There was a similar exodus to Britain and Pakistan from all boarding schools in north India. At the Lawrence School numbers were now so low that inter-house matches in all sports except boxing had to be abandoned. But most schools soon filled up with well-off Indian pupils, a transition symbolised by two prefect lists at Auckland House; in 1947 all the names were English and in 1948 all were Indian. House and team photographs of Bishop Cotton School show a similar development. Today most of the old British foundations, in their spectacular mountainside sites, feature in the *Guide to Good Schools of India*. They may be 'cultural heirs to a colonial legacy' but, concludes K. J. Parel, the Indian version of the British public school 'seems to have flourished well on our soil'.[68] Like their British counterparts they have become rather more humane over the years. The boys I observed at Bishop Cotton in 2003 looked cheerful in their open-necked blue shirts and were welcome to walk through the open door of the headmaster's study. The school's continued attachment to English culture was shown by the fact that the senior boys were rehearsing for a performance of *Macbeth*.

So various factors determined parents' choices about their children's education: economic necessity, family tradition, religious faith, social snobbery, racial prejudice, physical dangers or simply their own convenience. Of course, they also had their children's interests at heart. But they rarely consulted their sons and daughters or even took account of their experiences at the schools selected for them. To redress the balance, the rest of this chapter will use memoirs, letters and oral testimony to convey the child's view of an Indian education.

It was most unusual for parents to be as responsive as Donald and Maisie Langham Scott. Their decisions about the education of their only child, Dorothy, are revealed in Mr Scott's letters from India and in their daughter's unpublished memoir. Mr Scott was a postmaster whose begging letters to his brother suggest that he was often short of funds. His wife was probably Eurasian – to judge from her lack of English relations, her daughter's appearance in photographs and the couple's meagre social life. Based in Quetta in 1926, the Scotts sent Dorothy to the local convent, removing her when she became fearful of going to Hell because of not being a Roman Catholic. She then settled in quickly at Quetta Grammar School, coming home for lunch every day but going back early so that she could play with the other children. But her rather puritanical mother worried about her being in a school with boys, with whom she played games like 'kissing kook'. After Mr Scott's transfer to Rawalpindi in 1928, Dorothy (now ten years old) was sent to board at St Denys' Anglican Convent, a few hours' drive away at Murree. While Mrs Scott trembled 'at the idea of leaving her in other people's charge', Dorothy herself was 'as happy and excited as she can be'.[69] The school was typical of its day with its 'near-Spartan conditions', dull curriculum, and petty restrictions – like not allowing the pupils to read *Schoolgirls' Own* comic. Helped no doubt by her parents' regular visits in the early months, Dorothy thrived there. She was top of her class, won prizes, became 'part of a fairly tight-knit group' of friends and found the holidays 'rather lonely'.[70]

So there Dorothy stayed, twice rejecting the option of changing schools. Faced with the prospect of her father's being moved in 1930 she was adamant that she wanted to stay put: 'I pleaded hard and earnestly to be allowed to return to Murree wherever my parents might be transferred to, and finally they gave way.' Later the head-mistress offered to take Dorothy, by now their star pupil, to England so that she could have the advantage of attending a sister-school in Wiltshire. But, her father wrote, 'Madam Doll says she is not going to be separated from us for three years and would rather stay in India.'[71] Emerging from St Denys' in 1933, having taken her Senior Cambridge Certificate early, Dorothy did not have many other advantages in life. She was lanky, bespectacled, plain and poor. Her father said that she was a Saturday's child who would have to work hard for a living. He was probably right since she supported herself (and later her widowed mother) by working in the English Civil Service. But she had had a happy, secure childhood with parents who listened to her opinions. Her eloquent memoir reveals balanced views and an independent mind. There is no sign that India had morally contaminated her in youth after the fashion so dreaded by European parents.

Memoirs like Dorothy's are often more revealing about school experiences than juvenile letters. Children at boarding school, whether in India or in Britain, could seldom honestly express their feelings in the weekly letter home, which would usually be censored if it was at all critical of the school. In any case, wrote George Orwell (né Eric Blair) in a famous essay about his Edwardian schooldays, a boy could never think of asking his parents to take him away 'since to do so would have been to admit yourself unhappy and unpopular, which a boy will never do'. Eric's letters to his mother (who had left her husband in India in order to be with Eric and his sisters in England) reveal nothing of his 'desolate loneliness and helplessness' at St Cyprian's prep school in Eastbourne.[72] The recourse adopted by some desperate children was to make a bid for freedom, but that was likely to occasion extreme reprisals. When young James Butler tried to escape from Mount Abu High School in 1935, the Christian Brothers flogged him until he was unconscious. They also forbade him to communicate with his younger brothers, his fellow fugitives, for the remaining eight months of term. Meanwhile his parents, oblivious of their sons' torments, 'considered us to be in good hands'.[73] Butler eventually published a memoir, *Incense and Innocence*, in which he sought to put the record straight.

James was one of the eight children of an Irish captain in the Indian Army. All but the youngest were educated at Roman Catholic schools in India and three, including James, have talked to me about their experiences. They went first as day-pupils to local mixed convents wherever their father was based and then to boarding schools run by the Irish Christian Brothers or by nuns. Between 1926 and 1936 batches of the older boys attended St Fidelis' School in Mussoorie and then Mount Abu High School. St Fidelis' was set up in 1863 as a charity school to run next door to the more exclusive St George's. Both James and his oldest brother Joseph were aware of keen competition between the two establishments, at which the Brothers wore different-coloured sashes, but neither thought of theirs as an inferior school. This was because of its academic rigour, which meant that when each boy in his turn graduated at fourteen to Chepstow Army College he was well up to standard compared to other lads. They both left school with fluent Hindustani, which they were able to use in their army careers. Also they were well grounded in religious knowledge, for which Joseph won a silver medal in an All-India schools competition.

The price they paid for this learning was high. Joseph tells of his finger being broken by a science master who was caning him for not getting his homework right. Although the finger has remained bent ever since, Joseph is philosophical: 'That was just taking my punishment.'[74] James is less forgiving. He laments the 'long and laborious hours of intense work' and wryly sums up the Brothers' recipe for academic achievement: 'Fear of a good beating tended to make us more inclined to learn subject matter off by heart.' Sometimes miscreants were flogged with an eighteen inch strap in front of the whole school and no doubt the boys, with their 'lust for blood', enjoyed the spectacle as much as they did 'a fight in the bogs'.[75] Joseph learnt this to his cost when he first arrived at the school aged nine. He was lured into an ungloved boxing match with Fatty Stephens, who had a two-stone advantage over him. After four rounds, during which Joseph lost two teeth and was covered in blood, the bigger boys stopped the fight. The matron patched him up and no master ever commented on the episode. Joseph simply assumed that 'this was something you did at boarding school' and he decided to take boxing lessons. The experience did not apparently make him miserable at the school, where he always excelled in sport.[76] James, on the other hand, was sent there at six and remembers crying at night. He found no comfort in Matron, who regarded all boys as 'unruly, ill-mannered, dirty little baggages'. They had to be inspected daily and were humiliated if they wet the bed.[77]

Common to both the Butler accounts is the memory of acute hunger. As Joseph puts it: 'You were always trying to get food and you'd sell your boots to the cook for a jam sandwich.' Their staple fare at school was dhal and rice with 'jam halves' and cocoa for supper – while at a separate table boys who paid more were served with 'mouth-watering delicacies' like fish curry. When funds allowed, the Butler boys consoled themselves with Indian sweetmeats or curry and bread bought from a vendor known as Charlie Bootlace. And there were many sources of boyish enjoyment to be had in the Mussoorie hills – just as there were for Stalky & Co. on the Devon coast. There were stag beetles to be raced and put to fight, birds to be shot with catapults and their feathers displayed on hats, butterflies to be caught or swapped for items of school clothing, and snakeskins to be collected. James admits that they were 'a sadistic lot towards the lesser creatures on this earth'.[78] But the Christian Brothers, typified by the massively built principal Brother Burgin, more than matched them in savagery. After all, as Brian Moore wrote, 'no boy was stouter than a good cane'.[79]

In addition to some fearsome beatings James endured two instances of sexual abuse. One was at St Fidelis' in the guise of private Latin lessons and the other took place at Mount Abu High School under the cover of his being examined for a grumbling appendix. These manifestations of Christian Brotherly love accentuated his isolation for he could tell no one about them. 'I had to bear this intolerable burden alone.' It was no consolation to James that he was closer to home than his contemporaries who had been sent to England; he simply longed for the time when he and his brothers could be released from this 'mental torture'. In fact Captain Butler heard that he was to be transferred to England in 1937 and the boys left Mount Abu at the end of 1936 with certificates of good character and 'broad grins all over their faces'.[80] James's memories are more painful than those of his stoical older brother (who never attended the harsher Mount Abu School) and the two men have agreed not to discuss their differing recollections. Surprisingly, it is James who preserves the link; he belongs to the Manorite Association of St Fidelis' and St George's, which are now amalgamated. He even takes an interest in the present fortunes of the hated school at Mount Abu. Ex-pupils' correspondence in school newsletters contains some happier reminiscences of the Brothers. One old boy (1940–7) recalls 'with great affection' dear old Brother Darcy, who 'always smiled when he caned you'.[81]

One of the regrets of Wyn Munro, the older of the two Butler girls, was that after the early convent days she was always separated from her brothers. She went alone (for her sister was still a baby) to the Jesus and Mary Convent, Simla and then to St Mary's, Naini Tal.[82] Unlike Joseph, Wyn did not enjoy her train journey up into the hills at the beginning of March. She used to count the tunnels, dreading the moment of arrival at a freezing cold school where icicles hung from floor to ceiling in the lavatories. But what upset her more was the lack of emotional warmth. There was 'no contact whatsoever with home'. Letters to parents were always checked and rarely answered. Friendships did not last because 'you didn't see the same girls year in and year out'. And at neither school did she encounter 'a single kind nun'. More than her brothers, Wyn resented the 'demeaning' practice of differentiating between rich and poor pupils. At her schools the richer ones wore smarter clothes as well as getting better meals. Being made to eat up all her helpings of boiled liver and potatoes or turnip stew has made her fussy about food to this day. Even more of a penance for Wyn, a gifted needlewoman, was to be given bundles of socks to darn whenever she was discovered doing her own embroidery. The nuns were following the principle expressed by Mother Percival in Antonia White's autobiographical novel *Frost in May*: 'It is a hundred times better to knit a pair of socks humbly for the glory of God than to write the finest poem or symphony for mere self-glorification.'[83]

Unlike her brothers Wyn does not remember having any fun at school. Nor did she much enjoy the Christmas holidays, when she saw little of her parents who were 'going to all the socials' while she had to look after her younger brothers and sisters. But Wyn was a clever girl. She passed her Junior Cambridge exams with five distinctions at the early age of thirteen. Eventually she found scope for her natural talents as needlework editor of *Woman* magazine. She also published several books and has established herself as an artist. Wyn Munro would not want to go through her affectionless childhood again. But she did gain something from it. 'I learnt to stand on my own feet. There was no shoulder to cry on and so I had to bear my own troubles.'[84]

A much happier experience of convent schools was that of the actress Felicity Kendal. During a childhood spent travelling around India with her family's acting troupe during the 1950s she attended Loreto schools all over the country. Her mother refused to send her to boarding school. Felicity was always 'made to feel most welcome' at the convents, even though her father was not paying a single rupee for this exclusive education. He talked the nuns into accepting performances in lieu of fees. Despite having always to catch up during her first few days at a new school, Felicity loved learning and did well when it came to examinations. She attributes her lack of anguish to being 'a cheerful child'. After all, she was free to return to her eccentric family every day and had not been 'captured' (to use Wyn Munro's evocative phrase). It may also be that the schools were less harsh in Felicity Kendal's day than they had been two decades earlier.[85]

The British Army was nearly as peripatetic as the Kendals' theatre company. Jack Moore, the son of a gunner in the Royal Field Artillery, writes in his unpublished memoir that he had 'lived in thirteen different houses by the age of ten'.[86] By then most military cantonments had schools, although they were often somewhat rudimentary. Jack attended his first one at Aden in 1912 but he remembers more about being part of a gang which organised 'a supplementary signalling station' at the barracks than about his lessons. In 1913 his father was stationed at Quetta, near the Afghan border. Here too Jack seems to have learnt more outside the classroom than in it for Dadoo, one of the Battery messengers, became his 'very first tutor in the Hindustani language'. At Lahore, where Gunner Moore was sent at the outbreak of war, 'no schools had been organised and I spent a lot of time exploring on my own'. By the end of that year the family had moved to Delhi and then to Agra without there being time for Jack to get settled into schools. No doubt this is why he was sent to the Lawrence boarding school at Ghora Gali near Murree. It was, in Jack's view, 'a grim establishment'. When his parents learnt of 'the bad (and insufficient) food, primitive accommodation, freezing conditions, brutal canings for misdemeanours and the overall excessive regimentation' they took him away, an unusually humane decision for this time. After a year's absence Jack returned to his family (now in Quetta), glad to be 'back again where I was loved'.[87]

Granted 'an idyllic sabbatical year at home', ten-year-old Jack attended another army school in Quetta. His main memory of this is 'an enormous map of the world so developed that the red colouring representing the British Empire appeared to extend as a wide irregular swathe from end to end of the frame'. Meanwhile he learnt a good deal from accompanying his father on inspection tours of mountain villages and from acting as a Boy Scout dispatch rider for the station. After this Jack, now aged twelve, was readier for boarding school and he did not find it difficult in 1917 to settle at St Joseph's College, Naini Tal. In fact he concluded that the Christian Brothers there provided 'a kindly, caring community', from which he derived 'a deep fulfilment, both emotional and spiritual'. Jack Moore's memoir, written in his 'declining years', gives no details of St Joseph's but he was evidently luckier in his teachers than James Butler.[88]

Army schools do not seem to have changed much by the Second World War when they taught Brian Outhwaite, the son of a quartermaster-sergeant in the Green Howards. He describes them as similar to village schools, with one or two teachers instructing children of all ages in the same room. They followed an English curriculum and used the Army to enforce discipline when necessary. Brian changed schools every six months and sometimes missed periods of formal education altogether. In 1946, when there was no suitable school at Barrackpore, he and another eleven-year-old lad spent the whole year roaming around, playing football and cricket with Indian boys, making competition kites, hunting butterflies and attending the camp cinema which showed a different film every evening. 'It was Paradise,' said Brian. But it was worrying for his parents, who could not afford to send him to boarding school, the Lawrence Military Asylum having moved upmarket by this time. In any case, boarding school 'was not part of their culture'.[89] Still, Brian would soar ahead once he attended English schools – after his family's homecoming at the time of Independence.

An exact contemporary of Brian Outhwaite was Michael McNay, whose father was an army major with enough family money to send his three sons to the Lawrence establishment at Sanawar. The two older boys, Peter and Harold, apparently loved it there. Michael went off eagerly in 1943 because 'that's what a real boy would do'. But the military regime, severe discipline and strong sporting bias (all reinstated by Principal O'Hagan after the sudden and mysterious retirement of the liberal Evans) did not suit Michael. A 'skinny kid' who preferred reading books to playing games, he was literally sick with misery for most of his first year. In his first letter to his mother he wrote: 'I am very happy but I am in hospital because I keep vomiting.' After that he found some pleasure in the 'fantastic cama-raderie among the kids', the spectacular military parades put on for special occasions and the beautiful position of the school. There were also some 'really great guys on the military side who told us amazing tales after lights-out about their experiences in places like Singapore'. But Michael never adjusted to the 'rampant' physical punishment for minor misdeeds (like swearing during a hockey match) and he still finds it painful to recall such incidents. His experience of the school was further blighted by a near-fatal bout of typhoid.[90] Nevertheless he did well academically and still possesses his form prize: a copy of *Emil and the Detectives* signed by O'Hagan. For Michael, as for the Butler brothers, his father's home-posting was to give a reprieve.

It may have been easier for children to adjust to boarding schools which were not run by the Army or the Catholic Church, for they did not try to fit their pupils into such tight moulds. The current prospectus of Bishop Cotton School refers simply, in words which could have come from the mouth of the Bishop himself, to producing 'men of honour'.[91] Arthur Jones, Treasurer of the Old Cottonians, says that 'respect and discipline' were the qualities inculcated by the school. And his wife Shirley adds that she has never met a Bishop Cotton boy 'who isn't a gentleman'. Arthur, who attended the school in the 1940s, also stressed its high academic standards. 'People would have given their right arm for that education with Cambridge-educated masters.' Arthur preferred to use his right arm for cricket, boxing and the other sports at which he excelled. His name still adorns all the team boards in the dining-hall – but he possesses no Junior or Senior Cambridge Certificate.

Arthur's lack of concentration in lessons could well have had some-thing to do with his unusual family circumstances. The last of seven children, he was adopted at the age of six months after the death of his mother. He wanted for nothing with his new parents (a foreman on the North Western Railway and his wife) but he was never told of his adoption, which he discovered by accident from a cousin. 'Maybe that unsettled my life quite a bit in the early years,' he says. His lack of qualifications made it hard for Arthur to find employment in Britain after he had done National Service. Nor was his quest eased by his Indian birth and dark good looks, which suggested Eurasian ancestry. He did eventually pursue a successful career but to this day Arthur Jones (né Hine) has not been able to establish whether his original family had any Indian blood.

Arthur did not learn his lessons any better for being caned – as when he was unable to read a passage in Urdu. 'There was plenty of caning', he remembers, and not just for academic lapses. He was once beaten in front of the whole school for stealing *bhutta* (corn-on-the-cob) from local farmers. For more serious offences the penalty was expulsion, as occurred in 1949 to an Indian pupil who was discovered at night in the house of a young female teacher. On the other hand, masters turned a blind eye when Arthur and other senior boys broke bounds by going to Davico's in Simla, where they ordered beer, disguised as 'a pot of tea for four'. Arthur's memories of Bishop Cotton are, on the whole, cheerful ones. He saw no bullying, 'didn't starve' and kept very fit in the mountain climate. He preferred this to the Lawrence Memorial School at Ghora Gali, where he spent a couple of years. Here, apparently, the food was 'diabolical', they could only change their ill-fitting clothes once a week and the boys were known as 'hard nuts', from whom station vendors would flee as the Ghora Gali train approached.[92]

Arthur Jones must have overlapped at Bishop Cotton with Michael Foss and his brother, who there received for one nine-month term 'the full British treatment'. The Foss boys had loved 'the loose, messy entanglement of India', and resented being torn away from its embrace. They found it odd to be taught to recite 'all the dates of the reigns of the kings of England' while learning nothing of 'Chandragupta or Ashoka, or Akbar or Aurangzeb'. And they were not sorry to be parted from Bishop Cotton's 'puritans with canes'. This happened at the end of the war, when Major Foss was moved to Delhi, and they were left to roam the city. On their father's next posting to the south the boys were sent to the Highlands School at Coonoor, 'a small enclave of white boyish faces that studiously followed the pattern and ethos of the British prep school'. Again Michael had a sense of something missing from this education, in which the pupils never learnt anything about

India. The boys were once more removed when their father was posted elsewhere, even though they were boarding at the school. It can only be assumed that the Foss parents preferred their sons to be near them even if this meant a fractured education. Or it may be that they found it difficult to pay boarding school fees. In the event, although they were somewhat cut off from its culture, the brothers became 'bathed with India'. They were delighted no longer to be 'unnecessary prisoners bound by rules irrelevant to the continent we inhabited'.[93]

A school which prided itself on a more liberal ethos was Woodstock at Landour above Mussoorie. It had gone through various phases and by the 1930s it was run by American Presbyterians primarily for the children of American missionaries based in India. As ex-pupil Carol Pickering (née Titus) points out, American parents did not make their offspring bear the emotional cost of their own vocation by sending them home. It was too long a journey and there was almost no tradition of boarding school education in the United States. Nor did Americans in India share the English fear of mixing with Indians and Eurasians, who were welcomed at Woodstock; Nehru's nieces were among Carol's fellow-pupils. One Indian nationalist father sent his children there in the 1940s because they would be 'the equal of any other child', whereas in English-style schools there was 'constant conflict for the Indian children who refused to sing the British national anthem and salute the Union Jack'.[94] When Carol eventually went to the United States in 1943 she was appalled by the racial prejudice she found there.

She had loved her years at Woodstock (1934–41), settling in quickly each term after initial homesickness – compounded by travel sickness on the tortuous lorry journey up from Dehra Dun. Parting from her beloved missionary parents was eased by the knowledge that they would come up at some point during the nine-month term to rent a house and give her a respite from boarding, a practice which the school encouraged. Carol reckons that she had a 'sound academic education' as well as plenty of opportunity to take part in plays, concerts and day-long picnics. Of course, like everyone else, she began from early December to 'count the days until Going-Home Day'. But Woodstock remains part of Carol Pickering's life to this day, as does India itself.[95]

Unlike Carol, who remembers all her teachers and school-fellows, Dick Whittaker cannot recall a single name or bring to mind any particular friendships. Not that his time at Woodstock (1937–40 and 1941–3) was unhappy, for he too appreciated the liberal policy of racial integration and the enlightened practice of giving children as much freedom as possible. Dick especially loved being allowed to go off camping in the wilds at weekends (as long as he took a couple of chums) and he does not remember encountering any dangers. The Revd Frank and Mrs Whittaker, English Methodist missionaries based in Hyderabad, would also come up to Mussoorie during the summer so that Dick and his brother could live with them for a month or so. Dick has no complaints about Woodstock: it was not cold or uncomfortable, he was never ill, and he does not recall any corporal punishment. Academic achievement was encouraged with special pins, prizes, reports and scholarships. Looking back, he regrets only that there were no languages in the curriculum. But unlike Carol Titus and many other graduates of Woodstock, Dick did not become deeply attached to the place. He always suffered from severe insomnia, a symptom perhaps of missing his extremely happy home life, three days' journey away in Hyderabad.[96]

Although Woodstock provided a rather more progressive environment than most schools in the 1930s and 1940s, there was a grim side to life that Dick and Carol never experienced. One ex-pupil recalls instances of beating, usually with a belt or slipper, but it was 'rarely severe' and left 'no welts or black and blue spots'. More sinister retribution was administered by the students themselves; for talking in the study hall 'the guilty boy had to run the gauntlet once on a Saturday evening'. The other students would make a double line and hit him with knotted towels. And, as at all schools, some pupils were victimised. An Austrian boy, who was not a 'brilliant sportsman', considers that 'teasing and bullying was more rife than it should have been'.[97] The writer Jamila Gavin, daughter of an Indian Christian and his English wife, considered that her year at Woodstock in the early 1950s was the most miserable of her school career. She made no friends there and found herself longing to be American. She thinks now that she was the victim of the racism so often experienced in those days by Eurasians. 'In betweeners weren't much regarded; it helped to be something – Indian, English, American, or even Canadian.' For some children Woodstock might have been 'Paradise' but Jamila was much happier as a day-pupil at St Mary's Anglican School in Poona, where her father was headmaster.[98]

Some of the happiest memories of school in India are those of non-boarders – although the schools themselves always preferred their charges to be in residence. Many pupils enjoyed riding or walking to Auckland House, which is in the centre of Simla near the ramshackle

Lakkar Bazaar and the imposing Victorian Christ Church, Rosooa Ormond (née Chiesman), whose father was a judge in Simla, used to persuade her *syce* (groom) to stop in the bazaar to buy sweetmeats which she could distribute around the class. And Jennifer Perrin (née Gibbon) was pleased when her father was posted to Simla so that she and her sister could live at home, with the freedom to visit the ice-skating rink and the Gaiety Theatre. Ann MacDonald (née Bullock) is typical of the 1940s 'Aucky' graduates who have deposited their memoirs in the India Office Library. She writes fondly of classrooms invaded by monkeys, hillsides riotous with scarlet rhododendrons and so much religious education that she was way 'ahead of the game' when she came to England. Others stress the high standards of music and drama, though some regret the lack of science and classics, which were not then thought to be useful qualifications for future housewives and mothers. There is no mention of corporal punishment and the girls, in the chocolate-brown and yellow uniforms that are still worn today, seem to have been remarkably happy. Even the boarders write of the kindness they received from teachers and Matron when they were homesick.[99]

Some Anglo-Indian parents were uneasy about such surrogate relationships and wished to maintain greater contact with their offspring. The father of Agnes Heron (née Barratt), who was Chief Engineer for Carnatic Mills in Madras and a keen musician, would not send his daughter away because he was determined to supervise her musical education. So, unlike most girls of her acquaintance in the 1920s, Agnes was not packed off to England or even to St Hilda's at Ootacamund (known as Ooty). At first she was instructed at home by a young woman who was a qualified piano teacher. When Agnes was about ten the family moved to Poona for the sake of Mrs Barratt's health and she went as a day-girl to St Mary's, her mother's old school. Her fellow-pupils were English and Eurasian girls from military and planting families. Agnes took all her Trinity College and LRSM music examinations there and qualified as a music teacher. She has no regrets about growing up in India. 'It was a lovely, free, happy-go-lucky life with excellent schooling.'[100] When, after many years of married life in Darjeeling, Mrs Heron eventually settled in England with a sick husband and three children she managed to support the whole family by her teaching. She has not a trace of the dreaded chi chi accent.

During the 1930s Agnes Heron's first job had been teaching class music in the Cathedral School, Bombay. It was this establishment to which Bill Newman referred when he told me: 'I had a wonderful childhood but I didn't have a wonderful schoolhood.' Bill's problem was that he had been taught by his Indian/Portuguese mother up to the age of nine and was not familiar with the whole English curriculum. Its most challenging aspect was Latin, which he had to take (rather than Hindi or Urdu) as a second language. Thanks to the help of a devoted Indian teacher, who coached him in Cicero's orations, Virgil's *Aeneid* and Caesar's *Gallic Wars*, he got through his Senior Cambridge examinations. Bill gained a lot from the Cathedral School, including an enduring love of literature, but he was disappointed to find that the Latin and his Cambridge certificate did not automatically qualify him for Cambridge University, as he had been led to believe. However, he was able to get into a technical college and to pursue a successful engineering career in Britain.[101]

Naomi Good (née Judah) had a more realistic grasp of the entrance requirements of ancient British universities. She was born in Bombay, where her Iraqi Jewish father had a flourishing medical practice. Dr Judah was a wealthy man but he was not part of the Raj establishment. When called to an English patient who had been taken ill at the Yacht Club he was not admitted to these exclusive premises. His wife was the first Indian woman to graduate from Bombay University and his three children attended the Cathedral School, where as 'non-whites' they had to pay double fees. The only boy, Jack, was sent to England at the age of eleven, so that he could qualify as a doctor. But his older sister Naomi had developed her own ambitions. Inspired by school stories such as those of Angela Brazil, she wanted a share in the jolly hockey-sticks. She also wanted desperately to go to Oxford. Although Cathedral School pupils followed a curriculum so English that one examination essay topic was 'The English Hedgerow', Naomi felt that they were 'on the fringe'. She believed that an English public school was more likely to get her into Oxford – a tall order for a girl in the 1930s. She was probably right, although she does know of one Indian girl who arrived at the dreaming spires from the Bombay Cathedral School. Naomi herself realised that ambition – after spending two rather disagreeable years at Wycombe Abbey in Buckinghamshire with girls whom she found unwashed and unsophisticated.[102]

Her eleven-year-old sister Rachel took one look at Wycombe Abbey and told her mother never to send her 'to a place like that'. She was a home-loving girl who did not try very hard at the Cathedral School, where she was always being compared with her clever sister. By the age of sixteen she had had enough of slogging through Mowat's *English History* and left without matriculating. After attending art school, spending some time in England and working for All-India Radio, Rachel married an Englishman, Vlad Grenfell, who worked in Bombay.[103] Her daughter Ana, another independent-minded child, was to follow in the footsteps of her aunt and uncle. She chose to move from the Cathedral School to Cheltenham Ladies' College, where any homesickness for India was eased by yearly flights home to Bombay; she went on to qualify as a doctor. The traditions of the Raj are slow to die and a partly English education is still greatly prized in India.

These various stories show that going to school in India, though less traumatic than a 3,000-mile separation of several years, could also have its problems. Among these were harsh boarding conditions, minimal contact with parents, lack of provision for day-pupils and uncertain career prospects. Many children had enough emotional and intellectual resilience to win through but others were scarred for life. In view of these difficulties it is surprising that more mothers did not teach their children at home, at least until they were ready for boarding school. For, as Pat Barr and Margaret MacMillan have shown, the memsahibs often 'grew bored with seeing the same faces day after day' and needed more to occupy their minds.[104] Mrs Margaret Hinds (sister of Eryk Evans, headmaster of the Lawrence School) certainly put her mind to good use during three years (1933–6) spent in Peshawar with Captain Hinds and their two daughters. She taught her younger daughter Alison to read by the time she was three and instructed her older daughter Margaret in English, French and history between the ages of eight and eleven, while her husband filled in with maths and a friend with geography. When the family went to the hills in Kashmir Mrs Hinds, who had been a teacher, started a small school for British children.[105] For women who did not feel equal to this task there were efficient schemes of home education. The writer Penelope Lively, for instance, was brought up in Egypt by her English nanny, who educated her with the help of textbooks, timetables and tests supplied by the Parents' National Educational Union (PNEU), 'a do-it-yourself education kit' for expatriate parents.[106]

But most mothers in India, like Penelope Lively's in Egypt, were too busy with their social engagements to take on this weighty commitment. In her investigation of the use of the PNEU, Elizabeth Buettner found that there were never more than a hundred or so colonial parents using it at any one time.[107] Moreover, the scheme had its limitations, as Monica Clough (née Francis) discovered when her mother used it with her in south India in the 1920s. Monica remembers that the geography course was boring to a child who had grown up on a tea estate and 'seen it all' and that the nature study was 'wholly geared to the English countryside and very remote from the jungles of Travancore'. But Mrs Francis could apparently make 'the tedious and prolix books of the PNEU come to life'.[108] Gladys Nightingale (née Krall) also recalls that she and her sister enjoyed their PNEU lessons with an English governess in Agra even though 'she was quite strict and made us do our homework'.[109] Anne and Trish Battye, who had PNEU lessons in India with their mother throughout the Second World War, still bless the system for the excellent memory training it gave them.[110]

Another woman prepared to dedicate time to educating her children was Freda Wenger. She and her husband Leslie, who were Baptist missionaries in Bengal, did not want their children to go through a miserable separation such as Leslie and his sister had endured as children. They tried sending their oldest daughters, Margaret and Janet, to Mount Hermon School at Darjeeling, either as boarders or as day-pupils living with their mother in a rented house. Neither arrangement lasted for long. Janet was unhappy as a boarder and 'decided to be ill' for a time, inventing pains so that she could be kept in the sanatorium.[111] Freda Wenger hated being separated from her husband and from her own work in the mission. And both girls missed their father, wishing that he could be with them in the mountains to see 'the snows peeping behind the clouds'.[112] So for most of their time in India during the 1940s Janet and Margaret were taught at home: 'We had a proper time each day with special desks.'

The Wengers had always wanted their children to have a secondary education in India, but when the time came schools were in the difficult transition stage between English and Indian management. In 1950 Freda Wenger made the painful decision to be 'a good mother' and 'a poor wife', and she came to live with the girls in England.[113] She had obviously done an efficient job with their education since both sisters won scholarships to an academic girls' day school in Norwich. Their achievement, like those of other able children cited in this chapter, throws some doubt on the necessity for the costly schooling and separation so prized by most Anglo-Indian parents. In addition the girls had precious memories of a prolonged period of family life in India. Janet Bottoms (née Wenger) will never forget her expeditions to Bengali villages with her father, either on the back of his bicycle or in a boat during the monsoon. In the villages she would be surrounded by inquisitive Indian girls and on the weary journey home she and her father would sometimes sing hymns together. The next chapter will examine further the experience of growing up under the Indian sun.

❦

SIX

'Kites as Brilliant as Butterflies'

White Children in India

> I keep my memories in a large wooden Chinese chest with a brass
> lock which my parents acquired in Chittagong in 1938. . . . Sandal-
> wood lines the interior, perfuming everything in it.[1]

T
hus Yoma Crosfield Ullman opens her unpublished memoir and
her remembrance of things past is characteristic of those who
spent their childhood in India. In this they resemble Marcel
Proust, whose past was 'hidden somewhere outside the realm, beyond
the reach of intellect' until the taste of a madeleine cake soaked in tea
released from their thousand sealed jars the colours, scents, hungers
and desires of his childhood.[2] While doing the interviews for this book,
I myself witnessed recollections and emotions triggered by the sight
and feel of treasures brought back from India long ago.

Pat Harrison (née Foster) showed me her christening mug carved
from coins melted down by the people of her village, as well as the
brass flask and cup which her missionary father took with him on his
travels. The items prompted a flood of reminiscence. Sue Batten (née
Portal) was moved at the sight of a Sikh sword in a purple velvet cover
which her father's regiment had presented to her when she left India.
Linette Peter (née Purbi) hunted down her photographs, stored in the
canvas-covered leather case which had accompanied her on childhood
sea voyages between Britain and India. One of the photographs showed
a lamp made from a camel's stomach, which was given to her Kashmiri

father. It now has pride of place in her sitting room. Gillian Beard (née Northfield) treasures the sari in which she was photographed on her fifth birthday. And Jane Hudson (née Anson) delighted in showing me the glittering glass bangles which she had collected as a child in Calcutta markets. Others have told me of sounds, tastes or smells experienced in England which remind them strongly of India: the crowing of a cock, the clip-clopping of a pony and cart, the sweetness of mangoes, the scent of a wood fire and, of course, the spicy aromas wafting from Indian restaurants.

Looking further back we find that written memoirs often mention the magic of certain objects brought home from India. Emily and Georgina Metcalfe had rosewood boxes containing some rupees and gold *mohurs* (coins), which they would look at 'with reverence and love as part of our Indian belongings'. A century later Mollie and Bets Kaye cherished a soap box in which they kept flowers, leaves and grasses collected from their Delhi garden just before they left. 'Whenever we felt homesick or lost or forgotten we had only to open it and the past was there in our hands.'[3] A railway map of India, pinned on the inside of his school desk, enabled Alan Ross to 'make imaginary journeys from Delhi to Amritsar, Cochin to Ooty, Calcutta to Patna and Allahabad'.[4] In Lee Langley's autobiographical novel, *Changes of Address*, Maggie's mother does not bother to pack a collection of shells the child had gathered on the beach at Madras. She is devastated. 'Unimportant in themselves, the discarded armour of dead molluscs, fragments of carbonate of lime and conchin, shards and discs and spirals, the shells were all I had to remind me of a world left behind.'[5]

Jeremy Milne Gibbon must have felt a similar absence of mementoes after being sent to England in 1946. He wrote from Mill Hill School asking his parents to send him something typically Indian, adding as an afterthought: 'I suppose Daddy hasn't got a spare hookah!?' Jeremy had just been reading Kipling's *Second Jungle Book*, which had made him 'long for India and especially the hills'.[6] Adults in England did not always encourage such daydreams. Wilfred Bion's music teacher poured scorn on his choice of 'Summer Suns are Glowing' at hymn practice on a grey, drizzly day at his prep school. For Wilfred it brought back 'the fire of that wonderful sun, the great leaves drooping in the heat, the flowers blazing in colours of unimaginable splendour' — but he never asked for that hymn again.[7]

All these people had a large store of childhood memories of India gathered at different times but possessing a perennial nostalgia for the flora and fauna, and the timeless artefacts and customs of the subcontinent. This chapter uses oral and written memoirs like theirs to recapture Indian childhoods over the ages and to see whether growing up in India was as harmful as most British parents feared. Illustrative examples come from the whole period of the Raj, during which the family life of Anglo-Indians changed hardly more than that of their subjects. Anxious though parents were, they could not avoid keeping their children in India for shorter or longer periods. Before affluent children were sent home they spent what were probably their most formative years in the subcontinent. Youngsters whose parents could not afford an English education passed most of their childhood under the Raj and, in Spike Milligan's view, they 'may well have fared better than the more privileged children'.[8] In 'domiciled' families, like the Lukers, with a long history of Indian residence, 'there was never any thought of leaving India'; thus Lilian Ashby (née Luker) did not 'set foot on land that was not my India' until she went to visit her grandchildren in California.[9]

As we have seen, when school years coincided with the two World Wars children often stayed longer in the tropical sun. But there were sometimes reasons less obvious than maritime perils for wanting to keep children in India. As Leslie Wenger explained in a radio interview, he was determined that his children should 'have it a bit easier' than he and his sister Marjorie had had.[10] Some parents were keen not to repeat mistakes they had made with an older child, as Felicity Kendal explains: 'Having left Jennifer in England during the war, nothing would induce [my mother] to leave me.'[11]

Others could not bear to be parted from all their children at the same time and would keep their daughters and sometimes younger sons with them. Lord Mayo, who was appointed Viceroy in 1869, 'wrenched himself away from the assembled group of [his] children' but took his small son Terence to India with him. Every evening 'Terry-boy' would perch on top of a chest-of-drawers while his father got dressed. He would act as the Viceroy's 'quite discreet' confidant, listen to his stories from the Old Testament and Shakespeare and pin on his Star of India, 'a great and regularly demanded treat'.[12] Later Viceroys, Lord Lytton, Lord Lansdowne, Lord Elgin, Lord Curzon and Lord Hardinge, were accompanied by young daughters. The humourless Hardinge found the presence of his daughter Diamond a great help when he had to entertain the Maharajah of Gwalior, who shared her enjoyment of practical jokes.

Some officials chose to take all their offspring with them to India, complete with a governess from home. Lady Lumley, whose husband was Governor of Bombay from 1937 to 1943, explained to Iris Portal that they would never have taken the job if they had had to leave their children behind. In the opinion of Mrs Portal (who was just about to take her own daughters to England): 'It is easier for them than for lesser mortals and perhaps lucky that their three eldest are girls, so the school problem does not arise. They have brought a governess and the precious only boy is still in the nursery stage.'[13] Lady Lumley's letters to her husband's uncle, Lord Scarbrough, show special concern for the son's educational progress, saying little about the girls' schooling though a lot about their performances in gymkhanas. In 1942, as it happened, their daughter Elizabeth added to her cups for horse-manship the distinction of passing her School Certificate 'in the highest possible grade'.[14] Lesser mortals who found it impossible to abandon their offspring did take more of a risk. When E. L. Turner's father accepted a job in the printing department of *The Times of India* in Bombay, he and his wife did not want to be separated from their sons, aged twelve and two. They could not afford tutors but the older boy (author of an unpublished memoir) soon became the only white printing apprentice in all India and received 'some sort of education' from his manager.[15]

The children who appear in this chapter come from different levels of the Anglo-Indian hierarchy, having spent varying amounts of time under the Raj between the reign of George III and that of George VI. How did they fare?

The first year of an Anglo-Indian baby's life was the most worrying time of all. There are many sad family stories about this fraught period, such as that of the Revd Worthington Jukes, a missionary on the north-west frontier. In July 1883 he and his wife lost their six-month-old son Cyril and three years later they 'were called to face another sorrow' with their second child, Eileen: 'She was a strong and healthy babe, and daily took her rides in her perambulator, by the side of another little Eileen of the same age, the daughter of Colonel and Mrs Harvey, great friends of ours. But the babies sickened at the same time, died and were buried side by side in the cemetery on the Taikal Road.' It is not surprising that the Reverend decided at this point to resign his post, reluctantly leaving the local mullahs to 'their ignorance and fanaticism'.[16] But, even if we accept the most pessimistic of the infant death rates quoted from Dr Fayrer in Chapter Three, most families had happier stories to tell. Sheila Bevan's grandmother, Mary Rice, 'had a baby nearly every two years for twenty years and never turned a hair'. All ten children, born in late-Victorian times, apparently lived into their eighties.[17] Christina Leadlay told me that her cousin thinks herself particularly lucky to have been introduced to life under the Indian sun. All her siblings had been born prematurely in England, where they soon died. She was born in India and believes that her survival was due to the heat, which performed the function of an incubator.

Most baby experts during the time of the Raj advised Anglo-Indian mothers to breastfeed their babies. 'All mothers should persevere in nursing their children', insisted *The Complete Indian Housekeeper and Cook*. They should not be put off by 'gay friends' saying that they would be tied down and lose their figures; the authors advised that 'the nursing mother retain her usual occupations and amusements in moderation'.[18] Diaries and letters suggest that most mothers suckled their babies if they could. Sophie Plowden took her new baby, William, when she accompanied her husband on a trip along the Ganges between October 1787 and January 1789. An extract from her diary conjures up the difficulties she encountered in nursing the child: 'We heard a general alarm while I was suckling my little William. I was struck by the idea of it being a dacoit boat but in fact Khannah [a servant] was surprised by a tiger returning from the banks of the river where it had been to drink and rushed back to the boat spreading alarm as he ran.' The next day Mrs Plowden had 'a most providential escape' from being bitten by a snake lurking in her sewing drawer. On another occasion storms forced her to leave the boat and to spend the night in a cow shed. When they reached Lucknow the couple had to attend lengthy entertainments put on by the local Indian prince. Mrs Plowden's persistence was rewarded, however, when friends complimented her 'upon the good looks of my little William and his rosy appearance which they attributed to my nursing him'. Five months after arriving home in Calcutta Mrs Plowden gave birth to her eighth child; luckily her milk was sufficient and 'the little one quite satisfied'.[19]

At about the same time, Charlotte Dick, the doctor's wife encountered in Chapter One, successfully breastfed her little William and then his sister Elizabeth, each for a period of thirteen months. Clementina Benthall was another memsahib who was relieved to avoid the necessity of hiring an 'Oriental foster mother', her disparaging term for an Indian wet-nurse or dhye.[20] In the twentieth century mothers gained new insights into the psychological advantages of breastfeeding. Joan Battye felt that 'the mother has to relate closely to her baby and breast feeding is the best way'.[21] She suckled her babies even on long wartime train journeys, much to the surprise of Indian fellow-passengers who did not expect such conduct in a memsahib.

In practice, as Mrs Sherwood's story showed in Chapter One, it was often beneficial to resort to a dhye. In 1837 Julia Maitland hired a nurse to 'perform the part of a Cow' for her daughter Henrietta, who thrived under the regime.[22] The delicate Amy Macnabb tried in May 1863 to feed James, her second baby. At first she produced so much milk that she had 'to call in a little black boy to help Baby', so that she herself was the wet-nurse, but after an attack of dysentery and fever in June she had to give up and call in a dhye. Despite being 'thin and wee' at this stage, James survived and by the autumn he was 'quite round and fat [with] a jolly contented look on his face which shows he is well-fed and all right'. In January he was still thriving and Mrs Macnabb decided 'to keep on the dhye until the worst of his teething is over'.[23]

Maternal ill health was not the only reason for hiring a wet-nurse. During her husband's term as Viceroy, Lady Lytton found that 'official engagements made it impossible' for her to feed Victor, who was born in August 1876. Having already lost two little boys in England, she was most reluctant to hand Victor over to 'a horrid, dirty woman with a baby'. When she saw him again in December she lamented 'how little one knows a baby one does not nurse'. By January 1877 she feared that the dhye had 'transferred her dullness to the baby'.[24] But at least her milk enabled the Lyttons' son and heir to survive infancy – he may also have imbibed a love of India, for he returned to the country as Governor of Bengal.

Modern scientific opinion endorses the protective value of breast milk and suggests that a wet-nursed child might gain as a bonus its own 'resistance to organisms and diseases of the community'.[25] It was almost certainly safer in India than cows' milk during the eighteenth and nineteenth centuries, or than the proprietary milk powders which became fashionable in the 1920s and 1930s. Netta Brown, for instance, makes no mention of trying to breastfeed her first baby, George, who was born on home leave in 1922. She took tins of Glaxo baby food back to India with her but then became worried about getting further supplies. She bought several tins in Bombay but discovered that they were 'very musty'. And she found it difficult to keep the milk sterile in a bungalow infested with white ants. Anxiously Mrs Brown weighed up the alternatives: should she get supplies of baby food sent from England or acquire a cow or buffalo? As no letters survive after December 1922 it is not clear what she decided but we do know that George grew to adulthood, as did his three younger siblings.[26] In fact there were no infant deaths in any of these seven families that wrestled with the problems of feeding babies in India.

It is unlikely that Victor Lytton or James Macnabb had any recollection of their dhyes but, almost without exception, baba log remember their ayahs. They were children's first emotional tie with the subcontinent. Many would have shared Felicity Kendal's view of her ayah, Mary: 'It was through her that I experienced my India'.[27] Perhaps it was for this very reason that authoritative voices had always encouraged the hiring of respectable British nannies. Maud Diver insisted that 'where money permits' an English nurse was 'a step in the right direction' for the Englishwoman in India, who should guard her children 'from promiscuous intimacy with the native servants'.[28] This message was spelt out more crudely by a journalist known as Eha in an article on 'The Ayah' for *The Times of India*:

> The great bare arms of the pachyderm were loaded with bangles of silver and glass, which jingled with a warlike sound as she hugged her little charge and plastered its pretty cheeks with great gurgling kisses, which made one shudder. ...What if the impress of those swarthy lips on that fair cheek are but an outward symbol of impressions on a mind still as fair and pure, impressions which soap and water will not purge away?[29]

Eha's articles, first published in 1889, were apparently so popular among the Anglo-Indian community that they were issued as a book called *Behind the Bungalow* which was still in print in the 1930s.

It is not surprising, then, that better-off Anglo-Indian mothers chose a British nanny, especially if that was the family tradition. Iris Portal, while regretting that her own Scottish nanny had prevented her from having 'close contact with Indian servants', knew that 'it was thought snobbish to have a Nanny' – and promptly acquired one for her own children.[30] She had no complaint about the appointed woman but her daughters had a different view of her. Jane Williams (née Portal) recounts that Nanny 'was physically cruel and beat me'. Each evening she meant to tell her mother, whom she saw between five and six, but she never managed to say anything 'before the hands of the clock went up and down'. When left with Nanny up in the hills Jane would long for her parents to come. Her younger sister Susan, who was a delicate child, does not recall any corporal punishment but she remembers being locked in the bathroom and let out by Jane.[31] The Kaye girls experienced a more extreme 'reign of terror' under their Nurse Lizzie, who resembled Lord Curzon's notorious Nanny Paraman or P. G. Wodehouse's true-to-life Nurse Wilks. Nurse Lizzie habitually beat the girls' bare bottoms with a hairbrush 'until they were sore and scarlet'. She deliberately burned Mollie's precious silver-spangled scarf. And she often made her take castor oil before going out for a walk, with disastrous and humiliating results. When Mrs Kaye, who had left the children in Simla with Lizzie, found out about all this, she dismissed one she had believed to be 'a treasure of a nanny'. During most of their Indian childhood the Kaye sisters had ayahs, and they 'felt truly sorry for the nanny-children'.[32]

Part of the trouble with English nannies in India was that they were in short supply. Yoma Crosfield says that her parents did not dare to dismiss or even criticise her intimidating nanny who was 'a less than ideal caretaker for me [and] would never let me think or speak for myself'. So Nanny stayed for nine years (1936–45), allowing Mrs Crosfield to get on with her work in the Girl Guide movement and insulating Yoma from India.[33] But of course many Anglo-Indian children had happy memories of British nannies, just as Winston Churchill did of Nanny Everest at Blenheim Palace. In Lahore Hilda, Philip and Lesley Reid had a 'kind but very strict' Nanny whom Hilda fondly describes in a charming book of paintings lent to me by her great-nephew. This nanny sounds typical of her profession, whether practised in India or England: 'She made them mind their manners, and eat up their dinners, and put their toys away before they went to bed, and not spoil their clothes. When they were good she played with them, and amused them and told them stories about when she was little and had a cruel stepmother.'[34] Lorraine Gradidge (who gives no maiden name) was fond of 'Nana in her stiff Eton collar and cuffs'. She took Lorraine and her brother to Eden Gardens in Calcutta every afternoon but never allowed them to play with 'white children whose parents could only afford an Indian ayah'. Naturally, when Mrs Gradidge had her own children in India in the 1930s, she never considered having an Indian nanny.[35]

Yet, many mothers had cause to be grateful to their ayahs. Hilda Bourne's 'dear Ayah', whom she does not name, was 'a rock in the background' when she had her first baby in Madras in 1904. 'She was a born nurse and had had much practice with other English babies, so knew exactly what to do. She taught me so much, bless her!' This woman looked after all her four 'beautiful queenies' (calling one of the girls Tittipu – sweet flower) and helped Mrs Bourne to carry on after the death of her husband in 1918. 'She was so wonderful; she talked about the children [three of whom were by this time in England] and how Master would want me to live for them now and her own simple faith in the Almighty. It was a real lesson to me.'[36] Viola Bayley found similar qualities in her 'truly first-class' ayah. Her name was Mary and she 'adored the children, often going around with the smallest tucked blissfully into the back of her sari, but could also keep discipline'.[37]

It was for comfort and support rather than for stern authority, that their charges remembered most ayahs. Grace Rorke, growing up in Burma, always turned to Ayah (and not to her mother) when she was 'hurt or afraid'.[38] Gladys Krall and her sister had cause to be grateful to servants who 'often helped us avoid the wrath of the grown-ups when we had slipped up a bit'.[39] Joyce Wilkins, born into a missionary family in 1904, was 'a naughty girl' to her mother but 'Joycie-baba' to Emily-ayah. 'Ayah was the one who looked after me, and she had to be patient and kind and try to cajole me into good behaviour, for she was the one who would be scolded for not controlling me when I was naughty.'[40] An indulgent ayah might suffer more than a scolding. The ayah of Beatrice Coates (née Turner) had been her 'sole companion' for her first fourteen months; but she was sacked in 1928 because 'Father said she spoilt me'. Instead Beatrice was looked after by a maiden aunt 'who didn't like life in Ceylon'.[41] To fend off parental wrath, children and ayahs sometimes kept secret any practices of which Mother and Father would disapprove. Jane and Peter Anson kept a sharp lookout when they played cards with the servants during their parents' evening visits to the club. When they were alone in the house Joyce Wilkins and her sister Phyllis would speak English with Emily (a practice which was often forbidden for fear of children learning to speak with an accent). They also learnt from her the hymn 'Rock of Ages', which gave Joyce 'an awful sense of guilt for my own wickedness and for the fact that I was deceiving Mother by speaking to Ayah in English'.[42]

Secrets and songs feature in many memories. Monica Francis loved Mary-ayah, who bought her bangles which Mother considered 'too Indian' and sang her Tamil lullabies when her parents were out. On these occasions Mary's husband Anthony would play the *tabla* (an Indian musical instrument), another native practice to which Mrs Francis 'had a rooted objection'. Monica considered herself lucky to have an ayah rather than an English nanny. It meant that, despite her mother's fears, she experienced 'the Indianness of India' – and she also learnt to speak some Tamil.[43] It was common for children who had ayahs (or sometimes male bearers for boys) to learn the local Indian language. George Roche and his brother Paul, visiting England at the ages of three and two, 'spoke Urdu much better than our mother tongue'.[44] Youngsters would often retain this linguistic proficiency for years. Kipling was surprised to find that he could still understand and speak vernacular Hindi when he returned to India at sixteen, so that in his work as a journalist 'he had access to an India never approachable by most Europeans'.[45] When I met Frances Moxon and Jane Davenport (nées Labey), both in their eighties, they could still sing all the words of the lullaby 'Nini Baba Nini', even though they left India when they were seven. They and their ayah, Margaret, who was 'never cross', also used to keep secrets from their strict mother.[46]

There were some secrets which would have realised Anglo-Indian mothers' worst fears about ayahs. Felicity Kendal describes in detail the process of making *pan* with tobacco and betel leaves shown her by Mary, who was addicted to chewing this mixture. But Mary would always say: 'Not for you, darling. Tobacco not for you. You can have sweet pan.' That concoction, which was made with spices, does not seem to have done any harm to Felicity or to Lilian Luker, who delighted in mixing and chewing the contents of her ayah's pan-box.[47] I have discovered only two instances of one habit widely attributed to ayahs: feeding babies with opium to make them sleep. Patrick Gibson was told that his ayah in Burma was dismissed for secreting opium under her fingernails and administering it to him as a baby. And a memoir by Mrs M. D. Dench recounts a similar incident but recognises that most ayahs 'were entirely trustworthy and devoted to their charges'.[48] On the other hand, Patricia Hyde was later told that the reason for the sudden disappearance of a hated English nanny, who looked after her in Jubbulpore in the 1940s, was that she was discovered 'shooting herself up with heroin'.[49]

It was often from ayahs (and other household servants) that Raj children learnt the facts of life, which their parents were too inhibited to discuss with them. One little girl was surprised when her syce explained that her pony's increasing fatness was due to there being a baby inside her – though she still did not understand how a full-grown foal had got there. Guy Wheeler (a lonely child who had been adopted by his mother's sister because he was illegitimate) 'shrieked with laughter' when his ayah taught him how to make grass horses with erect penises. But he was careful not to mention this game to any white grown-ups. In fact Guy was soon to learn rather more about such matters from the rude rhymes circulating in a Scottish orphanage at which he was left in Bombay and from homosexual practices among the choirboys at the Cathedral School.[50]

Usually English children, like Hannah Tewson (née Bridgman), felt 'safe and happy' when left alone with Indian servants.[51] Jane Portal had a sense of complete security when she was gathered up in the arms of Kattarah Singh, her syce, after she fell from her bolting pony on the Bombay racecourse. Wyn Butler was grateful to servants who (unlike her teachers) never slapped her or gave her inappropriate food. In his south Indian plantation home, Robert Baker always felt protected by Govinda Pillai, the old bearer who slept on the floor beside his cot by night and told him stories by day. George Kennedy, whose father managed a jute mill on the Hooghly, spent much of his time as a small boy with the gangs of workers who pulled in the jute-laden boats; he remembers that they were always kind to him and that his mother never worried about his safety. But sometimes children were mistreated by servants in India, just as they were on occasion in the large households of Victorian and Edwardian England.[52] Pat Foster was sexually abused when she was about six, not by one of the trusted family servants, but by a local youth her parents had hired to look after her when they were in the Nilgiri hills. She vividly remembers 'the scratchiness of the heather and the pain and the fear'. But she adds that it didn't really worry her all that much afterwards and that it was her only unhappy experience in India. Sworn to secrecy, Pat did not tell anyone about it until she was married. Although she has never forgotten the incident, it has not prevented her from getting on with her life – a more mature approach towards such incidents, one can't help feeling, than the current hysteria about paedophilia in the popular press. Pat and her husband, staunch Methodists like her parents, are still devoted to each other after sixty years of marriage.[53]

A more common danger was that cherished baba log would learn bossy imperial habits, for they were often indulged by Indian servants. Many memoirs give instances: a Bengali cook (with one eye and one leg) making special creations of spun sugar for a delicate child; a Sikh gravely saluting the son of a judge as he pedalled past in his little red car; an elderly bearer being made to pull his charges up a steep hill by his coat-tails; an ayah buying dolls' furniture in the Simla bazaar out of her own meagre wages. Such practices could give a child a very great idea of his own importance.[54] And the spoilt infant sometimes grew into an 'imperious, commanding' adult, like Vivien Leigh (whose childhood was spent in Calcutta) or Alexandra Curzon (always known by her Indian baby name, Baba), who treated the staff of Save the Children as her servants when she became the charity's Vice-President.[55] There was a ring of truth in Frances Hodgson Burnett's famous portrayal of Mary Lennox as 'a disagreeable child' arriving in England unable even to dress herself.[56] But, as one historian writes, the fault lay more with parents for 'teaching English children that they are superior beings'.[57] Julia Maitland did not object, for instance, to little Etta bossing the servants 'like a grown woman' whenever she saw a dirty spoon.[58] To be sure, Anglo-Indian children did not normally sustain such behaviour for life – unless, like the beautiful film star, the rich Curzon heiress or some of the women who returned to India as memsahibs, they continued to be indulged as adults. In later life Patricia Hyde recalled with shame an instance of her juvenile despotism:

> I clapped my hands in the middle of the day and yelled 'Pannee Wallah' and a few minutes later this little old man came scurrying along with two tubs of hot water hanging from a wooden yoke thing. Of course it wasn't my bath time and Rose [her Burmese refugee ayah] wasn't too pleased by my behaviour.[59]

And it did not take long for Terence Milligan to learn that if you clapped your hands for a servant in Catford 'you'd get a clip round the ear-hole'.[60]

Some children mixed with Indians on a more equal basis even though they were discouraged from doing so by adults like Mrs Labey, who was determined that Frances and Jane should not acquire a chi chi accent. Young children at home sometimes slipped away to the servants' huts. There they would taste their curries and hot sweet tea, roast corn cobs or cashew nuts on the courtyard fires or play games with their children, who always allowed them to win. Pepita (Pip) Lamb (née Mirrell) recalled that she and her brother, Desmond, sneaked out to the servants' quarters most afternoons while they were supposed to be having their rest. She also admitted that, away from their parents' presence, they would lapse into a chi chi accent because they wanted to conform.[61] Also unknown to her parents were Gladys Krall's visits to Burra Bundhu, a servant at Agra College where her father was a professor. A rather unhappy child who did not feel loved by her stepmother, Gladys enjoyed Bundhu's stories about his family; she told me that he was respectful with her and never tried to explain to her the erotic pictures of Hindu gods which adorned the walls of his hut. She felt safer with him than she did later on with her English step-grandfather, who would put his hands down her stockings. At the age of eighty-five, Gladys still remembered Burra Bundhu with great affection.[62]

As they got a little older, children often formed friendships within their own age groups, without taking any account of racial barriers. Milligan's first companions were two Eurasian boys with whom he 'ran wild' in Poona and attended 'two-anna picture shows'.[63] Raleigh Trevelyan's best friend in Gilgit (where the only English children of his age were two girls) was Amin Khan, the youngest son of the Mir of Hunza. The only trouble was that the journey to Hunza involved crossing the river on a rope bridge, which Raleigh's parents would not allow him to do. So he could not visit Amin at his home where they could have ridden yaks, and 'this made me lose face with him'.[64] There was no such problem when Anne Battye was invited to play with the daughters of the Prince of Bastar, in whose state her father served as Resident. Later on her younger sister Trish had a similar relationship with 'Kitten', the daughter of His Highness Bahadur. And missionaries' children like Pat Foster and Gillian Northfield were allowed to play with their Indian Christian contemporaries in the compound.

As schools became more racially mixed in the 1930s and 1940s pupils of different colours often became friends, as we saw in Chapter Five. At Auckland House Roessa Ormond remembers no racism – while at home she played with her ayah's young niece, who was her own age but already 'an apprentice learning how to look after children'.[65] Lilian Luker's favourite playmate was also the niece of her ayah, with whom she would re-enact Indian weddings for their dolls. This friendship was encouraged by Mrs Luker, who thought fat little Golab's good appetite would stimulate Lilian's. At the Cathedral School in Bombay Guy Wheeler was conscious that 'Indian children paid fees twice as high as ours' (confirming Naomi Judah's experience), but that did not stop him playing with them or with children of any other race: 'Despite my mother's contempt for natives, I had absolutely no racial prejudice. Chandravarki, Akbar, Munji, the Hovsepians [two Armenian brothers] and the Japanese dentist's son, Murai, were all friends of mine.'[66]

Even children who were more closely guarded sometimes managed to establish some kind of communication with their Indian fellows. The Godden sisters, who were forbidden to play with Indians or Eurasians, acquired kites made of coloured paper and fine bamboo which were 'as brilliant as huge butterflies and almost as light'. They would fly these from the roof, challenging other children to contests in which the aim was to bring down the enemy kite: 'We were linked in the kinship of enmity with other unknown flyers and other unknown roofs, those invisible children. Indeed the kites could have been taken as a symbol of our lives.'[67] Twenty years later, as a child in Calcutta during the 1940s, Harry Webb played exactly the same game, which he describes as 'a real art form'. He too sees kites as symbolic of his early life of sunshine and play: 'India to me means kite-flying'.[68] Six-year-old David Wilkins so much enjoyed his kite games with a boy called Harv (whom he met when on holiday with his mother) that he painted his father a picture of it.

Such peculiarly Indian memories of people and places abound: hill-sides shimmering with oil lamps at Diwali, a procession of elephants all decked in turquoise and gold, the brilliant colours of saris worn by women picking tea, cricket on the *maidan* (public ground) thronged with people in the evening, and overnight train journeys with the smell of dung fires and spices and ghee pervading the carriage. Wilfred Bion, who often went on camp with his ICS father, conjures up one nocturnal memory with special clarity: 'Intense light; intense black; nothing between; no twilight. Harsh sun and silence; black night and violent noise. Frogs croaking, birds hammering tin boxes, striking bells, shrieking, yelling, roaring, coughing, bawling, mocking. That night, that is the real world and real noise.'[69] Whether travelling across India with their families, walking with their ayahs, riding their ponies or bicycles, or being carried in a *dhooly* (covered litter) or bullock cart, children observed everything and carried the images with them when they left India. What they valued, as they write or say quite independently of each other, was the freedom of living so much out of doors.

Boys had the greater measure of liberty, especially relished by Michael Foss: 'Beyond the gate was a universe to be cracked open and savoured each day, as tasty and full of promise as a newly baked bun.'[70] For Brian Outhwaite 'life was a tremendous adventure', which might involve gathering delicious sugar cane (like Kim) but getting covered with leeches in the process. Dick Whittaker spoke of the 'enormous space' around Hyderabad where he and his brother 'went off on our bikes wherever we wanted'.[71] In the cities, too, many boys seem to have been free to roam even during the war years. In Karachi Michael McNay spent the holidays riding around on his bike, hanging on to the back of trams, going to Tarzan movies and stripping a crashed Dakota on the edge of the neighbouring desert. Perhaps he came across Gordon Honeycombe, the future broadcaster, who also had 'a great deal of freedom' in wartime Karachi, where he was allowed 'to roam at will' from about the time he started kindergarten.[72]

But girls too could experience India for themselves. Di Turner's letters to her grandmother tell of the endless fun she had with her brother and sister in Baluchistan on the war-torn north-west frontier. At the turn of the nineteenth and twentieth centuries there was no Victorian respectability for them. She and Alice wore their home-knitted jerseys with 'navy blue bloomers and no dresses' as they pretended to be jackals or ogres in mountain caves.[73] For Jon and Rumer Godden, 'walking through the bazaar could start a whole tale of imaginings'. Monica Francis enjoyed 'unalloyed happiness' on the tea estate which was her kingdom.[74] Even the cocooned Yoma Crosfield discovered on a train journey to Darjeeling that there was 'all India to watch': 'Great trees isolated in the flat expanses, reedy marshes snowy with egrets, miles of baked mud, the brilliant green of rice paddies. All were mine as I lay peering around the blinds before the rest of the compartment woke up.'[75] Felicity Kendal never felt alone in India, where 'comfort and security lay in the people around me and the very countryside we travelled through'.[76]

There were also penalties to be paid by young British residents in India, which their memoirs are not too rose-tinted to mention. Tropical illness was always a risk, even though medical progress meant that by the later nineteenth century Anglo-Indian children seldom died or suffered permanent damage to their health. Those living in the south were particularly prone to bouts of malaria. Monica Francis in Travancore and Dick Whittaker in Hyderabad had recurrent attacks and Richard Murphy developed 'a terror of dying in Ceylon' during a serious outbreak there in 1935.[77] But most Anglo-Indian children were protected from it by regular doses of quinine (sometimes on a sugar-

Left A City Childhood: Jane and Sue Portal celebrating Christmas with their mother and servants, Bombay, 1935

Above A Cantonment Childhood: Brian Outhwaite, sporting his father's hat and baton, watched by his mother, Dagshai, 1939

Above A Plantation Childhood: Robert and Beatrice Baker riding with their father, Travancore, c. 1919

Right A Peripatetic 'English' Childhood: Rosie and Mavora Harrison taking tea with their dolls in a bungalow garden, Pakistan, c. 1951

Left A Missionary Childhood: Pat Foster with family and Indian friends, inspecting a leopard, shot because it was threatening the compound, Nagari, 1928

Left Early Deaths: the grave of the three Daniell children (cousins of Admiral Jackie Fisher), who died within hours of each other of 'Asiatic cholera', Ceylon, 14-15 September 1866

In memory of Alice Emma, who died at Hellebodde Sept 14 1866 Aged 4 years

Georgiana Margaret, who died at Hellebodde Sept 14 1866 Aged 1 year and 9 months

Lindsay Murray, who died at Delta Sept 15 1866 Aged 2 years and 8 months

Lovely and pleasant in their lives and in their death they were not divided
II Sam. I. 23

In their mouth was no guile for they are without fault before the throne of God
Rev. XIV. 5

The loving and beloved children of Lindsay Harrison Daniell and Alice Caroline, his wife

Right The Mutiny: Gerald and Richmond Ritchie, dressed in miniature volunteer uniforms, taunting a disarmed sepoy, Barrackpore, 1857

Below The Mutiny: embarking on the boats to escape from Cawnpore, 1857

Left Travelling in the Himalayas by Dhoolie: Hilary Johnston, c. 1933

Below The Fancy Dress Party, including Robert and Beatrice Baker: Kodai, c. 1919

Above The Child Left Behind: Eric Wilkins after the departure of his sisters, Orissa, c.1911

Right The Golden Afternoon: Otto and Frank Anson taking tea with their parents and dogs, Raniket, 1880s, some years before Mrs Anson's fatal fall from an elephant

Above Henry and Charles Doherty, painted by their mother, Bangalore, 1819

from David.

A picture of Haru and me flying kites on the Kuha.

your own son
David Gordon Wilkins

Mummy × × × × × × × × ×
Daddy × × × × × × × × ×
Robert × × × × × × × ×
Brian × × × × × × × × ×

Mummy   Brian   Bobby   Daddy

David

Above Drawing by David Wilkins, 1943: Kite-flying with Haru

Above right Drawing sent by David Wilkins to his parents from Woodstock School, 1945: Coming Home

FATHER BEING HAPPY.

~ THERE WAS NO WAR THEN
SO THEIR FATHER DID NOT
HAVE TO GO AND FIGHT;
BUT HE HAD LEARNT TO BE
A SOLDIER WHEN HE WAS
YOUNG IN CASE A WAR
SHOULD START.
~ WHAT HE LIKED BEST
WAS TO GO INTO THE
JUNGLE ON AN ELEPHANT
AND SHOOT TIGERS.
~ WHAT HE LIKED NEXT
BEST WAS
POLO,
AND CRICKET,
AND ROWING ~
~ AFTER THE CHILDREN WERE
BORN HE HAD NO TIME
FOR THESE AMUSEMENTS.
~ HE HAD TO SPEND ALL
DAY AT HIS WORK, WHICH
WAS BEING A JUDGE.

Above and below From 'Once there were three children', an illustrated memoir of Lahore in the early 20th century written by Hilda Reid in later life for her niece and nephew

JUNGLE TALES

~ ONLY AT THE BEGINNING
AND THE END OF THE DAY
HE COULD STOP BEING A JUDGE
AND PLAY WITH THE CHILDREN.
~ EVERY MORNING BEFORE
BREAKFAST HE USED TO
TAKE EITHER PHILIP OR HILDA
FOR A RIDE WITH HIM.
(NOT LESLEY, BECAUSE
SHE WAS TOO YOUNG).
~ EVERY EVENING BEFORE THEY
WENT TO SLEEP HE USED TO
TELL THEM STORIES ~
~ EXCITING STORIES ABOUT
THE JUNGLE
OR
FUNNY STORIES ABOUT
Mrs A. and Mrs B.
~ THE FUNNY STORIES WERE
SO FUNNY THAT THE
CHILDREN USED TO LAUGH
TILL THEY NEARLY ROLLED
OUT OF THEIR BEDS

Girls at Play in front of the Lawrence Military Asylum, 1864

St John's College, Agra, built in the 1850s by the Church Missionary Society in the style of the Akbar's Palace at Fatehpur Sikri

Top Arthur Jones (far left, bottom row) representing Bishop Cotton School in the Hockey Team, 1949; *Left* Mrs Margaret Hinds teaching her daughter, Alison, and other children, Gulmarg, c. 1934; *Below* Jim, Pat and Mick Butler at Mount Abu High School, 'the year we ran away', 1935 *Bottom* Penny Elsden-Smith rehearsing for a troop concert at the Hilltop school, Kalimpong, 1943

I have not been done to what this Illustration Sheros but I daresay I shall

Clockwise from top left Constance Halford-Thompson, aged 10, the first child to take an unaccompanied flight by KLM to India, 1938; Archibald Campbell writing home from his prep school, East Sheen, 1877; William Brown, a 'small man' of six at Craigflower Preparatory School, c. 1930; Letty, Tutu and Willie Beveridge at school in Southport, 1885; Leslie and Marjorie Wenger, 'solemn-faced while under the care of "Aunt" Jennie Bliss', 1916 lump), the application of citronella oil, confinement to the house after dusk and mosquito nets over their beds. Some imagined the nets to be a comforting protection against other dangers that might be lurking in their nurseries. One wrote:

> When I go to bed at night
> I'm fastened in all smooth and tight,
> My net is like a castle wall
> No tigers can get in at all.
>
> No jackals, prowling, yowling round,
> No serpents, creeping on the ground,
> No one can get through at all
> My NET that's like a castle wall.
>
> I am as safe as safe can be,
> Where only 'squiters' hum to me.[78]

Other dangerous diseases could be prevented by inoculations developed in the late nineteenth and early twentieth centuries. Patricia Cartwright (née Hutcheson) was in Jodhpur during the First World War when cholera became so widespread that 'even the monkeys collapsed and died after falling off the trees'. She and the family she was staying with (while her mother did war work in Mesopotamia 'so that she could see more of my father') were quickly injected with the new cholera vaccine, which gave protection for six months.[79] Eric Wilkins, a missionary doctor in the 1930s and 1940s, had his own family regularly injected against typhoid, while regretting that he did not have the resources to do the same for the pupils of the local mission school in Orissa. In the 1930s Lorraine Gradidge had her children inoculated against cholera, smallpox and plague – only to have her daughter Penelope nearly die of diphtheria, an illness which still caused over two thousand deaths a year in Britain. In fact, this too could be rendered less severe by injections, as the Langham Scotts realised in 1930. Their daughter contracted the illness from a school-friend in Murree. 'It turns out that Dorothy's flu is really diphtheria,' wrote her father, 'but the injection saved her and she is quite all right now.'[80] In the next decade the danger of dysentery in young children was reduced by new drugs. When Joan Battye tried out a sulphonamide-based medicine on five-year-old Anne who was 'fading before our eyes' in 1943, the child 'did not look back'.[81]

Both Penelope Gradidge and Anne Battye apparently contracted their illnesses by swimming in contaminated swimming-pools. But most of the time Anglo-Indian mothers took elaborate precautions. They made chamois-leather waistcoats as protection against the cold in the hills. They washed children in Dettol, oiling their bodies to prevent dryness. They generally insisted on the wearing of topees. They boiled all drinking water and milk, washing fruit and vegetables in permanganate of potash – or 'pinky pani' as children called it. Monica Francis's mother was so preoccupied by germs that even coins for the church collection had to be washed in 'pinky'. Robert Baker and his sister Beatrice Broad remembered that they were not allowed outside at all in the heat of the day – between nine in the morning and four in the afternoon. Nor could they swim in the snake-infested lake beside which their idyllic plantation bungalow was built.[82] (In the 1950s, however, Robert and Paula Baker's children enjoyed a more relaxed 'childhood by the lake', which now had a bricked-off section for swimming.[83])

Memoirs show that children were aware of these safety measures and also of prohibitions on buying Indian goodies from the bazaar, brightly coloured drinks being especially suspect. Spending the hot months in the hills was also supposed to do children good. Lord Hardinge always found Diamond 'looking quite splendid' when he joined her in Simla.[84] Dick Whittaker recalls being 'fantastically fit' in Mussoorie.[85] The bitter cold could, however, cause problems for some children. Michael Foss suffered from bronchitis when in Simla. Joanna Lumley fell seriously ill with whooping cough when she was taken as a small baby into 'the high alpine air' of Gulmarg.[86]

No doubt as a result of parental precautions (as well as resistance acquired in infancy), many children enjoyed good health in India. It could even improve. Alison Newton (née Hinds) remembers that her eight-year-old sister Margaret was suffering from tuberculosis when the family went out to India in 1933 'but came back healthy' after three years on the heights of the north-west frontier.[87] Of the fifty or so 'Indian children' I have interviewed most said that they suffered only the odd bout of sickness or fever. Hilary Sweet-Escott (née Johnston) reports that she never had anything wrong with her at all and Valentine Davies (née Morice) is sure that her lifelong good health is due to immunities developed during her Indian childhood. A few were less lucky. Sue Portal did not thrive as a young child; Michael McNay nearly died of typhoid caught from drinking stream water;

and Penny Eladen Smith suffered from recurrent amoebic dysentery in Calcutta and Darjeeling, although she was much healthier once she was sent to school in Kalimpong.

Illness was not the only maternal anxiety. During the monsoon there were (and are) terrible dangers, especially in the hills. During Carol Pickering's time at Woodstock several pupils were killed in landslides. Hilary Johnston lost her three-year-old brother Bill at Darjeeling when he 'slipped into the roaring torrent' of rainwater gushing down the steep hillside and was swept 'down the 1000 foot of *khud* [hillside]'. Discovering that many Indian children had already died in this way, Hilary's father, who was District Commissioner in Darjeeling, designed special drain-grids which 'would have an excellent chance of holding the body of even a small child'. They also served as a memorial to young Bill.[88]

In the north-west frontier region there was the additional hazard of earthquakes. Walter and Olive Trevelyan and their younger son John survived the massive one at Quetta in 1935 but Olive was so distressed that 'she could not bear to go on living in India any more'. Their older son, Raleigh, heard about it back in England and wrote simply: 'Dear Mummy and Daddy, I hear you have had an earthquake. I am third this week. I have two tulips out in my garden and another is in bud.'[89] Because his prep school teachers had prevented him from reading about the disaster in the newspapers, the boy did not realise that among the 30,000 fatalities were about 200 Britons and Eurasians. They included four-year-old Imogen Wakefield, daughter of the District Officer, and her chums, Pleasant Williams and 'the little Francis girl'. The three girls had been 'photographed together at a children's party the day before because they were such friends'. The headmaster of Quetta Grammar School lost two of his five daughters but all the boarders and masters at the school were dug out 'little worse for their ordeal'.[90] The Gradidge and Battye families experienced a milder tremor in 1940. While Anne Battye was young enough to find it 'good fun jumping over the cracks', Mrs Gradidge was so frightened that she gave premature birth to her third child, which survived. But Europeans (and rich Indians) were relatively safe since their 'earthquake-proof bungalows withstood the shock'.[91]

Olive Trevelyan and Lorraine Gradidge were not the only mothers to worry. Joyce Wilkins observed that her 'mother's anxieties extended to much that she saw in the world around her in India'. These included snakes in the bathroom, 'creepy-crawlies' on the verandah, scorpions in the shoes, tree frogs on the mosquito nets, pariah dogs in the neighbourhood, half-starved cows among the crowds and all the 'sights and smells and sounds in the bazaar'.[92] George Roche thinks that his mother 'tended to over-dramatize the danger to us of confrontations with wild animals, filling us with alarm about what could happen to small boys'.[93] But such fears are understandable, especially when families lived miles from the nearest hospital and when children did not share adults' caution.

Many had narrow escapes, especially with snakes. At Nundy in the Nilgiri hills Constance Maude and her sister 'used to have competitions to see who could kill the greatest number of snakes before breakfast'; one would jump on the head, the other on the tail and then they struck the snake with a dog whip.[94] The gentler Monica Francis nearly put her hand into a leafy bed she had made for her dolls, in which 'half a dozen baby cobras were sitting up weaving [*sic* – waving?] their tiny heads'.[95] Two adult cobras terrified Lillan Luker when they appeared in the bathroom and started to sway to the music of the mouth organ she was playing. George Roche and his brother, though trained to distinguish poisonous snakes, were tempted by the bright emerald pattern on some baby vipers, which they put into their pockets. Yet I have only come across two children who were bitten by snakes; both Joe and Jim Butler apparently survived three bites each while under the care of the Christian Brothers. It was, however, quite common for youngsters to be bitten by stray dogs or by wild animals like squirrels and baboons, incurring the urgent necessity for a series of painful anti-rabies injections in the stomach. Understandably some children had nightmares about Indian fauna, as Alan Ross did after a cobra slithered from the water tank while he was in the bath. Richard Murphy, who went to Ceylon at the age of four, found that 'more things frightened me than in Ireland' and he was convinced that there was a tiger living under his bed.[96]

Despite such fears, childhood memories tend to focus not on the dangers but on the wonders of the local animal life. In Burma Terence Milligan was fascinated by frogs, fish and snakes. At Guntakal, a southern railway junction, the Bourne children collected a family of animals including buffalo, baby spotted deer, tortoises, quails, rabbits and a spaniel. At Kulu, in the Himalayas, Marjory Fyson developed 'a great interest in creatures indoors and out', singling out rats, bats, mice, lizards, flying foxes and butterflies.[97] At Gilgit Raleigh Trevelyan enjoyed the company of 'a great number of pets, always fluctuating and including a fox cub, a wolf cub, a young markhor, a cat and some geese'.[98] Even Hilda Reid, who led a thoroughly English childhood in Lahore with her ponies and teddy-bears, had a green parrot whom she 'loved best in all the world next to her dear family'.[99] Other children, admittedly, were keener on the slaughter of animals. Tommy Usborne, having been given a Winchester rifle and boxes of bullets, remembers shooting pigeons, a jackal and a vulture at the age of six: 'I was in fact a blood-thirsty and heartless brute, but I was given parental encouragement in this addiction.'[100]

The fact is that Raj children were much better-protected from physical danger than are many Indian children today. Every year thousands still contract malaria, cholera, dysentery, typhoid, smallpox, tuberculosis, tetanus and plague because their parents cannot afford, or are ignorant of, the simple precautions available to their British rulers a hundred years ago. Less commonly appreciated were other hazards for children living under the Raj. The danger of losing a beloved parent persisted even in the late nineteenth and twentieth centuries. This was because adults could not shield themselves as effectively as they did their offspring. Missionaries, tea planters and railway engineers were out in all weathers. Civil servants went on lengthy tours in primitive parts of the country, often accompanied by their wives. Viceroys and Governors were exposed to assassination, as were their overdressed consorts, who also had to endure a punishing round of social engagements in the heat. Women often had babies without access to medical help. Thus a surprisingly large number of the children who appear in this chapter suffered bereavement while they were in India. Darkness could descend on the golden afternoon represented in a teatime scene photographed outside the Himalayan bungalow of Major George Wemyss Anson, his wife Katherine, their sons Otto and Frank and three dogs. In 1892, some years after this photograph was taken, family life was shattered when Mrs Anson died as a result of a fall from an elephant. Otto, Frank and their three younger siblings were hastily sent to live with their mother's relations outside Edinburgh.

Another tragic blow was that which fell on Terry Mayo, whose father was assassinated in 1872 while visiting a prison on the Andaman Islands. An observer describes the Viceroy's funeral in Calcutta: 'This morning at the final ceremony poor little Terence walked as chief mourner after the coffin, his two hands clutched together behind him. I can hardly bear to think of it. ... The walk in the sun was terribly trying to the poor little chap.'[101] Later viceregal offspring, Mary,

Cynthia and Alexandra Naldera Curzon (the last named after her parents' favourite place in India), mourned for their mother. The beautiful Vicereine, who had adorned many a glittering occasion and endured two difficult pregnancies (one ending in miscarriage), died of a heart attack at the age of thirty-six shortly after arriving home in 1906. Diamond Hardinge came close to being orphaned during her father's term of office. Lord Hardinge was seriously injured in 1912 when a bomb was thrown at his elephant during the Viceregal entry into the new capital of Delhi. Diamond apparently remained calm enough to make up a bed and prepare a hot-water bottle for her father. And when her mother died in 1914, partly as a result of the shock, this rather stiff and remote Viceroy 'was only saved from collapse by the untiring kindness and sympathy of Diamond, then only fourteen years old'.[102]

Working in India often fatally weakened the health of European adults. Jim Bourne, for instance, could not guard against mosquito bites when he was surveying, building and repairing railway lines in southern India. He died in 1918 after repeated attacks of malaria, though his four daughters living in the same area had escaped the disease. Another railway engineer to die prematurely was the father of Drusilla Harrington-Hawes. She remembers 'a wonderful expedition with him in a trolley' which was propelled down the line by 'coolies behind pulling levers back and forth'. When she developed boils (a common affliction in India) she was quickly taken home by her mother, sadly leaving behind a beautiful doll's house made especially for her in the railway workshops. She did not realise that she was also saying a final goodbye to her father, who died of typhoid while on the way to join his wife and daughter.[103] Guy Wheeler does not remember saying any farewell to his adoptive father, a telegraph engineer who died in a Bangalore sanatorium in about 1928. It was this death that caused Guy to be placed in a Bombay orphanage while his mother tried to sort out their future. As usually happened in those days, nothing was explained to the child, who simply felt betrayed. Gladys Krall was also left in the dark about her mother's death in childbirth when she was three years old: 'I was told that my mother died of pneumonia and I never knew for years that there had been a child.'[104]

Equally mysterious was the sudden withdrawal of George and Paul Roche from 'a grey, cold spell of existence' at a prep school in St Leonards-on-Sea. As George concludes, 'parents of their generation did as they thought fit'. In any case the boys were delighted to return to their parents' 'magnificent new bungalow' at Poona, where Captain

Roche was designing a new station for the Great Indian Peninsular Railway. But this 'halcyon time' was not to last for long. In February 1927 their mother contracted smallpox while on holiday at Mahabaleshwar and died soon after returning to Poona. Since neither of her sons nor her daughter caught the illness, it must be assumed that they had been vaccinated against it. The stricken family returned to England where the boys again went to boarding school, an experience George would 'prefer to forget'.[105] A similarly sad homecoming was that of the Foster family to Ireland in 1929. The Revd Foster had developed a tubercular kidney while serving as a stretcher-bearer in the First World War and the condition worsened during his strenuous missionary years in India. He was forced to abandon that work and died soon after his return at the age of forty. The death of her adored father is a much more upsetting memory for Pat than that of the sexual abuse in the heather.

Pat Foster's only consolation was that she had not lost years of her father's company by being sent away from India. She and her brother and sister could remember him reading them poetry and inventing games. Nor did Terence Mayo forget his daily sessions with his father. Mayo's friend and biographer, W. W. Hunter, tells how a year after the Viceroy's death 'the little man repeated to me wonderful fragments from a repertory of tales'.[106] George Roche had the more sensual memory of his mother 'always looking beautiful in her evening dresses and smelling of tantalizing perfume'.[107] Parental loss must have been harder to bear for Lord Mayo's 'dear Old Boys', his older sons who were at Eton, far away from any comforting arms, or for the three oldest Bourne girls who had not seen their father for six years or their mother for three. When they were eventually reunited with Mrs Bourne Tittipu did not even recognise her mother, who was 'dressed in black from head to foot with a widow's veil'.[108]

Less tragic, but hurtful all the same, was the parting of friends. Children in India often lost track of playmates because of the constant movement involved in their fathers' jobs. Military men and civilians were always transferring from one cantonment or station to another. This was obviously hard on their wives, whose job was to 'pay, pack and follow', but their children also suffered. When the Milligan family left Poona for Burma in 1924, Terence thought his parents had no 'idea what it cost me to say goodbye to the first friends I'd ever made'. Luckily, his mother was also much attached to Poona (where her own family lived) so that she and the children continued to spend time there.[109] With each of Gunner Moore's many moves his son Jack 'sought new friends and inevitably discarded those we left behind'. Jack seems to have been good at finding companions (both Indian and European), with whom he enjoyed kite fights, tipcat games, bicycle rides and sport of all kinds in every new location.[110] Brian Outhwaite was similarly adaptable, engaging in just the same games thirty years later.

'We took it in our stride,' writes Barbara Donaldson (who gives no maiden name), 'because each place we landed in was "home" and made familiar even if it was a tent.' Barbara was obviously a sociable child, taking part in dancing classes and joining the Bluebirds (the Indian version of Brownies) at each successive station. When she returned to India as a young memsahib she found that 'one by one little girls I had played with turned up', having married, as she had, into the ICS. Her own children in their turn did their fair share of travelling. They accompanied their parents on winter tours of duty, which Mrs Donaldson describes as 'bliss'.[111] But for most peripatetic children there must have come a time when they felt, like Michael Foss, that they 'were travelling too much [and] wanted to settle down'.[112]

Children's best chance of meeting each other was probably at the hill stations, where English mothers and their offspring congregated during the hot months. At Dalhousie, Margery Fyson found, a child's existence 'was just as gay and frivolous as that of its mother. Tennis parties for her – tea parties for the child; grown-up race meetings – children's events; amateur theatricals – and a fairy play for the juniors'.[113] At Simla too, according to M. M. Kaye, 'the children of the Raj led a very social life'.[114] Nancy Vernede remembers the many activities organised at Naini Tal to keep children 'busy and happy' among those of their own class.[115] Some naturally enjoyed them more than others. Sue Portal loved fancy dress parties and still remembers her elf costume with its special green shoes. But Raleigh Trevelyan dreaded the hectic summer at Gulmarg, preferring to ride his pony 'in the pine forests and across the flower meadows' rather than being in 'a crush of children dressed as columbines and pierrots'. He particularly hated one party where he was disguised as Felix the Cat and had to wear a mask.[116]

All over India British clubs organised similar events for children. But it was rare for youngsters to cross the social barriers, which were as rigid as racial ones. The experience of E. L. Turner's four-year-old brother on the family's second journey to India was unusual. He had a toy motor car while the son of the aloof Viceroy, Lord Halifax, who was also on board, was the proud owner of a London bus. 'Although first and second class were segregated (we were second),' Turner writes, 'these little boys rode their toys all over the ship, changing them from time to time, completely unconscious of class or station in life.'[117] No doubt some of the grown-up passengers disapproved of such unorthodox behaviour, which could never be repeated once the children were on dry land. White children in India seldom had playfellows of their own age, let alone of the same class or race. Monica Francis attended annual Christmas parties at the High Range Club in Munnar, where 'Father Christmas appeared on horseback or motor bike or by T-model Ford, according to the taste of the disguised tea-planter'. But, like Raleigh Trevelyan, she was quite happy playing on her own and 'it didn't matter that I only occasionally saw another white child'.[118]

Cultural poverty as well as social isolation could be a problem for British children in India. Discouraged from absorbing indigenous culture and cut off from Western arts and literature they might, like Beatrice Turner, lack 'mental stimulus'. Her normal routine as an only child on her father's Ceylonese tea plantation consisted of 'dreary lessons' with Aunt Vera, a weekly visit from another child and occasional parties in Kandy at which she 'clung to Vera'. Meanwhile her parents were busy with *thés dansants* and tennis parties, although there were a few 'blissful moments' when her mother played cards or did jigsaws with her 'between the emergence from resting and afternoon tea'. Yet amid the 'solitary hours and childish frustrations' Beatrice had more elevating experiences which she treasured after leaving Ceylon in 1934. Her father read Kipling to her as they watched the sunset from the terrace. They made excursions to archaeological sites and botanical gardens. And they often went to the cinema in Kandy.[119]

Since most twentieth-century cantonments, cities and hill stations had a cinema, films were frequently children's main link with the West. Viola Bayley remembers taking her four-year-old son to his first film in 1942. It was an Abbott and Costello comedy which the child found 'so ecstatically funny that he could hardly stay on his chair'.[120] Mr Honeycombe, who worked for an American oil company, even had his own ciné-projector on which he showed Charlie Chaplin films, to the delight of Gordon and his friends. But these were rare treats for most children who, like the Godden sisters, 'had so little of theatre, music or cinema that anything we did see or hear of them made an impression that lasted for months'. They were completely dazzled, for instance, by an amateur performance of the operetta *Veronique* at Darjeeling. Like young people everywhere, they relished whatever opportunities for amusement they could find. Jon and Rumer wrote – 'poems and stories poured out of us' – as did Margaret and Janet Wenger, who set up their own publishing company. From Mount Hermon School in 1948 seven-year-old Janet wrote her father a secret letter telling him that she 'had made up a lot of stories' and was going to turn them into a book; the next year Margaret reported that she had written four chapters and Janet eleven.[121] By the time he left India at the age of nine Gordon Honeycombe had written poems and 'Chapter One of a story called Mole'.[122] Penny Elsden-Smith (who is now a consultant in puppetry) first got 'theatre in her blood' through her parents' involvement in Calcutta's ambitious amateur dramatics.[123]

Many girls used pencil, paint or camera to portray their beautiful environment. Sixteen-year-old Christian Bruce, in the midst of the rather tedious social round involved in being a daughter of Viceroy Lord Elgin (1894–9), took landscape and portrait photographs. When she showed them in the Simla Art Exhibition, her proud sister records, she received a prize and 'many congratulations'.[124] For families who possessed a piano, music offered cultural diversion. Donald Langham Scott's letters give an attractive picture of his home life at Quetta in the 1920s. Dorothy had piano lessons at home and took Trinity music exams, so that her 'days are very full now, with school homework and music practice'. Mr Scott loved to join in Dorothy's music lessons and was delighted when he played his first duet with her: 'It was a great success and Maisie encored twice.'[125]

All these children read whatever books they could get hold of. By the age of five or six Monica Francis and Margery Fyson knew their Beatrix Potter books off by heart and were embarking on the classics: *Alice in Wonderland*, *The Wind in the Willows*, *The Water Babies*, *The Jungle Book*. In addition there were publications like *The Children's Newspaper* to be devoured. It is true that boys were often more like George Roche, who 'found it wearisome to read . . . and wanted to be up and doing something, anything, so long as it was something active'.[126] In fact many were slow to learn their letters, largely because their mothers found it hard to discipline them. As we have seen, despairing parents, like the Nicholls in Calcutta, the Lindsays in Cawnpore and the Kiplings in Bombay, lamented the recalcitrance of sons in whom they could not instil reading skills. But there is no evidence that this male backwardness was peculiar to India; boys in Britain today apply themselves to their studies more slowly than girls.

The fear that growing up in India would stunt children's cultural development was one of the main reasons for sending them back to Britain.[127] Parents need not have worried so much, since enterprising children found stimulation wherever they were. Many who stayed in India after the crucial age of seven went on to become writers, actors, academics, musicians and artists or simply people who love opera and theatre, books and pictures. Often they are all the richer for having been brought up by their parents and for having absorbed some of the 'vast and varied' culture of the Indian subcontinent as they travelled its length and breadth.[128] Elinor Tollinton (née Astbury) concludes that her Indian childhood, prolonged by the First World War, 'had so much to offer children whose imagination was not cluttered up with images of Walt Disney'. 'We were fancy free and wild: to us the Secoree Wolf Pack was real not fiction. We had faced the blazing eyes of Shere Khan. With others we had stood in awe before the Piper at the Gates of Dawn.'[129]

The longer they stayed, however, the more likely children were to see 'the misery and poverty that is so much part of India'. The Godden sisters knew that in the subcontinent 'death was as casual as life, part of every day'. George Roche had a 'macabre fascination' for the funeral pyres he saw beside the Bhima River near his house. He and his brother developed 'a phobia about death and germs, imagining that the air around the corpses would be full of the most dreadful germs ready to make a beeline for us'.[130] In a routine letter to her grandparents eleven-year-old Di Westlake included a story about a Muslim fanatic terrorising their village in Baluchistan with a sword: 'Mummy said it was all right for us because they don't kill ladies and children because that doesn't count.'[131] As a small child Mrs Cartwright made a train journey through areas that had been flooded and she can still see in her mind's eye 'the corpses of poor fellows floating down in the muddy waters'.[132] It was normal, says Morvyth Seely (née St George), for urban children like her and her brother in Bombay to 'learn to turn away from the sight of horribly maimed beggars with the remains of bloody severed limbs'.[133] For the Kims of India, who lacked for some reason the protection of parents, there could be no turning away. Lee Langley's *Changes of Address* portrays a girl who, like herself, spends her childhood on the move with a careless alcoholic mother. In fact Maggie comes to little harm, despite spending long periods on her own in various Indian cities. She often finds comfort among the crowds: 'There were always Indians around, there were stories to be heard, things to observe, mysteries to ponder, magic to believe in.'[134]

Peter Greave's autobiography tells a more alarming tale. He was born in 1910 and spent his first few years in the peace and comfort of Calcutta's Ballygunge suburb. His mother's greatest desire was to make a home for her children but her husband's restless pursuit of increasingly wild business ventures, not to mention his disastrous compulsion to expose himself to women, made that well-nigh impossible. Once when he deserted the family Peter and his brother were left at a charity boarding school run by the Christian Brothers in Darjeeling, for which Peter felt 'a deep and unchanging hatred'. After some months of enduring 'the humiliations, the petty restrictions, the ghastly food and the hostility of most of my companions', the thirteen-year-old boy took flight. Armed only with seven rupees, several bars of chocolate, a map of East Bengal and a copy of *Sexton Blake among the Parsees*, he too came to no serious harm. In one village he was 'touched and astonished' by Indians' hospitality and help. His bid for freedom succeeded and he spent six months of 'almost flawless happiness' with an American couple who took him into their house in Assam before restoring him to his reunited parents.

After another two years of steadfast struggle against the odds, Mrs Greave died and the two teenage boys were left to seek their own fortune. Because they were white and 'spoke without an instantly recognisable chi chi accent' they were disqualified from Eurasian preserves like the railways and customs, while their lack of an English education excluded them from higher posts. Thus Peter descended to the 'economic level of the indigenous population', working closely with Indians and finding that 'they were astonishingly like other human beings'. But the effects of poverty, as well as an insatiable sexual appetite, took their toll. In 1939 Peter Greave contracted leprosy, a disease dreaded for its infectiousness and incurability. He entered a 'twilit, fugitive world' in Calcutta but found some love and friendship among its other unfortunate inhabitants. Before being rescued in 1946 by an English doctor, Peter himself was one of the 'sickening sights' from which European children were shielded.[135]

They might, however, have been more upset by 'diseased cattle and carcasses alive with vultures and flies'.[136] Like many children then and now, Terence Milligan was particularly distressed by 'needless cruelty' to animals, whether it was the Indian servants decapitating live chickens or the British Army shooting 'no-collar' dogs. His biographer thinks that this led to his lifelong involvement in animal welfare.[137] Pip Mirrell never wanted to have snake charmers at her birthday parties because she considered it a cruel practice. Gladys Krall would protest when the driver hit the thin pony which was pulling the family in a *tonga* (light carriage). Sometimes children also observed British efforts to relieve both human and animal suffering. Aged about nine or ten and still living at home, Penelope Gradidge must have known about the Hospital for Animals which her mother set up in Quetta. Mrs Gradidge had been 'appalled by cruelty to animals' during all her time in India (as child and woman) and her hospital attempted to alleviate 'some of the misery suffered by the donkeys, ponies, bullocks and camels in that harsh land'. It did not seem to her any contradiction that at the same time she gloried in traditional Raj blood sports such as jackal-hunting and pig-sticking.[138] Janet Wenger was certainly aware of her parents' charitable efforts for she was in Bengal during the famine of 1943. Her father provided twice-weekly meals at the mission for large numbers of children. 'They were all sitting in rows on the verandah with large leaves as plates and I would go round and dollop some food on these.' Despite the happier times she had with her family Janet says that she would find it 'disturbing' to return to Calcutta now. Too many memories would be brought back by 'the crows flying over at dawn'.[139]

Although they glimpsed the darker sides of Indian life, most of the people I have mentioned still grew to love the country of their childhood. M. M. Kaye says that she 'learned very young to accept the beauty and wonder of that most beautiful and wonderful of lands, and with it the ugliness and cruelty that was an integral part of it'.[140] A couple of stories epitomise such mixed feelings. While admiring the Taj Mahal Carol Titus saw turtles pulling at a partly cremated body in the river: 'These two pictures in juxtaposition in my memory, the one of beauty and sublimity, the other seeming to represent suffering and degradation, symbolize India for me, a country of extremes and contradictions.'[141] About ten years later, in 1947, Jamila Gavin was in Bombay with her brother and English mother. They were on their way to England (leaving her Indian father behind) because of the communal riots which had broken out prior to Partition. Jamila witnessed a great deal of violence as they waited for their boat, but what she remembers most clearly is this image:

A tiny, ragged beggar-girl, carefully carrying in both hands a saucer of milk, steadfastly crossing a busy street, with bicycles and lorries and rickshaws swerving around her, and setting it down before a scraggy, starving, mewling little kitten, and seeing the contentment on her face as she stood back with hand on hip and watched it lap.

She concludes that 'India is dangerous, beautiful, cruel, serene and always exciting' – very different from the 'ordered, law-abiding' country in which she was soon to arrive. Once there she found it necessary 'to hang on to some kind of magic' and her belief in fairies, demons and ghosts helped to take her out of the 'grey, drab post-war life of Britain'.[142]

Not all Yoma Crosfield Ullman's experiences of the subcontinent were happy. She had been a 'sickly child' suffering from undiagnosed allergies; she had seen little of her Guiding mother; and she had lacked the company of other children. But Burma and India had seeped under the edges of her 'British carapace' and indelibly marked her being. Nothing could ever obliterate the glory of her train journeys, the splendour of Hindu festivals she had seen, the excitement of jungle safaris with her father, and the magic of exotic names – including her own Burmese Christian name. When Yoma left in 1945 she followed the Anglo-Indian tradition of throwing her topee into the sea on entering the Mediterranean, not realising that she was 'tossing away the most vivid and light-filled years' of her childhood.[43] But she still had her wooden 'treasure house' to keep her memories fresh. Adults who saw only the menace of India failed to perceive the bounty which it could bestow – an enchanted childhood.

SEVEN

'Other People's Houses'

Separated Families in the
Early Twentieth Century

According to a popular book published to mark the end of the last millennium, the twentieth century was 'greatly influenced by Dr Freud'.[1] Certainly in its first three decades Sigmund Freud's lectures and publications had important implications for the upbringing of children, including those sent back from India. In his writings as well as in his own psychoanalytical experiments, he drew attention to the significance of early experiences: the trauma of birth, the relationship between parents and babies, and infantile sexuality. In one paper, for example, he explored the consequences of children being beaten; not only did the practice signify 'a deprivation of love and a humiliation' but, he claimed, it could lead to adult neuroses and perversions.[2] In fact intelligent and open-minded people were beginning to reach similar conclusions for themselves, as is suggested in an incident recounted by Leonard Woolf, friend of Lytton Strachey and future husband of Virginia Stephen. After graduating from Cambridge, Woolf sailed out to Ceylon in 1904 to take up a post in the Civil Service. On board the ship he became 'painfully aware' that the army captain in the next-door cabin was regularly beating his small daughter for wetting the bed. Although he had not at this point read any of Freud's works he was convinced by the child's hysterical shrieks and sobs that 'beating was not the right way to cure bed-wetting'. He even managed to persuade the captain to desist from this practice but his wife 'was enraged with me for interfering and pursued me with bitter hostility until we parted for ever at Colombo'.[3]

As this woman's reaction suggests, Freud's new theories were slow to make their mark. Even in his home town, Vienna, only three people turned up to a lecture on 'The Interpretation of Dreams' in 1900 and Freud's book of that title only sold 228 copies in the two years after its publication. When his British disciple, Ernest Jones, was lecturing on the same subject in New York he met with a positively hostile response. One woman insisted that Freud's filthy theories applied only to Austrian dreams: 'he had no business to speak of the dreams of Americans ... [and] she was certain that all her dreams were strictly altruistic'.[4]

Undaunted, Jones worked hard to get his master's ideas accepted, setting up the British Psychoanalytical Society in 1919 to promote them. By 1939 all Freud's works had been published in Britain, at first by the Society and then by Leonard Woolf himself, who founded the Hogarth Press. Thus in 1930 Dorothy Wilkins, a missionary's daughter whose childhood features in this chapter, suggested that her troubled younger sister should read Freud's *Introductory Lectures on Psychoanalysis*.[5]

Most middle-class women of the inter-war years were less conversant with Freudian ideas than Dorothy, who had trained as a psychologist. If they could afford it, British mothers (in India and England) still left their children in the care of nannies, who rarely held with new theories and continued to be 'punctiliously strict' with their charges – especially about such matters as eating up all their porridge.[6] If they took anything as their guide it was the popular *Mothercraft Manual* written in 1924 by Dr Frederic Truby King. This recommended practices which Freud regarded as dangerously inhibiting: rigid potty-training aided by 'the soft rubber nozzle of a small bulb-enema' and the suppression of thumb-sucking and masturbation, if necessary by the use of hand and leg splints.[7] Truby King's disciple, Mabel Liddiard, gave similar advice in a manual of 1936 but by then a rival and more Freudian expertise had begun to emerge. In *The Nursery Years* (1929) Susan Isaacs advocated gentler methods of toilet-training and suggested that the 'strain of accepting adult standards too early' could lead to mental illness.[8] Even Truby King's daughter Mary toned down her father's message: splints should be used only in cases of 'pernicious' thumb-sucking and punishment should not be administered for masturbation or bed-wetting.[9] Most Raj children of the time seem to have endured the regime of Truby King. They tell of being fed by the clock every four hours, put on the potty until they performed, punished for wetting the bed or 'playing with themselves' and made to eat all the food on their plates even if it made them sick. One who was brought up in this way thinks Truby King should not take too much blame: 'That man has much to answer for – but with hindsight, along with emotional crippling came an adult ability to endure and keep the stiff upper lip.'[10]

Empire parents who did manage to read Freud's early works would not have been deterred from their time-honoured custom of sending their children away from home. In 1905 Freud actually warned against 'an excess of parental affection'. Not only would this cause 'precocious sexual maturity' but it would make a child 'incapable in later life of temporarily doing without love or of being content with a smaller amount of it'. It was not until 1926 that Freud began to think that such anxious over-dependence was more likely to be caused by separation from 'someone who is loved and longed for' than by too close a relationship.[11] There is no evidence that this rather obvious new idea gained much acceptance in Britain.

It remained common, for instance, for unwanted offspring to be put into children's homes or simply given away. Desirée Battye told an astonishing story in an interview in *The Oldie*. Her mother died in the influenza epidemic of 1919 when Desirée was aged about two. Within three years her father had remarried and Desirée and her brother Maurice had been turned out of the house by 'Steppie', 'who couldn't stand us any more'. For some years they lived in a home 'run by a clergyman who took in children who had nowhere to go', where they were 'terribly miserable and unhappy'.[12] Eventually their grandmother took Desirée to live with her in France while Maurice stayed at his prep school in England. The actress Geraldine James recounted a similar experience in a BBC interview. When their new stepmother refused to have them back at the family home during school holidays she and her sister were made wards of court. The rejection had a devastating effect on the young Geraldine, who took to the stage to disguise her insecurities: acting, she said, was 'a way of presenting myself to the world'.[13] The same fate nearly befell the cookery writer Nigel Slater even in the 1950s, as he revealed in his autobiography. After his mother's death and his father's remarriage he was told very seriously that if he did not try harder to get on with the new wife he would have to go into care. 'Getting rid of me has apparently always been an option.'[14] Wicked stepmothers did not only exist in the realms of fairy tales like *Hansel and Gretel*.

When the circumstances of the world wars produced more unwanted children than ever, mothers were encouraged to put them into orphanages, on the understanding that they would be adopted or fostered. In practice, thousands of them became child migrants. They were sent off to the colonies just as some 'street arabs' had been by Dr Barnardo and other philanthropists in the nineteenth century. Thousands ended up in Australian orphanages or farm schools. Their function was to prevent the British Dominion from being swamped by what the Archbishop of Perth called 'the teeming millions of our neighbouring Asiatic races'.[15] To this end they were separated from siblings, used for long hours of heavy work, denied a proper education, prohibited from free communication with family or friends, refused access to their birth certificates until they were twenty-one and, in many cases, sexually abused. Nothing was done to put a stop to this cruel flouting of juvenile rights and the practice only came to an end after 1967 because Australia no longer needed labour. Only in recent years has the story of these lost and unloved children been revealed.[16]

Just as Victorian child neglect extended into the twentieth century so too did the separation of Raj children from their families. Indeed, it actually became more common for youngsters to go to unknown guardians and to holiday homes in Britain. Of course, respectable sons and daughters of the Empire cannot be compared too closely with the 'Home kids' packed off to Australia.[17] It is true that both sets of children endured journeys to distant lands, the dispersal of their families, long spells in forbidding institutions and the lack of a home and possessions. But young exiles from India exchanged fond letters with their parents, knew that they would be reunited eventually and could look forward to a good career or marriage. In fact, their circumstances were strikingly similar to those of their nineteenth-century counterparts. Expensive sea passages (£40–£60 one way) still prevented frequent reunions with parents. Letters and telegrams continued to be the only means of communication as transoceanic telephone cables were not laid until the 1950s.

During the First World War contact became more difficult since passengers and mail were put at risk by mines and torpedoes. When the India-bound passenger liner *Persia* was sunk in December 1915, the 192 victims included many parents and children.[18] Also 'lying at the bottom of the Mediterranean Sea in the *Persia*', incidentally, were unmourned school reports on Dorothy Wilkins and her two sisters.[19] After 1919 when a Handley Page biplane made the first flight to India, landing bumpily at Karachi, it became technically possible for both passengers and mail to travel by air. From this aircraft Sir Henry Lawrence (Commissioner of Sind and great-nephew of his famous namesake) received his first 'aerial letter'. His wife proudly stuck this into their young son's diary with the comment: 'Some day when we are all flying it may be of interest to read of this first flight to India.'[20] That day did not come for some time and it was unusual for families to use airmail or aeroplane travel before the Second World War.

The young Dorothy Wilkins expressed the frustration of many children of her time when she wrote to her parents in 1909: 'Oh I wish I could see you. There are so many questions I should like to ask you but by the time I can get an answer from India I have almost forgotten the question.' In any case, she wrote a few years later: 'Letters tell nothing.'[21] However inadequate Dorothy may have thought her epistles, her father carefully stored them at his mission station in Orissa. Together with those of her sisters Joyce and Phyllis (and a few from their younger brother Eric) they survive today, forming an invaluable record of their exiled years. Joyce herself drew on them, as well as on her memory, when she wrote her *Child's Eye View* in 1992. Sadly, the other side of the correspondence does not exist because the girls had no home in which to store their parents' letters. In 1915, while staying at school for the Easter holidays, Dorothy made a bonfire of her collection: 'I had such a horrid job to do the other day. I destroyed nearly all the letters I've been keeping from you for several years. I had a huge pile and they were getting a bother to keep as I have no room in my drawers. So I set to work and read and burnt and read and burnt until I nearly put the fire out!'[22]

Dorothy had travelled to England with 'Nana' (her step-grandmother) in 1905 when she was seven and she soon started boarding at Walthamstow Hall, the fees for which were paid by the Baptist Missionary Society. Her sisters followed in 1908 and 1911 and all were to spend ten or eleven years at the school, seeing one or both of their parents every three or four years. In a brisk, no-nonsense way Walthamstow did its best to provide a home for all its missionary daughters and also to educate them for an independent career. The headmistress, Sophie Hare, was renowned for her 'complete renunciation of all forms of sentimentality'. Many pupils found her all too bracing, although she could be 'a jolly and friendly companion' to the little ones and 'a great friend' to talented sixth-formers.[23] The Wilkins girls also reacted differently to the school and its staff. Dorothy was a perceptive, capable girl who matured early and tried 'to be as brave as I can and help Joycie to bear it'.[24] Joyce, frequently ill and dyslexic long before the condition was recognised, suffered greatly at school, where reports labelled her careless, unpunctual and disobedient. Her letters reveal an affectionate, public-spirited girl who threw herself enthusiastically into school activities, especially its war efforts after 1914. Phyllis, the cleverest of the three, was probably the happiest at school for she loved academic work and music. She also made a number of close friends, one of whom died in the bed beside her during a measles epidemic in 1917. Phyllis felt everything passionately, veering quickly between the 'very bluest depths of misery . . . and the seventh heaven'.[25]

In such a copious and freely expressed record (for there seems to have been no censorship at Walthamstow) it is possible to pick out from the normal school news the factors which made girls in their position yearn for parental support. Unlike some Empire children, they had no special guardian in England and during the school holidays they either stayed at school or dispersed to various aunts and uncles. They sometimes felt that they were a burden, as Dorothy explained:

> These people only have us out of kindness. You are the only ones we belong to. To others we are somewhat of a nuisance [which] it is their duty to put up with out of charity. Still we can't be with you and I hope I don't make it harder for you. . . . I seem to have spent most of the holiday reading or darning stockings. . . . PS Don't let anything I say trouble you. We haven't seen each other for so many years and letters often give the wrong impression.[26]

It is clear that the relations did their best to care for the girls but that they had worries of their own; during the war, for instance, one family had three sons at the front. Anyway, the sisters had no one to see them win prizes or perform in concerts on Public Days, and there was no one to turn to in times of crisis. When Dorothy was suspected of stealing some money in 1910 she was desperately worried that her parents might believe the unjust charge but told herself bravely that 'a clear conscience can laugh at false accusations'.[27] Towards the end of her school career she longed for more guidance than letters could

give. She wanted to be a doctor so that she could 'ease bodily suffering
... and perhaps as a woman make more bearable those ills which
doctors cannot cure'. But, unable to gain a scholarship for the five-
year course and feeling that her father objected to it, she abandoned
the ambition and settled for a London degree in Psychology. This was
an unusual choice for that time, suggested by Miss Hare. Dorothy
worried that she had 'decided a great many things without [her
father's] permission or wishes being known'. She looked forward
nevertheless to the next stage in her life but longed for her mother's
help in getting together the necessary clothes for college, which
included in those days an evening gown. As it was she felt that 'nobody
is in the least interested here'.[28]

As well as sorting out her own problems, Dorothy 'helped and
strengthened' Joyce, who was always getting into trouble for lateness
and untidiness and going to the Cottage (the school sanatorium) with
spots and headaches. Joyce sent her parents texts to correct and desperate pleas that they should still love her when she got bad reports
or failed her exams. Her lowest point came in September 1917, when
she had to stay down a year after failing the Junior Cambridge exams
and to prepare for Matriculation in the same class as Phyllis. She
needed her parents badly at this time, as this letter in her own dyslexic
spelling demonstrates:

> Oh – is there? Is there any chance of you comming home before
> Xmas? If only you could! I heared a rhumer that you might! O! Do!
> Do! ! Do! ! ! School is so horrid this term with no Dorothy, and being
> in another form with such easy work. . . . Still I know I have to lump
> it – but oh, it is so beastly! I think I should sooner of left than come
> back to this.[29]

As she knew, the war and lack of funds made a parental visit unlikely
and she had to soldier on but Dorothy's daughter tells me that Joyce
was very depressed at this time. When she took and failed Matriculation in 1920 her parents were on furlough (home leave). Although
she did a year's training in speech therapy, she lacked the confidence
to pursue a career in England and went back to India with them to
teach in a mission school for Eurasians. Candid though she was about
her troubles, there were some she had never been able to mention. In
her memoir Joyce tells of being treated for the 'unspeakable crime' of
self-abuse by having her arms strapped to boards. In addition, the

miserable girl thought that she would never now be able to have her own children. 'Anyway,' she thought, 'I could not bear to think of a child of mine suffering as I was suffering.'[30]

Phyllis disclosed similar anxieties to her oldest sister later on but there is certainly no mention of masturbation in her Walthamstow letters. Her mind was on higher things. Aware that her father expected much of his 'Precious Pearl', especially in matters of religion, she often worried that her faith was not strong enough and sought his spiritual guidance. In this letter she asked what it means to love Jesus and ended with this heartfelt lament: 'Oh! I do so wish you here because there are some things I can't ask Dorothy and even she is going away very soon. I feel so stranded when I think of it and I do want someone to ask questions and confide in. Do please love me very much in your next letter, for I'm feeling a bit miserable and "down in the dumps".'[31] Even so, Phyllis managed to set up a religious discussion group for the younger girls. She also got a sweepstake stopped at the ungodly Clapham High School which she attended in 1921–2 to cram for Oxford Entrance. Indeed, all the Wilkins children found comfort in their parents' Evangelical faith. Nine-year-old Eric, newly arrived at Eltham College in 1915, was 'thankful to Jesus for giving me the strength and courage to bear his cross'. Probably he needed every bit of this help to cope with the 'monastic' and 'Spartan life' described by old Elthamians of his generation.[32] Perhaps, though, Dorothy was beginning to resent her parents' devotion to Christian duty. In 1917 she reminded them, 'You belong to us . . . as well as the Mission.'

Teachers also provided solace – unlike the starchy matrons whose 'bracing jests banished self-pity'.[33] Just before leaving school Dorothy went for a picnic with Miss Burtt, who 'has helped me a lot telling me the sort of things I shall need'.[34] When Joyce was seriously ill in 1914 she found that everybody was kind to her and even 'Miss Hair [*sic*] came to see me once!' At the convalescent home to which she was sent for several months of that year she longed to be back at 'dear old Sevenoaks'.[35] And Phyllis had a 'delightful secret understanding' with her music teacher, Doreen Anstey, which brought utter joy to her last months at Walthamstow. She poured out her happiness to her mother, who was in England at that time: 'Miss Anstey gets more topping every day, or every night rather! She is just the best friend any girl could have to help her in every way, and she is the dearest pal I ever had!' To her father she admitted that she did not know how she would exist without Doreen, with only letters to replace 'the lovely long talks we have every night'.[36] The fact that she wrote so frankly to her parents about her teacher's nocturnal visits suggests that they involved nothing more than deep discussions.

It was, however, on the subject of 'sexual perversion' that Dorothy, who had now managed to qualify as a psychiatric doctor, advised the adult Phyllis in 1930. As well as recommending the works of Freud, she assured her sister that homosexuals could often reach 'an irreproachably high standard of mental growth and development'.[37] Indeed, Phyllis went on to become a headmistress but she remained guilt-ridden about her sexual inclinations. Dorothy's skills were also in demand during a nervous breakdown which Joyce suffered while she was teaching in India. Dorothy tried to explain her sister's irrational fear of knives. Eventually, after a course of psychoanalysis, Joyce was able to pursue a successful career as a speech therapist. When, in her nineties, she was interviewed for television she pronounced a verdict on her childhood (and that of her siblings)· 'The parents had a call and they made a big sacrifice; they went out to preach to the heathen. But the sacrifice was also of the children.'[38] Since only one sister married and none of the girls became missionaries they did not have to make the same choice – although Dorothy was devastated when her son and daughter were evacuated during the next war.[39] But Eric Wilkins did return to the mission field in Orissa, where he and his wife had three sons. Would the cycle of separation begin again in the next generation of the Wilkins family?

The Wilkins sisters are unusual both in the frankness of their letters and their subsequent use of Freudian analysis to come to terms with their childhood experiences. Joyce, for instance, later saw her attempt to curl up inside the 'safe and comfortable' bottom drawer of her washstand in the Walthamstow Kindergarten as a desire 'to return to the womb'. All she got was a 'tremendous scolding' from Matron after the washstand tipped over, smashing the basin and ewer.[40] No doubt Freud would have made something of that.

A much more typical account of the years before and during the First World War is the matter-of-fact memoir of Esmée Mascall (née Cra'ster). In 1904, at the age of eight, she was left at a 'homely type of school' called The Lawn. She did not see her mother again until 1906 because 'the sea passage cost so much that on an army officer's pay one would have to scrape and save for *just one parent*, not both, to come Home to the children every other year'. She comments on the separation: 'The Stiff Upper Lip which was a child's duty in those days no doubt prevented us from making much fuss about it.'[41] Iris Portal (née Butler) was similarly stoical when remembering her unnamed school, another refuge for 'orphans of the Empire': 'It never occurred to any of us to blame our parents for leaving us ... We were taught to be very proud of our parents' share in the Empire and to feel that we were doing our bit by being left behind.' She says virtually nothing about her ten years at the school – a case of Freudian suppressed memory perhaps. But she does admit to singing 'Lord dismiss us, *what a blessing*' (instead of 'with thy blessing') with special fervour on the day she left in 1922.[42] In his autobiography John Christie also accepts unquestioningly his parents' decision to consign him in 1913 to St Cyprian's, Eastbourne, where he had 'spells of acute misery and loneliness' and missed camp life with his father's Indian regiment. But he has no sympathy for former pupil Eric Blair, with his 'outsize chip' on the shoulder, stoutly insisting that his own seven years at the school 'were, on the whole, happy' and blessing it for knocking into his head enough knowledge to gain him a place at Eton.[43]

For Douglas Jardine, son of a Bombay lawyer, it was cricket that softened the blow of separation. After he got into the First XI at Horris Hill Prep School in 1912, 'not a match was lost'. At Winchester he became 'one of the best schoolboy batsmen ever'. He also learnt, according to his biographer, a 'monumental toughness and unfailing confidence in one's convictions'. This enabled him, as England's cricket captain, to remain 'outwardly impervious to the waves of hate' that greeted his team's use of body-line bowling in Australia in 1932.[44] On the other hand Hugh Gaitskell, who followed Jardine to Winchester after many itinerant years away from his Burma-based parents, played sports 'without enthusiasm'. He distinguished himself as a combative debater but was otherwise, according to his housemaster, 'a quiet, modest and undemonstrative boy of whom no one would have predicted his future [as leader of the Labour Party]'. Gaitskell always maintained that he had 'a conventionally happy childhood'. But it is clear that he was a lonely lad, with no family life after his beloved older brother and sister had left England. Winchester was not much help. After leaving the school Gaitskell wrote to his brother: 'I believe that Winchester destroys, ties up, suppresses the natural vitality of almost all who go there.'[45]

School was no comfort to his fellow-exile, Wilfred Bion. In his autobiography Bion claims that until he became good at rugby and athletics the only redeeming feature in the 'appalling period' of his life at prep and public school (1905–14) was 'sex, wiggling of whatever variety'. 'Games were substituted for sex', he later wrote, having by then become a professional psychiatrist. For 'in those pre-Freudian days sex, nurtured and cosseted and titillated by the segregation of boys in public schools, was a PROBLEM'. But sport did not solve all Wilfred's problems, because they went too deep. Even becoming captain of the First Rugby XV in his last year was 'dust and ashes'. Reunited with his parents after many years apart he found that he was 'imprisoned, unable to break out of the shell which adhered to me'.[46] His hasty departure for the war and long service in the trenches only accentuated this tendency. More than most traumatised soldiers, Bion felt estranged from his family when he came home on leave: 'relations with anyone I respected were intolerable, notably with my mother'.[47] He longed to be back at the front.

The war, which provided Bion's psychological escape route, accentuated the difficulties of a new wave of young exiles whose parents seized the chance to get them to Britain while they could. They coped with these new circumstances as best they could and by no means all of them suffered the traumas of young Wilfred. Kissane Keane was only fourteen months old when she journeyed with her pregnant mother from Agra to Dublin, leaving Michael Keane to his work in the Indian Civil Service. The war, which was declared on the same day as Kissane's sister was born, was to shape the childhood of both little girls. Not only had it hastened their departure from India but it also deprived them of two grandmotherly homes. First they had to leave their paternal grandmother's home in troubled Dublin because the war gave Irish nationalists the opportunity they sought to rebel. The younger Mrs Keane took her daughters to live with her own mother in Devon before setting off on the dangerous sea voyage around the Cape to rejoin her husband in India. It was not long before the war forced the sisters out of this home too. Their Devon grandmother suffered a breakdown after losing three sons in combat and the girls were sent off to stay with a series of relations and friends, many of whom they had never previously met. Yet, far from regarding herself as a victim, Kissane remembers their wanderings as an adventure. The girls often travelled by train in the charge of the guard and, on one occasion when nobody was there to meet them at a Bedfordshire station, they spent the night in the cosy warm kitchen of the signalman's house, 'head-to-toe on an old couch'.[48] Kissane reports that 'no one was ever unpleasant to us' – apart from a few of the children required to share their nurseries with two strange girls who had no toys or possessions to recommend them.

Eventually the war brought a reprieve from this itinerant life. An Irish family friend, a war widow who wanted companionship for her wild fatherless son, took them into her Cornish farmhouse. They were joined by a baby brother whom they hardly knew. He had been born in England just after the war, when their mother briefly returned, and left in the care of his nurse so that Mrs Keane could go back to India. This time in Cornwall was 'a really good period', during which the girls walked daily to St Catherine's PNEU school in Bude (at which they had previously boarded) and had adventures on the farm and seashore. Their teenage years were, however, blighted by their being moved to an 'upper-crust' girls' boarding school in Surrey, where the motto admonished them to embrace a life of *Service and Sanctification*. Unlike her more rebellious sister, Kissane stuck it out until Matriculation. When she passed, her father summoned her to stand in for her mother, who had had enough of India. On the outward journey Kissane received a telegram saying that Sir Michael Keane (as he now was) intended to spend six months' leave in England before taking up a new post as Governor of Bengal and required her to turn round at Bombay and go home again. Aged eighteen, she asserted her hard-won independence and insisted on awaiting her father's return in India. 'I had grown up living with strangers,' she told me triumphantly, 'and I could do a bit more of it.'

Kissane found 'memories just pouring out' as she spoke and wrote about her unsettled and mostly homeless childhood. There is not a hint of self-pity or criticism in her account. Her greatest sadness is that her adored father died only two months after his retirement. She insists, as do so many Raj children, that the experience of separation was worse for her mother than for her. (Ironically, it was Mrs Keane who had most strongly favoured the arrangement because she herself had grown up in India, envying her brothers who had been sent to school in England.) The only clue to the girls' nagging anxiety about the long absence of their parents is their obsession with the hymn, 'Eternal Father Strong to Save'. At boarding school they would sing it every night in the dormitory until an exasperated matron stuck her head round the door and said: 'For goodness sake, children, go to sleep – your parents can't *still* be in peril on the sea!'

Another mother who risked peril at sea was Edith Brown, the wife of Bengal missionary Revd James Brown. In 1916 she brought her two youngest children, eight-year-old Charlie and four year old Leila, to join their older sisters, Olive, Joan and Marjorie, in England. They had to wear life jackets and their boat was nearly torpedoed. Leila's most painful memory, however, is not of that voyage. It is of her mother's walk away from Walthamstow Hall towards Sevenoaks station at the start of her journey back to India in 1918: 'I never really got over that.'[49] At the age of ninety-two, Leila still gets upset when she recalls that parting. She saw her parents only once during her time at the school for they were busy helping others. As her father wrote in his memoir, his wife could be a 'better colleague and helpmeet' now that she didn't have to nurse the children through 'infantile complaints', which had often caused great inconvenience. When, for instance, Joan had suffered from dysentery at the age of two they had prayed that Mrs Brown would not have to miss an important missionary convention. 'If Joan got worse,' her father noted in his memoir, 'all our arrangements for our guests and the meetings would be upset and spoilt.' Once all the children had left, though, 'my wife entered fully into all my work'.[50]

After her mother's departure, Leila languished at Walthamstow Hall, where one of her first experiences was contracting influenza in the post-war epidemic, during which a teacher and a pupil died. She describes herself as a 'nasty, shy child wondering why my parents had left me'. Soon after she arrived Miss Hare was replaced by Miss Euphemia Ramsay, who receives many plaudits in the school's official history. But Leila thought of her as 'the battering ram' because of her unjust (though not corporal) punishments. Leila was once banned from swimming for three weeks because she had gone to collect her swimming-costume at the wrong time. A keen patron still of the glorious outdoor pool in Cambridge, which is a hundred yards long, she has never forgotten being deprived of one of her few pleasures at school. It also still rankles that Miss Ramsay did not try to get her a grant for university, as she did later for her cousin. She feels that she 'was not worth bothering about'.

By the time her parents returned to live in England in 1929 Leila was an independent young woman with a secretarial qualification which enabled her to stay in work all through the Depression. She lived with her parents for some time but never re-established a close relationship with them. Like her three sisters she remained single, another legacy of First World War slaughter. Their spinsterhood was also a result, Leila considers, of spending the school holidays with a guardian who would not let them meet any young men. At no point in my interview with her did she repine about her own childhood. But she did say that both Charlie and Marjorie had 'needed parents very badly' and suffered as a result. As for herself, she revealed that she is not as good a churchgoer as she should be because 'Christianity to me means that parents were in one place and you in another'. Without using any Freudian language, Leila demonstrated the long-lasting effects of an insecure childhood.

While these children in Britain endured the wartime hardships of dangerous journeys, longer separations, lost letters, food shortages and preoccupied guardians, those who remained in India were hardly aware of the conflict unless they had friends or relations at the front. Margaret Tait, daughter of a college principal, stayed in Bangalore, enjoying 'gorgeous parties', 'military spectacles and sports' and the care of her sweet-tempered ayah. But her unpublished memoir also describes daily trips to the newspaper office with her father. As they read the casualty lists 'it sometimes seemed as if all our soldier friends had been killed or wounded'.[51] Diamond Hardinge, whose father's term as Viceroy was extended because of the war, lost one of her brothers in 1914, the year that her mother died. For most children in India, however, the victory celebrations in 1918 made more of an impression than the war had done. In Simla, Colonel Cecil Kaye (father of Mollie and Bets) sounded a Burmese gong which could be heard all over the town, soon to be 'decked out with coloured bunting and strings of coloured flags' for two days of 'non-stop *tamashas* [celebrations]', services of thanksgiving and victory parades.[52] Pamela Kirkpatrick (née Watson) recalls that one of her last experiences before being sent back to England was taking part in the grand pageant at Poona, where her father was stationed as an officer. Her beautiful mother, who was always 'a bit of a star', appeared as the British Empire, while eight-year-old Pamela represented France.[53]

The Kayes and the Watsons, like other parents, were relieved that they could now send their children to British schools in the normal fashion. Pamela Watson simply accepted the inevitable while the Kaye sisters hoped that all the boats would be too full to take them. Most expatriates did not realise how altered Britain would be. Many of the households which children now joined were affected by bereavement, the dearth of men, physical and psychological damage, prolonged rationing and, after a brief post-war boom, rising unemployment. The sober mood was reflected in the Cenotaph, designed by Sir Edwin

Lutyens, and in the dignified ceremony organised by Lord Curzon to inaugurate it in 1920. The 'stark simplicity' of both contrasted with the grandeur with which both men had celebrated the Raj – Curzon (as Viceroy) with his spectacular 1903 durbar, and Lutyens (son-in-law of another Viceroy, Lord Lytton), with the construction of New Delhi.[54]

Among the children packed on to post-war boats there were several who later made their names: Mollie Kaye, facing her 'bleak years of separation'; John Masters, a competitive boy who 'needed to run faster, to bowl faster' than anyone else once he got to Wellington; Vivien Leigh (née Hartley), a 'delicate, sensitive and shy' girl bound for the Convent of the Sacred Heart at Roehampton; and Sonia Brownell, later married to George Orwell, who was off to join the 'lonely little schemers' at the same school. Their stories are told in published works.[55] Less well known are the experiences of Robert and Beatrice Baker. In 1921, at the ages of seven and five, they departed from their south Indian plantation to board the *Morea* with their mother, nurse and baby brother David. Two years later Mrs Baker left Robert and Beatrice with relations in Essex and took young David back to Kumerakom. Like Eric Wilkins, another child forsaken by his older siblings, he was consoled with an expensive toy pedal car. It was the photograph of David in this car, still displayed in the Bakers' bungalow after its conversion into a luxury hotel, which led me to David's sister, Beatrice Broad, and to his brother's widow, Paula Baker. Through conversations with them and through the late Robert Baker's oral and written memoirs (1983), I found out about their childhoods before the Second World War and about those of the next generation.

The Bakers, who had worked as missionaries and planters in south India since the early nineteenth century, had always sent their offspring home to be educated. But for some reason George Baker, father of Robert, Beatrice and David, had not been dispatched until he was over twelve, with the result that he always carried with him the taint of having been 'country-born'. So Robert's memoir accepts that his father was right to avoid the 'primrose path' of keeping him in India, even though his English exile took him over some rough and thorny ways. He was sent to King's School, Canterbury, in those days 'a savage, backward place' where he was sometimes 'unhappy beyond words'. He suffered from beating, bullying, 'gross injustice' and acute acne for which his housemaster prescribed a trough of cold water.

Luckily, Robert was good at games, despite being permanently hungry: the only food provided after the midday meal was cocoa and biscuits. His prowess at rugby meant that in the end he could look back on his schooldays with some pleasure.[56] The same cannot be said of the holidays when, both his sister and his widow told me, he was 'miserable as sin'. He usually stayed in Shoeburyness with his father's cousin and her husband, whom he describes as 'a good man with no great social standing'. Robert remembered no diversions except five church services most Sundays, games of bagatelle, gathering mushrooms and occasional visits to the cinema. But what made him unhappy was the sense of being an intruder, a 'feeling of not being at home'. He tells of various occasions when he was severely reprimanded for mistakes 'which would have been understood by a parent'. At least, though, rationing ended in 1921 and he could look forward to high tea when Aunt Kitty served 'huge quantities' of buns, jam, butter, cakes, cold ham and kippers.[57]

Robert's only other consolation during the holidays was that he could bicycle every day to see Beatrice, who lived with their grandmother and unmarried aunt. The brother and sister understood that it was impossible for them to be together because 'two children extra would have been too much to ask of anyone'. Nevertheless there was between them the 'very strong bond that children have for each other who are away from their parents'.[58] Beatrice looked forward to Robert's visits all the more keenly since her over-anxious grandmother would never allow her to play with neighbouring children. It was a rather dull life for a child, with little to do except attend frequent church services and read to her grandmother. She envied the life described by her mother in weekly letters from Kumerakom. But it was not until she moved to Malvern Girls' College that Beatrice became positively miserable. The headmistress at that time was only interested in 'girls who were clever or musical or had important parents'. Beatrice's skills in tennis and dancing did not bring her much credit – nor did it help that her father, whose estate was affected by the trade slump which began in 1930, was sometimes slow to pay the fees. She was further embarrassed by having to explain to the Ling sisters, with whom she now boarded in the holidays, that their bill would be paid late. Clothes were another problem, as they were for many girls with no mother on hand to give advice. Neither the Misses Ling nor Grandmother had much idea. So when Beatrice had to dine with the headmistress her afternoon dress was 'not quite the thing'. Still, her python-skin shoes put up her stock – they had been made from snakes killed on the plantation.

With some reluctance, Beatrice told me her childhood was deprived and endorsed her son's assessment that she had lacked both love and money. She grew up into a beautiful young woman and, on returning to Kumerakom, she was 'overwhelmed by the loveliness of it all'. It would not have been difficult for her to find a husband there for she had many admirers. But she did not want to marry and settle in India, and to repeat the same pattern of separation. Instead Beatrice returned to England and, when war broke out, she joined the WRAF. Her brother, David, entered the RAF and was killed on duty. Beatrice had adored him and was completely devastated by his loss but later in the war she met her future husband, Vivien Broad, another pilot. When they married and had children, she tried very hard, her son Graham testifies, to give them a 'good home and plenty of love'. She was determined to provide the material and emotional support which she had lacked during her twelve years of exile.[59]

Another child afflicted, like the Bakers, by inter-war tribulations was seven-year-old Frances Labey. She was the daughter of a Hooghly River pilot and her parents brought her to England in 1927. For the next five years Frances alternated between a South Coast boarding school and her aunt's house in Surrey, without seeing her parents. As she told me, this is 'a long time for a child'. Frances was much younger than any other child in the school and she was to some extent mothered by the older girls. But she had to endure an exhausting, cold and comfortless regime and she longed for the physical and emotional warmth of her Indian home. The only thing she remembers with pleasure is a beautiful green woodpecker on the front lawn, which reminded her of the colourful little parrots she had loved in Calcutta. Her memories of Aunt Reeny's house are bleak. She was compared unfavourably with her three girl cousins, especially the one nearest her in age who was 'brilliant and beautiful'.

Like Robert Baker, Frances feels that she was judged harshly and tells a story strikingly similar to one of his. Whereas he was rebuked for picking up a hot gas-mantle which disintegrated into powder, Frances was scolded for spilling the potatoes when she was startled by the gas popping. Both incidents, unimportant in themselves, betray their common feeling of being guests in other people's houses, where they had to be on their best behaviour. In fact Frances was a highly responsible child, sharing with Beatrice Baker an unusual understanding of adults' problems. She was aware, for instance, of the effects the war had had on her father and on her aunt's husband. She wept as she remembered her father's waking up with terrible nightmares in their Calcutta flat and her uncle's struggling to earn his living in the City despite the after-effects of gas poisoning. She told me, 'It's quite hard to realise how poor everyone was after the war and how mentally shattered all the men were.'

Frances was rescued when her mother brought her sister Jane to England in 1932. She was shocked by her daughter's general unhappiness and her raw chilblains, made worse by tight-fitting combinations which no one had bothered to replace. Mrs Labey at once removed her from the school. The arrangements she made this time were much happier. Both her girls were taken to live in Jersey with a Professor Stapleton, who 'never talked down to children', and his wife, who 'loved children and animals'. Frances can still feel her relief at having considerate guardians and the company of her sister. But Jane, newly delivered from the care of an indulgent ayah, speaks of her 'traumas and night-fears' at the Jersey boarding school they both attended: 'You were taught not to show your emotions and had to be repressed.' However, both women are sorrier for their mother than they are for their young selves. For Mrs Labey came close to losing her husband even though she had, as was usual in those days, placed his interests before those of her children. Frances had been promised that on leaving school she could go back to India with the 'fishing fleet', but when the time came her father 'didn't want any of us out there because he was falling in love with someone else'. So Mrs Labey took her older daughter to France to go to a business school and then set up house in Jersey, where her errant husband eventually joined her after his retirement. The island is still home for Frances and Jane. They have never returned to India but maintain links with the country through an Indian who was once an apprentice of their father's on the Hooghly. Today Frances speaks with pride rather than bitterness about George Labey's work in the Bengal Pilot Service.[60]

The inter-war period did not affect all families adversely. Those with safe jobs, who had not been caught up in the First World War, often benefited from the falling prices which accompanied the Depression. Many senior ICS men and Indian Army officers felt no economic hardship during these years. Ruth Quadling (née Starte) told me, for instance, that her father 'never had to worry about money' after he joined the ICS in 1919, even though he came from a poor family. As a district judge in the Bombay Presidency Harold Starte could afford a spacious bungalow and plenty of servants, including both an English nanny and an Indian ayah for his three children. Although they had been healthy and happy during their first few years in Dharwar, the oldest two, Ruth and Roger, were brought to England in 1927 at the ages of six and five. They were luckier than many children in that they both stayed (with Nanny too) at the home of their grandmother and maiden aunt in Leamington, where they were joined later by their younger brother Gordon. Moreover they were not at first sent away to school and their mother could afford to visit the children regularly. According to Mrs Starte's own notes these English trips were biennial (1930–31 and 1933). In Ruth's memory they happened every year, perhaps because the seaside and farm holidays they all spent together were very important to her. In between times, however, Grandmother ('a real old-fashioned person') and Aunt Freda (a trained infant teacher) ruled with a rod of iron and without much obvious affection.

Eventually, the children became 'too naughty', Ruth remembers, and had to be sent to boarding school. Ruth, now about ten, survived after an initial period of misery but Gordon, who was only six, never adjusted to his prep school, from which he sent sad letters home saying that no one would play with him. Ruth thinks that this is why her parents quitted India in 1934, even though her father loved his work there. The children left their boarding schools and grandmother's regime to live with their parents. Now they could all have a pet of their choice and a room of their own, while attending private day schools close to home. Mr Starte had obviously retired on a good pension for, as far as Ruth recalls, there were still 'no money worries'.[61] And all three children went on to university, an opportunity denied youngsters like Leila Brown, the Labeys and the Bakers. So for the Starte children the blow of separation was softened by parents who were willing and able to respond to their emotional needs. This was unusual but not unique. When the time came for Richard and Jill Sarson to go to school their Norwegian mother came to England with them, leaving her husband, a retired colonel, to take up a new post as tutor to a maharaja. Richard thinks that she must have had a lonely time, living in a flat in Bournemouth for two years before her husband left India in 1936 – but he is glad not to have been 'badly damaged' as were some of his contemporaries.[62]

In general, parents preferred to stress the need for self-discipline and courage in the face of adversity. Armine Mathias often had to call on these qualities after she was brought to England from north India in 1926 aged three. It was her mother who insisted that she should be 'brought up English' from such an early age. Her father, an officer in the Indian Army and 'a perfect English gentleman', would have preferred to keep her (and later her brother Quentin) in India, where he himself had been educated. As there were no suitable relations available to look after Armine she was left with family friends in Norfolk who had a child of her age. 'They were wonderful to me', Armine told me, 'but they weren't my parents and I never had my own home, which does have an effect.' The first effect was that she earned a reputation as 'a naughty child' who had to be withdrawn from smart parties in big houses when she got over-excited. It is not clear whether this behaviour was the reason for Armine's being placed in a different family (of army friends) when her mother returned to England for the birth of Quentin. The new arrangement was less satisfactory because all the children were younger than Armine. But at least she was now happy at a co-educational Quaker boarding school.

After a delay caused not by the needs of her children but by the Quetta earthquake of 1935, Mrs Mathias returned to India with Quentin. By now his sister had become deeply attached to him, another effect perhaps of her rootless upbringing. She collected into an album all the photographs of him sent by her mother from India. Once Quentin was brought over to school in his turn, Armine had someone to love and it is obvious from all she says that she adored and mothered this 'good little boy'. The Mathias's army friends having been posted abroad, Armine and Quentin lived for a time with their grandfather, 'who didn't like children'. Later they stayed with the Archdeacon of Durham and his 'delightful' family, who had answered their parents' desperate advertisement for guardians. Quentin was to remain with this family all through the war, after Armine's return to India. But although they loved him dearly he was always 'a lone child', unhappy at his various boarding schools.

By the time she was seventeen Armine had lived in four different households, with occasional periods of staying with cousins. She had travelled the country alone by train, endured several painful illnesses without complaint and put up with the unsuitable clothes that guardians invariably provided. She had eventually learnt to control her feelings and to behave 'like a soldier's daughter'. In 1940 she returned at her parents' bidding to India, where she quickly fell in love and became a soldier's wife in 1941; when her fiancé was ordered back to

Europe who got married at four days' notice wearing a converted evening dress. The very next year, tragically, Armine lost her second chance of a happy family life. Her young husband was killed while fighting in North Africa.

Apparently her mother did not even consider coming to England, where Armine was now living, to administer comfort to the soldier's widow. In due course Armine joined the Institute of the Blessed Virgin Mary (IBVM) religious community, which has been her family ever since. She still maintains that the long separation was worse for her parents than for her: 'They don't have that intimacy with their grown-up children when they come back from India that they might have had. My mother had a mental picture of their retiring and us being there for them but we weren't. They weren't there for us and we weren't there for them.' On balance, though, she is glad that she was not brought up in the 'idle and opulent' milieu of India's officer class, arguing that 'it's not good for children to have servants and everything done for them'. But she is pleased too that all this is 'a thing of the past'.[63]

The dearth of suitable relations, apparent in several of these stories, was a common problem for Raj families in the twentieth century. Since many ICS men and army officers now came from quite ordinary backgrounds, their British relations lived in smaller houses which could not easily accommodate several extra children. This was also the case with most missionaries' families, as the Wilkins sisters found when they had so frequently to move bedrooms or houses during the holidays. And now that the two-child family had become the norm, there were fewer siblings to look after nephews and nieces from abroad. To respond to the need there grew up a network of holiday homes which took in strangers' children. Many of those interviewed by Laurence Fleming spent their holidays in such establishments, which sometimes even accommodated 'babies and toddlers who were looked after by Norland Nannies'.[64] Sonia Brownell's mother made a living after her divorce in 1930 by providing Indian exiles with a second home. A friend of Mrs Kaye also 'eked out her small income ... by looking after the left-behind children of friends and relatives'. The only trouble was, in the view of Mollie Kaye, who was one of her charges, that 'Aunt Bee ... didn't know the first thing about children and she did not want to'.[65]

There were certainly no checks into the suitability of these guardians, on whom many expatriate parents now relied. The dangers of private fostering, which is still a common practice today, were emphasised in a 1997 government report. It concluded that unregulated fostering puts children at 'very considerable risk' and should be made illegal. This recommendation was not implemented and after the death of Victoria Climbié at the hands of her foster parents in 2002 Lord Laming was appointed to investigate the circumstances behind the tragedy. In her evidence to his inquiry a health visitor observed that West Africans who have their children fostered in Britain aim to give them an educational head start. She could have been commenting on ambitious Anglo-Indian parents a generation earlier.[66]

It is impossible to say whether fostering children with strangers was more or less hazardous during the time of the Raj than sending them to live with family members. Relations, whom expatriate parents did not always know very well, could turn out to be unkind or negligent while paid guardians could, like Mrs Brownell, offer 'kindness and understanding to lonely children'.[67] The children I have studied had a range of experiences. At one extreme a boy developed long-term mental illness as a result of the neurotic obsessions of his carer, who was a family member. At the other is Jack Judah (brother of Naomi and Rachel, who appeared in Chapter Five), who hated being sent away from Bombay but was relieved that he did not have to spend the holidays with his Orthodox Jewish relations. Instead he and Naomi stayed with a guardian they nicknamed KM, standing for Kind Mother. Jack says that he was very close to her and that her children were 'like brother and sisters'.[68] Somewhere in between the two extremes was Pamela Watson, who had two sets of loving grandparents to act as a refuge from 'the toughest girls' school in the country where nothing mattered except games' and she was 'bullied unmercifully as a dud'. She considers herself lucky but she did suffer from always being with old people: 'I never met any young men until I went back to India at eighteen.'[69]

An alternative to foster parents were home schools in which children stayed all the year round. They sound like a perpetuation of Dickensian establishments such as that run by Mrs Pipchin, but I have discovered no instances of cruelty to match hers. According to a memoir written by Margot Maxwell-Gumbleton (née Bell) about St Catherine's at Bexhill-on-Sea, the priorities were 'manners, religion and patriotism'. This school was chosen for Margot and her three older siblings because Granny Bell was too old and her house too small to accommodate them all. Jessie, Billy and Robert were left there in 1913 when they were

twelve, seven and five. Jessie fared well but Robert cried himself to
sleep every night. In Margot's opinion Billy 'faced it with more bravado
but was affected as deeply'.

She herself went to St Catherine's in 1923 when she was seven,
having failed in her attempt to persuade her parents to take her back
to India with them. She was left 'sobbing in the rather beautiful
drawing-room of the Misses O'Sullivan'. But she soon merged in with
the other children of 'Civil Servants, Engineers, Bankers, Army Officers, Forestry Officers, Police Officers, or the 101 other occupations
that kept the Empire running smoothly'. Weekly letters were
exchanged but Margot admits that 'both children and parents were
hard put to it to think of anything to write about'. The ten years of
her education (the last three being spent at Sherborne with holidays
at St Catherine's) 'passed in a grey fog'. Writing as though she is
describing someone else, Margot sums up her childhood: 'Since the
age of seven she had been in one school or another. She had lived in
school uniforms, in school routines, and knew nothing about living in
a family; and very little about either of her parents. She had met up
with them twice in ten years.' Despite having been so thoroughly
institutionalised, Margot was nevertheless able to resume a relationship with her parents when she returned to 'an extremely pleasant
life' in India. After her mother's death in 1934 she stayed on until 1937
as companion and consort to her father, R. D. Bell, who was completing
his career in the Bombay Civil Service.[70]

Home schools were an unsatisfactory solution, though doubtless the
pupils often had fun together – as the Wilkins sisters did when they
had to spend the Easter holidays at Walthamstow. Peter Lloyd claims
that he was quite happy when he sometimes had to stay on for the
holidays at his prep school. As soon as the rest of the boys had left the
building the headmaster 'transformed himself into a distant but benign
uncle'. Peter and any other boys left after the end of term were allowed
to roam in the woods with a rook rifle all day 'as long as we presented
ourselves reasonably clean and tidy at meal times'.[71] That was all very
well, but parents understandably preferred their children to be cared
for in private homes rather than institutions. The trouble was that it
often involved moving between different guardians (professional or
private), frequently travelling around the country in the care of Universal Aunts, ladies who were paid to step into the breach. How well
children survived this gypsy life depended on their physical and
mental stamina.

Raleigh Trevelyan spent the 'years of blankness' from eight to fourteen alternating between the 'Spartan' Horris Hill prep school and the 'various relations and friends' with whom he was boarded during the holidays. Like most children he accepted it all at the time 'as a kind of inevitable turn of the wheel in my existence'. It was only when looking back that he realised how much he had disliked school life (which still caused him nightmares as an adult) and what he had missed 'by not having had a home for six years'. Two memories capture the embarrassment and insecurity felt by Raleigh and by many other children in this position. One, predictably, involves clothes: he was upset by having to wear the cast-offs of older boys in the families with whom he boarded and hated with particular passion an overcoat with a velvet collar. The other memory (which Trevelyan still finds distressing) consists of a remark which he overheard one relation make to another: 'It's your turn to have Raleigh for Christmas.' The lonely child took refuge in dreams of Gulmarg and Gilgit, where he had once been so happy.[72]

The poet Alan Ross described a similar response in his autobiography *Blindfold Games*. He too dreamed of India during his years of 'alienation from all family life'. 'The very sight of the word Bengal began to induce an obsessiveness close to morbidity.' Between 1929 and 1940 he was sent to three different boarding schools (ending up at Haileybury) and farmed out with two different families, in Cornwall and in Surrey. 'Strangers were always good to me,' he recalls, 'but however well you are treated, you never lose the feeling of being a paying guest.' There were good times, playing games or going for bicycle rides with guardians' children and developing a lifelong passion for cricket at his various schools. Ross also tells of bad times when he learnt not to place any trust in those around him. At school he was told by a prefect that he was 'wanted down by the bushes' – where he was promptly ambushed and assaulted by a group of older boys. And at his second foster home he was cast out of the affections of the homely Mrs Brack when her favourite son arrived on the scene. By the time he went to Oxford he had become detached not only from his parents (who were now the strangers) but from everyone else. During his wartime service in the Navy he felt this lack of involvement acutely: 'If anyone was expendable it was I.'[73]

Trevelyan and Ross emphasise the psychological toll of a childhood divided between institutions and other people's houses. For children who were physically frail such a regime could prove exhausting.

Travel-sickness, which afflicted many of these peripatetic youngsters, made matters worse. Joyce and Eric Wilkins were often sick on train journeys and had to cope as best they could without adult help. Roger Moore, the only child of a Madras businessman, who was 'farmed out to various people' during his English schooldays in the 1930s, told me two poignant stories of physical and emotional discomfiture. When he was only six he had to stay on at school during the Christmas holidays because he had scarlet fever. He remembers being so bored that he broke into a torch he had been given, spilling the black battery liquid all over the bed, a misdemeanour which got him into 'big trouble'. On a later occasion he was riding in the front of a two-seater car with a couple whom he 'didn't know at all well'. He did not dare tell them when he began to feel queasy and after he had been sick, he was put into the dicky at the back of the car for the rest of the journey.[74] His parents, Humphrey and Nora Moore, returned to England for good in 1937 when Roger was ten. But, as the next chapter will reveal, the Second World War was to bring him further heartache.

The consequences of a nomadic childhood could be more serious than fatigue or car-sickness. William Brown was one of the less fortunate ones. In 1929 he was brought back at the age of four from Bombay, where his father was a district collector. For several years he and his siblings boarded with a kindly Scottish woman who ran a 'home from home' for young children. Things changed when he was seven and considered old enough for Craigflower prep school and holidays spent in the Highlands with various aunts and uncles 'who did what they could to take the place of parents'. William thinks that he was not ready for the tough environment of Craigflower, which treated the boys 'like small men': 'I was too young but what else could [my parents] do?' The constant activity from 7 a.m. to 8 p.m., the freezing cold dormitories and the frigid atmosphere (in which close contact between brothers was frowned on) took their toll on William. He developed a limp and it was eventually discovered that he had juvenile arthritis, which caused him to be in hospital on and off until he was sixteen and deprived him permanently of the use of his left arm and leg. The cause of this illness is still unknown but doctors believe that 'physical and emotional stress play some part in setting off attacks'.[75] William himself thinks that it could have been triggered by his misery at school. 'If it had been possible for me to stay in India,' William concludes, 'I probably wouldn't have the disability I have.'

But there was an emotional bonus to compensate for his physical suffering. When William was ten, Leslie and Netta Brown decided to retire early so that they could look after him. They took him on a recuperative holiday to Switzerland and Mr Brown, who was a classical scholar, taught him at home for six or seven years. William passed his exams and took a university degree by correspondence. He considers himself luckier than his brother George (the Glaxo-fed baby mentioned in Chapter Six), who spent years at a boarding school he disliked. In adult life William himself worked for the British Council in India, which meant that he sent his daughters to Walthamstow (now open to non-missionary families). Unlike his own parents, he and his wife saw their offspring three times a year when they came out for the school holidays, at government expense, and had 'a grand time'. With characteristic generosity, William insists that the long separations of the past were felt more deeply by parents like his own than by children like himself. He bears no grudge and does not really accept Leslie Brown's description of him as 'a casualty of the British Empire'.[76]

Beatrice Turner is less forgiving. She was born a year later than William Brown, in Ceylon, where she spent her first eight years. She came to England in 1934 and went to a boarding school chosen for her by post. In this Anglican convent she spent four or five years, escaping from the repressive rules and the bullying of other girls by dreaming of Ellagalla, her old home. Bitterly she writes in her unpublished memoir: 'I do not think children should be put into situations beyond their control by parents who . . . have organised their children's lives to give themselves the minimum amount of trouble.' She expressly likens her situation to that of Rudyard Kipling as portrayed in *Baa Baa, Black Sheep*, a comparison which William Brown emphatically rejects in his own case. Yet Beatrice spent all her holidays with the same 'gentle, loving' Aunt Vera who had been her nanny/governess in Ceylon and who tried hard to amuse her niece with outings and walks at the grandparental home in Scarborough. What Beatrice resented was that her mother 'was simply *not there*'. She claims to have been 'brought up by correspondence', through her parents' 'unemotional and undemonstrative' missives and her own letters from school, in which 'no one could ever . . . give a hint of unhappiness'. When Mrs Turner did come to visit in 1936, Beatrice recognised her only by the clothes she wore: 'If Mother had been wearing different clothes I would not have given her another glance.'

After both parents came home on leave in 1939, however, Mrs Turner did not return with her husband to 'the social sunlit life of

Ellagalla', feeling it her duty to be with her daughter in wartime
Britain. She and Beatrice, who was now happier in the more liberated
atmosphere of Headington School, lived together during the holidays,
sharing lodgings 'in other people's houses'. But the separation had
already done irreparable harm, as Beatrice tries to explain:

> The reason for her not returning with Father and missing the war
> was me. She assumed full responsibility for me when I was thirteen
> and she had never been totally in charge of me on a one-to-one basis
> before. We had only had a few months in each other's company
> since 1934 when I was eight. The distance between being eight
> years old and thirteen years old represents a spectacular range of
> development in the human child.

With no settled home and no siblings to create a diversion, mother and
daughter were locked into a difficult relationship. Eventually Beatrice
escaped into the WRNS. After the war she went to London where she
trained as a radiographer. Now she sensed that her mother was both
jealous of her independence and disappointed in the way she had
grown up: 'Instead of a well-polished, accomplished young lady I
had emerged as a tongue-tied, hoydenish young female.' On her part
Beatrice felt that she was a 'Colonial-born', caught between two worlds.
At the age of twenty-eight she decided to escape from both by emi-
grating to New Zealand. Her memoir was written for her own children,
who are New Zealanders and with whom she has tried to forge a better
relationship than she was able to have with her own absent parents.
'If the exposure of the chip on my shoulder helps some other child
through life, then the soul-baring will have been to some purpose.'[77]

You don't have to read Freud (or Philip Larkin) to know that parents
are, at best, a mixed blessing. When the two generations are living
together as a family there is usually friction. This is what the Wilkins
sisters found in the scattered years of furlough when they were
reunited with their parents. 'We frequently quarrelled among ourselves and had rows with Mother,' Joyce remembers. But because their
parents had to go back to the mission field in India the girls were
plagued with guilt.[78] Quarrels are bad enough when a family is
together, but worse when they are separated. Then there can be no
kissing and making up. This is obviously what an old boy of Eltham
College had in mind when he recalled that there was always something
missing in his childhood: 'That something was Home; a base among

the lovable, irritating males and females who collectively make up a family.'[79]

For all their faults and failures, parents are 'a uniquely caring force in a child's development'. As John and Elizabeth Newson concluded from their extended observation of Nottingham parents and children in the 1970s: 'The crucial characteristic of the parental role is its *partiality* for the individual child. That is why all the caring agencies that we can devise can never be quite as satisfactory as the "good-enough" parent. ... A developing personality needs to know that to someone it matters more than other children.'[80] And so children who had to live as guests in other people's homes, doing their best to be inconspicuous, can rightly be described as casualties of Empire. It was not enough to send across the oceans 'as much love as the ships will hold'.[81]

EIGHT

'The Last of the Empire's Children'
World War II

'We were the last of the Empire's children, fashioned for a world of certainties but living in a world of transition.' Stephen Brookes's comment hardly conveys the agony of his own family's escape from Burma 'through dense jungles and swamps, across mountains and rivers for three hundred miles in the rainy season'.[1] But it does describe the general experience of children born into stable Empire families and jolted into a world war which would threaten their homes in both Europe and Asia. Some had to risk their lives in adventurous journeys by sea or air. Some had to endure prolonged separation from parents, rendered more painful by uncertain communication. Some were terrified (though others were excited) by the sound of sirens, the sight of bomber-planes or the prospect of invasion. Some lost years of schooling, some lost their freedom, and some, like Stephen Brookes, lost everything.

A global war which endangered civilians as much as combatants prompted much thought about human rights in general and about the needs of children in particular. Sigmund Freud had come to Britain in 1938 to escape Nazi persecution of Austrian Jews. He died soon after the beginning of the war but his daughter, Anna Freud, carried on his work. She also set up residential nurseries in Hampstead for children parted from their parents by wartime circumstances. She noted (with some surprise) the anxiety they suffered and published her findings during the war.[2] Another psychologist, John Bowlby, extended his pre-war research on the effects of separation. His interest may have sprung from his own childhood, during which he saw his mother for an hour a day and became very attached to a nursery maid who left the family in 1911 when he was four years old.[3] While working in the London Child Guidance Clinic after 1936, then as an army psychiatrist during the war, he observed that children and young adults who were referred to him for repeated stealing had often had severely disrupted relationships with their mothers. His conclusions were published by the World Health Organization in 1951 and came out in an abridged, popular version entitled *Child Care and the Growth of Love*. When the United Nations added to its post-war Declaration of Human Rights a list of the fundamental rights of the child it proclaimed: 'A child of tender years shall not, save in exceptional circumstances, be separated from its mother.'[4]

Meanwhile families had to cope as best they could in unpredictable and dangerous times. As the conflict approached, Raj parents had to make painful decisions about what were the safest havens for their offspring. Linette Purbi's mother was so worried about rumours of war that she brought her twelve-year-old daughter back to Kashmir in 1935. When hostilities became imminent Britain clearly seemed less safe than India and many children of the Raj were, like Laurence Fleming, allowed 'back into paradise'.[5] In July 1939 Pip and Desmond Mirrell, who had been in continuous residence at boarding schools on the Isle of Wight for the previous two years, were suddenly summoned to the seaplane aerodrome at Southampton. Journalists interviewed them, for they were the first children to make an unaccompanied flight from Britain. Knowing nothing of the menace of war, they were simply told that they would be joining their parents in India. It proved a thrilling experience for the two youngsters (aged thirteen and eleven), as Mrs Lamb explained in an interview for the British Empire and Commonwealth Museum. They stayed overnight at luxurious hotels in Rome, Alexandria and Basra (where they had dinner at the Captain's table) and landed for refuelling in Mediterranean harbours, the Sea of Galilee and the Persian Gulf. From Karachi they took a further flight in a tiny plane to Delhi, to be met by Mr Mirrell for the drive to their home in Dehra Dun. Here they rejoiced to see their friends, pets and servants and soon started school at the Jesus and Mary Convent. But by the time Pip matriculated in 1942 the war was close to home as Japanese troops approached India's borders. She joined the Women's Army Corps (India) and her first boyfriend was killed in fighting at Imphal, near the Indian–Burmese frontier.[6]

Other children, like Penny Eledon Smith and Roddy Gradidge, had not even crossed the threshold of their English boarding schools before they were hastily packed on to India-bound boats in the late summer of 1939. Penny, an only child who was devoted to her parents, is very glad now that she was not left in England at the age of eight: 'I don't know what I'd have done – I don't think I'd ever have accepted it.' Instead, her war years were divided between the Hilltop School at Kalimpong (where she could see the sun rise and set behind Kanchenjunga) and her parents' home in Calcutta.[7] On 3 September 1939, the day that war was declared, Lorraine Gradidge and her two children sailed for India – and a 'hazardous trip' it turned out to be. Their ship was twice chased by German submarines; on one occasion they saw a conning-tower and on the other they had 'the alarming experience of hearing a distinct scraping against the side of the ship'. During the voyage Mrs Gradidge heard that the *Athenia* (full of women and children bound for Canada) had been sunk – but she probably withheld this story from Roddy and Penelope, who never forgot their exciting journey.[8]

For parents based in India, far from enemy action in the early stages of the war, it was particularly difficult to decide on the best course of action. The Allans, a tea-planting family in Travancore, did nothing until early 1940, when they became worried about 'the phoney war in Europe breaking into open hostilities'. As their son Jimmy was already at school in Scotland they resolved that Mrs Allan (with six-year-old George in tow) should travel to Britain and there decide whether to retrieve Jimmy or to leave both boys to be educated in Edinburgh. George, who missed his brother's companionship, was delighted at the prospect of the reunion and the journey. The latter, which he describes in his unpublished autobiography, was a bit more than he (or his mother) had bargained for. They reached Paris on 10 May 1940, 'only to be told that the Germans had that day invaded Belgium and Holland'. At Calais they found that their intended boat had been bombed and 'was lying at the bottom of the harbour with only the funnel visible above water'. Back in Paris 'we experienced our first air raid'. They were lucky to get across the Channel before the evacuation from Dunkirk.

By the time they reached Edinburgh the German conquest of France was nearly accomplished and an invasion of Britain seemed imminent. Mrs Allan decided to take both boys back with her but the only passage they could find was one to Perth in Australia, from where they hoped to travel to India. George remembers that on the *Orcades* were '270 youngsters (some as young as five or six) who were being evacuated to Australia'. He has never forgotten the distressing sight of these children leaving their parents on the quay at Southampton or the sound of their homesick weeping during the voyage. He still wonders 'how many of them actually returned to the UK at the end of the war'. It was December 1940 before the Allans reached Perth (after a voyage around the Cape) and another six weeks before they were able to secure a passage to Colombo, where they were met by Mr Allan. The boys had many a tale to tell him – and they must have thanked their lucky stars in 1942 when they heard that both the ships on which they had travelled had subsequently been sunk.

George and Jimmy did not much enjoy the next two years, which they spent at the 'highly disciplined' Breeks Memorial School in Ooty. But there were consolations which they could not have experienced in Britain: scouting in 'an environment totally suited to this activity', collecting exotic beetles and lizards, mid-term breaks with their parents at the Coimbatore Club in the Nilgiri hills and the long Christmas holiday back on the High Range plantation. After 1942 fear of Japanese air or sea attack penetrated even to south India. George remembers 'Z-shaped trenches into which we all poured every time there was an air-raid alert'. Luckily he never had 'to contend with the real thing'.[9]

The evacuees pitied by young George on his journey were among thousands sent abroad privately or by the Children's Overseas Reception Board (CORB). They went to Australia, America, Canada, South Africa and New Zealand, far away from the bombs, shortages and anxieties that afflicted Britain in 1940. Unlike the Allan, Gradidge, Elsden-Smith and Mirrell children, the 'seavacuees', as they were often called, did not have parents accompanying them or waiting for them at the other end. Nor did they know much about the countries or families to which they were going. In fact they were in many ways akin to Raj children being sent to Britain in normal times: they were dispatched for their own good but without consultation; they travelled so far that returning home was virtually impossible; they did not know how long their exile would be; and they were told that if things went wrong they should remember that they were British and 'grin and bear it'.[10]

Things often went right. Most evacuees to Australia, for instance, found a warm welcome with relations or foster parents (who were usually more affluent than their own parents) They communicated regularly with home, enjoyed the opportunities afforded by the country's more varied educational opportunities, sunnier climate and more equal society and came home safely after the surrender of Japan in August 1945. (In all these respects their circumstances were quite different from those of the indigent child migrants mentioned in Chapter Seven.) But many evacuees paid a price for these advantages: acute homesickness on their departure and/or alienation from their parents on their return. Geoffrey Shaw, a teenager dispatched to Nova Scotia in 1940, illustrates both the gains and the losses. In 1942 he begged his parents to take him back as 'things aren't going as well as they ought to be' and he longed for 'the true sense of rest and well-being and happiness which are my sole memories of home'. Yet he soon got involved in the life of the community. He became a signaller in the cadets, took holiday jobs in a store and on a farm, and organised a local orchestra. He later concluded that in 'distant evacuation', far away from the influences of home, 'a large amount of independence is required and initiative developed'.[11]

Child psychologists took a great interest in evacuees but their views were predictably various. While Dr Josephine Barnes emphasised that 'being sent away from home could be beneficial', Bowlby voiced reservations from the start and continued to argue that 'evacuation was a bad mistake'. Anna Freud observed that the separation of children from their parents was 'far more distressing to them than the bombs from which they were being protected' and this was borne out by the return of many inland evacuees to their city homes during the Blitz.[12] Jack Rosenthal's play *The Evacuees* (based on his own wartime experience) tells the story of two evacuated Jewish brothers who manage to convey their misery during their mother's visit through a game of Consequences; once she realises their plight she takes them straight back to Manchester with her. As Angus Calder observed, 'Families . . . preferred to die together, if they must'.[13] This was a feeling shared by my own mother as she took me into bed with her when German bombers flew over Exeter.

Overseas evacuation from Britain was virtually abandoned after the death of seventy-seven Canadian-bound child evacuees in the *City of Benares*, which was torpedoed in September 1940. The scheme involved few Raj children, who (after the fall of France) were encouraged and helped by the India Office to return to their families.[14] But for Roger Moore that was not possible, since his parents had retired from Madras in 1937 and settled near Oxford, as described in Chapter Seven. He was pleased to have them back although it took time to get to know them again, for he was still at boarding school. Moreover his mother was a semi-invalid who spent a great deal of time resting and his father was involved in academic work. At the outbreak of war twelve-year-old Roger looked forward to a bit of excitement: 'When the Germans invaded I was going to become a messenger for the Home Guard riding on my bicycle.' Instead, to his fury, he was evacuated to America in 1940 on a scheme by which Yale University took in children from Oxford and Cambridge. 'I was separated from my parents for another three years, which seemed like an age.'

It could have been worse. Roger was taken in by the 'very nice family' of Dr Jackson (whom he always addressed thus) and got on well with their son Pete, who was about his own age. His main memories are of the escapades he led Pete into: excavating an air raid shelter under a derelict house, burying containers which they had filled with petrol in case of emergency and cutting down full-grown pine trees with which to build a log cabin. Just as unexpected and unexplained as Roger's sentence of exile was his reprieve. In 1943 an uncle who was a navy captain suddenly summoned him to board the *Newcastle*, which sailed to England via Bermuda, with Roger and eight other lads acting as crew. After arriving at Plymouth in December he made his own way to Oxford, walked to the college where his father was a Fellow and greeted him in an American accent.

This twang probably did not help Roger to fit in at Uppingham, Humphrey Moore's old school, to which he was now dispatched. It was difficult to make friends with boys who had been there two years already but luckily he found a companion from former years, the son of his favourite foster parents. Another problem was that since Roger had been following the American curriculum, which included neither Latin nor geometry, he was put into the 'Removes' and made to feel stupid. He was relieved to reach the age of seventeen, when at last he could do his bit in the war. Volunteering for the Marines in April 1945, he was sent to India, so that he was able to reacquaint himself with the land of his birth. But he never re-established a close relationship with his parents. While recognising that they acted in what they thought to be his best interests, Roger concludes that his rather drifting expatriate life (with HSBC) and his difficulty in forming close friendships stem from the frequent separations of his youth.[15]

The family biography written by fellow seavacuee, John Catlin, provides a strikingly similar analysis of his own character and up bringing. He was the son of the writer, Vera Brittain, who helped to organise CORB. As a child John and his younger sister Shirley (who became the politician Shirley Williams) led their own life, seeing their busy mother only after tea. At the ages of ten and seven the children were sent to separate boarding schools, a decision which John thought quite unreasonable. In 1940 they were evacuated to the United States where John 'never felt homesick'. When summoned back three years later he did not want to leave 'the freedom of the Mid-West' and felt that he was 'not the same John who had sailed from Liverpool'. In his book he concluded that his 'floating free independence' and 'detachment from close relationships' sprang from his transient childhood.[16]

The guardians of children who had not been evacuated, even though they lived in vulnerable parts of Britain, often shielded them from undue anxieties. Sydney Butler, who had charge of Iris Portal's daughters, told her sister-in-law in November 1940 that their country life at Stanstead Hall in Essex was 'genuinely normal', despite stray bombs intended for London or for Duxford airfield. 'For your children anyway,' she wrote, 'war is only in the background'. Nevertheless Mrs Butler was concerned about the prospect of an invasion. So without informing her nieces, she quietly made arrangements to send them, if necessary, to 'a place of greater safety' − Savernake Forest, where they would stay with another aunt. Meanwhile Mrs Butler had been receiving emotional letters from Iris Portal in India who assumed that they were all 'living in an atmosphere of dramatic and historic discomfort and excitement'.[17] Jane and Susan also got effervescent epistles from their mother, telling them that the war was 'all a great adventure', 'one of the most thrilling moments in our history', and that 'the best and finest place' to be spending it was in England. Iris Portal wished that she too could be 'part of history' and was 'FURIOUS' that she had never experienced an air raid.[18] Evidently Mrs Butler calmed any perturbation that their mother's missives might have caused the girls. Iris Portal herself was disappointed that her daughters' ordinary little letters did not emulate her histrionic tones. They simply told her about such everyday activities as playing netball at school in Cambridge or riding ponies at Stanstead Hall.

In fact the war visited both places and some of their schoolfriends left for safer locations such as Cumberland, Kenya and Canada. The Portal girls' letters mention spending nights under eiderdowns in air raid shelters, having half-terms cancelled 'as people have been asked not to travel', waiting ages for letters to come, knitting jumpers for refugees, and seeing tanks 'lovely and big and camelflaged [sic]'.[19] In 1941 their aunt removed Jane and Susan from their Cambridge school, where the headmistress, Miss Tilley, had 'with mistaken kindness taken in some Jewish refugees with little or no fees and is trying to run the boarding-house on the cheap'.[20] They were sent to St Mary's School at Wantage, which was less likely to suffer air raids. Now Sydney Butler had the worry of finding enough clothes coupons to kit them out in the new school uniform. Luckily they were allowed to carry on wearing their old overcoats instead of the 'lovely dark blue cloaks with light blue lining' which Susan had coveted.[21] Mrs Butler hoped that Eton, which her oldest son Richard was about to attend, would also relax its uniform requirements – though in fact many schools did not do so. The boys of Christ's Hospital, for example, still wore Tudor gowns and looked as if they 'were expecting the Spanish Armada' rather than the Wehrmacht.[22] It was also difficult for Mrs Butler to find enough petrol to visit children in three schools, but she always did her best to turn up for concerts and Parents' Days.

Although sheltered as far as possible from the worries and perils of war, Jane and Susan still had to cope with the enforced absence of their parents. There is no hint of misery in their letters and in one of them Jane expressed the hope that 'we will like each other better if we are separated for a little time'.[23] The girls always referred to Stanstead Hall as home and enjoyed school holidays there with the Butlers' three sons and a Polish boy to whom they had given refuge. Pony club rallies and dances continued despite the war and Jane and Susan much enjoyed the company of their uncle, Rab Butler, when he could get away from his government duties in London. Rather to the disapproval of his more proper wife, he would sometimes entertain the children at lunch by pretending that his spoon was a looking-glass and combing his hair with his fork. His lack of pomposity is suggested also by a family joke about the Cabinet post he was given in 1941: 'Rab is Board of Education and Richard [his eldest son] is bored with education.'[24] Once the children were old enough they were allowed to attend dinner parties with important political guests.

Sydney Butler's letters reveal the great care she took with her nieces' physical and social welfare. She made sure that Jane was properly prepared for the onset of her 'monthly affairs'. She took both girls home when they had measles at school, where they were just regarded

as 'a great nuisance'. And she defended their apparent naughtiness
against Miss Tilley, who seemed to have a down on them. Susan was
accused of boasting and lying, for instance, when she innocently said
that her Daddy had been made a general when in fact he was only a
colonel. Nevertheless, Mrs Butler's stoical belief that 'children and
parents should be independent of each other' made her seem rather
distant and austere. Susan remembers that 'Sydney never once kissed
me' and that 'there were no cuddles'.[25]

Iris Portal returned to England in 1943 when her husband was sent
to fight in the Middle East and she could not 'face being without *any*
of my three most precious creatures'. Susan did not at first recognise
her mother at the railway station but she settled down quite quickly,
although she now found that she was homesick when she went back
to school. She told me that the separation had been easier for her than
for Jane because she had always had an older sister to sort out problems. And Iris Portal was clearly concerned about her relationship
with Jane who had, by her own admission, been 'an unsettled child'
back in India, longing for more of her mother's time and attention.
Mrs Portal had written to her earlier, wondering 'if we shall have to
get to know each other all over again when we meet once more'. Now
she had her answer. Fifteen-year-old Jane found it very hard to leave
the Butler household and to adjust to sharing a house with her mother
who, she felt, had been living 'in another world'. Jane says that she
became 'impossible at school' – although her reports from St Mary's
refer only to difficulties in concentrating on her work. Susan remembers that her parents had 'terrible problems' with Jane at home,
especially when the whole family settled at Blakeney after the war.

Like Roger Moore and some of the evacuees returning from Australia, Jane found that the bonds with her mother 'never mended' and
she had to overcome serious psychological problems in later years. But
the two daughters' verdicts on the years of separation from their
parents have something in common. Susan feels, with the loyalty
typical of Raj children, that it was 'much worse for them than for us
to miss out on their children's development'. Jane also recognises that
it was not easy for adults. But she emphasises juvenile needs: 'Parents
found it difficult to realise that if they let their children go for that
length of time they will forge other loyalties and affections because
they need surrogate parents.'[26]

Some Anglo-Indian children seem to have developed the stiff upper
lip with greater ease, as Iris Portal herself had apparently done in her

own childhood exile. Peter Clark, sent to Britain in 1938 from India, in which he had spent the first eight years of his life, does not remember any regrets about leaving home and family. He enjoyed three weeks of fun on the journey, settled down easily at his 'happy' prep school and liked the kind Irish woman who looked after him (and other boys) in the holidays. At the time he 'just accepted it all' – although now he wonders whether 'the shock of separation may have blanked out' both his early years in India and the experience of parting.[27] Once the war started, the spirit of the Blitz helped to carry Peter through Wellington College, where the pupils spent many nights in the cellars and the headmaster was killed by a stray bomb. The war also brought him the bonus of some family life between 1940 and 1944, for Mrs Clark came to England while her husband was posted to Europe.

With the same kind of bulldog pluck, seven-year-old Gillian Beard (née Northfield) told herself, when her mother left her in England to return to the Bengal mission field in 1939: 'You had to stand on your own two feet.'[28] It helped that her two older sisters, Margaret and Anthea, were at Walthamstow School with her and that 'everyone else was in the same boat'. She also found Miss Ramsay 'a wonderful headmistress'. Perhaps the 'battering ram' had softened during her long service at the school since Leila Brown's day. She had extended her stay so that she could see the school through the war, during which she apparently showed 'Churchillian qualities' and an 'imaginative sympathy with human suffering'.[29] In other respects Gillian's circumstances were not altogether easy. There being no relations who could take her, she spent her holidays with the Martins, a childless Baptist couple in Sevenoaks. They were kind to her but she always felt that she had to be on her best behaviour. Her greatest delight was to play endless tomboy games in the woods with her brother Tony (who also had guardians in Sevenoaks). This rather disappointed Mrs Martin, who had hoped for a little girl whom she could dress up in pretty clothes. Instead she had to cable Mrs Northfield for permission to allow Gillian to wear shorts.

While the war cast its shadow over the childhood of Gillian and her siblings it also aroused in them an enthusiastic patriotism. Because Sevenoaks was in the battle zone, Walthamstow Hall was used as an air raid wardens' post and it was bombed in 1940, though without any serious injuries to girls or staff. Gillian remembers that the atmosphere was 'very fraught': Mr Martin built a shelter in the garden and she was 'frightened of Germans climbing up the drainpipe'. Letters to her parents were written as airgraphs, which were shrunk down to the size of a postage stamp to be enlarged at the point of arrival and Gillian was aware that they were censored by the authorities. After the bombing the junior boarders (including Gillian and one of her sisters) were evacuated to Pontesford House in Shropshire, a rural arcadia which ex-pupils remember 'with a Wordsworthian ardour'.[30] Gillian feels that she had 'a very good war' in Pontesford, where the villagers were sympathetic towards children whose parents were so far away. But for the holidays she and Anthea had to travel back to Sevenoaks in blacked-out trains full of soldiers. Like many children's wartime journeys, these were both thrilling and alarming. Gillian admits that it was a relief when her mother, who was suffering from tropical sprue, had to come home for good in 1943. Now the Northfields could live together as a family again with the freedom 'to fight like cat and dog', in the normal fashion of brothers and sisters.

In the lands of the Raj, as in Britain, the war made varying demands on children. Some hardly noticed the conflict while others were tested to the limit. The first area to be considered dangerous was Ceylon, an important British naval base. In the summer of 1941, months before Japan bombed Pearl Harbor, British women and children were evacuated from Colombo to South Africa or Australia. Among them was five-year-old Lesley Dowling (née Hayward). She had only just lost her mother, who died suddenly the night after taking Lesley out for a picnic from the Hill School at Nuwara Eliya. The headmistress gave the news to Lesley who was told nothing about the funeral: 'my father never came to see me at the school'. Nor did she ever learn anything about the circumstances of her mother's death at the Hill Club. When informed a month or so later that she was to be taken away to the safety of Durban in South Africa, Lesley was 'hugely excited about the whole adventure' and not at all bothered about leaving her father, 'a very forbidding character'. She claims to have 'no bad memories' of South Africa, where she lived in the hills with a farming couple and several other refugee children. They walked every day to the local school, learning to avoid green and black mambas along the way and turning into 'a gang of little thugs'. For their frequent misdemeanours the children were beaten 'on our backsides with butter pats'. It was a loveless time for the young child. She told me that she did not receive any letters from her father: 'I do not remember being homesick for him, or grieving for my mother.' When, after two years, she was told that she was going home her main feeling was regret at leaving her pet cow and its new calf.

Lesley's homecoming in February 1944, after a long journey via Bombay, was full of surprises. At Colombo station her father introduced her to his new wife, Mollie, whom he had married in June 1942, and back at home there was a month-old baby brother. This could have been very upsetting for an eight-year-old child but Mollie was a remarkable character. She presented her stepdaughter with a doll for which she had made 'an exquisite set of clothes' and suggested that she call her Mummy. Lesley does not remember Mollie ever taking more notice of the baby than of her. She herself was an adaptable and cheerful child who enjoyed the rest of the war, although there were few treats now that shortages and rationing were affecting Ceylon. She revelled in sport and music back at the Hill School, received 'love, cuddles and attention' from her stepmother and shared an ayah with her brother. The ayah was a Catholic and Lesley remembers lying in bed watching her say her rosary. (It may be no accident that she herself converted to Catholicism in later life even though her father was vehemently opposed to Rome.) All this compensated somewhat for the strictness of her father and for the absence of her older sister, Liz, who had been at school in the Lake District since 1939. They were not reunited until after the war.[31]

Another area where Raj families felt vulnerable was north-east India. As Japanese troops advanced through Burma in the early months of 1942, it seemed likely that they would cross the frontier into Bengal. Don and Tony, the two young sons of Dr and Mrs Bottoms, a Baptist missionary couple working in the Chittagong hills near the Burmese border, were evacuated with their mother to Shillong in Assam. There a baby sister was born. Dr Bottoms soldiered on at the missionary hospital, adding to his list of patients RAF personnel from an observation post that was established nearby. Later, the family returned and one of Tony's most vivid early memories is of sitting on the verandah watching a Japanese plane fly directly overhead. He supposes he must have been 'scared witless' by the experience to remember it so clearly, though he also recalls his father's reassuring remark that the plane was flying too high to drop bombs.[32] Meanwhile in Darjeeling children were 'forbidden to buy Japanese sweets because the Japanese might have poisoned them'.[33]

In fact it became clear in May that the Japanese had no immediate plans to follow up their conquest of Burma by invading India. But residents of Calcutta remained fearful. Because the city was the main port and railhead to be used in a future British counter-attack it was likely to be the target of Japanese bombing. Penny Elsden-Smith remembers being 'pathetically scared' when air raids did occur, even though 'for us there were merely some short dashes across the garden to our little Anderson shelter'.[34] Some families had reluctantly left the city. The Parkers, for example, had enjoyed a comfortable life there in a 'lovely cool house' fitted with the latest air-conditioning. But in the summer of 1942 Betty Parker took their three young children to the safety of Simla. By the end of the year her husband Tom had been transferred from ICI's Calcutta office to Delhi, and the whole family was settled into another 'delightful' house and garden.[35] The north-west, where for so long the British had feared Afghan or Russian incursions, was at that time one of the safest parts of India.

Christopher Parker, the middle child, who was only four when his family moved to Delhi, does not remember the war affecting his life at all.[36] And Betty Parker's wartime letters to her mother in Edinburgh are concerned mostly with the health, behaviour and development of the children, whom she was rearing by the new Susan Isaacs method. 'I feel that it is better on the whole,' wrote Mrs Parker, 'to err on the side of letting them be a little too free and easy, rather than too regimented.' Often she contrasted their lot with that of children who had been 'caught by the Japs or Germans or lost at sea'. Of course, as time went on, the family felt some effects of the war: petrol rationing, irregular post and staff shortages at the office which made Tom Parker's life 'one long, hard, relentless effort'. And the Parker children did have to be separated from their mother, for in April 1944 she was taken ill with tuberculosis and sent to an isolation clinic up in the hills at Kasauli. She worried dreadfully about missing their 'darling baby years'. In fact Susan, Christopher and baby Andrew were 'well, happy, loved and taught' by their Eurasian nanny back in Delhi.[37] They seem to have suffered no ill effects before Mrs Parker recovered in November – her husband thought that the Indian climate had done more for her than would 'almost any place in the world'. The end of the war found the family together at Simla, where the older two children went to school on a pony called Strawberry. 'Here conditions are, compared with the rest of the world, ideal. ...We are very far away from all the difficulties and terrors which have been and are so near to you.'[38]

Another family which spent the war safely in Simla and Delhi, as well as elsewhere in north-west India, was that of Gerald Curtis, an ICS District Officer. His wife, Decima, felt that they were lucky to have their four children with them during 'those anxious years', despite difficulties created by her husband's frequent re-postings and by the delicate health of her oldest son George. She did not follow the example of her friend May Almond, who decided in 1942 to take her children back to England even though they had places at Bishop Cotton and Auckland House Schools. 'The education in India is generally thought to be two years behind that in England and she had put the boys' names down for Winchester.' This decision nearly resulted in the death of all the Almond offspring, for the *City of Cairo* on which they sailed was torpedoed off Cape Town. Mrs Almond and the children were rescued by lifeboats after clinging to wreckage for two hours and it was a further twelve days before 'they were picked up by pure chance and taken back to Cape Town'. Mrs Curtis, who writes admiringly of her friend's courage, thought that their lifeboat 'was the only one left'. But I have discovered another mother and child who were saved from this shipwreck: Mrs Dulcie Kendall and her son Colin, refugees from Burma, whose story appears later in this chapter. No doubt there are more such tales of peril and survival yet to be told.

Meanwhile the Curtis family stayed together until the last year of the war when they sent their two oldest sons to Sheikh Bagh boarding school in Srinagar. Mrs Curtis must have been glad that they had not gone further away when, at the end of the long term, six-year-old Julian said to her: 'I used to wonder if I should ever see you again.'[39] Another pupil at the same Srinagar prep school was Roddy Gradidge, whose mother spent the war in north-west India where she and her fellow grass widows, 'white women living alone in a foreign land', were 'never molested in any way'. Like May Almond, Lorraine Gradidge seems to have been more worried about schooling than about the war, at least on her son's account. After Roddy had outgrown Sheikh Bagh she sent him to the Royal Indian Military College (RIMC) at Dehra Dun and moved to that town, where Penelope attended the local convent. Roddy seems to have been quite happy with this arrangement, telling his friend 'Gibbo' (Jeremy Milne Gibbon) that the RIMC was 'a jolly decent place' even though the pupils were 'under military disipline [sic]' and the food was 'absolutely putrid'. He obviously spent time with his mother, sister and baby brother and he also mentions seeing his father when he was home on leave. It must be said that Roddy's letters show a poor grasp of spelling and punctuation, although he was able to pass on to his friend the detailed information about liners which he had collected into scrapbooks.[40] Whatever the relative benefits and deficiencies of the RIMC, Mrs Gradidge decided in autumn 1943 to send Roddy back to England for a 'proper education' at Stowe. At that time 'the danger to shipping ... was still immense' and it was 'six anguished weeks' before she had news of his safety.[41]

Some parents with children in India had different priorities. Harry Southwell, the son of a ship surveyor, had hardly any schooling after being transferred from Bexhill to Bombay in 1940. His parents would not send him to any of the established European schools, like Bishop Cotton or the Cathedral School, for fear of his learning to 'speak chi chi'. Eight-year-old Harry was quite happy to go with his sister to a little British school in Bombay and to spend much of his time getting into mischief at Breach Candy Swimming Club. His favourite times were the long periods spent at his family's house up in the hills at Nasik, where he did not go to school at all but learnt to play a good game of golf. He was provided with an English governess, an Indian maths tutor and a French *mam'zelle* but he says that 'none of them did me any good'. Naturally, Harry took a great interest in the war, following events closely on the wireless. And he has never forgotten hearing the ammunition cargo ship *Fort Stikine* blow up in Bombay harbour and seeing the great tower of smoke rising from the docks.[42]

Hilary Johnston was another child kept in India for the whole war. Like Harry, she says that she 'didn't learn much at all' but she would not like to be without her 'irreplaceable fund of memories'. She was six years old when hostilities began (soon after the death of her little brother, described in Chapter Six) and does not remember much about the war before 1943, when the family moved to Jhansi in central India. Here she encountered troops who were training in 'the jungles, hills and rivers' of that area to fight in Burma. Her mother helped to organise a popular canteen (where the soldiers could consume eggs, bacon and chips) and she also gave tea parties for children who had escaped from Burma. 'I can still visualise my mother wobbling through the dust on her high old-fashioned bicycle on the way to do her stuff.' But Hilary's most vivid memory is of 'Dakotas towing gliders across the starry sky', for aeroplanes were still a rare sight.

Not so pleasant are her recollections of the Hallett War School in Naini Tal, which she attended from 1942 to 1944, when it closed down. She has never forgotten 'the absolute heartbreak of homesickness'. It was compounded by the unkindness of the headmistress, who sent her to Coventry for ten days, 'a very scarring experience for a young child'. There were better times when her parents came up for the June break and they walked and rode in the forest, or when she scoured the hills for holly to take home for Christmas. Like many who were children in this era, Hilary now finds that hymns trigger off memories. When she hears the carol 'It Came upon a Midnight Clear' she pictures herself looking out from school over 'the sad and lowly plains', with the lights of cities twinkling in the dark, and imagining that angels were hovering over them. She would then dream of her journey home from her 'eyrie on the mountain top'. Despite these desolate memories of school, Hilary is glad that her Indian childhood was extended by the war.[43]

The difficulty families had when trying to weigh up the various perils of war is illustrated by the story of the Whittakers. As Japanese pressure on the north-east frontier continued in 1943, the Revd Frank and Mrs Whittaker worried about a possible invasion. Even though they lived at Hyderabad in central India and Dick's school, Woodstock, was not in a danger zone, they feared that all European residents might be interned, as they had been in China and South-East Asia. In addition they may have been anxious about their son's health, for he had suffered a serious attack of malaria. In any case, they decided to send Dick (who was now fourteen) to join his older brother in England. Dick did not want to leave India, to which he was (and is) devoted, but he looked forward to the journey, the second he had undertaken in wartime. During the first, with his family in 1940, he had experienced a bombardment in Liverpool harbour, several submarine scares in the Atlantic and a hurricane in the China Seas. The better to face these maritime perils, Mrs Whittaker had even resorted to wearing trousers. Dick's 1943 voyage was also full of excitement. He was put in the charge of the captain, who came down from the bridge once he had navigated through the dangers of the Indian Ocean, and befriended the boy. He selected Dick as his quoits opponent, taught him to play chess and took him ashore when they docked at Suez. Once they had gone through the reopened Suez Canal and entered the Mediterranean, the captain had to return to his constant watch on the bridge. On the Libyan coast Dick saw scenes of devastation caused by the Battle of Tobruk. Back in England he and the captain remained firm friends.

The Whittaker brothers boarded in the holidays with their mother's sister and her clergyman husband, out of harm's way in the Lake District. The couple had once been missionaries but had come home for the sake of their son's education. Now Aunt Bessie felt that she had to 'do God's work' by taking in her sister's children. 'She was extraordinarily kind to us really,' Dick acknowledges, but he was aware that she saw looking after them as a duty, especially burdensome in time of war. He and his brother always took second place to their cousin, who never got into trouble as they did for making a noise when the parson was writing his next sermon. Nevertheless, Dick feels that he had 'a pretty good time' although his brother apparently felt 'a sense of deprivation'. Better still, Dick developed an aptitude and a love for classical languages at his Methodist boarding school. Despite not having studied Latin or Greek at Woodstock, he was able to race ahead and eventually became a Classics don at Cambridge University.[44] So the war had brought him a lasting bonus in addition to the memory of two thrilling odysseys.

For British children who had lived in Burma journeys were not so much an adventure as a terrifying ordeal. Those who left soon after the invasion of January 1942 had a relatively easy exit. In February Jill, Jennifer and Graham Parry were able to sail with their mother from Rangoon to Calcutta but in June their father had to trek out through the north of the country. Eleven-year-old Grace Rorke, who had been born and brought up near Rangoon, was at boarding school up in the hills at Maymyo when 'the war which had been taking place the other side of the world' came to Burma.[45] Soon her school was taken over as army headquarters, her sisters' university in Rangoon closed down and one of them joined up as an army nurse. Quite early on her parents decided to use a scheme by which Dakotas bringing troops into Shwebo airfield in central Burma would take women and children out. So Grace, her brothers and Grandma, in the charge of the remaining sister, flew over the Indian border to Chittagong and thence travelled by train and boat to Calcutta. They left everything behind apart from some clothes and a favourite toy dog or teddy-bear packed into light Burmese baskets. Not knowing whether they would ever see their parents again, the children were taken to Dehra Dun in the Himalayan foothills, where they had an aunt and uncle. Here the family dispersed – sister into the Army, brothers to a boarding school higher up in the mountains near Mussoorie and Grace to an exclusive school in a beautiful situation eight miles away. Grandma stayed in Dehra Dun. Meanwhile they heard that the Japanese were advancing further into Burma and had occupied Mandalay and taken Shwebo airfield.

As her memoir explains, Grace was now too anxious and unhappy to concentrate on lessons. After a time she heard that Mrs Rorke had caught the last plane to leave Myitkyina (the most northerly airfield in Burma) and had gone to Bombay. It was 'a hard blow' when Mother decided that the children should complete the long boarding school term. Furthermore, Grace's lack of suitable clothing caused her to be the victim of both bullying and acute bronchitis. 'The bullies more than met their match' but Grace could not tell her family about her untreated illness because 'letters we wrote home were always read, and if we wrote anything that was considered wrong, we were made to rewrite the letter'. She retaliated against the authorities by refusing to write any letters at all. The tactic worked, for Grandma eventually realised that something was wrong and took her out of school. By Christmas the family was reunited after Mr Rorke had made the dangerous trek out of northern Burma 'through jungle, marshes, bogs and rivers in flood'. In 1943 he joined the RAF and the three youngsters went to boarding school in Bangalore where they stayed for the next three years. They were not unhappy, though, as their mother came to stay nearby in the holidays. And the presence of many of their friends from Burma made school seem 'like home from home'.[46]

Most of those caught up in this 'forgotten war' have not written books about their distressing experiences. But in recent years the Imperial War Museum has encouraged some of them to write or record their memoirs, which are housed in the Museum's archive. Among them are records of the Powell, Kendall and McDougall children, who left Burma in February or early March by the same route as the Rorke family. All had their mothers with them but left their fathers behind to carry on civilian or military duties for as long as possible. For Nancie, Daphne and Dennis Powell this was their second long wartime journey, and they must have been anxious about it as they remembered what had occurred in their first. In 1940 they had been summoned to Burma from England by parents who did not want them to suffer the protracted separation they themselves had endured in the First World War. Daphne's account of the six-week voyage by convoy boat, train and seaplane reveals what a heavy responsibility it was for sixteen-year-old Nancie, who had taken her last School Certificate paper in geography a few hours before leaving. She still had with her the map used in that exam, which was confiscated at Liverpool 'because it could have aided an enemy'. At the end of the journey, during which the two younger children got measles, Nancie 'collapsed with nervous exhaustion'.[47]

It was just eighteen months later that they flew out of Shwebo with their mother. They could take nothing but clothes and one precious possession each – in Daphne's case a jade brooch her parents had given her at Christmas. Like many other refugee children they went to Mussoorie, where they were eventually reunited with Mr Powell: 'the most intense happiness I have ever experienced'. Later they moved to Simla, where Daphne attended Auckland House. There she tried to make up for her missed schooling, PNEU having proved inadequate in wartime because of the delays in correcting exam papers and sending study materials. When it came to her School Certificate, geography was the only subject she passed, for the paper included such topics as rice cultivation, irrigation, and sea breezes. 'I had *lived* my geography and in consequence I had a Credit.' Daphne's itinerant war had brought her this small benefit. But the family returned to Britain after VJ Day, considering that they had been 'extremely fortunate over the evacuation': 'Although we lost everything except what we could carry, we didn't have the pain and discomfort, the robberies and rains, the starvation and the trekking out.'[48]

Daphne's aunt, Dulcie Kendall, was much less fortunate. She was airlifted out of Burma at about the same time with her three-year-old son, Colin. She went to Mussoorie to join the Powells but in July she heard that her husband, Cyril, had contracted cerebral malaria during his belated escape through Upper Burma during the monsoon season. He died in a transit camp before Mrs Kendall could reach him. Understandably anxious to return to her family in England, she and Colin sailed from Bombay aboard the *City of Cairo* in October 1942. As we have seen, that ship was hit by a torpedo after leaving Cape Town. The mother and child managed to get into a lifeboat before a second torpedo sank the ship. They survived thirteen days at sea on very meagre rations before being rescued by a cargo boat and taken to St Helena. Mrs Kendall had kept Colin going by 'planning all the things we would do and eat when we reached land'. Perhaps the little boy did not remember much about his terrifying ordeal for 'with so little food he lost energy and slept a lot'. After three months on the island living in a bungalow near Napoleon's house, Colin was still very thin, 'but otherwise pretty well'. The mother and child were among sixty-three survivors taken back to Britain on the *Nestor*.[49]

The mother of the two little McDougall boys protected them in much the same way during several evacuations. Duncan and Hamish (together with Duncan's Benjamin Bunny) had already left Hong Kong and the Philippines, which seemed likely to be swallowed up in Japan's southwards expansion even before Pearl Harbor. They got out of Burma in good time and eventually reached Dagshai in the Simla hills, 'where the war seemed so remote that I almost feel guilty'. Barbara McDougall's account shows how aware she was of the children's insecurity: 'Duncan and Hamish were terribly upset at the awful upheaval of their little lives and I never left them for long.' Even so, they missed their Burmese amah, who was forbidden to travel with the family, and their father, who managed to get out of Burma in May. The family had lost everything but, luckily for posterity, Mrs McDougall had managed to bring out the letters, diaries and photographs on which her memoir is based.[50]

As appears from the experience of Cyril Kendall, it was a great deal riskier to leave Burma after the end of April 1942, when the Army began its withdrawal from the country. The Rorke family had been aware of the relatively easy western route to India when there were '*dawk* bungalows [rest-houses] on the way, villages to buy food from [and] bridges still intact'. Sixteen-year-old Fay Brown (née Foucar) and her mother managed to get out of Burma at this stage in country boats, 'using the river for everything – washing, swimming and drinking'. They made a final trek along the refugee route across the border to Imphal camp. Although they had lost all their possessions, they had enough money with them to pay boatmen and porters and to buy food. At camps along the way conditions were usually better for Europeans like the Foucars than for escaping Indians. This is illustrated by Fay's account of an incident in an unfinished camp which was only partially roofed: 'Some officious Indians crowded in under our cover and made themselves unpleasant. Only the efforts of the padres managed to move them on.'[51] Segregation of this kind was condemned by a young Indian official who was helping to set up transit camps as 'blatant discrimination' but he was unable to put a stop to it.[52] These westward journeys were later described by Europeans as 'one long picnic'. This opinion was echoed by Lieutenant-Colonel Westland Wright, who escorted members of his Burma Survey Department, as well as a British woman and her eighteen-month-old baby, out through the north of the country in April.[53]

After April the Japanese cut off the western route and advanced northwards while Burmans became more hostile towards European and Indian refugees. Moreover, the weather worsened with the intense heat and humidity of April to May and the monsoon rains of June to

September. The Governments of India and Burma, which had not foreseen the magnitude of the problem, now gave priority to military evacuation; 'civilians would have to take their chance'.[54] There were still tens of thousands trying to escape, most of them from Burma's million-strong Indian community, for whom evacuation by boat or plane had usually been barred. Many reached India and many others died en route, though little is known of their fate and estimates of the figures vary. Among the much smaller number of Europeans and Anglo-Burmese still stranded was eleven-year-old Stephen Brookes, who has published a graphic account of his experiences. He lived in Maymyo with his father Major William Lindfield Brookes, his Burmese mother, his older sister Maisie and his delicate fourteen-year-old brother George. His older married sisters and their families had already left Burma but his parents had delayed their own departure until the end of April, for reasons which were never explained to Stephen.

Even more incomprehensible to him was his mother's decision not to take an option still open to her of flying out with her children from a Chinese airfield. Instead the family stuck together and fled north by river steamer and ambulance train before advancing Japanese troops and beneath intermittent air bombardment. They reached Myitkyina airfield just before the last few Dakotas took off but failed to board one in the crush of desperate refugees. Stephen himself could have been pulled on to one by a helpful airman but let go of his hand, emotionally incapable of leaving without his family: 'I'd made it to the door on my own – yet I could not go, for what would my life be in a foreign land without my family? They were all I had left. We had come all this way together. Better to die together than alone.'[55] In fact that aeroplane was bombed before it could take off and no more were to leave Myitkyina. Now there was no choice but to join the mass movement of troops and civilians heading north through 'some of the wildest country in the world'.[56]

Unlike many others, whose corpses they constantly passed, the whole family survived a trek of 300 miles. They struggled through humid jungle, overcoming 'swollen rivers, swamps, starvation, disease and Chinese bandits', and finally reached the village of Shingbwiyang. Here a British major whom they knew well refused to help the family to complete their journey across the frontier. The rebuff was not explained to Stephen, who suspects that his mother's Burmese origins played some part. At this point the authorities, who presumably could not cope with the huge influx of destitute people, closed the route through the Pangsau Pass into India. So 45,000 refugees, mostly Indian families, crowded into the camp between July and October amid conditions of mounting squalor and disease.

It was here that Stephen Brookes became a man. For his father, an army doctor and the driving force of the family, died of blackwater fever. At the same time Maisie suffered recurrent attacks of malaria and George seemed to be fading. His exhausted mother said to her last-born child words he was never to forget: 'Stevie, you are the last Brookes.... We depend on you now. You must always do your best and never forget your family.' Stephen's family was allowed to leave the camp in October. But in their debilitated state, they still had to walk another 128 miles over the mountains into India. When they reached the border, the guards confiscated Stephen's 'silver-handled kukri [knife], which had been my constant companion for five months'. Now he had nothing left in the world except a torn shirt and threadbare shorts. Stephen had done his duty and looked after his family. Yet, when the war was over, the fifteen-year-old boy was left alone at La Martinière College in Lucknow while his mother, George and several other siblings returned to Burma. It is difficult to imagine that the schoolmasters were able to help Stephen deal with the painful visions of the trek which haunted him. He never met any of his immediate family again until the 1990s, when he summoned up the courage to write his remarkable story and to talk about it with Maisie.[57]

Professor Pearn of Rangoon University recorded an equally remarkable story of a refugee child who took on the responsibility of his family. After the death of his mother, fourteen-year-old Norman Richardson escorted three of his five brothers and sisters safely out of Burma by the terrible northern route. 'He carried a baby eleven months old for a week until it died, and on arrival at a camp would not only scramble for rations but would return two or three miles down the track to assist his grandmother to get in.'[58]

Meanwhile, European families who had not been able to escape by air, water or land faced years of internment. This was the fate of Cherie Crowley (née Walmsley), who had just left her convent school in Burma when the Japanese invaded. With her widowed mother, brother and sister she tried to escape along the western route but they found the great Ava bridge at Mandalay had been blown. They managed to trek to Myitkyina airfield, eating snake fillets along the way, but did not succeed in boarding the last plane to leave before the Japanese bombardment began. 'In a state of terror, thirsty and hungry, we fled down the line again, the way we had come in the first place.' Eventually they got on to a train which they fondly hoped was picking up refugees. In fact it was full of Japanese soldiers hiding under the seats, who proceeded to shoot or capture those who had swarmed on to it. Cherie, still wearing a cherry-trimmed straw hat which had been given her en route, was taken off in a cattle wagon to an 'uncertain future'. She survived the severe deprivation and brutality to which internees were subjected. And in 1996, after reading Fay Foucar's narrative in a Burmah Oil Company newsletter, she was inspired to tell part of her 'story from Hell'. The full story is perhaps wrapped in two army blankets, which she found beside the refugee road: 'I will *never* part with them, they perhaps can tell of more awful things than I can.' Mrs Crowley's own children used to be rather bored by her memories.[59]

Wartime circumstances forced many other youngsters (in Europe as well as Asia) to leave their childhood behind. Among them was Patrick Gibson, who has also told his story in print. In 1938, after he had spent three unhappy years at boarding school in England, he was told that he was to travel to Bangkok, where his father had been posted by his employers, the Bombay/Burma Trading Company. Presumably his parents realised that a European war was looming. Although not yet quite ten, he made this journey on his own, knowing no one on board ship and meeting only once the padre who was supposed to be keeping an eye on him. There was one treat, however: on his birthday, which he had not celebrated for three years because 'it fell during term time and was never mentioned', the crew provided a cake with ten candles. At Penang he spent a night alone in a hotel (where he ordered cucumber sandwiches and cakes for tea) and then flew to Bangkok in a Dakota plane which had to make an emergency landing in the forest. 'The journey taught me that I could stand on my own feet when travelling.'[60]

The outbreak of war found Patrick at the Highlands School in Sumatra, an 800-mile flight from his home, which he made alone four times a year, usually being invited into the cockpit – 'a wonderful experience'. By 1941 he had settled down at the school despite initial misery and attacks of asthma, neither of which could be described in his censored letters. Since Thailand (formerly Siam) was in thrall to Japan, Patrick was unable to fly to Bangkok at the end of the Christmas term. He spent the festive season with the headmaster and his wife – who with teacherly tact gave him a pack of Happy Families. The boy could not be matched up with his own Mr, Mrs and Master Gibson, whom he supposed to be in Rangoon, for the first flight he was able to board (amid the sound of artillery fire) was diverted to Calcutta. When he arrived there, clutching the small blue KLM suitcase in which his precious stamp album was packed, he was met by a representative of his father's company. This gentleman informed him brusquely: 'The news from Siam is very bad; we have good reason to believe that all British civilians have been executed and you will have to consider yourself an orphan. I know that it will not be any consolation to you at present, but your father's company will look after you until you reach the age of eighteen.' The company's first move was to pack Patrick off to a suitable family in Bombay while it made further arrangements for his future. There he amused himself, as did most European youngsters, at Breach Candy Swimming Club where three young Tommies befriended him. He invited them back to the grand home in which he was staying, only to be told by his hostess that she would not entertain 'any soldier below the rank of a Captain'.[61]

In due course Patrick was dispatched, with a sinking feeling in the pit of his stomach, to the Hallett War School at Naini Tal where the headmaster assured him that he would have nothing to fear as long as he worked diligently. But he simply could not concentrate in lessons and despite regular beatings he came bottom of the class. His anxieties must have been similar to those of many children orphaned or displaced by war: 'I was troubled by my thoughts. How had my parents and brother died? What was to happen to me when I left Naini? Past and future were all jumbled up in my mind making it impossible for me to learn.' Patrick spent the next Christmas at a guest house in the town, where he was presented with another pack of Happy Families! This made him sadder than ever as he remembered 'the happy times I had with my parents and brother before the Japs entered the war in the Far East'. His only consolation was that a family he met at the guest house offered to give him a home after the war.

In the end this was not necessary. In 1943 Patrick received a long-delayed letter from his mother telling him that she and his brother Jon were alive. They had been interned by the Japanese and later released, whereupon they had gone back to England. His emotions on hearing this news were somewhat confused:

> I somehow felt that I should be even happier, even more elated, than I was. ... I think that, in my subconscious, I had by now accepted the shock that I was an orphan and that my parents and brother were dead. ... This acceptance had now been overturned.

Would I really feel the same way towards them as I had once felt? They were alive, but would my old feelings return?

It was another year before Patrick could travel home from Bombay. He was in that port waiting for a passage in April 1944 when the *Fort Stikine* blew up killing thousands of servicemen, dock workers and civilians. Now aged fifteen, Patrick did his bit and spent several days helping at a mobile canteen for fire-fighters amid 'scenes of devastation and chaos'. On 1 June he arrived at Euston Station, where Mrs Gibson and Jon were waiting for him by the barrier. After all he had gone through, he later wrote, he found it difficult to believe that he really was seeing them. In September the family heard that Mr Gibson had been killed in the Japanese internment camp. 'To me it did not come as a shock, and I never shed a tear,' wrote Patrick, 'the hurt had died in February 1942.'[62] His reaction is strikingly similar to that of the Lindsay and Thornhill children orphaned by the Mutiny after they had been sent to England. It also resembles that of Lore Segal, a Jewish child evacuated in the *Kindertransport* from Nazi-occupied Vienna but reunited with her parents during the war. When her father died just before hostilities ceased Lore, too, found that she could not mourn, 'having cut myself off from my real feelings during that first separation from my parents'.[63] Children cannot cry, any more than they can rejoice, to order.

In 1944, when Patrick Gibson made his journey of reunion to England, Raj families were beginning to feel that their children's Indian reprieve had gone on long enough. Dangerous though the seas still were, the time had come for them to be banished to boarding school. Thus in the early summer of 1944, unaware of the secretly planned D-Day landings, the Allans set off from Travancore and the Elsden-Smiths from Calcutta. Mrs Allan and her two sons had the easier journey. Nevertheless they had to spend forty-eight hours in a British Army transit camp in the Suez Canal zone, to endure 'a massive smoke-screen' from British Navy vessels to protect them in the Gulf of Tunis, and to approach Liverpool by way of the long northern route. Mrs Allan returned to India on an oil tanker, leaving George to settle in at school in Edinburgh with the help of a kindly housemistress known as Ma Penman, who was 'very supportive to any boy who was homesick'. He was to spend ten happy years there but admits that he depended greatly on a Mr and Mrs Dobson, who acted as his foster parents at weekends and in the holidays. This was a relationship which Mrs Allan was unable to appreciate; on a subsequent visit she was livid when George asked Mrs Dobson for advice and would have nothing more to do with her. But George remained close to the couple until they died and still treasures his photographs of them.[64]

The Elsden-Smiths made their ten-week voyage aboard a 'sooty and smelly' Liberty cargo ship, the *Samthar*, on which Penny and her mother were the only females. Towards the end of an uncomfortable passage, food began to run out because their large convoy, with the *Samthar* in the lead, was diverted into the Irish Sea and all the way around the north of Scotland. While her ailing parents were 'pressed to the radio' for news of the fighting in France, thirteen-year-old Penny fell deeply in love with the second officer and 'never wanted the journey to end'. The sequel to this exciting voyage was confinement in Cheltenham Ladies' College and holiday release in the home of her house-proud grandparents. It all caused Penny 'deep culture shock'. 'This was *real* imprisonment, an enforced step backwards in my growing-up.' To her, as to other young people, the trials of war had given a reward. In her case it was the sweet memory of her first kiss beneath 'a huge golden moon'.[65]

The Wilkins family were not willing to make the journey home from Orissa until the war was over, even though their furlough was long overdue. Even if they had gone to England, Eric Wilkins, who had followed in his father's footsteps as a missionary, would have been reluctant to leave his children there. He did not want them to experience the 'enforced separation' which he and his sisters had endured during and after the First World War. Despite this resolve, it was difficult to keep the family together. In 1944 seven-year-old David was sent to Woodstock, 1,450 miles away, because there were no European schools in the remote Kond hills and Honor Wilkins was too busy with a new baby to teach him herself. His mother and baby brother lived with him in Mussoorie for the first four months, after which he 'got used to things', enjoying Sports Day and the Halloween party before setting out on the 'long journey home' at the end of November.[66]

When David returned to school in March 1945 (buying a model Spitfire in Calcutta en route) things did not go so well. His early letters home reveal a heartache which is never mentioned in the memoir his father wrote. The boy fell ill soon after his arrival and wrote a letter from hospital which vividly expresses the feelings of a child facing a nine-month stint at school:

I am feeling very homesick and am wishing school would stop so that I can come home and see you all. The time is passing very slowly and it seems as though the time will never pass. I hope it will pass very soon. I wish little boys didn't have to go to school and learn. I am always thinking of you and wondering when I will ever see you again.

By the next week he was out of hospital and sounding more cheerful – although it is clear that his normal school letters were read by teachers, who sometimes added corrective notes. In May he asked his parents whether they had 'any notion of when you will take me home from school'. He was clearly hoping that they would come up for the spring break but this was impossible because Honor Wilkins had not fully recovered from the difficult birth of a third son in February. David seems to have enjoyed himself, nevertheless, on the school picnic when they had 'hamburgers, cookies, fruit and lemonade' and played games near a cave which was inhabited by a bear, according to an American soldier they met. In subsequent letters he assured his parents that he was having fun (especially in the beetle season) although he was count-ing the hours to Going-Down Day. The school clearly kept the children informed about the progress of the war, during which an ex-pupil was killed in an air battle over the Pacific. In August there was a 'lovely victory celebration' for VJ Day: 'It began with a Thanksgiving Service. Later on in the evening we dressed up and had fights. We had two days holiday. . . . Aren't you glad that peace has come at last? I am. I expect that now that the war's over we'll be able to get a passage to go home to England soon.' With this letter David enclosed a crayon drawing of the long-anticipated homecoming, showing a house with his parents and two brothers at the four windows and himself at the front door.[67] By Christmas 1945 David was at home in Orissa after what he recalls as 'an eternity'.[68]

Unlike thousands of young refugees still displaced in Europe, most Raj children were now safe with their families, in India or in England. But they were not all in 'Happy Families'. Some had lost a father. Some were too disturbed to rejoice as wholeheartedly as was expected of them. Some were staying with relatives who were strangers to them. Some no longer had a proper home. And many faced upheaval as their families prepared to leave an increasingly hostile India. Indian nationalist sentiments had been exacerbated by the conflict, to which the Viceroy, Lord Linlithgow, had 'committed over 300 million Indians

... without consulting a single one'.[69] In the wake of war these subject people, so long regarded as 'grown-up babies' or 'large children' who should be made to eat up their supper, were to win the freedom they demanded.[70] But would the real children of the Raj, whose voices had usually gone unheeded in the past, win the right to be consulted in the post-war world?

NINE

'Is that the Same Moon
that Shines in India?'

The End of the Raj and Beyond

I ndia is a land of spectres and it was always haunted by memories of the Mutiny. That event pervaded Indian minds as a heroic battle for liberation and on the twenty-fifth anniversary of Independence its 'immortal martyrs' were added to the Victorian Mutiny monument in Delhi. For the British, the apparition rose anew with every outbreak of unrest in the subcontinent. During a violent strike at the Tata Iron and Steel Works in 1920, when her husband was attacked, Lilian Luker Ashby writes, 'the ghosts of the Sepoy Mutiny, never fully laid, were abroad in every home'.[1] Such fears increased as the nationalist struggle gathered force in the 1930s, reaching a climax during the Second World War. In 1942 Linlithgow told Winston Churchill that he was dealing with 'by far the most serious rebellion since that of 1857'.[2] Yet British families came to little harm in this 'Second War of Independence' and they made a safe exit when the nationalist cause triumphed in 1947. Some were able to stay on in independent India, Pakistan, Burma or Ceylon, where they perpetuated the Raj way of life in many respects, including the treatment of their children.

For the most part children were only dimly aware of the terrors that spooked their elders. But sometimes they experienced direct manifestations themselves. The formal beginning of the nationalist movement took place in 1885, with the foundation of the Indian National Congress; but during the late nineteenth and early twentieth centuries there were many more violent expressions of resentment against the Raj. Terrorists made isolated attacks on British officials. In 1912, for example, they attempted to assassinate the Viceroy, Lord Hardinge, nearly robbing Diamond of her father and probably contributing to her mother's death. The outrage prompted the British to mount a series of propaganda exercises aimed at promoting the Raj. Lord Hardinge's recovery from his injuries was celebrated on his birthday in 1913 by official entertainments for children all over the country. Six-year-old Margaret Tait attended one of these in Bangalore. She describes 'a colossal gathering of children of all races', who enjoyed bands, games, sideshows, swings and roundabouts, fireworks and a 'Wild West melodrama' enacted by soldiers. Later in the year Margaret was conscious of 'an electric thrill in the air' when Lord and Lady Hardinge processed through Bangalore with 'a splendid mounted escort'.

Margaret was still in Bangalore during the First World War, when one and a half million Indian troops fought for Britain. She remembers the 'quite remarkable' Armistice celebrations, which took the form of 'a parade of soldiers and schoolchildren, fireworks and a procession of Hindu deities'. In her view, which was probably taken from her parents, the idea of the pageant 'came spontaneously from local Hindu leaders in a desire to commemorate the Allied victory in a most fitting manner'.[3] The Taits, like many of the British in India, did not understand how eagerly Indians such as Nirad Chaudhuri had been 'looking forward to a great advance in self-government' at the end of the war. When their loyalty and sacrifice were not rewarded with the much-vaunted prize of self-determination granted to European national groups 'India was swept by the fury of disappointment and disillusionment.'[4]

Feelings were further inflamed in 1919 by the Amritsar massacre, in which hundreds of unarmed Indians were killed by British troops after nationalist rioters had murdered several Britons and attacked a missionary woman. During those riots British mothers had feared for the safety of their children. Lady Lawrence, wife of the Commissioner for Sind province, worried that Sir Henry might 'be struck at through Owen', their baby son. Melicent Wathen, who was married to the principal of a Sikh college, carried around a bundle of clothes and food in case it should be necessary to escape into the villages where 'with the families of some of our Sikhs we hoped the children at least would be safe'. After the massacre, in which she felt the 'blackguard leaders ... got their deserts', Mrs Wathen seemed to forget the trust she had

had in Indian villagers. Indeed, feeling that she could bear India no longer, she went home to put the children into English schools.[5] More enlightened people (including her husband) realised that 'India could not be held by force alone'.[6] Rosamund Lawrence, too, recognised that the causes of discontent went deep, 'high prices and hunger adding to the persuasions of the political few, and all this coming on top of the war and the ravages of influenza'.[7] Margaret Tait was right to conclude, in looking back on the immediate post-war years, that 'things would never return to their old pattern'.[8]

Spike Milligan expressed it rather more tartly in a poem about his boyhood spent in India and Burma between 1918 and 1933. The first verse refers to Poona, where he lived during his toddler years, and the second relates to Rangoon, where his baby brother had an ayah called Minema who lived in a *godown* (outbuilding). His father was one of the 'khaki men':

> As a boy
> I watched India through fresh Empirical eyes.
> Inside my young khaki head
> I grew not knowing any other world.
> My father was a great warrior
> My mother was beautiful
>   and never washed dishes,
>   other people did that,
> I was only 4, I remember
>   they cleaned my shoes,
>   made my bed.
>
> 'Ither ow'
> 'Kom Kurrow'
> Yet, in time I found them gentler
>   than the khaki people.
> They smiled in their poverty
> After dark, when the khaki people
>   were drunk in the mess
> I could hear Minema and
>   her family praying in their godown.
> In the bazaar the khaki men
>   are brawling.
> No wonder they asked us to leave.

By the time that the Milligan family reluctantly left the 'country where the white man fared so well' the campaign for self-government was well under way.[9]

As Milligan's poem confirms, the main contact English children had with Indians was with servants, through whom they would gain little understanding of Indian (or Burmese) nationalism. Although some managed to break down the racial barriers, most children thought it natural to be segregated in their white cantonments and clubs. Morvyth Seely has a clear memory of the notice at Breach Candy Swimming Club, where she spent so many happy days in wartime Bombay: *No dogs or Indians allowed.*[10] Many memoirs by children of the Raj loyally defend their parents' imperial role. M. M. Kaye regarded her father, Sir Cecil Kaye, as 'Perfection personified' and proudly quoted *The Times of India*'s tribute to his work as a 'disinterested servant of the public' in the Intelligence Department.[11] In similar vein, Norah Burke wrote in 1969 that she was 'proud of what my country, my family and my friends did for India'. Her conclusion is characteristic: 'British rule gave peace and justice and it is high time someone said so.'[12] The young Rab Butler also saw his father, a settlement officer, patiently dispensing those boons. But it seems that the boy felt more kinship with the Indian recipients whom Montagu Butler considered to be 'like children': 'My time as a small child in Kotah made me sympathetic by instinct and in my innermost being when in later life the Indians were seen to seek and expect self-government.'[13] Thus Rab Butler was 'deeply impressed' in the 1930s by the nationalist Mahatma (great soul) Gandhi, 'the current hate figure of many Conservatives and of his father'.[14]

Some young people sensed that not everything done by the British was peaceful and just. Monica Francis Clough is still haunted by the destruction of wild jungle involved in her father's job of clearing land for new tea estates. As fires began to devour the forest 'all the birds in the world cried in alarm'.[15] Monica did not blame her father for this devastation but Jane Portal did find her nanny guilty of racial prejudice. When they encountered sweepers cleaning and hosing Malabar Hill in Bombay Nanny would tell her to 'keep away from those dirty people, we don't talk to them'.[16] Pip Mirrell was uneasy about her parents' jackal hunt thundering across peasants' cultivated fields. Harry Southwell can only explain his father's resignation from the Bombay Club when it admitted Indians in 1946 by saying that he was 'a product of his time'. Harry himself knew no Indian boys – although he discovered later that one of his friends was Eurasian and should not have been allowed into Breach Candy. By the time Michael Foss was ten he began to be 'drawn into distinctions: brown and white, servant and master, native and European, them and us'. There were complications now in his friendship with the bearer's son: 'Rahul understood very well the unwritten protocols. He was my pal, but only up to a point. There were moments − only too easily reached − where life parted us. "No, no", he would say when my brother and I proposed some unthinking devilry, "that's all right for you sahibs. Not for me."' Rahul would go off and do his geometry homework, anxious about the grades, marks and certificates on which his future depended for, unlike Michael, he had 'nothing to fall back on'.[17] Thus their paths began to diverge.

Educated young Indians like Rahul were especially likely to join the independence movement. It is not surprising that Jaya Bolt (née Chandran) became a nationalist in her early adult life. She was one of a quota of Indian scholars at the Unitarian Clarence School in Bangalore during the 1930s, and was invited to a birthday party by Maureen, an English classmate. When seven-year-old Jaya arrived at the house, dressed in her best clothes and with 'a blue ribbon in my long black hair', she was turned away by Maureen's 'plump and pink' mother and jeered at by the white girls' ayahs who were 'squatting at one side of the porch'. This incident made a lasting impression on Jaya, who can still recall her own feelings of rejection and embarrassment and her mother's quiet anger.[18] And how must Vijaya Lakshmi Pandit have felt when she encountered park benches marked 'For Europeans Only'? Her own home in Allahabad contained a riding ring, indoor swimming-pool and fountain filled with ice and sweet-smelling flowers. Her brother was Jawaharlal Nehru, who had been to school at Harrow and became a Congress leader and first Prime Minister of independent India. Yet she was not thought fit company for a European.[19] Similarly, Nirad Chaudhuri, who as a student in Calcutta found himself rebuffed in areas which 'were roped off from us', grew to despise the British.[20] Other nationalists have recorded a youthful political awakening which resulted from witnessing 'the violence of colonial rule'.[21] 'Nothing', concludes one historian, 'excited so much anger among Raj subjects as racism.'[22]

Many children could understand injustice when they witnessed it but they were much less likely to follow the complicated political developments of the inter-war years: the failure of Royal Commissions and Round Table Conferences to satisfy nationalist aspirations; the growth of the Muslim League and calls for the separate state of Pakistan; and the ambiguous Government of India Act of 1935, which granted autonomy to the provinces while holding India to the Empire. But written and oral memoirs of the 1920s and 1930s often mention the popularity of Mahatma Gandhi and his campaign of *satyagraha* (peaceful resistance). Guy Wheeler, as a schoolboy in Bombay, actually saw him in action. On one occasion he came across 'vast crowds of natives with white Congress caps on their heads, listening to a bespectacled figure on a soap-box' and being watched by 'mounted English police'. Suddenly lines of 'Indian police advanced, lathis turning like propellers through seaweed'. As the crowds broke up, Guy and his friends were guarded by an armed and mounted English policeman who seemed to them like 'a knight in shining armour'. In fact, after Amritsar the British were reluctant to shoot on Indian crowds. Guy and the other boys were not worried by such gatherings. They even made a mockery of the Indian nationalists and bought themselves spinning-wheels (the symbol of Gandhi's boycott of foreign-made textiles), until they were accused by older boys of 'going native'. Sometimes Guy would idly wonder whether the Indian barber might use his 'cut-throat razors' against him. But in practice 'children were never molested'.[23]

Two British children living in Calcutta actually participated in a nationalist demonstration. Juliet Clough (whose father worked for a tea company and 'had many Indian friends') recalls this unusual scene, along with the normal memories of birthday parties at the Saturday Club and Christmas at Gobalpur: 'Well before dysentery banished us, aged four and six respectively, to the alien planet known as Home, my brother and I had spent a memorable day riding round Calcutta on a lorry draped with green and orange flags. "Jai hind!" we shouted: "Victory to India!"' Pupils at Woodstock School, which had some Indian pupils, also approved of the Mahatma. Henry Scholberg remembers that one of his classmates was a Gandhi follower and that he was 'with him all the way'.[24] At more traditional English schools (like the Lawrence Asylum or the New School) Gandhi's campaign 'did not attract much sympathy among the pupils' who had learnt to see him 'as poison not as a saint'.[25] Margot Bell's attitude was rather similar. When she returned to India in 1933 at the age of seventeen, her father, Sir Robert Bell, was a member of the Bombay Government and the 'civil disobedience movement was in full swing'. While she enjoyed her social life in the Poona Gymkhana Club and the Bombay Yacht Club, thousands of Congress members were imprisoned. Sir Robert was personally responsible for Gandhi who was in Yeravda Jail, next door to the Bells' house in Poona. Margot remembers overhearing a worried conversation between her father and the jail governor about the precarious health of the Mahatma, who was engaged on one of his life-threatening fasts. Yet, she remarks, 'he seemed to survive them better than his jailers.' She loyally defends the record of British officials like her father, who were mainly 'calm, professional, gentle, hard-working and devoted to the India they served'.[26]

Gandhi's own brand of moral force could not prevent the eruption of violence during and after the Second World War. In the 'Quit India' campaign of 1942 rioters attacked police stations, public buildings, trains and railway installations. Hundreds were killed when policemen and soldiers opened fire. To add to the misery, famine in Bengal caused about three million deaths in 1943. Many more lost their lives in the self-proclaimed Indian National Army which fought beside the Japanese under the slogan 'Asia for the Asiatics'. Much more blood was shed in 1946, when thousands were slaughtered in Calcutta alone during conflict between Hindus and Muslims. During the Bombay naval mutiny of 1946 ships' guns were trained on 'those twin bastions of the European community', the Yacht Club and the Taj Mahal Hotel, though neither was shelled.[27] According to Wilfred Russell, who worked for a firm of merchants in Bombay at that time: 'A Political Officer was burnt alive; the Master of the Hunt was knocked out by a brick hurled through the window of his car; nobody went to the office for three days. . . . Our rule was more unpopular than it had ever been since the East India Company established the first factory at Surat in 1612.'[28] Eventually the post-war Labour Government appointed Lord Mountbatten as the last Viceroy. He was instructed to engineer Britain's withdrawal and he hastened the inevitable by declaring that Indian Independence would take place at midnight on 14 August 1947. A separate state, Pakistan, was created for Muslims. In the prelude to, and aftermath of, this hurried partition communal violence, now also involving Sikhs in the Punjab, reached new heights. Perhaps as many as a million Indians died.

In the midst of this upheaval Anglo-Indian families continued to live much as they had always done. And teenage girls felt more at risk from British troops on leave or 'lorry loads of GIs' than from nationalist demonstrators.[29] But it was clear that the end of the Raj was near. 'This would be our last summer in Kashmir... the children were blissfully happy with their life of picnics and riding,' wrote Viola Bayley. Once back in Lahore she heard crowds shouting for the British to go, which 'made one picture only too vividly the days of the Mutiny'.[30] Another mother's memory reflects the same fear and it also illustrates the fact that most demonstrators felt little personal hostility to Europeans:

> One day we heard a chanting crowd coming from town and a procession of schoolboys of all sizes, carrying Congress flags and Quit India banners, came into sight. My little son escaped from his horrified ayah and, a toy gun on his shoulder, toddled up to see this fine sight; the boys started to laugh, gave a cheer and passed happily on their way.[31]

As one of Gandhi's followers explained to Lillan Luker Ashby, when she asked him why the Mahatma did not like the British: 'He doesn't dislike them. His good friends are English gentlemen. He likes them. He hates the rule.' The historian Trevor Royle, who grew up in India, concludes that 'dissatisfaction was aimed at the British government as the instrument of foreign rule and not at the British in India as people'.[32] Moreover, as the journalist Ann Leslie reflected when revisiting the land of her birth on the fiftieth anniversary of Independence, 'it was assumed that we were leaving anyway. ... We did not need to be ethnically cleansed.'[33]

Many children, then, were aware of frightening events but they rarely suffered harm. Morvyth St George was involved in an incident during anti-British demonstrations in Bombay, where both Gandhi and Muhammad Ali Jinnah (the Muslim leader) were living:

> My mother, brother and I were returning from a trip to the Army and Navy Stores, when we were stopped by a mob wielding lathis which they beat against the car. Our driver, Douglas, somehow quenched the fierce anger with a few quiet words, and swiftly drove us away, but it was an alarming moment, seeing people we children thought of as friendly suddenly turning into an angry, potentially violent mob.[34]

Train journeys were even more worrying. George Allan and his brother were fearful of taking the slow-moving funicular train down from the Nilgiri hills because they had heard about 'explosives being

used to blow up road and rail bridges'.[35] During the communal massacres of 1947 Hazel Hooper and her baby son were actually on board
a train to Madras when it was attacked by Muslims. She hastily hid
the Hindu ayah whom she had with her when assailants came to their
carriage: 'They had no quarrel with us, but if they'd seen my Ayah
they'd have killed her.'[36] A similar incident occurred on the Woodstock
school train which was attacked by Hindus: a group of students
covered up a Muslim fellow-passenger with a bed-roll and lounged on
top of him. A Muslim pupil was dressed in American clothes for Going-
Down Day and had his trunk marked with the name Smith. It was a
reversal of the situation in 1857, when Indians had often helped English
children to escape the violence.

Ann Leslie, who was a small child in India at this time, has an
enduring recollection of being on a train when it was held up by
Hindus: 'The long Indian train clattered and screeched to a halt somewhere in the middle of nowhere. A sudden silence. And then the
screams. My mother clutched me to her, covered my eyes, told me not
to be scared, there was nothing to worry about. And there wasn't: not
for us, at least.' Ann Leslie still feels 'an almost tearful relief' that her
father's bearer and her beloved protector, Yah Mohammed, was not
with them at that time; he, as a Muslim, would certainly have been
killed. It was only later that she was told the story of how Yah Mohammed had brought her home from a friend's garden during the Calcutta
killings of 1946. At great risk to himself he 'climbed over garden walls
and hurried down alleys, carrying the little white *missy baba* [young
girl] to safety on his spindly back'.[37]

Children with homes in or near Calcutta were particularly likely to
witness carnage or the results of it. Janet Wenger, who was living in
the mission compound at Barisal, has several vivid memories: seeing
villages burning on the other side of the river; taking bananas to two
Indian girls hidden under the stairs after they had fled from a riot; and
watching their Hindu cook look after a Muslim who had been beaten
up. But she always felt sure that Indians would never do anything to
harm children like her. Cliff Richard, who lived right in Calcutta at the
same time, claims in his autobiography that he revelled in hearing
gunfire in the nearby park: 'This was better than Cops and Robbers.'
He also remembers his family helping a Muslim on the run by lowering
food down to him over the wall and whisking him away in a lorry with
some of their Muslim servants.[38] Steve Turner's biography suggests,
though, that the boy was frightened when demonstrators shouted

insults at his mother in the street. Yoma Crosfield was not exposed to such scenes for she was forbidden to leave her house in Calcutta. She resented not being given any explanation of the riots: 'As usual, my grownups tried to shield me from knowing too much.'[39] Soon after the massacres Brian Outhwaite's father, based at Calcutta, was involved in the 'horrid, disgusting and thankless task' of clearing up the bodies left after the conflict.[40] At the same time Brian was not conscious of any anti-European feeling.

Iris Portal explained why she decided that it was time to go and at the same time she unwittingly illustrated why Indians 'asked us to leave'. In 1942 she came across a band of youths on the road shouting 'Quit India': 'I rode my bicycle straight at them. They fell apart into the roadside rubble and I went on, realising that they were right. The job was done – my job, Britain's job. The boys were right.'[41] It was at this point that Mrs Portal decided to return to her daughters in England. Four or five years later most of her compatriots followed her home, taking their children with them. The Parkers, for instance, came back with their three children in 1946 after spending the war years together in India. Christopher remembers hearing about the Partition troubles after they had arrived in Britain and being anxious to know whether their servants were safe. Ten-year-old Michael Foss, departing with his family in 1948, was aware that they were leaving behind them 'the tumult of partition' in which five million people in the Punjab became 'wanderers looking for home'.[42] Among these refugees were thousands of Muslim, Hindu and Sikh children displaced, abandoned, or killed in the mayhem. An Indian historian concludes that most of them have been 'lost to history'.[43] This is not the case for their British contemporaries, many of whom have left records and recollections of returning home.

There were some families, caught in the most violent north-west region, whose last weeks in India were fraught with anxiety, if not actual danger. When Patrick Brendon's first child was born in Delhi in February 1947, Hindu/Muslim conflict was just starting to become serious in and around the capital. As Deputy Commissioner for the Gurgaon region, Brendon was sent to deal with each new outbreak of trouble. En route to investigate a bazaar riot at Taoru, he stopped off to see his wife and baby at Willingdon Nursing Home. As he recalls in his memoir: 'I was very dirty and everyone there looked more than a little perplexed. New Delhi had not by then adjusted to communal fighting.'

After this the 'real slaughter' began and Brendon witnessed many villages blazing at night – 'a sight to which I never became hardened'. By June 'the civil administration was ... completely paralysed' and Brendon had become a 'public enemy' of the Hindus, whom he believed to be the aggressors in this area. Needing some respite after three months of arduous activity he went on leave, joining his wife and baby in Simla. There he decided 'to get my family and myself out of India before the situation became even worse'. To his great surprise a party of Hindus, including two whom he had sent to prison, came to say farewell. Nevertheless, he was glad to quit India's shores. 'We left just in time. A week later my wife would have been marooned in Simla.'[44]

This is just what happened in September that year to the family of John Christie (who had joined the ICS after his English education at St Cyprian's and Eton). He and his wife had taken their own four children and two of a friend's children to Simla for 'a short holiday – which, in fact, became a siege'. As Muslims migrated west and Hindus and Sikhs journeyed east after Partition, violence erupted in Simla and a curfew was declared. 'The feeding of the young menagerie was now a problem.' During the month that they were cut off the Christies had to dash out to the bazaars whenever the curfew was lifted, sometimes witnessing murders on the way. In October they went to Delhi by road, in a convoy escorted by Royal Scots Fusiliers, passing through 'country where the stench of death was evidence enough of the horrors of recent weeks'.[45] However the Christies had already decided to stay on in India and these events did not shake their resolve. Meanwhile other British residents were snatching a last holiday on houseboats in 'the cherished holiday resort' of Kashmir. This princely state was still precariously independent but both India and Pakistan laid claim to it. When fighting broke out in October 1947 British holidaymakers were much less at risk than Kashmiri refugees; but Field Marshal Auchinleck (the Commander-in-Chief) was moved by the plight of the British 'Kashmir wives', among whom was the family of his Director of Military Operations. So he ordered an airborne evacuation of 'the motley collection of women, children, cats, dogs, parrots and retainers'.[46]

For most returning expatriates, though, the 1947 experience was probably not very different from that of families who had packed up and come home in earlier years. Despite the communal cataclysm, Michael Foss observed, 'the transients of the Raj' endured no great hardship. Admittedly he himself was 'grouchy and fretful' to be leaving 'the vastness of open land under permissive skies where almost nothing was forbidden the privilege of boyhood'.[47] Departing from the shores of India was a mixed blessing, which could bring both sweetness and sorrow.

Homecoming had always meant the benefit of a settled family life, an end to what Henry Beveridge called 'the vagrant years'.[48] Some children experienced a particularly intense feeling of relief. Tom Stoppard had been forced by the war to leave homes in Czechoslovakia and Singapore before settling in Darjeeling in 1943. There he suffered the further blow of his father's death at the hands of the Japanese in Singapore. As soon as he arrived in England in 1946, accompanied by his mother, brother and English stepfather, Major Stoppard, he knew that he had found a home. 'I embraced the language,' he said, 'and the landscape.'[49] Stoppard found that the three years he had spent at Mount Hermon School ensured 'a smooth passage to an English prep school' but his Indian schooldays made an indelible impression on his mind. For example, he remembers vividly the boys having their hair dried by Matron on hair-wash night and says that 'the smell of damp hair cooking in the blast of an electric dryer is still a Proustian trigger for pleasurable and disturbing emotions'.[50]

Leaving India could be more painful for children who had always lived there. Yoma Crosfield had little idea of what 'Home' would be like; when taken to a Glasgow restaurant soon after arriving in 1946, she asked for *nimbu pani* (fresh lime juice) with ice. The same phenomenon was common in old boys of the Lawrence School at Sanawar who often had 'difficulty in settling down in England, as the Indian experience probably came in the way'.[51] Michael McNay, who left the school at the end of 1946 and secured a passage from India in the summer of 1947, is a case in point. He was glad to escape from the harsh regime of Sanawar depicted in Chapter Five and looked forward to living in England. But on arrival he was struck by the drabness: 'it seemed such a grey country when I had been promised it was green'. Although too old to take the 11+ exam introduced by Butler's Education Act of 1944, he was admitted to one of the new grammar schools. But because of the gap in his education he found it difficult to cope with the whole curriculum and was put down to the C stream. He failed his O-levels in most subjects. But such was his exceptional interest in, and aptitude for, literature that he gained a place to read English at Balliol College, Oxford. By that time he had got used to England although he still does not feel at home here. His two older brothers, who found it even more difficult to adjust, eventually emigrated to Australia and New Zealand. In former times, of course, they might well have returned to work in India, like so many earlier children of the Raj.

A particular problem for many families coming home during the years of Depression, war and post-war austerity, was that they were reduced to a lower standard of living than they had enjoyed in India. The contrast was most marked for ordinary NCOs who left servants and comfortable bungalows for a life of deprivation. The Milligans, thrust out by a reduction in troop numbers in 1933, returned to 'a slum' and 'a damp, dead greyness' in south London. Fifteen-year-old Terence was 'thrown into a state of shock from which I never properly recovered'. He spent long hours playing fantasy games with his younger brother about the 'land of Lamania' and failed to get into the RAF because of his 'impoverished educational background'. Then he took a series of unsuitable clerical and manual jobs and ended up in court for stealing cigarettes which he sold in order to save up for a trumpet. His father, who understood his confused state of mind, defended him before the judge on the grounds that 'he is an artist, Sir, and wanted only to enrich his life'.[52] It was the war that gave Terence the chance to do just that by becoming involved in troop entertainment. This was how Terence was transformed into Spike.

The Outhwaite family decided to return in 1944, making the journey in a convoy of troopships accompanied by destroyers and barrage balloons, a most exciting experience for nine-year-old Brian. They had no choice but to stay in the grandparents' two-bedroom miners' cottage in Pontypool. For the next two years 'there were never less than three to a bed' and washing took place at a bench in the garden. Conditions were so tough that the family took the risk of going back to India, only to be forced to leave when Independence came in 1947. Several years of peripatetic life in transit camps ensued. Brian, at least, was spotted as 'a clever boy' and passed the 13+ exam for late entry to a grammar school. But he still had to change schools frequently – with the result that he came to know a great deal about 'The Foreign Policy of Castlereagh and Canning' because 'they were always doing that topic when I arrived at a school'. These difficult years took their toll on his parents, who 'quarrelled incessantly'. So it was actually a relief to Brian when his father was posted to Hong Kong, to be left with foster parents in England, enjoying the benefit of an academic education which army schools in India had not provided. Now sixteen years old, he was ready to enjoy 'a measure of independence'. He went on to university and ended up as a History don at Cambridge.[53]

The Webb family's return in 1948 was no more auspicious. Both of Harry's parents had been born and brought up in India, where his father worked for the Kellner Company, well known in its day for railway catering. After witnessing much slaughter in Calcutta they decided to follow Mrs Webb's mother to England. Since Mr Webb had only £5 in his pocket and no prospect of a job, he and his family were obliged to share one room in his mother-in-law's Carshalton house, while trying to adjust to a country none of them knew at all. Harry found life particularly difficult in Carshalton because of the taunts provoked by his unusual background, as described in Chapter Two. He failed the 11+ but when his parents found a council house and work in Cheshunt during the 1950s he began to feel more secure. It was here, under the inspiration of Bill Haley's revolutionary 'Rock Around the Clock', that Harry Webb began to discover the talents which would turn him into Cliff Richard.

Homecoming was not usually such a problem for middle-class families. Viola Bayley, wife of an Intelligence officer in the Indian Police, had been bequeathed a house in Rye by her parents. It had, however, been reduced to squalor by troops quartered there during the war and Mrs Bayley, whose 'domestic abilities' were minimal, had to spend most of 1946 coping with the house and garden. Meanwhile their children, aged twelve, eight and four (who had stayed with their parents in India because of the war), took an 'absolute delight in the place which, shabbiness and all, they had instantly adopted as home'. Vernon Bayley was offered another post in Delhi after Independence but was declared *persona non grata* by the Indian Government when he got there. This spared the children the sorrow of separation – Mrs Bayley had intended to accompany her husband and to follow tradition by leaving them behind. The children may have been missing India more than their mother realised. One evening four-year-old Rosamund wistfully asked her old English nanny, 'Is that the same moon that shines in India?' Nanny was not certain but she reassured the child that there was at least this comforting link with her native land.[54]

Not all middle-class families were as lucky as the Bayleys in having a home to return to. More common was the experience of the St George family. When they left Bombay, where Mr St George had worked for twenty years on *The Times of India*, they had to live in a hotel until they found a house in Sussex, which then had to be furnished from scratch. But Mrs St George was, her daughter proudly told me, a Welsh woman and a good adapter. Despite having had servants for all her married life, she soon knuckled down to such tasks as cooking whale steaks and pickling eggs. Ten-year-old Morvyth also adjusted quickly, even though she had been heartbroken at leaving the family ayah and bearer, who had waved them off from Bombay docks. But she did not really say her final farewell to India until after her mother's death forty-nine years later. Then she and her brother revisited all the scenes of their childhood and had an emotional reunion with some of their Parsee friends in Bombay.

Another daughter who witnessed the problems of making a home in post-war Britain was Hilary Johnston, who has written sympathetically of her mother's struggles. Her parents had no private means but Ronald Johnston had saved up from his ICS salary to realise his retirement dream of setting up a commercial apple orchard in Dorset. Hilary, who was fifteen at the time, can still picture her mother's labours after they moved into a house which had been full of evacuees. She stripped floors with sugar soap and then polished them on her hands and knees. She haunted auction rooms for furniture. She washed clothes on a scrubbing-board with coarse yellow soap and got nail infections from gardening afterwards. Life was made all the more arduous by food and petrol rationing and shortages of such commodities as paint. Mrs Johnston coped with all this cheerfully for she was not 'a pampered woman'; her lonely life in remote *mofussil* postings had not been easy despite the loyal servants, who 'kept in touch for years via the bazaar letter writer'. In general, she found it a relief to be back in 'England's green, pleasant and friendly land', with the comfort of a village church and an intimate community. Another bonus was 'having her child at home' more frequently than had been possible in India with its customary nine-month school terms.

Hilary's experience was different. She had been at the 'cold and unfriendly' Sherborne School since 1945. There she toiled to keep up with lessons, tried in vain to make a friend ('there just wasn't anyone') and spent her holidays in Lyme Regis with her mother's unmarried sister. In fact, the unhappy girl had grown to love Aunt Constance, 'the best aunt you could ever have', who never chided her for 'dire' reports from Sherborne. Like other children who had made alternative attachments, Hilary found it hard to adjust to parents who were 'a bit demanding at times'.[55]

Returning Raj parents like the Johnstons usually carried on the boarding school tradition, although there were good private and state day schools such as those which helped Ruth Starte, Brian Outhwaite and Michael McNay to get into university. One historian judges that 'for the Imperial ruling cadre, the [public] school was of unmistakably paramount importance' and 'separation was a *rite de passage* as marked as a ritual of aboriginals'.[56] Thus, when the New School at Darjeeling closed at the end of the war, Mark Tully was sent to an English prep school 'behind high walls' and then became further 'institutionalised' at Marlborough.[57] Christopher Parker and his brother, who appear on home movie film with the Tully children in Delhi gardens and at Indian seaside resorts, were also sent to Marlborough after their parents' return to England. This was surprising in view of the fact that Mr Parker, a box-wallah despite his good job at ICI, had disliked the ex-public-school boys of the ICS who were so 'conscious of the social hierarchy'. In fact Christopher found that the school suited him pretty well – but he has not sent his own children to boarding school.[58]

In some instances it was difficult to find a suitably genteel establishment, especially for a boy like Harry Southwell, who was already fourteen when he came back to England after his scanty education in wartime Bombay. His parents eventually got him into a Berkshire boarding school. But 'it didn't work out' academically and Harry left without ever having sat an exam – though he later passed all his banking exams with no trouble and has been educating himself ever since. Still, his years at Breach Candy Club stood Harry in good stead by making him 'the best swimmer the school had ever known'. That sporting prowess helped to win him popularity. Despite this he found that he missed home much more than he had when originally sent to an English boarding school at the age of six. Eventually he put down roots in Newcastle, where his parents had settled, and he still thinks of himself as a Geordie, though he now lives in Cornwall.[59]

So it was that many Raj children did not actually spend much time with their families even after they had come 'Home'. They were in the same position as Winston Churchill, who concluded about his 'barren and unhappy years' at Harrow:

> I would far rather have been apprenticed as a bricklayer's mate, or run errands as a messenger boy, or helped my father to dress the front windows of a grocer's shop. It would have been real; it would have been natural; it would have taught me more; and I should have

done it much better. Also I should have got to know my father, which would have been a great joy to me.[60]

His feelings are echoed by some children of the Raj. For Roger Moore it was 'a big tragedy' that his father died in 1948, 'just as I was getting to know him'. And he found he had 'nothing in common' with his mother, who always treated him as though he was five – the age he had been when first separated from her.[61] Mark Tully too has admitted with regret that a distance developed between him and his mother, explaining that 'I didn't want any interference in my life'.[62]

As the twentieth century progressed, however, more imperial parents 'were trying to change this pattern of behaviour'. So said Anne Battye, who is descended on both sides from long-serving Raj families which had suffered lengthy separations between parents and children – the 'curse of the East'. Her great-grandfather was Legh Battye, one of the Victorian 'Fighting Ten' mentioned in Chapter Three. All ten Battye boys (and their one sister) had been sent from India to their grandmother's house in London, where they received maternal letters impressing on them 'the importance of saying their prayers and the daily reading of their Bibles'.[63] Anne's mother, Joan, was the daughter of Sir Robert Reid, Governor of Assam and Acting Governor of Bengal. When sent to Battle Abbey for her English education, Joan had been 'a lonely, miserable little girl'. After marrying Keith Battye of the Indian Army in 1937 she knew that she was in for a life of adventure. But Joan wanted to avoid being parted from her own children, Anne, Trish and Ian, who were born in 1938, 1941 and 1944. 'The war helped because it was so frightening to send a child away.' Despite all the difficulties, she gave Anne and Trish systematic PNEU lessons and tests before the whole family came home on post-war leave in 1946.

At the end of this furlough, spent mostly in helping the recently retired Reids to furnish and organise a large Suffolk home, Mrs Battye decided to leave eight-year-old Anne in England. Although Anne knows that her mother 'went through many a troubled time thinking about what to do with her', she has never really understood the reasons for her abandonment. Was it because there was 'little prospect of tuition' in India, as Joan Battye's memoir claims? Was it because of 'pressure from her own parents and the force of tradition', as Anne thinks likely? Or was it, she sometimes wonders, because she was not 'an easy child'? Whatever the truth, Anne put her foot down, refusing to be left at a PNEU boarding school in Sudbury, as had been planned.

She got part of her own way and lived with the Reid grandparents (whom she loved) in Holbrook House, being taught by her mother's old governess. In retrospect Joan Battye considered that 'it was a mistake as we were posted to Mount Abu where I could have got teaching help'. For her part, Anne still feels that 'any separation has a destabilising effect on relationships within a family' and suspects that her sister and brother forgot all about her when she was no longer there.

Indian Independence rescued Anne from exile since the rest of the family came back in 1947. For a time they all lived in Holbrook House, together with an uncle who had walked out of Burma twice. This became for her sister Trish, who had never lived anywhere long enough to put down roots, her first real home. She remembers it with photographic clarity: 'I could draw *everywhere* in it – all the pictures and wardrobes and everything.' But Keith Battye (whom Anne describes as 'a killer, mostly of animals') could not settle in England.[64] In this he was not unusual; there are many examples of men who found it hard to make the transition 'from Somebodies to Nobodies'.[65] Like other restless exiles from the Raj, Battye decided to seek adventure in colonial Africa, and the whole family moved to Dar es Salaam. This time no one was left behind, for Mrs Battye 'had had enough of separation'. Yet, after two years with Trish at Sao Hill School, to which they travelled by plane taking turns in the cockpit, Anne was sent to St Margaret's School in Ludlow. In the holidays she lived with her grandparents. Now twelve years old, Anne still disliked boarding school but she 'stuck it'. 'I found a way of dealing with it by playing music, reading books and hiding from people.' Trish joined her there a year later but the sisters did not get on well at this stage; Anne resented intrusion into her 'little kingdom' while Trish, by her own admission, 'preferred animals to people'. It was a help, though, that every year their mother came to see them or they flew out to Africa so that 'we were never separated for more than about half a year'.

After leaving school Anne went to join her parents in Africa. But she resented the fact that they wanted her with them at last just when she wanted to escape. While she was there her father, who hunted elephant in order to pay the school fees and air fares, was killed in a shooting accident. The family's attempt to establish a new *modus vivendi* had not been entirely successful and now ended in tragedy. Anne was left with the feeling that she 'was constantly being pushed away and then drawn back' to suit her parents, although she knows they did the best they could in the circumstances. But Trish, who was not sent to a separate country until she was ten, remembers 'a constancy within the family' despite its frequent moves. Both girls benefited from easier (though still expensive) international travel in the 1950s. And both retain wonderful memories of living in India and Africa.[66]

Once India became independent there was no further need for work like Keith Battye's: serving in the Political Department of the Army, he had acted as British Resident in various princely states. Others, however, were able to stay on in a land where the economy, the political and educational systems and the working language were familiar to them. Businessmen, planters of tea, jute, rubber and coconut, political advisers and missionaries (who were often teachers or doctors) could all earn their living in independent India and Pakistan; or in Ceylon and Burma, which both became self-governing in 1948. Thus Michael Thomas's father carried on his India-based career with Shell until 1953 – and also perpetuated expatriate English traditions in the education of his only child. Michael's older cousin was Roger Moore, who had gone to school in England in 1932. Much to Roger's envy, Michael was forced by the war to undergo an extended period of education in India. Actually Michael says that he wasn't particularly happy at his three Indian boarding schools: St Hilda's in Ooty, Tiger Hill in Coonoor and Sheikh Bagh at Srinagar. But he certainly had more parental contact than did Roger.

In 1946, when Michael was twelve, he went with his mother and father on the three-day journey by flying-boat from Karachi to England. Later in the year his parents returned to India, leaving their son at Rugby, which had not changed much since Mr Thomas's own time there. Like Roger before him, Michael spent his school holidays with different relations and family friends, his mother being anxious that he should not be too much of a burden to anyone. His favourite guardian was his mother's youngest sister, Auntie Val, who had never forgotten her own experience of being sent back to England at the age of three. His least favourite was an army officer friend of his father's, who made him feel 'a bit superfluous'. Michael saw his mother and father only when they came home on leave in 1948 and 1951. For firms like Shell did not yet pay for their employees' children to use costly international flights – these were all first-class, often in converted military planes, with cocktail bars in the gun turrets.

Michael Thomas gives a rational analysis of the social and cultural reasons behind his being sent back to England. He is clear that it was not done for reasons of health, as by that time there were injections against most illnesses, including plague, which broke out in India during his time there. He understands his parents' concern that he should not become 'Indianised' and realises that he has benefited from the conventional academic English education they provided. On another level he recalls that he spent his school years living 'out of a suitcase' with nowhere that he could call home. He did not send his own sons to boarding school, even though he acknowledges that they were by then 'much happier places with more access to parents'.[67]

It is often assumed that England-based children had frequent access to parents soon after the Raj ended. Trevor Royle, for instance, claims that 'thanks to air travel they could go out to India for the holidays'.[68] Closer examination reveals that it was not as easy as all that.

The historian Charles Allen, whose father stayed on as a political adviser, came to England in 1948 when he was eight and did not return to India until he was fourteen. In the meantime, he met his father at three-yearly intervals and never got to know him. He saw his mother when she came back by sea between furloughs and otherwise spent the holidays (with his brother) in the care of very strict 'Victorian' grandparents, who did not relate to children at all. Like so many youngsters before him, Charles was 'not quite unscathed' by his dismal Christmases and long periods of separation. It was only with their daughter, who was born in 1947, that the Allens broke away from Raj practice by taking the risk of an education in India.[69] But George Kennedy and his sister (born in 1945 and 1947) were each sent to Britain when they were seven, while their father stayed on as a manager in the jute business and as a European Member of the Bengal Assembly. In traditional fashion, Mrs Kennedy made regular sea journeys to visit their children, who did not return to India. George has only 'cheerful memories' both of his Scottish schools and of holidays with his aunt and boy cousins. He was apparently unharmed by the 'culture of the age' and went on to pursue a distinguished military career, ending up as a Major-General in the Gordon Highlanders.[70]

Lesley Hayward's post-war experience was similar to that of the Allen brothers and the Kennedy children. When her father and step-mother left her at Micklefield School, Seaford, in 1947 she 'hated saying goodbye to the family, knowing I would not see them again for three years'. There were consolations. She loved her new school and excelled in sport and music as she had at the Hill School in Ceylon. And she caught up with her glamorous seventeen-year-old sister, Liz, after a gap of seven years. But she dreaded the holidays with her 'incredibly strict' uncle and aunt in Surrey, where she was 'unhappy beyond words', especially after Liz returned to Ceylon in 1948.

In retrospect Lesley realises that it must have been difficult for her uncle and aunt, who were in their sixties, to cope with a 'pretty wild' teenager. 'She used to buy smock dresses for me when I was fourteen or fifteen and I would never dream of saying I didn't like them.' In any case there was no question of her flying out to join her family, whom she did not see until 1950. By this time, recalls Lesley, 'I was nearly sixteen years old and somewhat changed from the thirteen-year-old they had left.' Mr Hayward finally retired from the rubber business in 1953, by which time his daughters' childhood and adolescence were over. In that year Lesley began her nursing career and Liz got engaged to be married. The sisters have remained devoted to each other ever since and have fond memories of their stepmother but they never formed a close relationship with their father.[71]

Missionary societies were even less likely than Shell bosses or plantation owners to pay for luxurious air travel and they granted home leave only once every five years. So Tony Bottoms, who had travelled to England with his family in 1945 when he was six, remembers that he saw his parents together only twice between their return to the mission station in 1946 and 1960; he had his mother's company for a precious extra six months when she came back to nurse her dying mother. During the couple's second furlough in 1956, Tony and his brother and sister made it clear to their parents that they would prefer them to come home because they were so unhappy with the aunt who looked after them. By the time the doctor and his wife did take early retirement in 1960 Tony had left Eltham College (which had been his 'saving grace') and gone up to Oxford. But he was glad that he could now return to a loving home for his university vacations.[72]

David Wilkins, whom we saw arriving home from Woodstock School at the end of Chapter Eight, was much luckier in his post-war experience of England. Eric and Honor Wilkins came home on a troopship in 1946 but were confident that Indians would welcome them again 'knowing that those of us who came back had their welfare at heart'. After two and a half years of retraining in Britain they returned to the hospital they had built in Orissa, taking their two youngest sons with them and reluctantly leaving eleven-year-old David at Eltham. But Eric Wilkins remembered the past and prepared for the future. Because of his own years of 'enforced separation' and lack of home life, he decided not to 'impose this deprivation on our children'. So he broke the age-old pattern. He told the Baptist Missionary Society that he would go back to India only for three years, during which time David would remain in England under the care of Eric's unmarried sister, Joyce.[73]

Not only did David have the security of knowing that the parting was for a fixed period but he was also 'a lucky boy to have Joyce as a guardian'.[74] As we saw in Chapter Seven, Joyce Wilkins had suffered a great deal as a child and she still bore the scars of those days. In 1949 she had a nervous breakdown, of which her nephew was probably unaware. It is likely that her own experience helped to make Joyce an ideal aunt. She found it fun to have David to stay in the holidays. She was 'proud and pleased' to see him go up for the prizes he regularly won at Eltham and showed wisdom in guiding the adolescent boy. She allowed him to go off on long bicycle tours with his cousin John, son of her sister Dorothy. And she was tactful in her efforts to curb his extravagant spending habits: 'I try not to interfere too much, but to make him think a bit before rushing in to buy things.'[75] David's letters refer to gorgeous holidays 'full of fun and enjoyment'. He describes such boyish activities as midnight feasts, making fires, shooting air pistols and developing photographs. When, during the holiday that Joyce was ill, he went to some other relations he felt the difference between her and 'people who don't know me quite so well . . . and do not trust me to look after myself'.[76] In retrospect David pays heartfelt tribute to his aunt: 'I was the child she never had and she became a mother-figure. She had the knack of giving me leeway as an adolescent – she gave me a lot of freedom but there was always security.'[77]

Meanwhile, in India, Eric and Honor Wilkins were educating their younger sons by the PNEU system, thus earning the nickname 'pneumatic parents'. Judging by seven-year-old Bobby's nature notebooks, they seem to have been pretty successful. And David had obviously found his father's earlier instruction useful, for when he was given school lectures 'on the subject of sex' he found that 'there was nothing said that I didn't know from what you told me'.[78] In 1951 the Wilkins parents kept their word. They left Orissa 'with many regrets' and on the sea voyage home they prepared for their meeting with 'the young man who will greet us'.[79] In one way their arrival was a relief to David, for he had not liked Eltham where he was sometimes bullied and quite often caned; his housemaster would 'turn the screw' by making him wait all day for the punishment. David much preferred the co-educational Dorking County Grammar School, where he was picked out as 'Cambridge material'. The drawback of his parents' return was that he lost Aunt Joyce and had to adjust to his mother, who expected him 'to be the son of the house, do what I was told and be subservient to her will'. Of course it must have been hard for Joyce Wilkins too. She wisely retired from the scene so as to avoid any battle for David's affections, worrying at the same time that the boy might feel that she had deserted him.[80] Whether from innate sensitivity or from her acquaintance with Dorothy's work as a psychologist, Joyce seemed to understand the emotional conflict which could spring from family separations. David's younger brothers did not have to suffer this stress, though family life was not easy as their mother had to cope without servants and their father had to find a new job.

Eric and Honor Wilkins would not have made a different decision even if they had been able to avail themselves of BOAC's second-class tickets, introduced in 1952, for travel on a less lavish scale. During that decade flights also speeded up a little, though those who flew to India as children remember as many as fifteen stops in Europe and the Middle East. They also recall much excitement: pillow fights in the gangways, exotic food and plush hotels at the transit stops, and the sight of their parents waiting for them at the edge of the tarmac as they descended. From the parents' point of view air travel was still a worry, despite the care of bossy BOAC 'aunties'. Flying was seen as dangerous, especially when one of the new Comets crashed after leaving Calcutta in 1953. And even with the lower fares it was very expensive to fly several children out and back. Employers were slow to take on this cost. In 1954 HSBC, which had many employees in the East (including India), sought to attract recruits with the promise: 'If an officer wishes to bring his child/children out from home for a temporary visit instead of sending his wife home, the Bank will pay an amount equal to the wife's return air passage once during the officer's tour [of three years].'[81]

An Assam tea planter's daughter, who came to England in 1956, recalls that 'on each three-year tour you'd only get one passage home paid by the firm'.[82] She was lucky in that her grandfather paid for her to go out in the intervening years. Her experience accords with that of Agnes Heron's daughter, Elizabeth, who was sent to school in

England because the high altitude of Darjeeling was bad for her weak chest. She was able to fly out twice (in 1954 and 1956) to visit her mother and stepfather in Assam during her secondary school years. Mrs Heron, whose own entirely Indian childhood is described in Chapter Five, found it 'a big worry being that far apart', especially when she received 'terrible letters of complaint'. She would probably have kept her two sons in India if her husband's ill health and retirement had not forced the family to return to England in 1960.[83]

The Diplomatic Service Wives' Association (DSWA) had to wage a long campaign before it could persuade the Foreign Office to pay for more frequent family reunions. After all, the rules and allowances were determined by 'men with little understanding of what constitutes a normal family life ... whose only criteria were financial'. Lone mothers in India had a similar tussle with their husbands' firms to establish what the DSWA called 'an inalienable right'.[84] Jane Anson's mother taught at a Calcutta school and made all the family's clothes in order to pay for passages to Britain. After Jane and her brother started at English schools in 1951 Mrs Anson, who was a strong-minded woman, persuaded the shipping agents for whom her husband worked to pay for the children to fly out once every two years. Jane and Peter were delighted to return to Calcutta with its parties at the Saturday Club and swimming at the Tollygunge. Both these clubs, Jane remembers with surprise, were still restricted to Europeans.

Apart from these regular trips back to India, the Ansons' experience was not very different from that of Raj children in earlier days. When Jane arrived at Ashford School at the age of seven, all excited by boarding school tales she had read in *Girl* comic, she was terrified by the sight of an intimidating Matron standing at the door in her starched apron. She was so homesick in her first term that her mother decided to take her back to India for another year and a half – a small victory (like Anne Battye's) for the child's right to be heard. Ashford was not so bad the second time round but, even if it had been, Jane could not have told her parents so in the weekly air letter which was firmly censored. At one point, for instance, Jane 'got into terrible trouble' for telling Mrs Anson that Matron would not take her seriously when she reported (correctly) that she had a recurrence of a tropical eye disease. Sometimes communication was as slow and difficult as it had been in earlier years. A postal strike in India meant that when Jane fell ill with pneumonia and was sent to an isolation hospital, her parents knew nothing about it. One innovation was a five-minute telephone call booked for Christmas Day; but both brother and sister were so stunned that they couldn't think of anything to say.

Like many exiled children before them, Jane and Peter stayed in holiday homes because there were no relations who could cope with them on a regular basis. Jane remembers with great fondness one home which took in quite a few children from the East. At Hook Farm in Sussex, run by a kindly widow and her two sons, she would help with the milking, collect the eggs and feed the calves. When one of the sons got married she acted as bridesmaid, wearing an Indian muslin party dress. Eventually, though, her mother removed her because she thought there were too many boys among the other boarders and 'it was never so good after that'. On leaving school at seventeen, Jane returned to Calcutta to be with her parents. She loved them dearly but found at this stage that she needed more freedom. So she decided to go to Australia.[85] It was never easy for such youngsters to give up the self-reliance hard won during years of separation.

Old Raj habits were slow to die in most corners of the 'foreign field which was forever Esher' – as Ann Leslie recalled during a nostalgic visit to Ootacamund in 1997. She found that her old school, St Hilda's, had not changed much since she was there in the first few years after Independence. The girls still wore the same grey uniform, slept in the same dormitories, attended the same compulsory services in the same chapel and ran the same cross-country races. Traditionally English though it was, the school had not been deemed suitable in her day for the complete education of expatriate English girls. Ann Leslie remembered the two incidents which had precipitated (or given the excuse for) her own removal in 1951: a rabid dog bit her and a panther ate a friend's dog while she was taking it for a walk:

> And I knew that the hungry panther and the rabid dog meant that I would probably now be sent 'Home' ... never to live in India again, never to smell woodsmoke in the night villages, never to play with my pet mongoose, never to see the pale gold dust at twilight. ... And never to see my parents again except for once a year at most.

Thus the heartbroken nine-year-old girl followed the well-trodden path of exile and 'never felt truly at home anywhere else again'. When asked to select her most important record on *Desert Island Discs*, she chose Indian music by Ravi Shankar because 'it evokes the time when I was the happiest I have ever been'.[86]

Pukka British expatriates were even less inclined to keep their children at schools in India now that they were filling up with Indian teachers and pupils. They would certainly have had reservations about Bombay's Cathedral School as memorably evoked in *Midnight's Children* by Salman Rushdie, one of its alumni. Saleem Sinai and his friends troop off to 'Optional Cathedral' in 1957 'in a long line of boys of every conceivable religious denomination, escaping from school into the bosom of the Christians' considerately optional God'. All the boys look forward to the School Social at which they 'would be permitted to dance the box-step and the Mexican Hat Dance with the girls from our sister institution – such as . . . Elizabeth Purkis and Janey Jackson – European girls, my God, with loose skirts and kissing ways!' This opportunity was all the more welcome as Indian youngsters were still barred from the exclusively white Breach Candy Club.[87]

Few parents seem to have considered the new international schools which educated the offspring of ambassadors, businessmen and missionaries from other countries – they were thought to be too American. But John Christie, who was now working as adviser to the Central Commerce Committee, sent three of his children to one such school in Delhi where they 'happily mixed with every variety of race and language'. In the relaxed cosmopolitan atmosphere of the post-Independence capital (where clubs even admitted Indian women) Christie was tolerant of 'the polyglot riot of sound in the playground'. His autobiography does not record whether he kept the children there until he left India in 1959 or whether he sent them to England. Whatever the case, one of his sons reaped a benefit from his international schooling: he played cricket with the future captain of India, Tiger Pataudi, whom he was able to bowl out when they met later 'on more famous playing fields'.[88]

Families who went out to make a fresh start in the newly independent countries of Asia tended to follow the traditions of the Raj. Richard Walker, who could not settle in England after his wartime service in the Navy, trained as an accountant and travelled to Ceylon with his wife and two children in 1952. Like the many other 'Brits' there, the Walkers kept plenty of servants and enjoyed a busy social life in clubs which were still strictly reserved for Europeans. Their oldest child, Penny Smith (née Walker), is conscious that there were embarrassing disputes over whether *burghers* (mixed-race descendants of former Dutch colonials) could join the swimming club. It does seem, though, that Mr and Mrs Walker tried to educate their children in

Ceylon. Penny went to three schools, including Bishop's College in Colombo, where she enjoyed the curry and rice served to its racially mixed clientele. But she had to move on from each school because there were too few places for European pupils. For the same reason she could not get into the favoured Hill School even though her parents had bought shares in it. Thus the Walkers eventually followed the practice of most of their friends, sending Penny and her brother back home.

After three happy and largely healthy years in Ceylon (during which the new Queen was welcomed in Colombo harbour), Penny and Ian travelled to England with their mother and baby brother Rupert. Alarmed by news of several more Comet crashes, Mrs Walker travelled by sea. Penny remembers wonderful sights on the three-week voyage, including camels beside the Suez Canal – but not Naples because she and Ian had been naughty and were not allowed ashore. After their traditional journey home, the children faced other old-fashioned experiences. Penny was not permitted any items from home at her prep school (not even a teddy-bear) and at his school her brother was 'beaten for anything'. Like colonial children in the past, both of them were considered too thin and in need of building up with a daily pint of milk, which both of them now hate. Staff always checked letters received or written. On one occasion this proved to be helpful. Penny got a letter from her mother which said: 'Daddy has had a medical check-up. I think he'll live till Christmas.' It took much persuasion from the headmistress to convince the distressed child that the second sentence was meant as a joke. A telephone conversation would have been more reassuring but at £1 a minute this was still out of the question.

The Walker children's holiday arrangements also followed a familiar pattern. Relations were too busy with their own families to cope regularly with two rather 'tricky' extra charges – especially after Penny passed measles on to all her cousins. The most striking instance of continuity is that holiday homes were still making a profit out of taking in children from the former Empire. Penny and Ian were particularly unlucky in the one they stayed at during their first summer holiday. The couple who ran it neglected their boarders, leaving them to roam around York on their own all day. Later on the husband was found guilty of sexually abusing little boys, though Penny does not think her brother was among the victims. At least the Walker children were able to assert themselves by refusing ever to go back there.

For Penny, who was clearly as sociable and positive then as she is now, there were gains as well as losses. Despite the lack of home comforts she enjoyed her prep school in the Lake District, where she learnt to ride. She liked getting to know her cousins, aunts and uncles and grew to love Jersey while staying with her final guardian, Auntie Pegg. Through taking charge when she and her brother travelled on their own Penny became self-reliant. Best of all she relished the summer of 1958 when they flew out to Ceylon in an Argonaut plane. Richard Walker recalls that this cost him about £200 for each return flight (compared to school fees of £60 a term) and his wife's worries about safety were confirmed when one engine developed a fault and the children had to stay in a Frankfurt hotel for three nights. This holiday was Penny's last experience of wonders like the parade of the Buddha's tooth, kite-flying on Galle Face Green, the sight of huge fireflies at night or the sweet smell of temple flowers. For in 1959 Mrs Walker made the hard choice, faced by so many Raj wives before her, between husband and children. She came to England to start Rupert at prep school and decided to stay on so that she could give the other two a home for their holidays. This arrangement was a boon for all of them, especially for Ian who had not flourished under the previous arrangements.

Malvern Girls' College, to which Penny was now sent, was less of a bonus. She loathed its 'Victorian attitudes' and found it very restricting until she was given a little more freedom in her last term. Then, in theory, she was supposed to be preparing for Oxbridge entrance exams. In practice something much more exciting was on offer. She had met the dashing Henley Smith, who used to drive over from Cheltenham College in his friend Nick Parks's Austin A10. Penny and a schoolmate would say they were going out with relations, jump into the car, change out of their uniforms at the earliest opportunity and hide under the seats if they saw any lurking teachers. It was a bit more alarming if they were driving in Cheltenham, when the boys had to duck for the same reason while trying to keep the car on the road. Henley's visits did not do much for Penny's chances of getting into Oxford. In fact, she soon gave up the whole idea and, reader, she married him! These days Penny's international experience is reflected in her love of travel and in her work for the Medical Foundation for the Victims of Torture.[89]

Mrs Walker's decision to provide an English home for her children seems to have been more common in the late 1950s than in former years. This may well be connected with the more child-centred theories of parenthood current at this time. Dr Benjamin Spock's *Baby and Child*

Care, first published in Britain in 1955, emphasised children's need for 'continuity in their caregivers' and for frequent expressions of their parents' love. 'Even when attending school and becoming more independent they still ought to have a feeling that they belong somewhere, even if they forget to go there.'[90] The Wenger family story shows how hard it was for India-based parents to satisfy this simple need. Because of their determination that their children should not have to live with guardians, Leslie and Freda Wenger lived separately in the early 1950s while Janet and Margaret attended day school in Norwich. But their resolve broke after four or five years and Mrs Wenger returned to her husband's side in Bengal. The girls went to lodge with separate relations and their younger brother and sister boarded at Eltham and Walthamstow for their secondary education. The result was that, in Janet's opinion, they were 'more affected by not knowing their parents'. She herself missed them when she was at Oxford University. Her state scholarship had to be used to pay various aunts for her keep during vacations since it would not stretch to intercontinental air fares. Soon after taking her degree Janet created her own home by marrying Tony Bottoms, her fellow-exile from the Bengal mission field. It was a marriage so auspicious that Indian family friends thought it must have been arranged.[91]

Sometimes it was younger rather than older children who had their mother's continuous care after sad experiences of earlier partings. At the same time and for much the same reasons as the Kendals kept Felicity in India, the Harrison parents kept their two daughters with them in Pakistan. Their son, Gerald, was born in 1943 while Major Harrison was serving in the Indian Army. Loving the country, the Major decided to stay on after the war to work for the Imperial Bank of India. In 1947, in the midst of Partition, twin girls, Rosemary (Rosie) and Mavora, were born and the very next year Gerald was sent away from the family to school in England. The little boy, so confused that he woke up at night calling for *pani* (water), became devoted to the grandmother and aunt with whom he lived. He did not see his parents and sisters for about three years, by which time, Rosie Gutteridge (née Harrison) reports, 'he was a stranger'. Bonds severed so early in life were not easily mended, even when the Harrisons took Gerald on a three-week tour of Europe after their final return to England in the late 1950s, hoping 'to get to know him better'.

Meanwhile Rosie and Mavora returned to Pakistan, moving around from one lovely bungalow to another in Lahore, Rawalpindi, Nowshera and Karachi. They had suffered a serious attack of dysentery when they were six months old. And they grew up in troubled times, once or twice seeing terrible things in the refugee camps on the India/Pakistan border. Yet the twins were not sent home as Gerald had been. Rosie explains this partly by the lower priority given to girls' education but also by her parents' worries about the effects of separation. The twins have memories of a happy and secure childhood with loving ayahs, PNEU lessons (even in history of art), tea parties for their dolls in the garden and birthday celebrations at which each wore a miniature *shalwar kameez* (tunic and trousers). They grew to love the land of their birth. Rosie will never forget, for instance, the smell of water poured from buffalo skins on to dry dusty roads during the hot season. When the time came for secondary school Mrs Harrison came with them to England, leaving her husband alone in Pakistan until the time of his retirement. Even though she had never before used a saucepan and had to keep moving house, Mrs Harrison was able to give her daughters a loving home to which they could return at the end of the school day.[92]

By the 1960s several factors combined to persuade employers to finance annual reunions for separated families: pressure from parents, new ideas about childcare and cheaper fares. Some firms like Williamson Magor had started this practice in the 1950s, in time to benefit Valentine Morice whose father was a manager on its tea plantations in Assam. By the time Valentine left the 'heaven' of her Indian home she had been taught all about Hell at the Loreto Convent in Shillong. Apart from being scared by these terrifying visions, her eight early years in India had been 'too good to be true'. The Convent of the Holy Child Jesus at St Leonards, to which she was sent in 1956, could not match this idyll but Valentine was not unhappy there. She fitted in and made some good friends.

Nevertheless, she always missed her parents, especially her father, a 'distant knight in shining armour'. Most of all she missed them during holidays spent in Sussex with her grandmother. Granny was kind but inclined to be possessive, having lost two sons in the war. She was often difficult as Valentine began to grow up and once, when she arrived late after a delayed flight, Granny locked her out of the house. What kept Valentine going were her Christmases in Assam and her parents' summer visits to England, all now paid for by Williamson Magor. This was no help, though, to her older sister, who had left school by that time. And it was almost too late for her brother, whose relationship with his father was stormy. To Valentine the reunions were a great comfort. But, she explained, even two annual spells with her parents did not constitute family life: 'It wasn't safe because you'd be uprooted and set off again.' And that 'has consequences', which will be explored further in Chapter Ten.[93]

Another tea-planting firm, James Findlay, paid for the three children of Richard and Hannah Tewson to return every summer to the High Range in Kerala. Their younger daughter Susie Rook (née Tewson) was not sorry to leave St Hilda's, Ooty in 1963 at the end of a seven-year stint. St Mary's at Calne in Wiltshire (their mother's old school) was not much better. But she 'quite enjoyed it in the end', helped by maturity and by the presence of her older sister, Sally. The Christmas and Easter holidays presented Susie with problems typical for children whose parents were abroad. She often had to stay with a bossy aunt in Ireland 'who didn't kiss us' and 'made us feel a burden'. Another aunt called her a 'tart' because she wore eye makeup. And if invited to smart parties by schoolfriends, she never had suitable clothes. For one such occasion she sent away for a 'sew-it-yourself smock' but no one asked her to dance the whole evening because she 'looked like a sack of potatoes'. These were unhappy teenage times. Still, the Tewson children had the great compensation described by their mother: 'the excitement of flying out to see us, to their Home in India'. Susie remembers that these holidays were 'great fun', especially when she and Sally became popular with the young bachelors working on the estate. Here was an obvious improvement on the unbroken years of homesickness endured by their mother in the 1930s. But Susie would probably not agree with Mrs Tewson that her seven years at English boarding school had no effect on 'happy family relationships'.[94] And she suspects that her brother, who was 'a small pretty boy' with no sibling for comfort, had a much harder time at his school.

Even in these more liberal times, boarding schools were often insensitive to their pupils' feelings. Martin Baker, younger son of Robert Baker who was now running the family plantation at Kumerakom, had never been fond of them – when taken to Kotagiri Convent in 1963 his mother had to prise his fingers from the car door. The four-year-old boy found it oppressive there with 'the devil in the background' and 'an atmosphere of evil and good and ghosts over you'. At the age of eight he followed his brother Howard (and their father before them) to the junior school at King's, Canterbury, but he did not get on much better there. Because he was not considered to be up to the academic standard and because he 'dominated the playground', the headmaster persuaded his parents to withdraw him after two terms. Martin's name was put up on a list of leavers before he had even been told, an action which his mother, Paula, still describes as wicked.

Miserable though Martin's early school experiences were, he had at least a guardian aunt (Beatrice Broad) who understood the problems of separation. And he could always look forward to his summers at Kumerakom. Some of his troubles were assuaged by exciting flights in the pilot's cabin to Cochin. Back home he made rafts from banana trees, fished in the lake and enjoyed being with his family and with Sangrain, the servant to whom he was devoted. As all the family agrees, the Bakers' youngest child Paulette Bateman had the best of it: 'I was the lucky one, kept home with my mother until I was six years old; I was never bored or unhappy.' She was taught by the PNEU system and found that she was not at all behind when she came to England with her parents in 1962.[95]

The Bakers left their lakeside estate in that year because the Communist state of Kerala introduced land reforms limiting the size of agricultural holdings. In other parts of the subcontinent, too, life became less congenial for British expatriates during the 1960s as independent governments encouraged their own citizens to take over the reins in business and administration. Taxes were imposed on traditional perks like rent-free housing, expense accounts, free servants and passages to England. In addition, 'remittance difficulties presented grave problems when children came to school age'. For all these reasons, and because of the Chinese invasion of Assam in 1962, Himalayan tea planters 'were throwing in their hands and leaving India'.[96] At about the same time, after considerable pressure from the Indian community, clubs in Calcutta were removing their race barriers. At the Swimming Club, for instance, 'a winner of an Olympic gold medal had been refused entrance and squatted at the entrance eyeing venomously all those who entered'.[97] In Ceylon a heavy tax on the number of children persuaded Richard Walker to resign from his senior accountancy post in 1961. John Christie and James Anson were involved in disputes over their British nationality. 'It was galling', writes Christie, 'that families of pure British stock who happened to have served abroad for generations sometimes found it harder to be recognised as citizens of their homeland than to pass through the eye of a needle.'[98]

The process of Indianisation made Richard Tewson redundant in 1967 – though his hat still hangs in the bar of the High Range Club. The present Secretary of that club, Allan Oakley, told me of the different path which he has trodden since Independence. He was the posthumous son of a British soldier killed during the Burma campaign, whose mother decided to live on in India after the war with her five children. In his turn Oakley stayed on as a tea planter (taking Indian citizenship) and he can say today: 'My life in India has been an interesting one and the country has been good to me. India has been my home.'[99]

Allan Oakley's case is unusual. Most Britons still working in India, Pakistan, Burma and Ceylon returned to the home country in the 1960s, just as communication between the two continents was becoming easier. 'It was the end of an era', said Peter Clark, who spent his adult life as a tea planter in Ceylon, following in the footsteps of generations of missionaries and planters on both sides of his family.[100] Since that time the Foreign Office has agreed to finance three return fares a year for all diplomats' children and two for those over eighteen who are still in full-time education. Other public bodies (like the British Council) as well as private firms (like HSBC) made similar concessions to families based in any foreign country. Thus they implicitly acknowledged the loneliness endured over the centuries by all the offspring of parents working abroad. Katie Hickman, a diplomat's daughter sent back to school from Singapore in 1970, wrote that the pain she felt on being separated from her family was 'like a bereavement'.[101] In her opinion, one home visit a year was not enough to prevent severe damage to the natural bonds between children and their parents. Expatriate parents of the late twentieth century, like this HSBC wife, could not help comparing their children's experiences with their own: 'We thought they were lucky that we saw them every holiday. You see, I was at a holiday home and my parents didn't see their children for five years.'[102]

Nowadays, as Valentine Davies observed when living in Hong Kong, parents and children hop on to planes at the drop of a hat. Contemplating all those Raj children who had gone before she thought, 'What a different story.' The last chapter will assess the impact of that story on their lives.

TEN

'Did I Smell of Curry?'

The Abiding Effects of an
Indian Childhood

Clearly there was no whiff of the kitchen about the persons of those 'born in the territories of the British Raj', as Raleigh Trevelyan half fears at the beginning of his memoir, *The Golden Oriole*.[1] This chapter argues that certain other apprehensions also proved unfounded but that a Raj childhood nevertheless left an indelible mark.

British parents had often felt forebodings that their children would be permanently corrupted by the earthier aspects of Indian life, including its food. An article in *The Calcutta Review* warned that 'a child brought up in this country [presents] a fair prospect of becoming in after-life a lover of eating and of all other bodily experiences'. *The Complete Indian Housekeeper and Cook* was shocked that an English child should be allowed to eat his dinner 'off the floor', being fed 'spoonfuls of *pish-pash*' at any old time of the day.[2] This fear of over-indulgence did not quite accord with the widely held view that Anglo-Indian children were puny and pale, unlike the chubby, rosy-cheeked youngsters back at home. In practice, of course, all children were different. Cliff Richard admits to having indulged in India a 'passion for curry and rice' which he now has to curb in the interests of stardom.[3] Mollie Kaye, on the other hand, was pronounced by her English schoolmistresses to be 'much too thin, skinny and sallow' when she first arrived from India. They built her up so successfully with pints of rich milk and spoonfuls of cod liver oil and malt that she turned into 'one of those unfortunate fatties who spend half their life on a diet without ever achieving a slim figure'.[4] Two sisters sent to St Hilda's School, Ooty in the 1960s reacted quite differently to its Indian fare: Caroline (Caro) Kennett (née Paylor) had to be forced to eat her twice-daily helpings of curry and rice and drink nightly cups of hot goat's milk, while her sister Annie relished it all.[5] In fact most adults who have grown up in India preserve a taste for its culinary delights – but then the favourite dish of most Britons today is apparently chicken tikka masala.

Nor can a daughter of the Raj be distinguished by her clothing, even if 'her dress had hitherto been half Hindoostanee and half European' like that of Mrs Sherwood's fictional Lucy, who had spent too much time 'in the company of heathens'.[6] For the styles and fabrics of India have been fashionable in Britain ever since the nabobs sent back sprigged chintz and embroidered silk in the eighteenth century.

But what of the baneful 'moral miasma' which Eha saw rising from the servants' quarters behind the bungalow?[7] In this respect, too, it is hard to find proof of lasting damage caused by 'promiscuous intimacy with the native servants'.[8] I have found only two cases which give any weight to anxieties of this kind: the abuse of Pat Foster by a servant and the illicit anatomy lessons which Guy Wheeler received from his ayah, both described in Chapter Six. Pat was able to put the incident behind her. But Wheeler was seduced by homosexuals several times during his early years in India, where 'pricks were as plentiful as lollipops if you knew where to look'. At the end of his memoir he calls India a 'hot-house'. He understands 'why well-heeled colonials like to whisk their children out of the tropics as early as possible' and concludes, 'For me, it was too late.'[9] Of course there is nothing peculiarly Indian about such episodes – and in any case some of Wheeler's seducers were British. Abuse of children and homosexual experimentation in the 'hothouse society' of boys' boarding schools were not unusual in Britain during the period of the Raj.[10] Children who grew up in India probably did see, smell, hear and handle more raw life than their contemporaries in England. The three fair-haired Paylor sisters, for instance, were constantly touched by Indian men and women as they walked in the streets of Quilon and Cochin during the 1960s. Caro found this upsetting at the time but admits that this expression of curiosity was no threat to their welfare. Nor did Annie come to any harm on the many occasions when a local man took her horse-riding in the countryside around Ooty.

The truth is that parents had more influence than they realised. Most of the children I have studied grew up, whether in India or away from it, to adopt their parents' attitudes – often with astonishing fidelity. Leslie Wenger's two oldest daughters, Margaret and Janet, lived in India until they were twelve and ten but, far from being corrupted by 'all the dogmas and obscenity of [Indian] religion', they have remained devout Baptists all their lives.[11] Felicity Kendal provides another example of parents' standards of morality proving a stronger influence than any supposed Indian sensuality. She spent eighteen years amid 'new places, new faces, noise and animals, sweat and curry, with life and death as part of the everyday canvas'. When she returned, having been 'Made in India' and knowing nothing of the Swinging Sixties, she found that her Victorian ways were out of date. Lessons were well learnt on the maternal lap. 'Mother's morals had been firmly imprinted and it took me a long time to catch up.'[12]

Mothers and fathers also stamped their morals on the thousands of Anglo-Indian children sent to Britain at an early age. They made their mark (on the Bourne sisters, for example) with letters containing lectures on everything from 'being really good unselfish' children to 'sitting up beautifully to avoid growing permanently crooked'. The lessons were reinforced by the relations who were 'so good' to have them in the holidays and by schools selected for their 'strict discipline'.[13] Thus many children of the Raj trod in their parents' footsteps despite the distance separating them. For Leslie Wenger the idea of being a missionary was 'in the blood' even though his father was 'rather a stranger' to him. Countless other sons loyally followed their fathers into the Indian Army or Civil Service, creating long dynasties such as the Macnabbs, Metcalfes, Barlows, Benthalls, Lawrences, Yules, Thornhills, Battyes, Ansons and Butlers. Girls tended to marry into Anglo-Indian families although sometimes, like Beatrice Baker or the Wilkins sisters, they were deterred by the thought of imposing on their own offspring the separation they had suffered.

Peggy Lawrence (née Neave) strikingly exemplifies such a change of direction. She describes herself as 'a terribly family person'. But despite being part of the distinguished Lawrence line, she and her husband decided that it would best serve their daughters' interests for George to pursue an English career. Peggy had never forgotten departing with her brother from the shores of Madras when she was eight, watching her parents 'getting smaller and smaller as we disappeared'. She felt as though 'the end of the world had come' and still in old age hoped 'never to go through anything like it again'. She spent the next ten years in school and in 'various holiday homes'.[14] Such women knew the limitations of letters, however hard parents had tried to convey love to their 'darling treasures'. They remembered being told that they must wait patiently for wars to end and passages to become available before they could see their parents again. This was bad enough but some recalled having to stifle even deeper feelings. When their father died in India, for instance, the three oldest Bourne girls were urged 'not to grieve too much'.[15]

It was their reserve, rather than any physical or moral taint, that most exiled Raj children had in common. Over and over again, their oral and written memoirs show how they were drilled not to show their emotions. At school they had to write cheerful letters on safe subjects. It was seldom, for instance, that adolescents mentioned anything about their developing sexuality, with the result that it is hard to judge to what extent this aspect of their lives was affected by family separation. David Wilkins was unusual in telling his father about the signs of his pubescence and about a secret assignation he arranged with a Walthamstow girl – with strict instructions that he was not 'drop a brick' by mentioning any of this to his housemaster.[16] In the holidays they had to fit into other families' routines, trying (like Janet Wenger) 'not to ask any questions about what you were supposed to be doing'. Parents on leave were prone to dismiss any complaints about unkind treatment with words like 'Teachers have to be strict' or 'You're very lucky to have someone to look after you.'

These attitudes were slow to change even after the end of the Raj. Research into British boarding schools of the 1960s shows that most of them still censored pupils' letters home and made no telephones available. They also continued to administer corporal punishment and to insist on such formalities as the use of surnames even between brothers. Penny Henderson (née Fitzgerald), who spent much of her own childhood in 'arid' holiday homes, was one of the researchers. She told me how difficult the pupils found it to ask for help and talk about their problems. They felt that 'one should be able to cope' and preferred to 'sort things out for themselves' – in true Raj spirit.[17] For children whose parents were abroad this emotional independence was more pronounced. They usually saw their parents once a year but some, like this ten-year-old missionaries' son, had infrequent contact even at this late date: 'I only see them once every three years, sometimes I forget what they look like or speak like and this worries me. I wish there were heathen people in Scotland, perhaps Jesus could call them there.'[18]

Down the ages parents were naturally more aware of their own painful feelings about separation than of the hidden price their children would pay. Sir John Shore's distress after parting from his Caroline in 1792 was as heartfelt as Mrs Paylor's anguish when she left her Caroline for a nine-month spell at St Hilda's in 1962. Occasionally, though, parents showed an understanding of just what their offspring were missing when deprived of family life. In 1847 Mrs Sarah Terry and her three youngest children were living in Bombay, where her husband was engaged in the export trade. Their oldest daughter Amelia had been separated from the rest of the family for five years and was at that time staying with Mrs Terry's sister in Alexandria, pursuing 'sufficient education for her prospects in life'. At the end of a letter to Amelia containing the normal admonitions to good behaviour and correct spelling, Mrs Terry wrote a postscript addressed to her sister.

> I did feel very anxious about the dear child Amelia, but she says she is quite well and never mentions wanting to come here, but often when she writes of Mary [her sister] I see where her tears have fallen on the letter. She can never feel that love for the children that they have for each other and I know at Malta [in 1844] she did not like Sidney [one of her brothers] or Sidney her. Do you remember, dear Mo, how we used to fight and to play after we were in bed? Our children do just the same.[19]

Here Mrs Terry put her finger on the features lacking in the life of every young exile: the opportunity to complain, the freedom to quarrel – and to kiss and make up in the usual rough-and-tumble of family life.

A century and a half later the daughter of an Assam tea planter analysed the psychological effects of being sent away from a family home in India. In a university thesis, Valentine Davies used the records of past exiles like Rudyard Kipling and Vivien Leigh, interviewed some who are still alive and reflected on her own childhood. She found that children sent away from home acquired a 'premature independence' as a means of coping with the pain of separation, the fear that they were unwanted and the longing for a secure base. Their weeks with their families were too precious to be normal, as she recalls from her own experience: 'Not being there all the time it was the most terrible thing in the world to have rows and then just leave.' Valentine concludes that children of the Raj develop, to varying degrees, 'a detached character as a defence against the fear of rejection'.[20] This can make it hard for them to regain any intimacy with their families or to form lasting new relationships. She found a high rate of marriage breakdown in her sample. Her depressing conclusions accord with those of American sociologists who investigated the effects of separation on US 'missionary kids'. Their analysis of 282 replies to a questionnaire, couched in the jargon of their profession, found that about forty per cent reported 'a negative impact'. The researchers included in this category only those with altogether unhappy experiences. This was a typical response: 'I do not easily let others get close emotionally. I find it very hard to communicate in an intimate relationship for fear of rejection. It has crippled my marriage.'[21]

My historical inquiries have been of a different nature. Letters, memoirs and diaries do not usually include soul-searching of this kind and I did not specifically ask about the adult relationships of the fifty-seven 'Indian children' I interviewed. But the evidence they provided does not wholly confirm this bleak picture. Most of my interviewees have had happy marriages (thirty-one were still married and thirteen were widowed). Some told me that marriage and parenthood have been a refuge, making them feel needed and wanted after being sent away as children. A minority, however, suggested that their insecure childhood had led to 'trouble with relationships' in adult life, resulting in divorce or abstention from marriage – seven were divorced, four were single and two did not reveal their marital status. Family ties also varied; some had become exceptionally close to parents and siblings after long periods of separation while others had remained distant. Very few of the people I have read about or talked to were entirely negative about their childhood. Although British children were deprived of family life for longer and more unrelieved periods than Americans (or any other nationalities), they usually tell of blessings as well as hardships. There was nearly always a saving grace such as a helpful teacher, a kind granny or a good friend. Nevertheless, it has surprised me, as it did the American researchers, that separation continued to take a psychological toll despite the more frequent contact afforded by late-twentieth-century circumstances.

The contrast between British and American responses is significant. For it seems that the long British tradition of sending children away from their parents has helped to form the national character. It has perhaps produced the strong silent British type, with the familiar attributes of uncomplaining endurance, gritty determination and emotional reticence, not to say inhibition. Surely it was not just French prejudice which caused Victor Jacquemont to remark on these characteristics while travelling around British India in 1830.

> Even when Englishmen have really kind hearts, they are strangers to that tenderness, that sweet abandonment to which we other continentals owe so many pleasures or consolations. Their reserve certainly lends their domestic life a dignity which we forget in ours, but they purchase this outward semblance at the cost of many of the pleasures of the heart.[22]

In the language of psychotherapy this reserve could be termed 'detachment'. A child psychologist might argue (as does Sue Gerhardt) that people who have had insufficient mothering 'ignore their feelings in much the same way that their caregivers ignored their feelings'.[23] The tendency is more commonly known as the stiff upper lip.

It can be discerned, for instance, in Lieutenant-General Sir John Hearsey, who wrote of his period of harsh English schooling during which he received no kindness or protection from any grandmother or aunt: 'Perhaps the hardships I underwent did me a good turn for I undeniably became very hardy.'[24] Cyril Connolly tells the story of one of his persecutors at the brutally 'feudal' Eton of the 1920s, who afterwards joined his father's regiment and went out to India. He was awarded the VC after being killed in action on the north-west frontier: 'I have often thought of his death on that untenable hillside, outnumbered, putting heart into his troops by assuring them that help would reach them, though well aware that help could not, and dying covered with wounds after fighting all day.'[25] Traditionally, of course, the wounds of British officers hurt only when they laughed. On such hardiness the Empire was built.

The stiff upper lip also helped to give both civilians and servicemen the resilience needed in both the world wars of the twentieth century. Among the many examples which could be cited is that of Alfred Bestall, famous as the illustrator of Rupert Bear. Between the ages of five and eighteen, from 1897 to 1910, Freddie was at school in Britain while his Methodist parents carried out their missionary work in Burma. It is not clear how often they visited him but letters from his various guardians say that the 'little gentleman' thought 'a great deal of his absent mother'. In her honour he would choose her favourite hymn to sing on a Sunday evening, 'Abide With Me'. In 1914 the 'delicate, shy and retiring youth' volunteered for war service, but was rejected several times as unfit. He reapplied after each rejection for, according to the *Methodist Recorder*, the training he had received at Rydal Mount (his Wesleyan public school) 'had put iron into his blood'. His persistence was rewarded when he was sent to France as a driver/mechanic. He served there for the rest of the war, often under fire and always refusing to be promoted to a desk job. The rest of Bestall's life was uneventful. He never married but felt it a privilege 'to have made so many children happy'.[26]

In this respect he resembled Rudyard Kipling, whose special affinity with children is mentioned in Chapter Four. As it happens, Kipling's only son was, like Bestall, rejected as unfit in 1914. Kipling used his influence to get the short-sighted young man to the Western Front, where he was killed in his very first battle. Kipling endured the loss with an agonised stoicism summed up in his haunting poem 'My Boy Jack' (1916):

> 'Have you news of my boy Jack?'
>   *Not this tide.*
> 'When d'you think that he'll come back?'
>   *Not with this wind blowing, and this tide.*
>
> 'Has any one else had word of him?'
>   *Not this tide.*
> *For what is sunk will hardly swim,*
>   *Not with this wind blowing, and this tide.*
>
> 'Oh, dear, what comfort can I find?'
>   *None this tide,*
>   *Nor any tide,*
> *Except he did not shame his kind —*
>   *Not even with that wind blowing, and that tide.*
>
> *Then hold your head up all the more,*
>   *This tide,*
>   *And every tide;*
> *Because he was the son you bore,*
>   *And gave to that wind blowing and that tide!*[27]

Men did not have a monopoly of stoicism. The same quality can be seen in a 'soldier's daughter' like Armine Mathias, who gained from her lonely childhood the courage to face the loss of her new husband in the Second World War.

Many others have spoken or written of the resilience they learnt during the years spent without the care of parents. Ann Leslie said in a radio interview of her departure from India: 'Iron got into my soul.' This has enabled her to maintain the emotional detachment essential in a good journalist.[28] Julie Christie, sent home from Assam at the age of eight, soon learnt self-reliance in her English boarding schools: 'I was always scorned, mocked or punished by the authorities for extremist behaviour. After I'd been humiliated enough I turned introverted. . . . I learned to get along without my parents, without anybody.' Her biographers reckon that 'acting offered a refuge from the loneliness she so frequently felt'.[29] Julie Christie has not had children, feeling that motherhood was not for her unless she was prepared to devote herself heart and soul to it; she has dedicated herself instead to good causes. An obituary of the studio potter, Helen Pinchcombe, judged that her character was marked by being born into an 'empire-building family'. Sent from India to an Australian boarding school at the age of seven, she spent her holidays in the house of a Plymouth Brethren aunt, where she was 'so fearful of getting things wrong that she always said "Please, thank you, excuse me" to cover all eventualities'. The early separation from her parents 'turned Helen into a profoundly private person, self-sufficient and independent', who never married and whose passion was her work. In photographs she is 'often looking away as if trying to remove herself from the scene'.[30]

There was sometimes a high price to be paid for the stiff upper lip. Anglo-Indian written and oral records include cases of Raj children suffering acute disturbances in adult life. One of the Pemberton boys went insane after being imprisoned for debt. Trix Kipling had 'some sort of psychotic breakdown' and became inseparable from her mother, 'returning to a childhood she had not had'.[31] Joyce Wilkins had several spells in convalescent homes before she became matriarch of the family in whose honour 'Rejoyce' gatherings are still held. Several interviewees have told me about the therapy they have received for psychological problems arising from childhood separation and I am especially grateful to them for shedding light on this obscure part of the picture. One said that he was sure a number of people have been disturbed by these periods of banishment and I think this is true.

Without doubt there are many who are still too upset to tell their story.

Patricia Hyde, in her reply to Mary Thatcher's questionnaire for the Centre for South Asian Studies, wrote that her brother, whose 'personality was warped by his parting from Mum', refused to contribute to such an 'unscientific' record.[32] Other women have told me of brothers who suffered more than they did (often because of harsher treatment in school) and now felt unable to talk or even to think about it. One has 'gone off the rails with drink and drugs'; another refused to watch a ciné-film of his childhood; and yet another could not express sympathy to his father when his mother died. Still others choose not to remember anything of India. One woman told me that the family friend with whom she shared many childhood seaside holidays at Chandpur and Puri now recalls nothing about them. It seems that men are especially prone to bury their emotions in the manner taught by 'gruff and peppery' schoolmasters of the time.[33]

A common feature of Anglo-Indian childhood, whether in the subcontinent or in the home country, was what Julie Christie called 'the gypsy life'. In India fathers were always being moved from one part of the country to another while in Britain children usually lived out of a suitcase. This is largely a thing of the past for the British in India and now it is the sons and daughters of prosperous Asians who are likely to be packing school trunks for England. The families of Western diplomats, multinational business executives, members of the armed forces and charity workers still lead an itinerant life. These days they are likely to hail from the United States, which took over Britain's global role after the Second World War. American academics have coined the acronym TCK to describe a Third Culture Kid, who reflects the cultures of both his host-country and his home. The circumstances have changed as much as the people and the language. Nowadays three reunions a year are considered the right of separated children, who can also have rapid contact by telephone, text message or e-mail. Because of all this communication, even the most ancient boarding schools have had to open up to the world and they have correspondingly less hold over their pupils. Nor are they any longer the normal choice of expatriate families, for Americans are not wedded to the boarding school tradition and the three million who live abroad either send their offspring to schools in the host-country or follow home-schooling schemes.

An unsettled life, even when led in the company of parents and siblings, often has an enduring effect on the children of expatriates. They cannot put down roots in a home or neighbourhood and must adapt continually to new companions. Margery Fyson concluded that her early years on tour with her parents in the Punjab had bred in her a 'desert island streak'. 'I like to have my habits so ordered in civilisation that it wouldn't make a vast difference if I were wrecked on a desert island.'[34] Brian Outhwaite explained that his nomadic childhood with the British Army in India had affected him as an adolescent and a young adult: 'It made it difficult to establish friendships with people because it never seemed worthwhile.'[35] Rosie Gutteridge, looking through her mother's record of her (and her twin's) juvenile birthday parties, each year in a new place with different guests, understood why she sometimes feels a bit insecure.

Similarly, American children moving around the military bases, diplomatic enclaves, mission stations and business centres of the world feel like 'perpetual outsiders . . . flung into global jet streams by their parents' career choices'. The son of a Marine Corps soldier, for instance, thinks he and other military brats deserve some recognition 'for the sacrifices they made over and over again to the United States of America'.[36] And an Asian sixth-form boarder at St Mary's School, Cambridge, said to me: 'It's like being in two boxes. I don't belong in any one place.'[37] Her words reminded me of a former pupil of Auckland House School, a refugee from Burma, who wrote that leaving friends and moving on had made her wary of getting involved. She still felt an outsider after thirty-two years in Britain. In her study of the British Diplomatic Service Ruth Dudley Edwards concludes that this 'life of painful transit . . . tends to throw up quite a lot of disturbed children'.[38]

Still, most young people like adventure and novelty and, as long as they have enough family contact, they can gain as much as they lose. Or, as one American study puts it, there can be enrichment as well as estrangement. Captain Peter Collister counted himself among the enriched. He was brought from India as 'a tow-headed dumpling of a boy in a tweed pepper-and-salt outfit' and left at a Bexhill prep school, where his profuse curls provoked ridicule from the other boys. During a five-year stint there he received only one maternal visit before moving to Cheltenham College, where he was classed a dunce and put 'on the military side'. Yet, when he joined up in 1939 he found his upbringing an advantage: 'With a peripatetic background . . . I was able to merge into a new society, in a way that others who had had a static home life and who had been brought up in a particular religion or social ethos found it harder to do.'[39] Nor did Marjory Fyson regret her early travels: 'On the march I watched the grandest scenery in the world unfolding new each day.' Always after that she felt partly a Punjabi and spent much of her adult life working with blind children in Karachi and Lahore.[40]

It is the same with modern expatriates. HSBC wives feel that their children have relished the variety and excitement of their upbringing. Research in the 1990s demonstrated that Americans who spent their youth travelling the world with their parents were more international in outlook as adults than most of their compatriots. Significant numbers had jobs with a global dimension, supported protest activities like the anti-Vietnam War movement, spoke a foreign language or tried to 'introduce their offspring to the diversity of the world's people and cultures'.[41] And the Hong Kong girls I talked to at St Mary's felt that they were benefiting from the more open society and more liberal teaching methods of Britain. In addition, they say that being away from home has made them more grown-up and independent, bringing the unexpected bonus of better relationships with their parents. As one explained to me: 'You can express your feelings more on the telephone than you can face to face. . . . Before my mother was always giving me advice which I didn't always want to hear but now she's on my side.' She added that friends too 'treasure you more and treat you better because you have been away'.[42]

All the same, the equilibrium can be easily upset. These girls find their thrice-yearly home visits vital to their well-being despite feeling 'seriously homesick' after each return to school. When the outbreak of SARS stopped them from travelling to Hong Kong at Easter 2003 there were many tears. They need sympathetic friends and staff who will listen to worries which would otherwise be bottled up. 'It's better if you talk about it,' explained one girl, 'because then it feels like everything's gone out.'[43] Kay Hannaford, who has pastoral care of the boarders at St Mary's, agrees but she knows too that pupils from the Far East are often too proud or too reticent to ask for help when they need it. Like children of the Raj, 'they soldier on'.[44] There are other echoes from the past: some parents have inflated expectations and some guardianship agencies are greedy and ineffective. But the school has learnt, over three years' experience, how to help overseas pupils to deal with separation and culture shock so that their schooldays are happier than they could ever have been in the days of the Raj. Even though they miss their mothers' cooking and their brothers' teasing, the late-night shopping and the real *karaoke*, not one of the girls regrets the decision (made in discussion with parents) to come to school in Britain.

These ambitious young students, like Raj children over the centuries, react in different ways to family separation and cultural change. As Kay Hannaford reports, 'it varies according to the individual'. Victorian records can also reveal distinctive responses, even though they are overlaid by earnest expressions of Christian piety. The letters and journals of Minnie, George and Edward Thornhill, the Mutiny orphans featured in Chapter Three, show how the same legacy of childhood sorrow could produce very different adult consequences in brothers and sisters. All three spent their school years with their many cousins at Lyston, the home of their paternal grandmother in Essex. But it does not seem to me that 'the happiness of their Lyston days illuminated their whole lives', as one writer has claimed.[45] Minnie's diary for 1866 records, for instance, that she felt 'dreadfully lonely' after the death of 'Dearest Grandmama' in March. She had 'a sad day' when dear Ned followed George to New Zealand in September. And she found that when 'dear Ellen' (her closest cousin) married and left for India in November 'our room seemed so bare and wretched'.[46] The self-portrait which she drew on the opening page of her 1867 diary shows a sombre young woman in mourning dress. Still, for the next ten years Minnie entered gamely into the social life of Aunt George's household in Lambeth, gaining satisfaction from her Sunday school teaching and good works, even if she sometimes felt rather unwanted.

Meanwhile her brothers, lacking the willpower to succeed in their New Zealand farming venture, were reduced to penury. Less forbearing than their sister, they blamed their failure on the 'tainted place', with its demanding banks, unfavourable weather and high taxes. They also complained of their wealthy aunt's meanness: 'No one would ever think, even if they knew Aunt George had relations, that starving wretches like us could possibly be them.'[47] Nevertheless Minnie loved her profligate brothers and when George came to visit her in Lambeth with his new wife Esther (known as Tassy) in 1877, she gave them all she had. Not only did she lend George and Edward the £1,500 she had just inherited from her maternal grandmother but she took George's part in a quarrel, with the result that she was cast out of her aunt's house.

After confiding to her diary that losing her home had made her 'feel so unhappy', she conquered her emotions in the fashion taught by Dearest Grandmama and soldiered on.[48] At the end of 1878 she wished she had accompanied George and Tassy to New Zealand for she seems to have been disappointed not to receive a marriage proposal from Mr Rudolf, a fellow Sunday school teacher. Her secret is betrayed only by references in Tassy's sympathetic letters and by another expressive drawing in her diary: a young man kneels before a woman who looks very like Minnie. The diary also records that she received some 'Spiritual Counsel and Advice', the words of which are pasted over. It tells that she spent a 'sad dull Christmas' and saw in the New Year alone at her lodgings: 'I opened the windows to hear the bells. . . . It seems so sad the Old Year grief but such joy when the bells peeled out a welcome to the New Year.'[49]

For some years Minnie (now in her early thirties) led a nomadic life, staying with different relations, before finding a home as companion to Miss Minet, a charitable elderly spinster. But her quiet courage found its reward. In a letter to George written in 1881 she told of her forthcoming marriage to Charles Downe. George wished her joy, 'for your life has been anything but happy for many years'. But he added a self-pitying regret that he could not write to Mr Downe, 'for I should be sorry to let him know that he was marrying the sister of a pauper'.[50] After her marriage the lonely Raj orphan could at last give free rein to her affections, as one of her four children testifies:

> Hers was an ideal marriage and she was a devoted wife and mother, of a most loving nature; always bright and cheerful; deeply religious; full of hope and consolation in difficulties and troubles, unswerving in loyalty to her family, relations and friends. Everybody who knew her, loved her and felt better for having known her.[51]

Minnie continued to help her brothers, who were never able to repay her loan. George died alone in 1915, bitter that everyone except his sister had 'turned against him'. Ned was last heard of in 1918, running a billiard saloon but lamenting that he was 'very hard up' because 'almost half of the young fellows have left here for the front'.[52] Neither of them had been able to get over the early loss of love and support.

The twentieth century yields further examples of siblings with similar childhood experiences but dissimilar reactions. Among them are Joseph and James Butler, Jane and Sue Portal, Anne and Trish Battye or Penny and Ian Walker, whose stories have been told in earlier chapters. One of the sharpest contrasts is between Caro and Annie Paylor, who are mentioned earlier in this chapter. Their father dealt in tea, coffee and rubber for Harrisons & Crosfield and they spent their very early years in Indonesia. The family moved to India in 1962 when the sisters were seven and four. In 1963 Annie joined her big sister to become the youngest pupil at St Hilda's, Ooty. She soon got stuck into such joys as the school picnic with its waterfall walk and curry rolls – treats which Caro had always been too homesick to appreciate. While Caro had gravitated towards the only other English girl in the school, her tomboy sister joined the little boys in stilt-walking, collecting mice and making racetracks for toy cars. Thus one sister hated her every moment at St Hilda's and the other, though younger, regarded it as 'all a big party'.

Back home in Quilon and Cochin Caro remembers boring tennis sessions at the club, which did not welcome children. Annie's memories are of long bicycle rides, games of marbles and jacks with the servants and family evenings when 'Dad got out the Scalextric set and set it up' as a treat. But it was coming to England (one in 1964 and the other in 1966) that affected the sisters most differently. They attended the same prep and public schools, travelled to and from India on the same twice-yearly flights (paid for by the firm) and usually spent half-terms and occasional holidays with the same friends and relations. The older sister's memories are bleak: the sad Christmas of 1965, which she had to spend apart from her family because of the war between India and Pakistan; the guardian who nagged her about table manners; the teachers who told her she was stupid. Annie, on the other hand, traces her current expertise as an aviation journalist to the exciting nineteen-hour flights to Bombay and the freezing-cold Dakota journeys on to Cochin. (She has kept some of the tickets, which show that in 1967 a return fare for an Unaccompanied Minor from London to Cochin still cost about £200 on post-Raj exchange rates.) Annie loved school, where she shone academically. And she felt that 'Mum was always there' for her even when she was thousands of miles away.

Caro has only been able to talk about her childhood separations since she has found security in marriage and motherhood. Like Thackeray, she still cannot bear saying goodbye to people. But Annie blesses her childhood for giving her a sense of independence and an enduring respect for other cultures. She is glad not to be 'home-grown English'. What the two sisters share is their devotion to the family which is all the stronger, they suspect, for its earlier partings.[53] But the Paylor sister who feels most deeply for India itself is the youngest, Susie, who was born soon after they arrived there. She loved every minute of her first eight years, which were spent in Quilon and Cochin. She was never sent to boarding school because in 1970 the family came to the 'cold wet place' which they called home. Now married to an Indian, Susie Taylor celebrates all the Hindu festivals with her husband's family in London. She still cherishes her magical memories.[54]

Most children who left India, at whatever age, received this consolation prize. They brought back with them 'invisible luggage' containing their lasting remembrances of its culture, people, flora and fauna. In Paul Scott's novel, *The Birds of Paradise*, William Conway, who has been brought up in an Indian princely state, reflects: 'If I were to go into the forest now I could take a tiger with me. He is here, picked at random from the recollections I have brought with me … complete with his own Indian background of thorn-sharp fronds.'[55] Joyce Wilkins carried with her the memory of her last evening in Orissa:

> The servants had caught some fireflies and put them (unharmed) under a piece of fine green gauze in the centre of the dining table so that we could enjoy the beauty of a living table decoration. We were urged to look at them carefully – the little blue-green lights flashing under the gauze – and to remember the sight, for, they said, we would not see fireflies in England.[56]

This enchanting picture was to comfort Joyce during her years at Walthamstow Hall. Wyn Munro says that her parting gift from the Indians she knew was a 'built-in transcendental spirit', which has enabled her 'to live and let live'. She has also found artistic inspiration in the 'giant's paint-box' of India.[57] Raleigh Trevelyan took away lingering dreams of Gilgit high in the Himalayas: 'Could any place have been so beautiful? Could I ever have been so happy?'[58]

It is true that the invisible luggage sometimes had less welcome contents. Rather like fleas leaping out from a trunk delivered months after its owners' return from the tropics, distressing memories could spring into life. Even though all those I approached welcomed the opportunity to talk of their Indian past, they sometimes found it painful. Beatrice Broad, prompted by her son, acknowledged the economic hardship and social condescension often suffered by her coconut-planting family on their lovely Travancore estate. Linette Peter admitted that 'one was bored a lot of the time' in Kashmir despite its famous beauty.[59] Pamela Kirkpatrick had to admit that the India she loved as a child 'had a certain spookiness' and that she was terrified of ghosts.[60] Penny Francis shuddered as she recalled her frequent spells in hospitals and sickrooms. And Rosie Gutteridge did not dwell too long on her vision of a dead baby being thrown on to a bonfire in a refugee camp. Some, too, felt guilt at 'what our superiority and arrogance, often unconscious, had done'.[61] A verse from Alan Ross's poem, 'Indian Childhood', evokes such dark thoughts of the past:

> Time sifted the images, yet upsetting things,
> Like falling fortunes, lingered to remind
> – A chance remark, a suicide,
> A door one dared not look behind –
> Reappearing in sleep, a false world
> With dreams mysterious and deep.[62]

These haunting memories, both joyous and sorrowful, have often drawn Raj children back to the subcontinent. Raleigh Trevelyan returned eventually to Gilgit to 'watch the shadows of the mountains like folds in silk and hear the chukor calling in the cornfields' and he knew that 'Shangri-La had been real'. What is more, 'an oriole was singing in that same tree' in the garden of his parents' bungalow. At Gulmarg he found the family's summer home 'a jagged pile of ruins'; nevertheless he was deeply affected by the sight of the yellow flower that he had seen growing on his mother's grave in Cornwall: 'Now as I navigated the blackened bricks, old tins, bottles and more shit, I found what had been Olive's and Walter's bedroom, and there in the middle of this disgusting debris another verbascum was growing.'[63] Other pilgrims have come across powerful reminders of their Raj forebears. Anne Battye found that there was still a picture of her grandfather in the Reid Memorial Hospital at Shillong. She had more of a surprise when she called on the present Collector of Jagdalpur in central India. There, hanging on the wall, was a framed photograph of her father who had been the Resident in the 1940s.

Such encounters can arouse strong feelings. There were 'tears on both sides' when Martin Baker was greeted by Sangrain on visits to the family's former estate at Kumerakom. On one occasion, after the bungalow had been turned into a hotel, Martin stayed for a night in his old bedroom. That was a disturbing experience, which he does not want to repeat. His sister Paulette has returned too but 'it was horrible' not to be able to communicate with their former servants – she had

forgotten all her Malayalam.[64] Dick Whittaker's 1997 visit to Hyderabad, where his father served as Bishop of South India after Indian
Independence, was all the more traumatic because he was suffering
from a severe septic throat. In fact, the current Indian bishop diagnosed
the condition as an emotional reaction to being back there for the first
time since his boyhood. Suffering from a high fever, Dick was taken
on a motorbike to visit Medak Cathedral, at which his father had
officiated. He nearly fainted as he walked into the dark church and
saw a life-size and true-to-life portrait of his father: 'I felt distinctly
fuzzy; seeing my father like that as I walked through the door was like
a hallucination.' Some days later he went to visit his old house in
Secunderabad. By an extraordinary coincidence it was at that very
moment being demolished. 'I saw the great metal ball going into my
own bedroom and it was gone as I watched it.' However, these experiences have not dimmed Dick's love of India. He shares this with his
wife, Margaret, another Methodist missionary child, delivered into the
world at Secunderabad by Dick's mother and an early playmate for
Dick before her father, Dr Thompson, was replaced by an Indian doctor
in an early Indianisation drive. Mrs Thompson, who had lived in India
nearly all her life, brought Margaret up to think of India as 'the most
perfect place in the world'.[65]

For the Irish poet Richard Murphy the return to childhood haunts
produced heady emotions. News of violence and massacre during Sri
Lanka's civil war 'brought back a terror of my childhood – dying in
Ceylon'. He travelled to the country in 1984 in an attempt to purge
those fears and found them submerged by 'a wave of euphoria'. The
sound of monsoon rain falling on the roof 'as so often in my childhood'
gave him 'a feeling akin to *nanda*, one of the four cardinal virtues of
Buddhism, variously interpreted as bliss and universal love'.[66] Thus
inspired, Murphy (a divorcé with a daughter and an illegitimate Irish
son) took on the guardianship of a boy from an orphanage:

> Soon after you heard the genial warden call
>   'Nimal!' a slim dark boy with a sweet
>   Cup to offer came in his bare feet
>   From work in a spice garden: so beautiful
> His face, not yet street-wise, with institutional
>   Small scars, black irises watering to meet
>   A tall white guardian, that in withering heat
>   You swallowed more than nectar: all in all

> You found the cast-off natural child you'd come
>   Flying back fifty years to seek, who'd sprung
>   From bible mould of a mission compound left
> To soldier on when your people sailed home:
>   Whom fathering by word of mouth you bring
>   To love, leaving his native tongue bereft.[67]

Murphy returned to the country several times during the troubles, bringing back four more boys to be educated in Ireland as well as material for his collection of poetry, *The Mirror Wall*.

The poems of Murphy and Ross, Scott's novels and Trevelyan's family memoir provide further evidence of the way in which India coloured the minds of those who came under its spell in their formative years. M. M. Kaye's *The Far Pavilions*, Tom Stoppard's *Indian Ink*, Mark Tully's radio essays and Charles Allen's *Plain Tales from the Raj* are among many other literary creations to spring from childhoods passed in places which set imaginations ablaze. Like Kipling, after his second departure from India in 1889, they felt a yearning which would not go away:

> It's Oh to see the morn ablaze
>   Above the mango-tope,
> When homeward through the dewy cane
>   The little jackals lope,
> And half Bengal heaves into view,
>   New-washed – with sunlight soap.[68]

Paul Scott, who fell 'in love with India' as a young conscript, concluded that 'its possession had helped to nourish the flesh and warm the blood' of the British people.[69] It also did something to cure the heartache of children of the Raj.

'A Shift in the Balance of Power'?

After being transported in 1930 from 'the variety, colour and sheer excitement of India' to a 'desert of misery' at a Tonbridge prep school, John Harvey Jones sent his parents 'desperate SOS calls'. But, he recalls in his autobiography, they 'seemed to be consigned to oblivion for all the response I received'. It was three years before he saw his parents and they did not, as his mother had promised, 'go in a flash'. When Mr and Mrs Harvey-Jones did arrive back, 'visiting me was not the first thing they did' – they simply had not realised what an 'unhappy person' their son was. This child's experiences epitomise those of the children who lived in Britain's Empire. John spent an early life 'of security [and] privilege' in Dhar state, where his father was Resident; at the age of six he was taken without any discussion to Tormore prep school; he was beaten and bullied by the older boys but accepted his 'apparent abandonment' without question; he survived by finding a best friend and by developing the 'the habit of work' which enabled him to pass the entrance exam for the Royal Naval College at Dartmouth; he spent his holidays with paid guardians; he thinks that his need to prove himself in every area of his life can be traced back to his early days; and he retains a 'deep affection' for India.

Some fared better if they saw their parents more often, attended more congenial schools or enjoyed the care of loving relations. Others fared worse if they lost a parent, could not achieve their ambitions or suffered ill-treatment from adults. Over the two centuries examined here their joys, sorrows and desires tended to go unvoiced or unrecognised while nabobs sought their fortunes or sahibs shouldered the white man's burden. Their story sheds light not only on the nature of childhood but also on the character of the Raj. When sending their children back to Britain, upper- and middle-class parents were not concerned only with health and education. It was also racial exclusiveness which decreed that their children must be educated in Britain. There was no suggestion, for instance, that John Harvey-Jones could attend Dali College at Indore with his playmate, the young Maharaja of Dhar, even though it was a 'seedbed for the finest of India's youth'.[1]

The same prejudice applied in the mandated territories which Britain had acquired after the First World War, as Richard Crossman discovered while he was serving on an Anglo-American Commission in Palestine in 1946. When he remarked at a cocktail party in Jerusalem that it must be nice for British officials to be able to keep their children with them in the 'wonderful climate', one of the wives quickly disabused him: 'If they were kept here, they would grow up horrid little Levantines, and then where would we be?' She went on to explain that even if schools in Jerusalem were 'quite good' the children would 'mix with strange people, mature too rapidly, and get the wrong ideas.'[2] Clearly, old imperial attitudes had deep roots and would be slow to die.

Child-care methods also progressed tardily despite Dr Spock's new liberal ideas. Many children were still expected to be 'seen and not heard' in the second half of the twentieth century, even though this time has been identified by some historians as marking 'a shift in the balance of power between adults and children'.[3] Many of the childhood autobiographies which have multiplied since the Second World War reveal a sad lack of communication. Tim Jeal did not tell his parents about the bullying and beating he endured at prep school in the 1950s because 'if I told them how I really felt, and they failed to remove me, how would I be able to think they still loved me?'[4] The novelist Hilary Mantel was more outspoken. She told her parents how much she hated her teacher's habitual punishment of making the pupils sit with their arms folded behind their backs. 'But no one can have been listening; they were listening to something else at the time.'[5] Both these pleas, one silent and one spoken, echo the SOS calls written by John Harvey-Jones. They also bring to mind a scene depicted by Lee Langley in her novel *Persistent Rumours*. Young James Pilkington, recently arrived at boarding school from the Andaman Islands, has been summoned for a chat in the headmaster's study:

> The old man with the bushy eyebrows did not care, not really, how he was getting on. Just as his parents could not really and truly care

about him or they would never have handed him over to Mrs Etheridge on the Port Blair quayside, to be delivered to school like a parcel. He was just another piece of luggage: one tin trunk, one leather suitcase, one wicker tuck-box, one boy.[6]

The young have undoubtedly gained many more rights since the days of the Raj and these are enshrined in the UN's Convention on the Rights of the Child. Yet the rights are easily violated even in countries which have ratified this agreement. In 2003 the Children's Rights Alliance found that in the areas of juvenile imprisonment, asylum and corporal punishment, Britain was failing to protect children adequately. 'Children's rights are being sacrificed to adult public opinion.'[7] And there is a danger, too, that in the competitive modern world fathers and mothers are just as preoccupied with their parallel careers as their imperial forebears were with tours of duty and social functions. Sue Gerhardt expresses concern for young children 'who are increasingly being shunted to and from nurseries or childminding groups, plonked in front of videos, fitting around the parents' busy lives which are elsewhere'.[8] In such circumstances modern youngsters may be deprived, like Raj children, of the advantage of simply playing at home. They may feel, as Cyril Connolly did, after several 'brutal partings and long separations' in the early years of the twentieth century, 'that our parents are determined to get rid of us!'[9]

And how do children manage today when their parents are working abroad? An *Observer* investigation revealed that in 2004 the Foreign Office and the Ministry of Defence spent £100 million on sending the offspring of their foreign-based employees to boarding schools in Britain. Parents can claim this allowance, apparently, even when serving in European countries with good schools and sometimes after they have returned from foreign postings. The article suggested that it is still a privilege to be able to send children away and a penalty for them to live in foreign parts.[10] In truth, according to the Diplomatic Service Families Association, parents are increasingly inclined to keep their children with them. In any case, those who are sent to boarding school still have the right to three flights a year out to their parents' home. Diplomatic mothers often take advantage of cheap air travel to visit their sons and daughters at half-terms.[11]

If, in the meantime, the children are homesick, modern schools no doubt offer more expert pastoral care than was given by the old man with bushy eyebrows who asked James Pilkington how he was getting on. Some lessons have been learnt from the children of the Raj.

Notes

Introduction: 'We Indian Children' (pp. 1–10)

1 NAM, 1998-10-299, Charles Augustus Moyle, Memoir (1877).
2 G. Ray (ed.), *Letters and Private Papers of W. M. Thackeray* (1994), vol. I, pp. 3, 5.
3 Kristin van Ogtrop quoted in C. Hanauer, 'When the Yelling Starts', *The Guardian*, 8 March 2003.
4 *The Guardian*, 30 September 2002.
5 Pemberton Papers 7/5/9, F. Pemberton to his sisters, 7 February 1771.
6 Maria, Lady Nugent, *A Journal from the Year 1811 till the Year 1815* (1839), vol. 2, p. 352.
7 Private Papers, David Wilkins to his parents, 9 September 1945.
8 OIOC, Mss Eur C250, Terry Papers, Sarah Terry to her daughter, 20 January 1843.
9 OIOC, Mss Eur C354, Letters of Di Turner, Easter 1905.
10 K. Hickman in *The Sunday Times*, 11 July 2004 and Private Papers, Joyce Wilkins to her parents, April 1917.
11 OIOC, Mss Eur B298/18, Thornhill Papers, no date but during 1860s.
12 *Pictures in the Post: The Illustrated Letters of Sir Henry Thornhill* (1987), pp. 55, 97, 115, 152 and www.ultimategrandparent.com.
13 E. Buettner, *Empire Families: Britons and Late Imperial India* (2004), p. 269.
14 Lord Beveridge, *India Called Them* (1947), p. 2 and M. Foss, *Out of India* (2002), p. 191.
15 Buettner, *Empire Families*, p. 265.
16 Coe, *When the Grass Was Taller: Autobiography and the Experience of Childhood* (1986), p. 287.
17 Buettner, *Empire Families*, pp. 144–5.
18 J. Harvey-Jones, *Getting it Together: Memoirs of a Troubleshooter* (1991), p. 58.
19 CSAS, Turner Papers, 'Life Was Like That: The Anguish of a Colonial-Born Child', p. 22.
20 A. Graham, *Lindsay Anderson* (1981), p. 96; C. Headington, *Peter Pears* (1992), pp. 6, 14; article on Douglas Jardine in *Oxford DNB*.
21 See L. de Mause (ed.), *The History of Childhood* (1974), p. 33; J. Walvin, *A Child's World: A Social History of English Childhood 1800–1914* (1982); I. Pinchbeck and M. Hewitt, *Children in English Society* (1969–73).

22 E.g. G. Wagner, *Children of the Empire* (1982) and P. Bean and J. Melville, *Lost Children of the Empire* (1989).

23 H. Cunningham, *Children and Childhood in Western Society Since 1500* (1995), p. 77.

24 V. Davies, 'Children of the Raj', MA Dissertation for London University, 2000 and E. Buettner, 'Families, children, and memories: Britons in India, 1857–1947', Ph.D. Thesis for University of Michigan, 1998, p. 372.

25 Article in *The Week*, 4 September 2004.

26 M. Forster, *William Makepeace Thackeray: Memoirs of a Victorian Gentleman* (1978), p. 10.

27 Ray, *Letters and Papers of Thackeray*, vol. 1, p. 4.

28 J. and R. Godden, *Two Under the Indian Sun* (1966), p. 9.

29 N. C. Chaudhuri quoted in K. Amis, *Rudyard Kipling* (1975), p. 52 and R. Kipling, *Kim* (1981 edn), p. 89.

30 E.g. A. Burton, 'India, Inc.? Nostalgia, memory and the empire of things' in S. Ward (ed.), *British Culture and the End of Empire* (2001), p. 226.

Chapter One: 'The Cure for the Heartache' – Children of the Nabobs (pp. 11–40)

1 Sir John Shore's letters quoted in C. J. Shore, *Memoir of the Life & Correspondence of John Lord Teignmouth* (1843), vol. I, pp. 231, 246, 253, 324, 342.

2 CSAS, Hunter Blair Papers, Andrew Hunter to his cousin James Hunter, 17 November 1771.

3 Eleanor Eden (ed.), *Letters from India by the Hon. Emily Eden* (1872), vol. I, pp. 110 and 267.

4 CSAS, Hunter Blair Papers, Charles Stuart to James Hunter, 20 September 1768.

5 See P. Quennell (ed.), *Memoirs of William Hickey* (1960).

6 Letter from Hyacinthe to Lord Wellesley, May 1799 quoted in I. Butler, *The Eldest Brother* (1973), p. 152.

7 CSAS, Hunter Blair Papers, Andrew to James Hunter, 31 January 1785 and 17 November 1771.

8 Ainslie T. Embree on Sir John Shore in *Oxford DNB*.

9 CSAS, Hunter Blair Papers, Charles Stuart to James Hunter, 20 September 1763.

10 Pemberton Papers, 7/5/12, F. W. Pemberton to his father, 16 January 1774, 7/5/38, 7 February 1781 and 7/5/80, 11 January 1794.

11 Ibid., 7/5/38, 7 February 1781.

12 Ibid., 7/5/39, 15 May 1781 and 7/5/34, 14 July 1780.

13 Ibid., 7/5/32, 15 March 1780 and 7/5/65, 28 January 1787.

14 Ibid., 7/5/45, 17 November 1783, 7/5/63, 3 August 1786, 7/5/64, 10 December 1786 and 7/5/68, 11 February 1790.

15 See T. G. P. Spear, *The Nabobs* (1932), p. 68.

16 Pemberton Pedigrees.

17 OIOC, Mss Eur D737/1, Stuart Letters, H. Stuart to his daughter, 20 September 1780 and 10 June 1777.

18 Ibid., 20 September 1780.

19 CSAS, Macpherson Papers, Reel 9 Section T/1, 16 February 1790 and T/2, 19 September 1787 and 1 December 1793.

20 Ibid., Section T/1, 29 March 1792 and T/2, 19 November 1791 and 14 April 1790.

21 Ibid., Section T/2, 8 October 1796 and 26 September 1798.

22 Ibid., Section T/13, 26 March 1806 from Prince of Wales Island and 3 November 1812.

23 OIOC, Mss Eur F206/1 Macnabb Papers, J. Macnabb to his parents, 21 February 1797.

24 Ibid., J. Macnabb to Mr and Mrs Reid, 1 September 1806.

25 Ibid., F206/4, J. Macnabb to his parents, 4 September 1821 and 1828 and Jane Macnabb to her parents, January 1821.

26 M. Abbott, *Family Ties* (1993), p. 25.

27 *A Brief Sketch of the Services of Sir G. H. Barlow Governor of Madras* (1811), p. vi.

28 A. Spencer (ed.), *Memoirs of William Hickey* (1925), vol. IV, pp. 321–3, 169.

29 OIOC, Mss Eur F176/16, Barlow Papers, Eliza to her parents, 17 March, 6 April and 9 May 1801.

30 Ibid., F176/12, T. Barlow to G. Barlow, 1 March 1803, 11 July 1804 and 4 February 1806.

31 Ibid., F176/16, Eliza to her father, 8 April 1806 and F176/12, T. Barlow to G. Barlow, 4 February 1806.

32 Ibid., F176/7, W. Barlow to G. Barlow, 20 October 1804.

33 Ibid., F176/3, R. Barlow to G. Barlow, 18 February 1806.

34 Ibid., F176/66, William to his mother, 25 November 1806.

35 Ibid., F176/54, George to his father, 17 November 1806.

36 Ibid., F176/7, W. Barlow to G. Barlow, March 1806, 10 February 1803, 20 October 1804, 2 September 1805 and 1 August 1806.

37 Spencer (ed.), *Memoirs of William Hickey*, vol. IV, p. 343.

38 OIOC, Mss Eur, F176/7, W. Barlow to G. Barlow, 12 August, 20 August and 17 September 1807.

39 Ibid., W. Barlow to G. Barlow, 10 February and 12 July 1811 and 12 July 1812.

40 Ibid., W. Barlow to G. Barlow, 29 December 1811 and F176/16, Henry to his father, 24 January 1812.

41 Ibid., F176/7, W. Barlow to G. Barlow, 20 October 1807 and F176/8, W. Barlow to G. Barlow, 10 February 1811.

42 Ibid., F176/16, Louisa to her father, 1 February 1810 and 31 March 1812.

43 Ibid., F176/12, T. Barlow to G. Barlow, 2 July 1811.

44 Ibid., F176/36, Divorce Papers, pp. 93,78, 85.

45 Ibid., F176/3, R. Barlow to G. Barlow, 8 July 1810.

46 Ibid., F176/55, George to his father, 12 March 1812.

47 Ibid., F176/16, Louisa to her father, 30 March 1812.

48 Ibid., F176/47, G. Barlow to Eliza, October 1816 and Eliza to her father, 8 July 1818 and 22 January 1819.

49 Ibid., F176/96, Fanny to her father, 27 August 1846.

50 OIOC, Mss Eur D1160/2, Henry Prinsep Memoir, pp. 201–3, 251–2.

51 Ibid., D1160/3, pp. 133–5, 239, 246, 241.

52 Ray, *Letters and Papers of Thackeray*, vol. 1, pp. 8–9, 11 June 1818.

53 W. M. Thackeray, *Roundabout Papers*, ed. J. E. Wells (1925), p. 20.

54 R. Kubicek, *British Expansion, Empire and Technical Change* in A. Porter (ed.), *The Oxford History of the British Empire* (1999), p. 263.

55 Sometimes called variolation, inoculation involved taking pus from the scabs of someone suffering from smallpox and infecting a healthy person with it.

56 OIOC, Mss Eur F127/94, Diary of Mrs Plowden, 7 January 1789.

57 H. Morris, *Charles Grant: The Friend of William Wilberforce and Henry Thornton* (1898), pp. 15, 24, 18 and *Life of Charles Grant* (1904), p. 9.

58 W. R. A. Austen-Leigh, *Jane Austen: A Family Record* (1989), p. 15.

59 Pemberton Papers, 7/5/47, F. W. Pemberton to his father, 19 December 1783.

60 Spencer (ed.), *Memoirs of William Hickey*, vol. II, p. 140.

61 OIOC, Mss Eur A172, Diary of Lady Chambers, 21 March 1784.

62 See S. Taylor, *The Caliban Shore: The Fate of the Grosvenor Castaways* (2004), pp. 185, 177, 146. Charles Dickens later found the story of Thomas Law and Henry Lillburne so 'beautiful and affecting' that he wrote about it in *The Long Voyage* (1853).

63 Nugent, *Journal*, vol. 2, p. 358.

64 OIOC, Mss Eur C537, Journal of Mrs E. M. Doherty, 1820.

65 N. A. M. Rodger, *The Command of the Ocean: A Naval History of Britain, 1649–1815* (2004), p. 527.

66 W. H. Carey, *The Good Old Days of Honorable John Company* (1906), vol. I, p. 351.

67 OIOC, Mss Eur C537, February and August 1819, 7 June 1920.

68 OIOC, Mss Eur D888/1, Diary of Lucretia West 1822–8, 30 May 1827, 17 August 1828 and postscript by Cecil Powell, Fanny's son-in-law.

69 A. Price (ed.), *Letters from Madras* (2003), p. 160, J. Maitland to her mother, 9 January 1839.

70 BECM, Sound Archive 194.

71 Capt. Thomas Williamson, *The East India Vade-Mecum* (1810), vol. 1, p. 341.

72 S. Kelly (ed.), *The Life of Mrs Sherwood* (1865), pp. 267, 391, 406.

73 M. Sherwood, *Lucy and her Dhye* (1825), pp. 32, 40.

74 J. Lawson and H. Silver, *A Social History of Education in England* (1973), p. 232.

75 Kelly, *Life of Mrs Sherwood*, pp. 306–7.

76 J. J. Rousseau, *Émile* (1911 edn), pp. 65, 43.

77 Open University, *The Religious Revival in England* (1972), p. 52.

78 Lawson and Silver, *Social History of Education*, p. 256.

79 Quoted, ibid., p. 255.

80 OIOC, Mss Eur F176/60, June 1809.

81 Ibid., F176/8, W. Barlow to G. Barlow, 17 April 1809.

82 *Memoir of Lord Teignmouth*, vol. I, p. 324.

83 R. Bayne-Powell, *The English Child in the Eighteenth Century* (1939), p. 94.

84 OIOC, Mss Eur E357, Yule Papers, G. Yule to his father, 15 August 1829.

85 Footnote in Ray, *Letters and Papers of Thackeray*, p. 3.

86 Pemberton Papers, 7/6/14, H. Pemberton to F. W. Pemberton, 25 December 1792.

87 CSAS, Macpherson Papers, Reel 9, T/2, W. Dick to A. Macpherson, 8 October 1796 and 26 September 1798.

88 OIOC, Mss Eur F176/54, George to his father, 16 January 1806 and F176/30 George's judgement on Eton, June 1809.

89 Ibid., F176/16, Richard to his father, 3 March 1812.

90 Lawson and Silver, *Social History of Education*, pp. 208, 256.

91 OIOC, Mss Eur F176/12, R. Barlow to G. Barlow, 4 February 1806.

92 Lawson and Silver, *Social History of Education*, p. 256 and Bayne-Powell, *English Child*, p. 108.

93 OIOC, Mss Eur F176/12, R. Barlow to G. Barlow, 31 March 1804 and Anne Barlow to G. Barlow, 30 May 1805 and F176/16, Eliza to her father, 10 August 1807.

94 Ibid., F176/8, W. Barlow to G. Barlow, 12 July 1812 and F176/16, Frances and Louisa to their father, 16 and 25 January 1811.

95 OIOC, Mss Eur F228/9,

Kirkpatrick Papers, W. Kirkpatrick to Col. J. Kirkpatrick, no date.

96 Quoted in H. Pearse, *The Hearseys: Five Generations of an Anglo-Indian Family* (1905), p. 122.

97 CSAS, Macpherson Papers, Reel 9, T/2, W. Dick to A. Macpherson, 26 September 1798.

98 Lawson and Silver, *Social History of Education*, pp. 198–9.

99 W. H. Dunn, *James Anthony Froude* (1961), p. 32.

100 OIOC, Mss Eur E357/17, 12 August, 18 November, 2 December and 20 December 1826, 8 September 1827 and 29 March 1828.

101 See W. H. Dalgleish, *The Company of the Indies in the Days of Dupleix* (1933), pp. 122–3, 160 and OIOC, Mss Eur F193, Verlée Papers, 50 and 51 (wardship and tuition arrangements).

102 OIOC, Mss Eur F176/3, R. Barlow to G. Barlow, 22 December 1804.

Chapter Two: 'A Forlorn Race of Beings' – Eurasian Offspring (pp. 41–67)

1 H. A. Stark, *Hostages to India* (1926), pp. 2–3.

2 F. Henriques, *Children of Caliban: Miscegenation* (1974), p. 169.

3 Pearse, *The Hearseys*, p. 38.

4 J. Clay, *John Masters: A Regimented Life* (1992), pp. 12–13.

5 See, for instance, Henriques, *Children of Caliban*, p. 176, G. Moorhouse, *India Britannica* (1984), p. 137 and W. Dalrymple, *White Mughals* (2002), p. 51.

6 I. Edwards-Stuart, *The Calcutta of Begum Johnson* (1990), pp. vi, 4, 118.

7 S. Turner, *Cliff Richard* (1993), pp. 28–30, C. Richard, *Which One's Cliff?* (1977), p. 30 and T. Jasper, *Cliff: A Biography* (1993), p. 14.

8 Author's interview with Margaret Whittaker (née Thompson), 4 November 2003.

9 Both statistics come from C. J. Hawes, *Poor Relations: The Making of a Eurasian Community in British India 1773–1833* (1996), p. 4.

10 E.g. R. Hyam, *Empire and Sexuality* (1990), p. 116.

11 Henriques, *Children of Caliban*, p. 168.

12 Kelly, *Life of Mrs Sherwood*, p. 427.

13 Hawes, *Poor Relations*, p. 12.

14 CUL, SPCK Papers, Reports from Trichinopoly, 1 July 1818, Cuddalore, 13 February 1821 and Vellore, 13 August 1822.

15 Williamson, *Vade-Mecum*, vol. I, pp. 463–4.

16 Eden (ed.), *Letters from India*, vol. 1, p. 172.

17 Captain Bellew, *Memoirs of a Griffin* (written in 1843, 1880 edn), pp. 85–92. The word 'chi chi' is sometimes spelt 'chee chee' and may be hyphenated. It was a disparaging term in the days of the Raj. See H. Yule and A. C. Burnell, *Hobson-Jobson: A Glossary of Colloquial Anglo-Indian Words and Phrases* (1994 edn).

18 D. Arnold, 'European Orphans and Vagrants in India in the Nineteenth Century' in *Journal of Imperial and Commonwealth History*, vol. VII, 2, p. 113.

19 Kipling, *Kim*, p. 3.

20 OIOC, MSS Eur D547, Sutherland Papers, Gen. de Boigne to Col. Robert Sutherland, 7 and 8 January 1797. Quoted in Dalrymple, *White Mughals*, p. 144.

21 CSAS, Gardner Papers, W. Gardner to Mrs Claydon, 25 May 1815 and 1818.

22 NAM, 6305-65-5, Gardner Papers, W. Gardner to E. Gardner, 7 July 1821.

23 W. Dalrymple (ed.), *Begums, Thugs & White Mughals: The Journals of Fanny Parkes* (2002), pp. 235, 321–2.

24 Ibid., pp. 133, 199, 245, 311, 205.

25 Ibid., pp. 239–40.

26 OIOC, Mss Eur D547, pp. 133–5, D. Ochterlony to R. Sutherland, no date.

27 OIOC, Mss Eur E298.

28 NAM, 1952-05-19, Col. Skinner's Memoirs, p. 1.

29 Ibid., p. 147.

30 J. B. Fraser (ed.), *Military Memoir of James Skinner* (1955), Part II, p. 241.

31 Star Staunton quoted in L. Fleming, *Last Children of the Raj* (2004), vol. 2, pp. 219–20.

32 Letter of Lord Bentinck quoted in Fraser, *Military Memoir*, pp. 238–9.

33 OIOC, Mss Eur D443, 'The Palmers of Hyderabad' by Edward Palmer (1934), p. 8.

34 Hawes, *Poor Relations*, p. 106.

35 Pearse, *The Hearseys*, p. 38 and C. Hibbert, *The Great Mutiny: India 1857* (1980 edn), p. 64.

36 Pearse, *The Hearseys*, p. 94.

37 Private papers quoted in Dalrymple, *White Mughals*, p. 491.

38 Dalrymple, *White Mughals*, p. 390.

39 Lady Russell, *The Rose Goddess & other Sketches of Mystery and Romance* (1910), p. 7.

40 Private papers quoted in Dalrymple, *White Mughals*, p. 490.

41 Author's translation from V. Jacquemont, *Voyage dans l'Inde pendant les Années 1828 à 1832* (1841), vol. I, pp. 482–3

42 Pemberton Papers, 7/5/102, 27 March 1794.

43 Ibid.

44 Pemberton Papers, 7/8/6, 8 June 1810.

45 Pemberton Papers, 7/8/9, 14 January 1821.

46 W. Hunter, *The Thackerays in India* (1897), p. 157. This Victorian work does not mention Richmond Thackeray's illegitimate daughter.

47 See G. Ray, *Thackeray: The Uses of Adversity* (1955), p. 30 for details of Sarah's birth and marriage.

48 Ray, *Papers of Thackeray*, vol. I, pp. 208, 244–5.

49 Ibid., vol. II, pp. 32, 34, 367, 381.

50 Quoted by Alyson Price in her introduction to Maitland, *Letters from Madras*, p. xix.

51 Diary, 21 January 1795 quoted in P. Robb, *Clash of Cultures? An Englishman in Calcutta in the 1790s* (1998), p. 39.

52 BL, Add Mss 29178, Warren Hastings Papers, J. Palmer to W. Hastings, 1 January, 26 March 1802. Cf. S. Grier, *The Letters of Warren Hastings to his Wife* (1950), pp. 451, 9 and 21 August 1802.

53 K. J. Feiling, *Warren Hastings* (1954), p. 380.

54 BL, Add Mss 29180, W. Hastings to C. Imhoff, 24 January 1805.

55 BL, Add Mss 45418, W. Hastings to D. Anderson, 23 July 1805, D. Anderson to W. Hastings, n.d. and W. Hastings to D. Anderson, 13 August 1805. Dalrymple (*White Mughals*, p. 51 footnote) states that Hastings thought a Scottish accent to be as great a disadvantage in 1805 as 'a swarthy complexion'. In fact it was Anderson and not Hastings who voiced the fear about the Scottish accent and he was not comparing the two factors as impediments to success.

56 BL, Add Mss 29183, J. D. Perkins to W. Hastings, 26 November 1807 and 5 April 1808. Add Mss 29184, 8 November and 7 December 1808.

57 BL, Add Mss 29185, J. D. Perkins to W. Hastings, 6 January 1810.

58 E.g. William Dalrymple, 'White Mischief' in *The Guardian*, 9 December 2002: 'this was not an era when notions of clashing civilisations would have made much sense to anyone'.

59 F. North to his sister, 23 April 1801 quoted in E. F. C. Ludowyk, *The Modern History of Ceylon* (1966), p. 102.

60 BL, Add Mss 29185, W. Hastings to J. D'Oyly, 31 January 1810.

61 BL, Add Mss 29184, W. Hastings to C. Imhoff, 26 April 1809, W. Fitzjulius to W. Hastings, 7 July 1809 and S. Toone to W. Hastings, 21 April 1809.

62 Hawes, *Poor Relations*, p. 65.

63 BL, Add Mss 29184, S. Toone to W. Hastings, 22 April 1809.

64 BL, Add Mss 29186, W. Fitzjulius to W. Hastings, 13 January 1811. BL, Add Mss 29187, 7 December 1812.

65 BL, Add Mss 29188, J. Palmer to W. Hastings, 10 February 1813 and W. Fitzjulius to W. Hastings, 19 April 1813.

66 Grier, *Letters of Warren Hastings*, p. 451.

67 *The Prelude*, Book II, lines 241–4 in T. Crehan (ed.), *The Poetry of Wordsworth* (1965), p. 198.

68 CSAS, Edmonstone Papers, p. 36.

69 OIOC, Photo Eur 31/3, Hardcastle Family Records, C. Metcalfe to G. Metcalfe, 24 March 1823.

70 CUL, MS. Add. 7616, The Elmore Letters, Frederick to N. Edmonstone, 15 June 1811 and 19 February 1812.

71 Ibid., W. Shepherd to N. Edmonstone, 13 May 1813 and 26 January 1817.

72 Ibid., M. Baillie to N. Edmonstone, 28 May and 11 October 1813, 23 May 1811, 17 and 7 September 1813.

73 Ibid., M. Baillie to C. Edmonstone, 28 May, 1813, 23 May 1811 and Alick to N. Edmonstone, 29 May 1815.

74 Ibid., J. Baillie to N. Edmonstone, 15 January 1817.

75 C. Metcalfe to G. Metcalfe, 17 October 1819 and 4 July 1823 quoted in E. Thompson, *The Life of Charles, Lord Metcalfe* (1937), pp. 178–9, 234.

76 OIOC, Photo Eur 31/3, C. Metcalfe to Mrs G. Smythe, 12 March 1825.

77 C. Metcalfe to G. Metcalfe, 4 July 1823 quoted in Thompson, *Life of Metcalfe*, p. 234.

78 C. Metcalfe to G. Metcalfe, 27 May 1826, quoted in Thompson, *Life of Metcalfe*, p. 252.

79 Quoted in Thompson, *Life of Metcalfe*, pp. 353–4.

80 Quennell, *Memoirs of Hickey*, p. 88. The memoir provides many examples of Hickey's extravagance, gambling, promiscuity and drunkenness.

81 R. Vizram, *Asians in Britain: 400 Years of History* (2002), pp. 36–7.

82 Quoted in Hawes, *Poor Relations*, pp. 136–7.

83 Quoted in F. Anthony, *Britain's Betrayal in India* (1969), p. 52.

84 F. Shore, *Notes on Indian Affairs* (1837), vol. I, p. 110 quoted in Hawes, *Poor Relations*, p. 37.

85 BECM Sound Archive 547. Similar accounts are given in other interviews for which the museum holds no copyright.

86 CSAS, MT1 and 2, conversation between Miss H. G. Stuart and Mary Thatcher, January 1971.

87 CSAS, R8, tape recording by F. W. Rawding in Friends in Need Home, Madras, 1974, interviews with Andrew du Morius and Kenneth Cutler.

88 Jacquemont, *Voyage dans l'Inde*, vol. I, p. 328.

89 Williamson, *Vade-Mecum*, vol. II, p. 458.

90 Bellew, *Memoirs of a Griffin*, p. 186.

91 OIOC, Mss Eur C354, Turner Letters, p. 2.

92 Story told by Roy de Vandre in Fleming, *Last Children*, vol. 2, pp. 280–81.

93 G. Atkinson, *Curry and Rice* (2001 edn), pp. 53–5.

94 M. M. Kaye (ed.), *The Golden Calm: An English Lady's Life in Moghul Delhi* (1980), pp. 142–3.

95 Mrs Monkland, *The Nabob at Home* (1842), vol. I, pp. 68, 61.

96 OIOC, Mss Eur F351/2, Auckland House Memoirs, Margaret and Rachel Appleton.

97 E. Linklater, *Country-Born* in D. Dunn (ed.), *The Oxford Book of Scottish Short Stories* (1995), pp. 202–5.

98 Henriques, *Children of Caliban*, p. 185.

99 *Oxford DNB*.

100 M. Thomson, *The Story of Cawnpore* (1859), p. 23.

101 Author's interview with Bill Newman, 24 May 2003.

102 Rosalie Griffiths quoted in C. Younger, *Neglected Children of the Raj* (1987), p. 160.

Chapter Three: 'Alarming News' – The Mutiny and Other Perils (pp. 68–93)

1 J. Fayrer, *Recollections of my Life* (1900), p. 257.

2 J. Fayrer, *European Child-Life in Bengal* (1873), pp. 6, 30–31.

3 Fayrer, *Recollections*, p. 315.

4 OIOC, Mss Eur D634, Hutchinson Papers, Codrington Journal, 28 June 1840, 12 and 14 August 1839.

5 Lady Sale, *The First Afghan War: Journal of the Disasters in Afghanistan, 1841–2*, ed. P. Macrory (1969), 15 November 1841, p. 45.

6 NAM, 1997-12-67, Thomas Dunn, Journal of the First Afghan War, 24 October 1839.

7 OIOC, Mss Eur D634,13 July and 14 May 1840.

8 OIOC, Mss Eur C703, Journal of William Anderson, 7–8 January 1842.

9 Sale, *Journal*, 9 January 1842, p. 109.

10 V. Eyre, *Journal of an Afghanistan Prisoner* (1843, 1976 edn), p. 215.

11 C. Mackenzie, *Storms and Sunshine of a Soldier's Life* (1884), vol. I, p. 258.

12 Eyre, *Journal*, p. 242.

13 Ibid., p. 296.

14 OIOC, Mss Eur C703, 23 May 1842.

15 Lady Sale quoted in P. Barr, *The Memsahibs* (1976), p. 64.

16 OIOC, Mss Eur A186, Letter of Lady Sale to her husband, 8 May 1842.

17 Sale, *Journal*, pp. 130, 131, 139.

18 Mackenzie, *Storms and Sunshine*, p. 281.

19 Barr, *Memsahibs*, p. 64 and Sale, *Journal*, p. 154.

20 Eyre, *Journal*, p. 243.

21 Sale, *Journal*, p. 153.

22 OIOC, Mss Eur D634, Introduction by J. Codrington.

23 NAM, 1998-10-299, p. 41. Toby appears in early-nineteenth-century versions of Punch and Judy.

24 *Diary of the Doctor's Lady*, Colina Brydon's Diary compiled by G. Moore (1980), 17 August and 22 November 1857.

25 OIOC, Mss Eur D937, Nicholl Collection, T. Nicholl to his son, 21 October, 23 November,

5 December 1840 and 25 April 1841.

26 Ibid., T. Nicholl to his mother, 7 December 1857 and 26 January 1858.

27 John Rivett-Carnac quoted in E. Collingham, *Imperial Bodies* (2001), p. 98.

28 CSAS, Sampson Papers, William Sampson to his parents, 18 June 1857.

29 A. Ward, *Our Bones are Scattered: The Cawnpore Massacres and the Indian Mutiny of 1857* (1996), p. 88.

30 Brydon, *Diary*, 23 June 1857.

31 OIOC, Mss Eur F206/3, 23 May 1857.

32 Several such stones are vividly told in Hibbert, *Great Mutiny*, pp. 84ff.

33 OIOC, Photo Eur 313, 'The Story of our Escape from Delhi by Miss Wagentreiber', 1894, pp. 12, 24.

34 Hibbert, *Great Mutiny*, p. 94. But Hibbert incorrectly describes Theophilus as the nephew rather than the son of Sir Thomas Metcalfe. He was the cousin of the three Eurasian sons of Charles Metcalfe who appear in Chapter Two.

35 CSAS, Campbell-Metcalfe Papers, Box IV, G. Campbell to her husband, 24 July 1857.

36 Ibid., 2, 6 and 14 July, 19 August and 14 October 1857.

37 G. Ritchie, *The Ritchies in India* (1920), pp. 201, 257.

38 CSAS, Erskine Papers, May and December 1857.

39 CSAS, Stock Papers, A. Simons to H. Stock, 27 May 1857.

40 Ibid., C. Simons to her mother, 21 June and 4 October 1857.

41 Ibid., C. Simons to her mother, n.d. and 10 June 1857.

42 G. W. Forrest (ed.), *Letters, Despatches and Other State Papers 1857–58* (1893–1912), vol. II, p. 60 and vol. III, Appendix C, pp. vii–x.

43 CSAS, Huxham Papers, A Personal Narrative of the Siege of Lucknow, pp. 9, 12, 36–7, 29–30.

44 Ibid., pp. 33, 48.

45 Fayrer, *Recollections*, pp. 179, 196, 228.

46 Most guidebooks give a highly distorted and exaggerated figure; e.g. *Footprint India Handbook*, p. 142 states: 'of the 2,994 women and children who had taken refuge in the Residency, only 1,000 marched out'.

47 E.g. D. Hutchinson (ed.), *Annals of the Indian Rebellion 1857–8*, p. 267.

48 Forrest, *State Papers*, vol. III, Appendix C, pp. vii–x.

49 Brydon, *Diary*, 21 June 1857.

50 NAM, 6008-248, article from *Constantia*, December 1927.

51 S. David, *The Indian Mutiny 1857* (2002), p. 183.

52 J. W. Shepherd, *The Cawnpore Massacre 1857* (1886), pp. 26–7.

53 Moorhouse, *India Britannica*, p. 87.

54 Shepherd, *Cawnpore Massacre*, pp. 57, 62.

55 Captain M. Thomson, *Story of Cawnpore* (1859), p. 103.

56 OIOC, Mss Eur D1092/3, Lindsay Papers, 7 May 1851 and 8 June 1852.

57 Z. Yalland, *Traders and Nabobs: The British in Cawnpore 1765–1857* (1987), p. 150.

58 OIOC, Mss Eur D1092/3,17 April and 7 December 1856 and D1092/4, 19 May 1857.

59 Thomson, *Story of Cawnpore*, p. 109

60 Forrest, *State Papers*, vol. III, Appendix A, pp. xc–xci, Statement of Mrs Bradshaw and Mrs Letts.

61 Both stories have often been told. See, for instance, Hibbert, *Great Mutiny*, pp. 194–5 and David, *Indian Mutiny*, pp. 220–1.

62 Thomson, *Story of Cawnpore*, p. 217.

63 Forrest, *State Papers*, vol. III, Appendix A, p. xvi

64 CSAS, Mill Papers, pp. 17, 22, 23, 32, 48.

65 Pemberton Papers, 7/18/28, F. P. Campbell to his mother, 29 May 1858.

66 Ward, *Our Bones are Scattered*, p. xviii.

67 Brydon, *Diary*, 19 October and 2 November 1857.

68 Thomson, *Story of Cawnpore*, p. 97.

69 OIOC, Mss Eur D1092/5, Mr Beatley of the Bombay Mint to M. Drage, 29 July and M. Drage to her sister J. Boase, 8 September 1857. Both these quotations are used in *Our Bones are Scattered*, p. 516 by Andrew Ward, who saw the papers when they were in private hands.

70 OIOC, Mss Eur B298, Thornhill Papers, grandmother to Minnie Thornhill, 1859 and undated birthday letter. The locket is still listed with the papers but cannot at present be found.

71 OIOC, Mss Eur D1092/5, Mr Beatley to M. Drage, 29 July 1857

and M. Drage to J. Boase, 8 September 1857.

72 See B. Kerr, *The Dispossessed* (1974), pp. 194–5.

73 Queen Victoria to Lady Canning, 8 September, 22 October 1857 and 1 July 1858 in C. Hibbert (ed.), *Queen Victoria in her Letters and Journals* (1984), pp. 137–8.

74 Quoted in C. Hibbert, *Queen Victoria: A Personal History* (2000), p. 250.

75 Ritchie, *Ritchies in India*, William Ritchie to his sisters, 10 November 1858, p. 205.

76 CSAS, Wentworth-Reeve Papers, T. W. Daniell to his mother, 18 September 1866.

77 M. Harrison, *Public Health in British India: Anglo-Indian Preventive Medicine 1859–1914* (1994), p. 50. Harrison's reference is to Kaye (ed.), *Golden Calm*, p. 49.

78 CSAS, Campbell-Metcalfe Papers, Box IX, E. Bayley to her sister, n.d.

79 L. Pollock, *Forgotten Children* (1983), p. 127.

80 C. Allen, *A Glimpse of the Burning Plain: Leaves from the Indian Journals of Charlotte Canning* (1986), p. 91.

81 C. Woodham-Smith, *Florence Nightingale* (1964 edn), p. 311.

82 *Sanitary Report of the British Army in India* (1863), vol. 1. pp. 29, 101.

83 Ibid., p. 198.

84 F. Nightingale, *Observations on the Evidence contained in the Stational Reports submitted to the Royal Commission*, pp. 83–4.

85 Royal Governess Lady Lyttelton quoted in Hibbert, *Queen Victoria*, p. 154 and C. Dickens, 'The

Paradise at Tooting', 20 January 1849 *Miscellaneous Papers* (1911), vol. I, p. 157.

86 Fayrer, *European Child-Life*, pp. 7, 14 and *Sanitary Report*, vol. I, p. 15.

87 See E. D. Battye, *The Fighting Ten* (1984), p. 22 and general.

88 CSAS, Erskine Papers, Box 44A, Journal, June 1844, 17 March 1849 and 6 and 7 April 1854.

89 R. Keynes, *Annie's Box* (2002), p. 243.

90 OIOC, Mss Eur F206/131, James Macnabb to his mother, 5 May 1863 and Amy Macnabb to her mother, 16 February 1864.

91 A. Dutta, *Glimpses of European Life in Nineteenth-Century Bengal* (1995), p. 42.

92 OIOC, Mss Eur F206/191, Alice Macnabb's Diary, 23 March 1885.

93 Ibid., F206/131, Amy Macnabb to her mother, 26 June and 1 November 1864.

94 Ibid., F206/133, James Macnabb to his mother, 25 December 1869 and 16 September 1872.

95 See G. Tindall, *City of Gold* (1982), p. 133.

96 CUL, MS. Add. 7490, Mayo Papers, F. Nightingale to Governor-General Lord Mayo, 24 June 1870.

97 F. Nightingale, *How People May Live and not Die in India* (1864), p. 10.

98 Carey, *Honorable John Company*, vol. I, pp. 109–10.

99 Monkland, *Nabob at Home*, vol. I, p. 90.

100 Fayrer, *European Child-Life*, p. 30.

Chapter Four: 'A Horse Does Not Cry' – Young Exiles in Victorian Britain (pp. 94–123)

1 C. Dickens, *Dombey and Son* (Oxford India Paper edn), pp. 135, 143, 175.

2 Eden, *Letters from India*, vol. 2, p. 196.

3 M. Perham, *Lugard: The Years of Adventure* (1956), pp. 3, 10.

4 These sides of the boat were more expensive because they were cooler.

5 CSAS, Benthall Papers, C. Benthall to three-year-old Edith, 17 April 1848.

6 OIOC, Mss Eur C97, T. H. Prinsep, 'Three Generations in India 1771–1904', p. 313.

7 S. Mathur, *An Indian Encounter: Portraits for Queen Victoria* (National Gallery Catalogue, 2003), pp. 7, 11.

8 A. N. Wilson, *The Victorians* (2002), p. 507

9 Letter of 10 April 1894 in Hibbert, *Letters and Journals*, p. 328.

10 Letters to her daughter Vicky, 8 May 1872 and 5 January 1876 in Hibbert, *Letters and Journals*, pp. 228, 241.

11 *Leeds Mercury*, 11 September 1858 quoted in A. Briggs, *The Age of Improvement* (1959), p. 459.

12 Hibbert, *Queen Victoria*, p. 344.

13 D. Bennett, *Queen Victoria's Children* (1980), pp. 49, 110.

14 P. Quennell (ed.), *Mayhew's Characters* (n.d.), p. 88.

15 F. McLynn, *Stanley: The Making of an African Explorer* (1989), p. 18.

16 I am grateful to Tim Jeal for giving me the benefit of his research on Stanley's childhood in advance of the publication of his new biography.

17 Hannah More quoted in I. Bradley, *The Call to Seriousness* (1976), p. 150.

18 Quoted in Bradley, *Call to Seriousness*, p. 93.

19 E. Mack, *Public Schools and British Opinion since 1860* (1941), pp. 108, 126.

20 *St Paul's Magazine*, 1872 quoted in S. Bhattacharya, *Victorian Perception of Child* (2000), p. 8.

21 Wilson, *Victorians*, p. 334.

22 C. Dickens, *Great Expectations* (1985 edn), pp. 56–7.

23 Dickens, *Miscellaneous Papers*, vol. I, p. 163.

24 Letter to Vicky, 26 June 1875 in Hibbert, *Letters and Journals*, p. 239.

25 CSAS, Benthall Papers, Diary of Clementina Benthall, 9 December 1841. There are several versions of these diaries, which were copied later on, probably by members of the family. In the original MS diary their destination is clearly Jessore although the later typescript transcribes it as Ikpore.

26 Ibid., 8 May, 10 April and 3 October 1842.

27 Ibid., 27 June 1846.

28 Ibid., 1 July 1843, 17 December 1846 and 21 March 1845.

29 Ibid., 'Account of Separation from the Children', 1 December 1847–16 February 1848.

30 Ibid., C. Benthall to Clement, 17 August 1850.

31 Ibid., Diary of C. Benthall, September 1845. Only the original version of Clementina's diary includes references to the bankruptcy. This family disgrace was omitted in the later version of the diary.

32 Ibid., C. Benthall to Louisa, 31 October 1849 and to Aunt Thornton, 7 April 1851.

33 Ibid., E. Benthall to Clement, Ernest and Edith, 25 June 1854.

34 Ibid., C. Benthall to Clement, 23 May 1850.

35 Ibid., L. Benthall to E. and C. Benthall, n.d.; Clement to different members of his family, 6 March and 15 October 1859, 27 January 1866 and 6 August 1873; E. Fay, 6 December 1873 and L. Waterfield, n.d.

36 S. Butler, *The Way of All Flesh*, first published 1903 (Collins Library of Classics), p. 230.

37 R. Pears, *Young Sea-Dogs* (1960), p. 135.

38 J. Morris, *Fisher's Face* (1995), pp. 22, 23.

39 J. Fisher, *Records* (1919), pp. 10, 8.

40 Pears, *Sea-Dogs*, pp. 135, 138.

41 Quotations taken from Pears, *Sea-Dogs*, pp. 143–5 and Morris, *Fisher's Face*, p. 30.

42 See Paul Halpern in *Oxford DNB*.

43 Morris, *Fisher's Face*, p. 86.

44 J. Abbott, *The Young Christian* (1860), pp. 340, 264.

45 OIOC, Photo Eur 31/1A, autobiographical notes dictated by Emily Bayley, October 1847, pp. 89–90.

46 Ibid., pp. 91, 96, 98.

47 CSAS, Campbell-Metcalfe Papers,

Box IX, E. Metcalfe to her sister, 18 December 1849.

48 J. Lawrence and A. Woodiwiss (eds), *The Journals of Honoria Lawrence* (1980), pp. 15, 154.

49 M. Diver, *Honoria Lawrence* (1936), p. 140.

50 Lawrence and Woodiwiss, *Journals*, pp. 111, 170.

51 Ibid., pp. 195, 184, 205, 200, 235–7.

52 OIOC, Mss Eur F85/65, Lawrence Papers, Henry Lawrence to Alick, 15 January and F85/110, 1 May 1854.

53 Lawrence and Woodiwiss, *Journals*, p. 239.

54 Diver, *Honoria Lawrence*, pp. 450, 463.

55 OIOC, Mss Eur F85/53, Dr Bernard to Harry, 18 February 1863 and Honie to Harry, 14 February 1863.

56 *Memorials of the Life and Letters of Major-General Sir Herbert Edwardes by his Wife* (1886), p. 358.

57 Lawrence and Woodiwiss, *Journals*, p. 239.

58 Quoted in *Memorials of Sir Herbert Edwardes*, p. 361.

59 OIOC, Mss Eur F85/53, Letters to Harry Lawrence, 14 and 18 February 1863 and 11 October 1864.

60 Lawrence and Woodiwiss, *Journals*, p. 165.

61 Butler, *Way of All Flesh*, p. 158.

62 W. Arnold to his sister Mary, 29 January 1848 quoted in F. Woodward, *The Doctor's Disciples* (1954), p. 202.

63 CUL, MS. Add. 7349, Papers of Sir James Fitzjames Stephen, Box 1,

Stephen to his wife, 10 February and 16–21 December 1870.

64 See Bradley, *Call to Seriousness*, p. 194.

65 W. Arnold to his late wife's sister Matilda, 5 March 1859 quoted in Woodward, *Doctor's Disciples*, p. 225.

66 M. Holroyd, *Lytton Strachey: A Biography* (1979 edn), pp. 36, 46.

67 OIOC, Mss Eur F127/325, Strachey Papers, Dick to J. Strachey, 6 April 1867.

68 Holroyd, *Lytton Strachey*, p. 50.

69 OIOC, Mss Eur F127/325, Dick to J. Strachey, 7 February, 28 March and 9 April 1868.

70 B. Strachey, *The Strachey Line* (1985), p. 155.

71 OIOC, Mss Eur F127/438, R. Strachey to Dick, 26 March 1869, 9 March 1867, 9 February and 22 January 1868.

72 Ibid., F127/439, J. Strachey to Dick, 5 August 1868 and n. d.

73 B. Caine, *Bombay to Bloomsbury: A Biography of the Strachey Family* (2005), pp. 81, 88–9 and Strachey, *Strachey Line*, p. 155.

74 OIOC, Mss Eur C376/3 and 4, Wonnacott Papers, W. Wonnacott to his family, 8 and 20 December 1871, 16 September 1872 and June 1873.

75 Ibid., C376/5, W. Wonnacott to his family: 1 March and 3 July 1875, 14 July 1878, 12 April 1875, 10 April 1876 and 7 April and July 1878.

76 Ibid., W. Wonnacott to his family: 7 November 1875, 15 July 1877 and 27 January 1878 and T. Wonnacott to Mrs Short, 30 October 1878.

77 Quoted in J. W. Lambert (ed.), *The Uunbearable Bassington and other Stories* (1963), pp. 10–11.

78 A. J. Langguth, *Saki: A Life of Hector Munro* (1981), pp. 17, 13, 25, 28, 32.

79 G. Greene, *The Lost Childhood and Other Essays* (1962), pp. 82–3.

80 Saki, *The Complete Short Stories* (2000 edn), pp. 374, 376.

81 *The Story-Teller* in ibid., p. 354.

82 See R. McCrum, *Wodehouse: A Life* (2004), pp. 16–19 for an interesting discussion of Wodehouse's childhood during which his parents lived in Hong Kong.

83 Saki, *Short Stories*, p. 372.

84 C. Raine (ed.), *A Choice of Kipling's Prose* (1987), p. 91.

85 Quoted in J. Flanders, *A Circle of Sisters* (2002), p. 131.

86 Raine, *Kipling's Prose*, pp. 105, 98, 106.

87 M. V. Hughes, *A London Child in the 1870s* (1977 edn), p. 10.

88 E. L. W. Wenger, 'Ancestral Anecdotes: Records of the Wenger Line' (1996), p. 35.

89 Quoted in Flanders, *Circle of Sisters*, p. 133.

90 Raine, *Kipling's Prose*, pp. 92–3, 106.

91 Quoted in A. Wilson, *The Strange Ride of Rudyard Kipling* (1977), p. 32.

92 Flanders, *Circle of Sisters*, p. 170.

93 Wilson, *Kipling*, p. 32.

94 K. Amis, *Rudyard Kipling* (1975), p. 25.

95 Davies, 'Children of the Raj', p. 70.

96 J. Harris, *William Beveridge* (1997), p. 14.

97 Annette Beveridge quoted in Lord Beveridge, *India Called Them* (1947), p. 237.

98 These letters provide the 'direct record of those years', which Harris claims to be lacking in *Beveridge*, p. 13.

99 OIOC, Mss Eur C176/115, Beveridge Papers, Tutu to her parents, 18 and 20 October, 2 and 21 December 1884.

100 Ibid., C176/121, Willie to his parents, 8 March 1885 and W. Beveridge, 'Anglo-Indian Childhood' quoted in Harris, *Beveridge*, p. 50.

101 OIOC Mss Eur C176/115, Letty to her parents, June 1884; C176/121, 31 May 1885 and C176/125, 11 May 1886.

102 Ibid., C176/126, Annette Beveridge to her children, 10 January 1886; C176/62, Annette Beveridge's diary, 23 and 30 April 1886; C176/19, Annette to Henry Beveridge, 30 April and 9 May 1886.

103 Beveridge, *India Called Them*, pp. 321–2.

104 Harris, *Beveridge*, pp. 57, 101, 105, 114, 479.

105 Beveridge, *India Called Them*, p. 303.

106 G. Talbot to her parents, 2 March 1884 quoted in E. Buettner, 'Parent-child separations and colonial careers: the Talbot family correspondence in the 1880s and 1890s' in E. Fletcher and S. Hussey (eds.), *Childhood in Question* (1999), p. 122.

107 *Annals of the Society of the Holy Child Jesus in Hadham*, 1873. I am grateful to Hope Gilbert for this reference.

108 OIOC, Mss Eur E349, Campbell Papers, Archibald to Sir George and Lady Campbell, undated but probably 1877.

Chapter Five: 'Cold Showers and Porridge' – British Schools in India (pp. 124–55)

1 *Juvenile Missionary Herald*, October 1890, pp. 149–50.

2 Arnold, *European Orphans and Vagrants*, p 105.

3 CUL, SPCK Papers, Report of Vepery Mission School, 1819.

4 C. Dickens, *Hard Times* (1961 edn), p. 1.

5 H. Lovatt and P. de Jong, *Above the Heron's Pool* (1993), p. 109.

6 Kipling, *Kim*, p. 154.

7 CUL, SPCK papers, Annual Report for 1822, Regulations for the Boarders in the School at Vepery and Report on the School for 1823.

8 R. Llewellyn-Jones, *A Fatal Friendship: The Nawabs, the British and the City of Lucknow* (1985), pp. 26–7.

9 'Bengal Establishment', 23 July 1845 quoted in M. Khan and K. J. Parel, *Sanawar: A Legacy* (1997), p. 228.

10 OIOC, Mss Eur F85/62, Papers Related to the Lawrence Orphan Asylum, Commander of Artillery to Adjutant General of the Army, 31 October 1845.

11 Khan and Parel, *Sanawar*, p. vii.

12 Ibid., pp. 38, 46.

13 *The Lawrence Military Asylum* (LMA Press, 1858), pp. 60–61.

14 Ibid., pp. 55.

15 *The Times*, 26 August 1847.

16 Marriage Register in possession of K. J. Parel.

17 OIOC, Mss Eur F85/50, A. Lawrence to his brother Harry, 3 March 1861.

18 Ibid., F85/62, Edward Hathaway to Governor-General of India, 18 June 1859.

19 *Address from the Bishop of Calcutta on the subject of education for European and Eurasian children* (1861), pp. 9–10, 1–6.

20 Llewellyn-Jones, *Fatal Friendship*, p. 140.

21 See H. Innes Craig, *Under the Old School Topee* (1996 edn), p. 61.

22 Minute by Lord Canning quoted in full in *Report of Committee upon the Financial Condition of Hill Schools for Europeans in North India* (1904), vol. 2, Appendix I, p. 335.

23 *Address from Bishop of Calcutta*, p. 10.

24 A. J. Lawrence, *Report on the Existing Schools for Europeans and Eurasians throughout India* (1873), p. 18.

25 This is demonstrated in Buettner, 'Families, children and memories', pp. 144 ff.

26 *Report on Existing Schools*, p. 120.

27 Admissions Register at Bishop Cotton School.

28 Author's interview with Kabir Mustafi, 22 September 2003.

29 Current prospectus for Bishop Cotton School, p. 3.

30 *Report on Exiting Schools*, p. 124.

31 M. MacMillan, *Women of the Raj* (1996 edn), p. 55.

32 Hazel Innes Craig gives an excellent survey of these schools in *Under the Old School Topee*.

33 *Report on Existing Schools*, pp. 128–9, 214.

34 Wilson, *Victorians*, p. 289.

35 *Report on Existing Schools*, p. 39 and Parel and Khan, *Sanawar*, p. 111.

36 Woodstock School Archive, letter from Warston Andrews to Dr Wherry, 25 February 1913.

37 CSAS, Dunphy Papers, Prospectus of Panchgani Boys' School, c.1912.

38 *Report on Existing Schools*, p. 20.

39 Ibid., p. 19.

40 *Report on Financial Condition*, vol. 1, p. 2.

41 Quoted in Buettner, 'Families, children and memories', p. 149.

42 *Report on Existing Schools*, p. 108.

43 There was therefore no need for the reviewer of a recent biography of Milligan to wonder 'what was really going on there in girls' convents in the 1920s'. See S. Louvish in *The Guardian*, 20 September 2003.

44 *Report on Financial Condition*, vol. 2, pp. 16, 66–7, 121.

45 Ibid., vol. 2, pp. 12, 35, 203, 204.

46 J. Staines, *Country Born: One Man's Life in India 1909–1947* (1986), p. 88.

47 Author's interview with Peter Lloyd, 22 November 2004.

48 'A Day in the Life', *Cam*, Summer 2004.

49 *Report on Financial Condition*, vol. 2, pp. 31, 58.

50 Ibid., vol. 1, p. 11.

51 Ibid., vol. 2, p. 216.

52 M. M Kaye, *The Sun in the Morning* (1992 edn), pp. 194–5.

53 Goddens, *Indian Sun*, p. 63.

54 Kipling, *Kim*, pp. 175–6.

55 BCS Prospectus, p. 7.

56 Admissions Book and Prefect Lists at Auckland House.

57 Khan and Parel, *Sanawar*, pp. 149, 225.

58 E. Evans, unpublished memoir 'A Few More Years' (1974), p. 13.

59 CSAS, Bayley Papers, 'Memoir of Life in the Punjab, 1933–46', p. 57; unpublished manuscript lent by Andrew Best, L. Gradidge, 'The Last of the Raj Memsahibs'; author's interview with Penny Francis (née Elsden-Smith), 17 February 2004.

60 CSAS, Portal Papers, unpublished memoir, 'Song at Seventy', p. 114.

61 M. Foss, *Out of India* (2002), p. 66.

62 *The Sanawarian*, Midsummer and Midwinter 1940.

63 BBC, *Desert Island Discs*, 15 June 2003; Fleming, *Last Children*, vol. 2, p. 96 and author's interview with Michael Thomas, 3 October 2003.

64 Craig, *School Topee*, p. vii.

65 E. Jones, C. Wilkie and M. McGee, *Woodstock School: The First Century 1854–1954* (1954), p. 107.

66 Article in school magazine 1945, quoted in J. Lethbridge, *Harrow on the Hooghly* (1994), pp. 163–4.

67 R. Bond, *Scenes from a Writer's Life* (1997), pp. 51, 57–8.

68 Khan and Parel, *Sanawar*, pp. 226–7.

69 OIOC, Mss Eur D1232/1, Langham Scott Papers, D. Scott to his brother Bert, 1 and 12 March 1928.

70 Ibid., D1232/14, Dorothy Langham, 'Missie Baba and Family', pp. 134, 185–8.

71 Ibid., pp. 227, 247.

72 G. Orwell, 'Such, Such were the Joys' in *Collected Essays, Journalism and Letters* (1970), vol. 4, pp. 399, 382

73 James Butler, *Incense and Innocence* (1991), p. 115.

74 Author's interview with Joseph Butler, 16 December 2003.

75 Butler, *Incense and Innocence*, pp. 40, 28.

76 Interview with Joseph Butler.

77 Butler, *Incense and Innocence*, p. 32.

78 Ibid., p. 73.

79 This is the opinion of the Dean of Discipline at St Michan's, an Irish school evoked by Brian Moore in *A Moment of Love* (1965 edn), p. 156.

80 Butler, *Incense and Innocence*, pp. 39, 7, 150.

81 Manorite Association Newsletter, August/September 2003.

82 Author's interview with Wyn Munro (née Butler), 17 December 2003.

83 A. White, *Frost in May* (1978 edn), p. 180.

84 Interview with Wyn Munro.

85 F. Kendal, *White Cargo* (1999 edn), pp. 117–19.

86 CUL, RCMS 57, J. Moore, 'From Aden to Quetta to Lahore to Delhi to Quetta', p. 47.

87 Ibid., pp. 18, 30, 36, 46–7.

88 Ibid., pp. 51, 58, 63.

89 Author's interview with Brian Outhwaite, 23 July 2002.

90 Author's interview with Michael McNay, 1 August 2003.

91 BCS Prospectus, p. 8.

92 Author's interview with Arthur Jones, 9 December 2003.

93 Foss, *Out of India*, pp. 131–2, 156, 165, 178.

94 Author's interview with Carol Pickering (née Titus), 4 February 2003.

95 S. Stoddard et al. (eds), *Living on the Edge: Tales of Woodstock School* (n.d.), p. 70.

96 Author's interview with Dick Whittaker, 4 November 2003.

97 Stoddard, *Living on the Edge*, pp. 158–9, 58.

98 J. Gavin, *Out of India: An Anglo-Indian Childhood* (1997), p. 85.

99 OIOC, Mss Eur F351/5 and 11, Auckland House Memoirs.

100 Author's interview with Agnes Heron (née Barratt), 18 April 2003.

101 Interview with B. Newman.

102 Author's interview with Naomi Good (née Judah), 25 June 2003.

103 Author's interview with Rachel Grenfell (née Judah), 25 June 2003.

104 MacMillan, *Women of Raj*, p. 158.

105 Letter to author from Alison Newton (née Hinds), 30 June 2003.

106 P. Lively, *Oleander, Jacaranda: Growing Up in Egypt in the 1930s and 1940s* (1995 edn), p. 94.

107 Buettner, 'Families, children and memories', p. 107.

108 CSAS, Clough Papers, 'A Childhood in Travancore, 1922–31', pp. 58, 62.

109 Author's interview with Gladys

Nightingale (née Krall), 8 June 2004 and her unpublished memoir.

110 Author's interviews with Anne Battye and Trish Schreiber (née Battye), 21 July and 3 August 2004.

111 Author's interview with Janet Bottoms (née Wenger), 25 August 2002.

112 Private Papers, letters of J. and M. Wenger to their father, 12 May 1949.

113 Private Papers, letter of F. Wenger to her husband during journey to England, 23 June 1950.

Chapter Six: 'Kites as Brilliant as Butterflies' – White Children in India (pp. 156–84)

1 CSAS, Crosfield Papers, Yoma Crosfield Ullman, 'A Memoir of a Childhood in India' (1999), p. i.

2 M. Proust, *Remembrance of Things Past*, trans. C. K. Scott Moncrieff (1966 edn), vol. 1, p. 57.

3 Kaye, *Golden Calm*, p. 27 and *Sun in Morning*, pp. 297–8.

4 A. Ross, *Blindfold Games* (1986), p. 35.

5 L. Langley, *Changes of Address* (1987), p. 155.

6 OIOC, Mss Eur F392, Gibbon Papers, 25 August 1946.

7 W. Bion, *The Long Weekend 1897–1919: Part of a Life* (1982), p. 41.

8 P. Scudamore, *Spike Milligan* (1985), p. 23.

9 L. Luker Ashby and R. Whately, *My India* (1938), pp. 114, 345.

10 Tape 1 of interview with L. Wenger by Elizabeth Cornish lent by J. Wenger.

11 Kendal, *White Cargo*, p. 117.

12 W. W. Hunter, *The Earl of Mayo* (1891), vol. I, p. 111 and J. Rivett-Carnac, *Many Memories* (1910), pp. 227–8.

13 CSAS, Portal, 'Song at Seventy', p. 109.

14 OIOC, Mss Eur F253/32, Lumley Papers, Lady Lumley to Lord Scarbrough, 25 May 1942.

15 CSAS, Turner Papers, E. L. Turner, 'A British Civilian Family in India, 1920–1946', pp. 1–4.

16 CUL, RCMS 90, Revd Worthington Jukes, 'Reminiscences of Missionary Work 1873–1890' (1925), pp. 107, 148, 51.

17 S. Bevan, *The Parting Years: A British Family and the End of Empire* (2001), p. 2.

18 F. Steel and G. Gardiner, *The Complete Indian Housekeeper and Cook* (1898), p. 160.

19 OIOC, Mss Eur F127/94, Diary of Mrs Plowden, 24 and 25 October and 26 November 1787 and 25 June 1789.

20 CSAS, Benthall Papers, 14 April 1845. Pat Barr was mistaken in taking this to be a description of dhyes hired by Mrs Benthall. See *Memsahibs*, p. 67.

21 Joan Battye, unpublished memoir lent by Anne Battye.

22 J. Maitland to her mother, 6 July 1837 in Price, *Letters from Madras*, p. 67.

23 OIOC, Mss Eur F206/131, 20 May, 26 June and undated 1863 and 17 January 1864.

24 These comments are reported by Lady Lytton's granddaughter,

Mary Lutyens, in *The Lyttons in India* (1979), pp. 52, 77, 89.

25 V. Fildes, *Breasts, Bottles and Babies* (1988), p. 201.

26 Private Papers lent by George's brother, William Brown, Netta Brown to her parents, 31 October–13 December 1922.

27 Kendal, *White Cargo*, p. 48.

28 M. Diver, *The Englishwoman in India* (1909), pp. 35–6.

29 Eha, *Behind the Bungalow* (1916), pp. 89, 94.

30 CSAS, Portal, 'Song at Seventy', pp. 4, 70.

31 Author's interviews with Jane Williams (née Portal), 28 February 2003 and Susan Batten (née Portal), 30 April 2003.

32 Kaye, *Sun in Morning*, pp. 136–40, 86–7, cf. J. Gathorne-Hardy, *The Rise and Fall of the British Nanny* (1972), pp. 302–8 and McCrum, *Wodehouse*, p. 14.

33 CSAS, Ullman, 'Memoir of Childhood', pp. iii, 15.

34 Manuscript lent by Alex Reid: H. Reid, 'Once there were Three Children'.

35 Gradidge, 'Last of Memsahibs'.

36 H. Bourne, unpublished memoir lent by Rosie Gutteridge, 'It was Like This', pp. 38, 204, 217.

37 CSAS, Bayley, 'Life in Punjab', pp. 14–15.

38 G. Rorke, *A Child in Burma* (2002), p. 25.

39 G. Nightingale, unpublished memoir.

40 J. Wilkins, *A Child's Eye View* (1992), pp. 11, 14.

41 CSAS, Turner, 'Life Was Like That', pp. 8–10.

42 Wilkins, *Child's Eye View*, p. 27.

43 CSAS, Clough, 'Childhood in Travancore', pp. 24–6, 98.

44 G. Roche, *Childhood in India: Tales from Sholapur* (1994), p. 11.

45 Amis, *Rudyard Kipling*, p. 20.

46 Author's interviews with Frances Moxon (née Labey) and Jane Davenport (née Labey), 17 and 18 August 2002.

47 Kendal, *White Cargo*, pp. 48–9 and Luker Ashby, *My India*, p. 37.

48 See, for instance, M. Edwardes, *Bound to Exile: The Victorians in India* (1969), p. 40 where the author blames the deaths of British children on this practice. Cf. P. Gibson, *Childhood Lost: A Boy's Journey through War* (1999), p. 10 and CSAS, Dench Papers, Mrs M. D. Dench, 'Memsahib', p. 46.

49 CSAS, 'Women in India', Replies to Questionnaires: P. Hyde.

50 CUL, RCMS 52, Guy Wheeler, unpublished autobiography, 'The Pathography of a Cuckoo', pp. 20, 26, 47.

51 CSAS, 'Women in India', H. Tewson.

52 See, for example, Gathorne-Hardy, *British Nanny*, p. 99.

53 Author's interview with Pat Harrison (née Foster), 10 June 2003.

54 E.g. John Rivett-Carnac, interviewed by Charles Allen and quoted in *Plain Tales from the Raj* (1976 edn), p. 26.

55 H. Vickers, *Vivien Leigh* (1988), p. 11 and A. de Courcy, *The Viceroy's Daughters* (2000), p. 435.

56 F. Hodgson Burnett, *The Secret Garden* (1994 edn), p. 12.

57 A. J. Greenberger, *The British Image of India: A Study in the Literature of Imperialism 1880–1960* (1969), p. 31.
58 J. Maitland to her mother, 18 September in Price, *Letters from Madras*, p. 153.
59 CSAS, 'Women in India', P. Hyde.
60 Harry Secombe quoted in Scudamore, *Spike Milligan*, p. 7.
61 BECM, Sound Archive 363.
62 Interview with G. Nightingale.
63 Scudamore, *Spike Milligan*, p. 22.
64 R. Trevelyan, *The Golden Oriole* (1987), p. 8.
65 OIOC, Mss Eur F351/5, Roessa Chiesman.
66 RCMS, Wheeler, 'Pathography of a Cuckoo', pp. 52, 86.
67 Goddens, *Indian Sun*, pp. 44–6.
68 Richard, *Which One's Cliff?*, pp. 14–15.
69 Bion, *Long Weekend*, p. 18.
70 Foss, *Out of India*, p. 174.
71 Interviews with B. Outhwaite and D. Whittaker.
72 G. Honeycombe, 'Young Tales of the Raj' in NSPCC, *When we were Young* (1989), p. 97.
73 OIOC, Mss Eur C354, D. Turner, Christmas 1899 and May 1901.
74 Goddens, *Indian Sun*, p. 73 and CSAS, Clough, 'Childhood in Travancore', p. 26.
75 CSAS, Ullman, 'Memoir of Childhood', p. 50.
76 Kendal, *White Cargo*, p. 250.
77 R. Murphy, *The Kick* (2002), p. 37.
78 CSAS, Mrs S. Shoosmith, 'Poems of Childhood in India'.
79 CSAS, Cartwright Papers, Mrs P. Cartwright, 'Notes on Life in India', p. 3.
80 OIOC, D1232/14, Donald Langham Scott quoted on p. 247.
81 J. Battye, unpublished memoir.
82 OIOC, R214, taped interview with R. Baker and author's interview with Beatrice Broad (née Baker), 27 March 2003.
83 Author's interview with Paula Baker, 16 June 2003.
84 CUL, VP2, Hardinge Papers, Diary, 29 April 1910.
85 Interview with D. Whittaker.
86 J. Lumley, *Stare Back and Smile* (1989), p. 3.
87 Letter to author, 30 June 2003.
88 Hilary Sweet-Escott, manuscript memoir, p. 3 and Ronald Johnston, 'One Man's Life' (unpublished memoir), p. 226, both lent by Hilary Sweet-Escott.
89 Trevelyan, *Golden Oriole*, pp. 496–9.
90 Stories told in R. Jackson, *Twenty Seconds at Quetta* (1960), pp. 149, 91–2.
91 J. Battye, unpublished memoir and Gradidge, 'Last of Memsahibs'.
92 Wilkins, *Child's Eye View*, p. 16.
93 Roche, *Tales from Sholapur*, p. 60.
94 CSAS, Maude Papers, Constance Maude, 'Memoir', p. 7.
95 CSAS, Clough, 'Childhood in Travancore', p. 52.
96 Murphy, *The Kick*, pp. 31–2.
97 OIOC, Mss Eur D885/2, M. Fyson, 'Good Memory', p. 47.
98 Trevelyan, *Golden Oriole*, p. 37.
99 Reid, 'Three Children'.

100 Memoir lent by Christine Usborne, T. Usborne, 'Memories of my Father, Charles Frederick Usborne'.

101 CUL, MS. Add. 7349, J. F. Stephen, 18 and 23 February 1872.

102 Lord Hardinge, *My Indian Years* (1948), p. 97.

103 OIOC, Mss Eur C553, D. Harrington-Hawes, 'Drusilla's Memories', pp. 1–2.

104 G. Nightingale, unpublished memoir.

105 Roche, *Tales from Sholapur*, pp. 82, 87, 96, lxxiii, xvi.

106 Hunter, *Earl of Mayo*, vol. I, p. 200.

107 Roche, *Tales from Sholapur*, p. 115.

108 Bourne, 'It Was Like This', p. 220.

109 Scudamore, *Spike Milligan*, p. 22.

110 RCMS 57, Moore, 'From Aden to Quetta', p. 23.

111 CSAS, Donaldson Papers, B. Donaldson, 'India Remembered', pp. 2–3.

112 Foss, *Out of India*, p. 134.

113 OIOC, Mss Eur D885/2, Fyson, 'Good Memory', p. 81.

114 Kaye, *Sun in Morning*, p. 86.

115 CSAS, 'Women in India', N. Vernede, p. 7.

116 Trevelyan, *Golden Oriole*, pp. 7–8.

117 CSAS, Turner, 'Civilian Family in India', p. 8.

118 CSAS, Clough, 'Childhood in Travancore', pp. 88, 26.

119 CSAS, Turner, 'Life Was Like That', pp. 20, 30, 39, 37–9, 55.

120 CSAS, Bayley, 'Memoir of Punjab', p. 79.

121 Goddens, *Indian Sun*, pp. 158, 164; J. and M. Wenger to their father, 9 April 1948 and August 1949.

122 NSPCC, *When we were Young*, p. 98.

123 Interview with P. Francis.

124 OIOC, Mss Eur A144, Diary of Lady Elisabeth Bruce, vol. III, p. 64.

125 OIOC, Mss Eur D1232/1, Donald Scott to his brother Bert, 22 and 24 March 1926.

126 Roche, *Tales from Sholapur*, p. 102.

127 See, for instance, D. Kennedy, *The Magic Mountains: Hill Stations and the British Raj* (1996), p. 132.

128 R. Godden, *A Time to Dance, No Time to Weep* (1987), p. 2.

129 OIOC, Mss Eur D1197, Elinor Tollinton, Memoir (no page numbers).

130 Goddens, *Indian Sun*, p. 124; Roche, *Tales from Sholapur*, p. 104.

131 OIOC, Mss Eur C354, D. Turner, Quetta, 1900.

132 CSAS, Cartwright, 'Life in India', p. 2.

133 Letter to author, 9 August 2004 and interview with Morvyth Seely (née St. George), 3 August 2004.

134 Langley, *Changes of Address*, p. 72

135 P. Greave, *The Seventh Gate* (1978), pp. 76–7, 105, 113, 142–4, 170.

136 CSAS, Fyson, 'Good Memory', p. 27.

137 Scudamore, *Spike Milligan*, pp. 19–20.

138 Gradidge, 'Last of Memsahibs'.

139 Interview with J. Bottoms.

140 Kaye, *Sun in Morning*, pp. 287–8.
141 Henry Martyn Centre, Cambridge, C. Pickering, 'Goodbye India', p. 55.
142 Gavin, *Out of India*, p. 54.
143 CSAS, Ullman, 'Memoir', p. 77.

Chapter Seven: 'Other People's Houses' – Separated Families in the Early Twentieth Century (pp. 185–212)

1 H. Davies, *Born 1900* (1998), p. 222.
2 S. Freud, *A Child is Being Beaten* (1919) in Penguin Freud Library, vol. 10, p. 187.
3 L. Woolf. *Growing: An Autobiography of the Years 1904 to 1911* (1961), p. 13.
4 Quoted in P. Conrad, *Modern Times, Modern Places* (1998), p. 272.
5 Private collection of Wilkins letters lent by Dorothy's daughter Elinor Kapp: Dorothy to Phyllis Wilkins, 2 May 1930.
6 Gathorne-Hardy, *British Nanny*, p. 249.
7 Quoted by M. Abbott in *Family Affairs* (2003), p. 35.
8 See C. Storr, 'Freud and the Concept of Parental Guilt' in J. Miller, *Freud: The Man, his World, his Influence* (1972), p. 102.
9 M. Truby King, *Mothercraft* (1934), pp. 185, 198, 202.
10 Maeve Kelly quoted in Fleming, *Last Children*, vol. II, p. 267.
11 J. Bowlby, *Separation, Anger and Anxiety* (1998 edn), pp. 277, 428–9.
12 Interview with Mary Kenny in *The Oldie*, March 2004, p. 38.

13 BBC, *Desert Island Discs*, 31 May 2004.
14 N. Slater, *Toast: The Story of a Boy's Hunger* (2003), pp. 174–6.
15 Quoted in M. Blackburn, S. Humphries, N. Maddocks and C. Titley, *Hope and Glory* (2004), pp. 14–15.
16 See, for instance, Bean and Melville, *Lost Children* and M. Humphreys, *Empty Cradles: One Woman's Fight to Uncover Britain's Most Shameful Secret* (1994).
17 Florence Aulph in Bean and Melville, *Lost Children*, p. 11 uses this term to describe herself and other child migrants.
18 *The Times*, 7 January 1916.
19 Wilkins Letters, Phyllis to her parents, 1 February 1916.
20 Rosamund Lawrence, *Indian Embers* (n.d.), p. 367.
21 Wilkins Letters, Dorothy to her parents in India, 1909 and 2 July 1914.
22 Ibid., Dorothy to her parents, 31 March 1915.
23 Former pupils quoted in E. Pike et al., *The Story of Walthamstow Hall* (1973), p. 53.
24 Wilkins Letters, Dorothy to her parents, 1909.
25 Ibid., Phyllis to her father, 17 July 1921.
26 Ibid., Dorothy to her parents, 13 August 1914.
27 Ibid., Dorothy to her parents, 9 June 1910.
28 Ibid., Dorothy to her parents, 20 June and 22 August 1917.
29 Ibid., Joyce to her parents, 19 September 1917.

30 Wilkins, *Child's Eye View*, pp. 99–100.

31 Wilkins Letters, Phyllis to her parents, 30 May 1917.

32 Ibid., Eric to his parents, 12 November 1915 and C. Witting (ed.), *The Glory of the Sons: A History of Eltham College* (1952), pp. 168, 170.

33 Pike, *Story of Walthamstow Hall*, p. 59.

34 Wilkins Letters, Dorothy to her parents, 25 July 1917.

35 Ibid., Joyce to her parents, 26 March and 2 July 1914.

36 Ibid., Phyllis to her mother, 25 June 1921 and to her father, 17 July 1921.

37 Ibid., Dorothy to Phyllis, 2 May 1930.

38 From interview published in G. Wood and P. Thompson, *The Nineties* (1993), p. 134.

39 Information supplied by her daughter, Elinor Kapp.

40 Wilkins, *Child's Eye View*, p. 45 and Wood and Thompson, *Nineties*, p. 136

41 IWM, P121, Mrs E. Mascall, 'All Change: Memoir 1896–1949', p. 11.

42 CSAS, Portal, 'Song at Seventy', pp. 18, 21.

43 J. Christie, *Morning Drum* (1983), pp. 8–10.

44 C. Douglas, *Douglas Jardine: Spartan Cricketer* (1984), pp. 4, 12, 144.

45 P. Williams, *Hugh Gaitskell: A Political Biography* (1979), pp. 9–12 and B. Brivati, *Hugh Gaitskell* (1996), p. 2.

46 Bion, *Long Weekend*, pp. 47, 91–2, 103–4.

47 Ibid., p. 266.

48 Author's telephone interview with Kissane Probyn (née Keane), 20 January 2004 with additions in writing, March 2004.

49 Author's interview with Leila Brown, 4 February 2003.

50 W. Brown, memoir lent by L. Brown, 'Highlights in the Life of a Bengal Missionary', pp. 39, 61.

51 CSAS, Tait Papers, M. Tait, 'Memories of Bangalore', pp. 2, 6, 7, 9.

52 Kaye, *Sun in Morning*, p. 291.

53 Author's interview with Pamela Kirkpatrick (née Watson), 11 February 2005.

54 P. Clarke, *Hope and Glory: Britain 1900–1990* (1996), p. 85.

55 Kaye, *Sun in Morning*, p. 392, Clay, *John Masters*, p. 26, Vickers, *Vivien Leigh*, p. 16 and H. Spurling, *The Girl from the Fiction Department* (2003), p. 10.

56 R. Baker, unpublished memoir lent by Paula Baker, 'Early Memories', pp. 1, 6–7 11–13, 15, 21–2.

57 OIOC, R214, interview with Robert Baker.

58 Baker, 'Early Memories', p. 20.

59 Interview with B. Broad and her unpublished memoir, 'Fishing Fleet'.

60 Interviews with F. Moxon and J. Davenport.

61 Author's interview with Ruth Quadling (née Starte), 17 April 2004.

62 Author's interview with Richard Sarson, 12 May 2003.

63 Author's interview with Sister Armine (née Mathias), 2 May 2003.

64 Patricia Toft quoted in Fleming, *Last Children*, vol. I, p. 273.

65 Kaye, *Sun in Morning*, p. 369.

66 Report in *The Observer*, 26 January 2003.

67 Spurling, *Girl from Fiction Department*, p. 12.

68 Author's interview with Jack Judah, 7 July 2003.

69 Interview with P. Kirkpatrick.

70 CSAS, Maxwell-Gumbleton Papers, 'RD and Jay', pp. 110, 112–14, 118–19.

71 Interview with P. Lloyd and unpublished memoir, 'A Pinch of Salt'.

72 Trevelyan, *Golden Oriole*, pp. 1, 9–10, 491.

73 Ross, *Blindfold Games*, pp. 58, 68–9, 82, 245.

74 Author's interview with Roger Moore, 6 May 2003.

75 P. Wingate, *The Penguin Medical Encyclopaedia* (1988 edn), p. 411.

76 Author's interview with William Brown, 11 February 2003.

77 CSAS, Turner, 'Life Was Like That', pp. 58, 6, 64, 66, 85, 137, 70.

78 Wilkins, *Child's Eye View*, p. 68.

79 W. J. Thorne quoted in Witting, *Glory of Sons*, p. 176.

80 J. and E. Newson, *Seven Years Old in the Home Environment* (1976), pp. 405–6.

81 Wilkins Letters, Joyce to her parents, April 1917.

Chapter Eight: 'The Last of the Empire's Children' – World War II (pp. 213–40)

1 S. Brookes, *Through the Jungle of Death* (2000), pp. 98–9.

2 See A. Freud, *Infants without Families* (1939/45).

3 See J. Stevenson-Hinde and R. A. Hinde, 'John Bowlby' in N. J. Smelser and P. B. Baltes (eds), *International Encyclopaedia of the Social and Behavioural Sciences* (2001), p. 1314.

4 Principle 6 of the Declaration of the Rights of the Child, 1959.

5 Fleming, *Last Children*, vol. II, p. 47.

6 BECM, Sound Archive 363 and typescript of talk to the University of the Third Age given by R. Lamb.

7 Interview with P. Francis and her unpublished article, 'The Long Voyage', p. 1.

8 Gradidge, 'Last of Memsahibs'.

9 G. Allan, 'India 1934–1944', pp. 9–13, unpublished memoir lent by the author.

10 George Shakespeare, the organiser of the Children's Overseas Reception Board, quoted in E. Stokes, *Innocents Abroad: The Story of British Child Evacuees in Australia, 1940–45* (1994), p. 57.

11 IWM, 97/21/1, G. E. Shaw, letter to parents, 30 January 1942 and essay, 'The Effects of Evacuation'.

12 Quotations from R. Inglis, *The Children's War: Evacuation 1939–45* (1989), p. 154–6.

13 A. Calder, *The People's War: Britain 1939–45* (1992 edn), p. 128.

14 See CSAS, Dench, 'Memsahib', p. 110. Mrs Dench took her own children out to India in 1940 by this scheme and wrote about it in a patriotic magazine she started in Lahore: *Women in India*.

15 Interview with R. Moore.

16 J. Catlin, *Family Quartet: Vera Brittain and her Family* (1987), pp. 113, 135, 140, 148, 120.

17 Private collection of Portal letters lent by Susan Batten, S. Butler to I. Portal, 1 November 1940.

18 Portal Letters, I. Portal to Jane, 7 June, 21 July and 4 August 1940 and to Susan, 15 July 1940 and 26 July 1941.

19 Ibid., Jane to her mother, 3 June and July 1940 and Susan to her mother, 27 December 1941.

20 Ibid., S. Butler to I. Portal, 2 March 1941.

21 Ibid., Susan to her mother, 30 July 1940.

22 Quoted in Abbott, *Family Affairs*, p. 77.

23 Portal Letters, Jane to her mother, 30 May 1940.

24 Ibid., Jane to her mother, 10 April 1942.

25 Ibid., S. Butler to I. Portal, 14 August 1940 and 2 March 1941, note from Miss Tilley to I. Portal, 13 January 1941 and interview with S. Batten.

26 Portal Letters, I. Portal to Susan, 21 June 1942 and to Jane, 2 February 1941 and interviews with J. Williams and S. Batten.

27 Author's telephone interview with Peter Clark, 18 November 2004.

28 Author's interview with Gillian Beard (née Northfield), 19 March 2004.

29 Pike, *Story of Walthamstow Hall*, Part II by U. K. Moore, pp. 73, 81.

30 Ibid., p. 74.

31 Author's interview with Lesley Dowling (née Hayward), 31 July 2003. Before seeing me Lesley wrote out an account of her life.

32 Interview with Tony Bottoms, 24 April 2004.

33 BECM, Sound Archive 021, Mrs Rosemary Burton.

34 Francis, 'Long Voyage', p. 1.

35 Parker correspondence made available by C. Parker, B. Parker to her mother, 7 April 1941 and 13 February 1943.

36 Author's interview with Christopher Parker, 10 March 2004.

37 Parker correspondence, B. Parker to her mother, 7 September 1941, 13 February 1943 and 3 June 1944.

38 Ibid., T. Parker to his wife's sister, 17 May 1944 and B. Parker to her mother, 21 September 1945.

39 OIOC, Mss Eur C462, Decima Curtis, 'The Last Twelve Years of the British Raj', pp. 2, 57, 90.

40 OIOC, Mss Eur F392/3, Roddy to Jeremy Milne Gibbon, 1943.

41 Gradidge, *Last of Memsahibs*.

42 Author's interview with Harry Southwell, 21 June 2003.

43 Interview with Hilary Sweet-Escott, written memoir lent by her and article 'Indian Christmas' in *Beaminster Parish Magazine*, 1992.

44 Interview with D. Whittaker.

45 Rorke, *Child in Burma*, p. 106.

46 Ibid., pp. 136–9, 147.

47 IWM, 86/3/1, Miss D. M. Powell, 'Where the Flying Fishes Played', pp. 1, 9.

48 Ibid., 'East is West – Home is Best', pp. 13, 22, 32.

49 IWM, 03/42/1, Mrs D. Kup, Memoir, pp. 6–7.

50 IWM, 02/28/1, Mrs B. McDougall, 'Journey to Dagshai', pp. 130, 147, 156.

51 CSAS, Burmah Oil Papers, Fay Brown, 'Retreat from Burma', pp. 7, 11.

52 CSAS, Tayabji Papers, Captain N. S. Tayabji, 'The Burma Story', p. 21.

53 IWM, Westland Wright, 'Out of Burma 1942', p. 44.

54 J. Lunt, *A Hell of a Licking: The Retreat from Burma 1941–2* (1986), p. 270.

55 Brookes, *Jungle of Death*, p. 73.

56 Lunt, *Hell of a Licking*, p. 273.

57 Brookes, *Jungle of Death*, pp. 171, 204, 250.

58 Maurice Collis, *Last and First in Burma* (n.d.), pp. 177–8.

59 CSAS, Burmah Oil Papers, letter from Cherie Crowley (née Walmsley), 26 November 1996. For the horrors of internment see, for example, Ernest Hillen, *The Way of a Boy: A Memoir of Java* (1993).

60 Gibson, *Childhood Lost*, pp. 26, 48.

61 Ibid., pp. 48, 103, 111.

62 Ibid., pp. 126, 147, 155–7.

63 M. J. Harris and D. Oppenheimer, *Into the Arms of Strangers: Stories of the Kindertransport* (2001 edn), p. 222.

64 G. Allan, unpublished memoir, 'Off to School in Scotland', pp. 1, 8 and author's interview, 4 March 2004.

65 Francis, 'Long Voyage', pp. 1–4.

66 Letters lent by David Wilkins, 26 October and 30 November 1944.

67 Ibid., 14 April, 28 May and 20 August 1945.

68 Author's interview with David Wilkins, 7 April 2004.

69 L. James, *Raj: The Making and Unmaking of British India* (1997), p. 539.

70 T. Jesse and E. Thompson quoted in Greenberger, *British Image of India*, p. 122.

Chapter Nine: 'Is that the same Moon that Shines in India?' – The End of the Raj and Beyond (pp. 241– 73)

1 Luker Ashby, *My India*, p. 290.

2 Quoted in James, *Raj*, p. 567.

3 CSAS, Tait, 'Memories of Bangalore', pp. 2, 11.

4 N. Chaudhuri, *The Autobiography of an Unknown Indian* (1951), pp. 399, 401.

5 Diary of M. Wathen quoted in Trevelyan, *Golden Oriole*, pp. 478, 482.

6 T. Royle, *The Last Days of the Raj* (1989), p. 47.

7 Lawrence, *Indian Embers*, pp. 384, 391.

8 CSAS, Tait, 'Memories of Bangalore', p. 16.

9 'India! India!' quoted in Scudamore, *Milligan*, pp. 9–10, 32.

10 Interview with M. Seely.

11 Kaye, *Sun in Morning*, pp. 16, 454.

12 OIOC, Mss Eur C216, N. Burke, 'The Raj: India 1890–1920', pp. 152, 156.

13 R. A. Butler, *The Art of the Possible* (1971), pp. 5–6 and OIOC Mss Eur F225/1, M. Butler to his mother, 17 July 1919. I am grateful to Patrick Higgins for allowing me to see his notes from this archive.

14 Ian Gilmour in *Oxford DNB*.

15 CSAS, Clough, 'Childhood in Travancore', pp. 43–4.

16 Interview with J. Williams.

17 Interview with H. Southwell and Foss, *Out of India*, p. 178–9.

18 Unpublished memoir lent by Jaya Bolt, pp. 21–2.

19 V. L. Pandit, *The Scope of Happiness* (1979), p. 41.

20 Chaudhuri, *Autobiography*, p. 370.

21 S. Kamra, *Bearing Witness: Partition, Independence, End of the Raj* (2002), p. 223.

22 I. Copland, *India 1885–1947: The Unmaking of an Empire* (2001), p. 33.

23 CUL RCMS 52, Wheeler, 'Pathography of a Cuckoo', pp. 68–70.

24 Stoddard et al., *Living on the Edge*, pp. 61–2.

25 Lethbridge, *Harrow on the Hooghly*, p. 133 and interview with M. McNay.

26 CSAS, Maxwell-Gumbleton, 'RD and Jay', pp. 128, 134.

27 James, *Raj*, p. 594.

28 W. Russell, *Indian Summer* (1951), p. 10.

29 Fleming, *Last Children*, vol. II, pp. 237, 199.

30 CSAS, Bayley, 'Life in Punjab', pp. 124, 126.

31 CSAS, Donaldson, 'India Remembered', p. 6.

32 Royle, *Last Days of Raj*, p. 58.

33 A. Leslie, *Daily Mail*, 13 August 1997.

34 Letter to the author from M. Seely, 9 August 2004.

35 G. Allan, 'India 1934–44', p. 13.

36 Quoted in Blackburn et al., *Hope and Glory*, p. 36.

37 *Daily Mail*, 13 August 1997.

38 Richard, *Which One's Cliff?*, p. 18.

39 CSAS, Ullman, 'Memoir', p. 72.

40 Royle, *Last Days of Raj*, p. 137.

41 CSAS, Portal, 'Song at Seventy', p. 172.

42 Foss, *Out of India*, p. 196.

43 Urvashi Batalia, *The Other Side of Silence: Voices from the Partition of India* (1998), pp. 211, 215.

44 CSAS, Brendon Papers, P. Brendon, 'Disaster in Gurgaon', pp. 30, 32, 47, 64.

45 Christie, *Morning Drum*, pp. 107–10.

46 The story of Fey Williams told in Royle, *Last Days of Raj*, pp. 193–5.

47 Foss, *Out of India*, pp. 196–8.

48 Harris, *Beveridge*, p. 54.

49 Quoted in P. Delaney (ed.), *Tom Stoppard in Conversation* (1994), p. 233.

50 T. Stoppard, 'In Search of Childhood' in *The Independent*, 23 March 1991.

51 Khan and Parel, *Sanawar*, p. 198.

52 Scudamore, *Milligan*, pp. 35, 39.

53 Interview with B. Outhwaite.

54 CSAS, Bayley, 'Life in Punjab', pp. 128, 132.

55 H. Sweet-Escott, unpublished memoir and interview.

56 P. J. Rich, *Chains of Empire* (1991), pp. 94–5.

57 BBC, *Desert Island Discs*, 15 June 2003.

58 Interview with C. Parker.

59 Interview with H. Southwell.

60 W. Churchill, *My Early Life* (1959 edn), p. 46.

61 Interview with R. Moore.

62 BBC Talk, *Something Understood*.

63 Battye, *Fighting Ten*, pp. 18, 25.

64 Interviews with A. Battye and T. Schreiber.

65 See E. Buettner, 'From Somebodies to Nobodies: Britons Returning Home from India' in M. Daunton and B. Rieger, *Meanings of Modernity: Britain from the late-Victorian era to the Second World War* (2001).

66 Interviews with A. Battye and T. Shreiber.

67 Interview with M. Thomas.

68 Royle, *Last Days of Raj*, p. 229.

69 Telephone conversation with Charles Allen, 2 February 2005. Both Charles Allen's parents appear in his pioneering work of oral history, *Plain Tales of the Raj*, which was first broadcast on BBC Radio in 1974.

70 Author's interview with George Kennedy, 16 February 2005.

71 Interview with L. Dowling.

72 Interview with T. Bottoms.

73 E. G. Wilkins, *By Hands, Bullocks and Prayers* (1987), pp. 177, 174.

74 Private papers, Gordon Wilkins to Eric, 11 July 1950.

75 Ibid., Joyce to Eric Wilkins, 12 August 1949.

76 Ibid., David to his parents, 7 January and 20 April 1950 and 26 June 1949.

77 Interview with D. Wilkins.

78 Private Papers, David to his father, 11 November 1950.

79 Private Papers, Eric to David Wilkins, 17 April 1951 and 6 December 1950.

80 Interview with D. Wilkins.

81 Recruiting brochure quoted in S. Kinsey and E. Green, *The Good Companions: Wives and Families in the History of the HSBC Group* (privately published, 2004), p. 99.

82 Quoted in Davies, 'Children of the Raj', p. 147.

83 Interview with A. Heron.

84 Ruth Dudley Edwards quoted in K. Hickman, *Daughters of Britannia: The Lives and Times of Diplomatic Wives* (1999), p. 228.

85 Interview with Jane Hudson (née Anson), 27 July 2004.

86 A. Leslie in the *Daily Mail*, 12 August 1997 and on BBC, *Desert Island Discs*, 7 November 2004.

87 S. Rushdie, *Midnight's Children* (1982 edn), pp. 229–30.

88 Christie, *Morning Drum*, p. 114.

89 Author's interview with Penny Smith (née Walker), 17 July 2004.

90 B. Spock, *Baby and Child Care* (1979 edn), pp. 60, 68.

91 Interview with J. Bottoms.

92 Author's interview with Rosie Gutteridge (née Harrison), 3 March 2003.

93 Author's interview with Valentine Davies (née Morice), 8 September 2004.

94 Author's interview with Susie Rook (née Tewson), 18 February 2003. CSAS, 'Women in India'.

95 Author's interviews with Martin Baker and Paulette Bateman (née Baker), 16 June 2003.

96 Eric Hannay quoted in P. Pugh, *Williamson Magor Stuck to Tea* (1991), p. 130.

97 Ibid., p. 111.

98 Christie, *Morning Drum*, p. 139.

99 Author's meeting with Allan Oakley, 27 January 2002 and letter 11 March 2002.

100 Interview with P. Clark.

101 Hickman, *Daughters of Britannia*, p. 221.

102 Quoted in Kinsey and Green, *Good Companions*, p. 100.

Chapter Ten: 'Did I Smell of Curry?' – The Abiding Effects of an Indian Childhood (pp. 274–92)

1 Trevelyan, *Golden Oriole*, p. 1.
2 Collingham, *Imperial Bodies*, p. 97 and Steel and Gardiner, *Complete Indian Housekeeper*, p. 87.
3 Richard, *Which One's Cliff?*, p. 14.
4 Kaye, *Sun in Morning*, pp. 321–3.
5 Author's interviews with Caroline Kennett (née Paylor), 30 September and Annie Paylor, 8 November 2004.
6 Sherwood, *Lucy and her Dhye*, pp. 32, 40.
7 Eha, *Behind the Bungalow*, p. 96.
8 Diver, *Englishwoman in India*, p. 36.
9 CUL RCMS, 52, Wheeler, 'Pathography of a Cuckoo', pp. 16, 75, 109.
10 R. Lambert, *The Hothouse Society* (1968), pp. 277 (reference by pupil to 'hothouse society'), 317–41.
11 *Domestic Guide to Mothers in India* (1848) quoted in Collingham, *Imperial Bodies*, p. 97.
12 Kendal, *White Cargo*, pp. 239, 209–10.
13 These examples are taken from Hilda Bourne's letters to her three daughters in England, CSAS, Bourne Papers, 9 December 1914 and 25 April 1918 and Bourne, 'It Was Like This', p. 120.
14 BECM, Sound Archive 638.
15 CSAS, H. Bourne to her daughters, 5 June 1918.
16 Private Papers, David to Eric Wilkins, 23 July 1950 and 29 June 1952.
17 Author's interview with Penny Henderson, 19 October 2004.
18 Lambert, *Hothouse Society*, p. 214.
19 OIOC, Mss Eur C250, Terry Letters, S. Terry to her sister Mary (at end of letter to Amelia), March 1847.
20 Interview with V. Davies and thesis 'Children of the Raj', p. 133.
21 Survey of 1986 cited in David C. Pollock and Ruth E. Van Reken, *Third Culture Kids: The Experience of Growing Up Among Worlds* (2001), Appendix A, p. 302.
22 V. Jacquemont, *Letters from India*, ed. C. A. Phillips (1936), p. 134.
23 S. Gerhardt, *Why Love Matters: How Affection Shapes a Baby's Brain* (2004), p. 94.
24 Pearse, *The Hearseys*, p 122.
25 Connolly, *Enemies of Promise*, p. 202.
26 Letter from guardian, 26 January 1906, *Methodist Recorder* 1925 and *Surrey Comet* 1970 quoted in C. Bott, *The Life and Works of Alfred Bestall* (2003), pp. 7–9, 19–20, 101.
27 R. Kipling, *The Years Between* (1919), pp. 61–2.
28 BBC, *Desert Island Discs*, 7 November 2004.
29 T. Ewbank and S. Hildred, *Julie Christie: The Biography* (2000), pp. 5, 7, 8.
30 H. and L. Rothschild in *The Guardian*, 1 February 2005.
31 Flanders, *Circle of Sisters*, pp. 289, 316.
32 CSAS, 'Women in India', P. Hyde.
33 Connolly, *Enemies of Promise*, p. 176.
34 OIOC, D885/2, Fyson, 'Good Memory', p. 115.

35 Interview with B. Outhwaite.

36 F. Eidse and N. Sichel (eds), *Unrooted Childhoods: Memoirs of Growing Up Global* (2004), pp. 1, 116.

37 Author's interview with Livia Lai, 28 July 2004.

38 R. Dudley Edwards, *True Brits: Inside the Foreign Office* (1994), p. 219.

39 IWM, 83/46/1, P. Collister, 'Then a Soldier', pp. 6, 11, 53.

40 OIOC, D885/2, Fyson, 'Good Memory', p. 57.

41 tckworld.com: Ann Baker Cottrell and Ruth Hill Useem, 'ATCKs maintain global dimensions throughout their lives'.

42 Author's interview with Karen Chan, 28 July 2004.

43 Author's interview with Maggie Lai, 28 July 2004.

44 Author's interview with Kay Hannaford, 18 October 2004.

45 Kerr, *Dispossessed*, p. 39.

46 Minet Library, Lambeth IV/3, Diaries of Henrietta Thornhill, 18 March, 30 September and 9 November 1866.

47 CUL, RCMS 304, letters from Thornhill family in New Zealand, George to Minnie, 16 July 1895 and quotation in Kerr, *Dispossessed*, p. 240.

48 Minet Library, IV/14, Diaries of Henrietta Thornhill, 18 November 1877.

49 Ibid., IV/15, 22 November, 19, 25 and 31 December 1878.

50 CUL, RCMS 304, Thornhill Letters, G. Thornhill to Minnie, 11 March 1881.

51 Ibid., Mabel Downe to archivist D. Simpson, 21 July 1976.

52 Ibid., E. Thornhill to Minnie, 16 December 1918.

53 Interviews with A. Paylor and C. Kennett.

54 Telephone interview with Susie Taylor (née Paylor), 26 November 2004.

55 P. Scott, *The Birds of Paradise* (1967 edn), p. 22.

56 Wilkins, *Child's Eye View*, p. 29.

57 Interview with Wyn Munro.

58 Trevelyan, *Golden Oriole*, p. 10.

59 Author's interview with Linette Peter (née Purbi), 19 January 2004.

60 Interview with P. Kirkpatrick.

61 Kristin Squire quoted in Fleming, *Last Children*, vol. II, p. 289.

62 From 'Indian Childhood' quoted in Ross, *Blindfold Games*, p. 22.

63 Trevelyan, *Golden Oriole*, pp. 489–90, 37–8, 167–8.

64 Interviews with M. Baker and P. Bateman.

65 Interviews with D. and M. Whittaker.

66 Murphy, *The Kick*, pp. 339–93.

67 R. Murphy, *Collected Poems* (2000), p. 168

68 Quoted by D. Gilmour in *The Long Recessional: The Imperial Life of Rudyard Kipling* (2002), p. 106, to illustrate Kipling's persistent nostalgia for India.

69 H. Spurling, *Paul Scott: A Life* (1990), pp. 145, 24 and P. Scott, *A Division of the Spoils* (1977 edn), p. 103.

Epilogue: 'A Shift in the Balance of Power'? (pp. 293–6)

1 Harvey-Jones, *Getting it Together*, pp. 25, 40, 54–8, 73, 21, 27.

2 R. Crossman, *Palestine Mission* (1947), p. 140.
3 Cunningham, *Children and Childhood*, p. 182.
4 T. Jeal, *Swimming with my Father* (2004), p. 73.
5 H. Mantel, *Giving up the Ghost* (2003), p. 92.
6 L. Langley, *Persistent Rumours* (1999), p. 113.
7 Carolyne Willow reported in *The Guardian*, 9 October 2003.
8 Gerhardt, *Why Love Matters*, p. 214.
9 Connolly, *Enemies of Promise*, p. 174.
10 A. Barnett and M. Bright, Special Investigation, *The Observer*, 23 January 2005.
11 Information supplied by Tina Attwood, Education Officer of the DSFA.

Bibliography

Unpublished Sources

Auckland House School, Shimla
Admissions Book
Visitors' Book

Bishop Cotton School, Shimla
Admissions Register, 1863–

British Empire and Commonwealth Museum (BECM), Bristol
Sound Archives, 021, 194, 363, 547, 638

British Library (BL)
Anderson Papers, Add Mss 45418
Dropmore Papers, Correspondence with Gen. Nugent, Add Mss 59004
Warren Hastings Papers, Add Mss 29178–29188

Cambridge University Library (CUL)
Edmonstone Papers (The Elmore Letters), MS. Add. 7616
Hardinge Papers, VP2
Mayo Papers, MS. Add. 7490
Royal Commonwealth Society Manuscripts (RCMS), 52, 57, 90, 304
SPCK Papers
Stephen Papers, MS. Add. 7349
Sanitary Report of the British Army in India (1863)

Address from the Bishop of Calcutta on the subject of education for European and Eurasian children (1861)

Centre for South Asian Studies, Cambridge (CSAS)
Bayley Papers
Benthall Papers
Bourne Papers
Boyes Papers
Brendon Papers
Burmah Oil Papers
Campbell-Metcalfe Papers
Cartwright Papers
Clough Papers
Crosfield Papers
Dench Papers
Donaldson Papers
Dunphy Papers
Edmonstone Papers
Erskine Papers
Fyson Papers
Gardner Papers
Hunter Blair Papers
Huxham Papers
Macpherson Papers
Maude Papers
Maxwell-Gumbleton Papers
Mill Papers
Mosse Papers
Portal Papers
Sampson Papers

Shoosmith, 'Poems of Childhood in India'
Stock Papers
Tait Papers
Tayabji Papers
Beatrice Turner Papers
E. L. Turner Papers
Wentworth-Reeve Papers
Women in India Questionnaires
Tape recordings, MT1&2, R8

Henry Martyn Centre, Cambridge
Titus Papers

Imperial War Museum (IWM), Department of Documents
The papers of:
Capt. P. Collister, 83/46/1
Mrs D. Kup, 03/42/1
Mrs E. Mascall, P121
Mrs B. McDougall, 02/28/1
Miss D. M. Powell, 86/3/1
G. E. Shaw, 97/21/1
Westland Wright, 'Exit from Burma 1942'

Lawrence School, Sanawar
Baptismal certificates
Marriage Registers
Sanawarian, 1941, 1944, 1945

Minet Library, Lambeth
Diaries of Henrietta Thornhill, IV/18/1-16

National Army Museum (NAM)
Constantia, 6008-248
Dunn Journal, 1997/12-67
Gardner Papers, 6305-65-5
Moyle Memoir, 1998-10-299
Skinner Memoir, 1952-05-19

Oriental and India Office Collections (OIOC)
William Anderson Journal, Mss Eur C703

Auckland House Memoirs, Mss Eur F351
Robert Baker Interview, R214
Barlow Collection, Mss Eur F176
Beveridge Collection, Mss Eur C176
Lady Elisabeth Bruce Diary, Mss Eur A144
Norah Burke Memoir, Mss Eur C216
Campbell Collection, Mss Eur E349
Lady Chambers Diary, Mss Eur A172
Decima Curtis Memoir, Mss Eur C462
Mrs E. M. Doherty Journal, Mss Eur C537
Margery Fyson Memoir, Mss Eur D885
Gibbon Papers, Mss Eur F392
Hardcastle Family Records, Photo Eur 31
Harrington Hawes Memoir, Mss Eur C553
Hutchinson Family Papers, Codrington Journal, Mss Eur D634
Kirkpatrick Collection, Mss Eur F228
Langham Scott Papers, Mss Eur D1232
Henry Lawrence Collection, Mss Eur F85
Lindsay Papers, Mss Eur D1092
Lumley Collection, Mss Eur F253
Macnabb Collection, Mss Eur F206
Nicholl Collection, Mss Eur D937
Ochterlony Papers, Mss Eur E298
Palmer Family memoir, Mss Eur D443
Henry Thoby Prinsep, 'Three Generations in India 1771–1904' Mss Eur C97
William Prinsep Memoir, Mss Eur D1160
Lady Sale Letter, Mss Eur A186
Shore Papers, Mss Eur E307
Strachey Collection, Mss Eur F127
Stuart Letters, Mss Eur D737
Sutherland Papers, Mss Eur D547
Terry Papers, Mss Eur C250
Thornhill Papers, Mss Eur B298

Elinor Tollinton Memoir, Mss Eur
  D1197
Dorothy Turner Letters, Mss Eur C354
Verlée Papers, Mss Eur F193
Wagentreiber Memoir, Photo Eur 313
West Papers, Mss Eur D888
Wonnacott Collection, Mss Eur C376
Yule Collection, Mss Eur E357
The Lawrence Military Asylum, T20231
*Report of Committee upon the Financial
  Condition of Hill Schools for
  Europeans in North India* (1904),
  V/26/861/1&2
A. J. Lawrence, *Report on the Existing
  Schools for Europeans and Eurasians
  throughout India* (1873), V/27/861/1

Pemberton Papers
F. P. Campbell Correspondence,
  7/18/28
F. W. Pemberton Papers, 7/5/1-109
H. J. Pemberton Correspondence,
  7/6/1-16
Nancy Pemberton Correspondence,
  7/8/6-10
Ann Ward Correspondence, 7/7/1-4

Woodstock School, Mussoorie
Annual reports
Correspondence
Handbooks
Quadrangle

Private Papers
George Allan, Memoir
Robert Baker, 'Early Memories'
Joan Battye, Memoir
Jaya Bolt, Memoir
Hilda Bourne, 'It was Like This'
Beatrice Broad, 'Fishing Fleet'
Netta Brown, Letters
W. Brown, 'Highlights in the Life of a
  Bengal Missionary'
Eryk Evans, 'A Few More Years'

Freda Evans, 'Freda's Story'
Penny Francis, 'The Long Voyage'
Lorraine Gradidge, 'The Last of the Raj
  Memsahibs'
Ronald Johnston, 'One Man's Life'
Elizabeth Knopp, Memoir notes
Pepita Lamb, 'To India by Imperial
  Airway'
Peter Lloyd, 'A Pinch of Salt'
Gladys Nightingale, Memoir
Betty Parker, Letters
Portal Family Papers
Hilda Reid, 'Once there were Three
  Children'
Patti Rundall, 'A Very Catholic
  Marriage'
Freda Starte, 'An Account of a Visit to
  India 1926-7'
Hilary Sweet-Escott, Memoir
Tommy Usborne, 'Memories of my
  Father, Charles Frederick Usborne'
Wenger Family Letters
E. L. W. Wenger, 'Ancestral
  Anecdotes and interview with
  Cornish
Wilkins Family Letters

Unpublished Theses
E. Buettner, 'Families, children, and
  memories: Britons in India, 1857-
  1947', Ph.D. Thesis for University of
  Michigan, 1998
V. Davies, 'Children of the Raj', MA
  Dissertation for London University,
  2000

Author's interviews
George Allan, 4 March 2004
Sister Armine (née Mathias), 2 May
  2003
Martin Baker, 16 June 2003
Paula Baker, 16 June 2003
Paulette Bateman (née Baker), 16 June
  2003

Susan Batten (née Portal), 30 April 2003

Anne Battye, 21 July 2004

Gillian Beard (née Northfield), 19 March 2004

Janet Bottoms (née Wenger), 25 August 2002

Tony Bottoms, 24 April 2004

Beatrice Broad (née Baker), 27 March 2003

Leila Brown, 4 February 2003

William Brown, 11 February 2003

James Butler, (telephone) 30 December 2003

Joseph Butler, 16 December 2003

Peter Clark, (telephone) 18 November 2004

Jane Davenport (née Labey), 18 August 2002

Valentine Davies (née Morice), 8 September 2004

Lesley Dowling (née Hayward), 31 July 2003

Penny Francis (née Elsden-Smith), 17 February 2004

Naomi Good (née Judah), 25 June 2003

Rachel Grenfell (née Judah), 25 June 2003

Rosie Gutteridge (née Harrison), 3 March 2003

Kay Hannaford, 18 October 2004

Pat Harrison (née Foster), 10 June 2003

Penny Henderson (née Fitzgerald), 19 October 2004

Agnes Heron (née Barratt), 18 April 2003

Jane Hudson (née Anson), 27 July 2004

Arthur Jones, 9 December 2003

Jack Judah, 7 July 2003

George Kennedy, 16 February 2005

Caroline Kennett (née Paylor), 30 September 2004

Pamela Kirkpatrick (née Watson), 11 February 2005

Peter Lloyd, 22 November 2004

Michael McNay, 1 August 2003

Roger Moore, 6 May 2003

Frances Moxon (née Labey), 17 August 2002

Wyn Munro (née Butler), 17 December 2003

Bill Newman, 24 May 2003

Gladys Nightingale (née Krall), 8 June 2004

Brian Outhwaite, 23 July 2002

Christopher Parker, 10 March 2004

Annie Paylor, 8 November 2004

Linotte Peter (née Purbi), 19 January, 2004

Carol Pickering (née Titus), 4 February 2003

Kissane Probyn (née Keane), (telephone) 20 January 2004

Ruth Quadling (née Starte), 17 April 2004

Susanna Rook (née Tewson), 18 February 2003

Richard Sarson, 12 May 2003

Trish Schreiber (née Battye), 3 August 2004

Morvyth Seely (née St George), 3 August 2004

Penny Smith (née Walker), 17 July 2004

Harry Southwell, 21 June 2003

Students at St Mary's School, 28 July 2004

Hilary Sweet-Escott (née Johnston), 1 May 2004

Susie Taylor (née Paylor), (telephone) 26 November 2004

Michael Thomas, 3 October 2003

David Wilkins, 7 April 2004

Jane Williams (née Portal), 28 February 2003

Dick Whittaker, 4 November 2003

Margaret Whittaker (née Thompson),
November 2003

Published Works

Abbott, J., *The Young Christian*, 1860

Abbott, M., *Family Ties*, 1993

    Family Affairs, 2003

Allen, C., *Plain Tales from the Raj*, 1976
edn

    *A Glimpse of the Burning Plain:
Leaves from the Indian Journals of
Charlotte Canning*, 1986

Allen, L., *Burma, The Longest War
1941–5*, 1984

Amis, K., *Rudyard Kipling*, 1975

Anthony, F., *Britain's Betrayal in
India*, 1969

Arnold, D., 'European Orphans and
Vagrants in India in the Nineteenth
Century' in *Journal of Imperial and
Commonwealth History*, vol. VII

Atkinson, G., *Curry and Rice*, 2001 edn

Barr, P., *The Memsahibs*, 1976

Batalia, U., *The Other Side of Silence:
Voices from the Partition of India*,
1998

Battye, E. D., *The Fighting Ten*, 1984

Bayne-Powell, R., *The English Child in
the Eighteenth Century*, 1939

Bean, P. and Melville, J., *Lost Children
of the Empire*, 1989

Bence-Jones, M., *The Viceroys*, 1982

Bennett, D., *Queen Victoria's Children*,
1980

Bevan, S., *The Parting Years: A British
Family and the End of Empire*, 2001

Beveridge, Lord, *India Called Them*,
1947

Bhattacharya, S., *Victorian Perception
of Child*, 2000

Bion, W., *The Long Weekend 1897–
1919: Part of a Life*, 1982

Blackburn, M., Humphries, S.,

Maddocks, N. and Titley, C., *Hope
and Glory*, 2004

Bond, R., *Scenes from a Writer's Life*,
1997

Bott, C., *The Life and Works of Alfred
Bestall*, 2003

Bowlby, J., *Separation, Anger and
Anxiety*, 1998 edn

Bradley, I., *The Call to Seriousness*,
1976

Briggs, A., *The Age of Improvement*,
1959

Brivati, B., *Hugh Gaitskell*, 1996

Brookes, S., *Through the Jungle of
Death*, 2000

Buettner, E., 'Parent-child separations
and colonial careers. the Talbot
family correspondence in the 1880s
and 1890s' in Fletcher, E. and
Hussey, S., *Childhood in Question*,
1999

    'From Somebodies to Nobodies:
Britons returning Home from India'
in Daunton, M. and Rieger, B.,
*Meanings of Modernity: Britain from
the late-Victorian era to the Second
World War* , 2001

    *Empire Families: Britons and Late
Imperial India*, 2004

Burton, A., 'India, Inc? Nostalgia,
memory and the empire of things'
in Ward, S., *British Culture and the
End of Empire*, 2001

Butler, I., *The Eldest Brother*, 1973

Butler, J., *Incense and Innocence*, 1991

Butler, R. A., *The Art of the Possible*,
1971

Butler, S., *The Way of All Flesh*, first
published 1903, Collins Library of
Classics

Caine, B., *Bombay to Bloomsbury: A
Biography of the Strachey Family*,
2005

Calder, A., *The People's War: Britain 1939–45*, 1992 edn

Carey, W. H., *The Good Old Days of Honorable John Company*, 1906

Catlin, J., *Family Quartet: Vera Brittain and her Family*, 1987

Chaudhuri, N., *The Autobiography of an Unknown Indian*, 1951

Christie, J., *Morning Drum*, 1983

Churchill, W., *My Early Life*, 1959 edn

Clarke, P., *Hope and Glory: Britain 1900–1990*, 1996

Clay, J., *John Masters: A Regimented Life*, 1992

Coe, R., *When the Grass Was Taller: Autobiography and the Experience of Childhood*, 1986

Collingham, E., *Imperial Bodies*, 2001

Collis, M., *Last and First in Burma*, n.d.

Colmcille, M. M., *First the Blade*, 1968

Connolly, C., *Enemies of Promise*, 1961 edn

Conrad, P., *Modern Times, Modern Places*, 1998

Copland, I., *India 1885–1947: The Unmaking of an Empire*, 2001

Coveney, P., *The Image of Childhood*, 1967 edn

Cunningham, H., *Children and Childhood in Western Society since 1500*, 1995

Crossman, R., *Palestine Mission*, 1947

Curtin, P., *Death by Migration*, 1989

Dalrymple, W. (ed.), *Begums, Thugs & White Mughals: The Journals of Fanny Parkes*, 2002

Dalrymple, W., *White Mughals*, 2002

David, S., *The Indian Mutiny 1857*, 2002

Davies, H., *Born 1900*, 1998

de Courcy, A., *The Viceroy's Daughters*, 2000

Delaney, P., (ed.), *Tom Stoppard in Conversation*, 1994

Dickens, C., *Dombey and Son*, Oxford India Paper edn

Great Expectations, 1985 edn

Hard Times, 1961 edn

'The Paradise at Tooting', 20 January 1849 in *Miscellaneous Papers*, 1911

Diver, M., *The Englishwoman in India*, 1909

Honoria Lawrence, 1936

Douglas, C., *Douglas Jardine: Spartan Cricketer*, 1984

Dudley Edwards, R., *True Brits: Inside the Foreign Office*, 1994

Dutta, A., *Glimpses of European Life in Nineteenth-Century Bengal*, 1995

Eden, E., *Letters from India by the Hon. Emily Eden*, 1872

Edwardes, M., *Bound to Exile: The Victorians in India*, 1969

Edwards-Stuart, I., *The Calcutta of Begum Johnson*, 1990

Eha, *Behind the Bungalow*, 1916

Eidse, F. and Sichel, N. (eds), *Unrooted Childhoods: Memoirs of Growing Up Global*, 2004

Ewbank, T. and Hildred, S., *Julie Christie: The Biography*, 2000

Eyre, V., *Journal of an Afghanistan Prisoner, 1843*, 1976 edn

Fayrer, J., *European Child-Life in Bengal*, 1873

Recollections of my Life, 1900

Feiling, K. J., *Warren Hastings*, 1954

Fildes, V., *Breasts, Bottles and Babies*, 1988

Fisher, J., *Records*, 1919

Flanders, J., *A Circle of Sisters*, 2002

Fleming, L., *Last Children of the Raj*, 2004

Forster, M., *William Makepeace Thackeray: Memoirs of a Victorian Gentleman*, 1978

Foss, M., *Out of India*, 2002

Fraser, J. B. (ed.), *Military Memoir of James Skinner*, 1955

Freud, A., *Infants without Families*, 1939/45

Freud, S., *A Child is Being Beaten*, 1919 in Penguin Freud Library, vol. 10

Gardam, J., *Old Filth*, 2004

Gathorne-Hardy, J., *The Rise and Fall of the British Nanny*, 1972

Gavin, J., *Out of India: An Anglo-Indian Childhood*, 1997

Gerhardt, S., *Why Love Matters: How Affection Shapes a Baby's Brain*, 2004

Gibson, P., *Childhood Lost: A Boy's Journey through War*, 1999

Gilmour, D., *The Long Recessional: The Imperial Life of Rudyard Kipling*, 2002

Godden, J. and R., *Two under the Indian Sun*, 1996

Godden, R., *A Time to Dance, No Time to Weep*, 1987

Graham, A., *Lindsay Anderson*, 1981

Greave, P., *The Seventh Gate*, 1978

Greenberger, A. J., *The British Image of India: A Study in the Literature of Imperialism, 1880–1960*, 1969

Greene, G., *The Lost Childhood and Other Essays*, 1962

Grier, S., *The Letters of Warren Hastings to his Wife*, 1950

Harris, J., *William Beveridge*, 1997

Harris, M. J. and Oppenheimer, D., *Into the Arms of Strangers: Stories of the Kindertransport*, 2001 edn

Harrison, M., *Public Health in British India: Anglo-Indian Preventive Medicine 1859–1914*, 1994
Climates and Constitutions, 1999

Harvey-Jones, J., *Getting it Together: Memoirs of a Troubleshooter*, 1991

Hawes, C. J., *Poor Relations: The Making of a Eurasian Community in British India 1773–1833*, 1996

Headington, C., *Peter Pears*, 1992

Henriques, F., *Children of Caliban: Miscegenation*, 1974

Hibbert, C. (ed.), *The Great Mutiny: India 1857*, 1980 edn
Queen Victoria in her Letters and Journals, 1984
Queen Victoria: A Personal History, 2000

Hickman, K., *Daughters of Britannia: The Lives & Times of Diplomatic Wives*, 1999

Hillen, E., *The Way of a Boy: A Memoir of Java*, 1993

Hodgson Burnett, F., *The Secret Garden*, 1994 edn

Holman, D., *The Life of Col. James Skinner*, 1961

Holroyd, M., *Lytton Strachey: A Biography*, 1979 edn

Hudson, K. and Pettifer, J., *Diamonds in the Sky: A Social History of Air Travel*, 1979

Hughes, M. V., *A London Child in the 1870s*, 1977 edn

Humphreys, M., *Empty Cradles: One Woman's Fight to Uncover Britain's Most Shameful Secret*, 1994

Hunter, W. W., *The Earl of Lord Mayo*, 1891
The Thackerays in India, 1897

Hyam, R., *Empire and Sexuality*, 1990

Inglis, R., *The Children's War: Evacuation 1939–45*, 1989

Innes Craig, H., *Under the Old School Topee*, 1996 edn

Jackson, R., *Twenty Seconds at Quetta*, 1960

Jacquemont, V., *Letters from India*, ed. C. A. Phillips, 1936

335

Voyage dans l'Inde pendant les Années 1828 à 1832, 1841.

James, L., *Raj: The Making and Unmaking of British India,* 1997

Jasper, T., *Cliff: A Biography,* 1993

Jones, E., Wilkie, C. and McGee, M., *Woodstock School: The First Century 1854–1954,* 1954

Kamra, S., *Bearing Witness: Partition, Independence, End of the Raj,* 2002

Kaye, M. M. (ed.), *The Golden Calm: An English Lady's Life in Moghul Delhi,* 1980
The Sun in the Morning, 1992 edn

Kelly, S. (ed.), *The Life of Mrs Sherwood,* 1865

Kendal, F., *White Cargo,* 1999 edn

Kennedy, D., *The Magic Mountains: Hill Stations and the British Raj,* 1996

Kerr, B., *The Dispossessed,* 1974

Keynes, R., *Annie's Box,* 2002

Khan, M. and Parel, K. J., *Sanawar: A Legacy,* 1997

Kinsey, S. and Green, E., *The Good Companions: Wives and Families in the History of the HSBC Group,* privately published, 2004

Kipling, R., *Baa Baa, Black Sheep* in Raine, C. (ed.), *A Choice of Kipling's Prose,* 1987
Kim, 1981 edn

Lambert, R., *The Hothouse Society,* 1968

Langguth, A. J., *Saki: A Life of Hector Munro,* 1981

Langley, L., *Changes of Address,* 1987
Persistent Rumours, 1999

Lawrence, J. and Woodiwiss, A. (eds), *The Journals of Honoria Lawrence,* 1980

Lawrence, R., *Indian Embers,* n.d.

Lawson, J. and Silver, H., *A Social History of Education in England,* 1973

Leslie, A., *Daily Mail,* 12 and 13 August 1997 and BBC, *Desert Island Discs,* 7 November 2004

Lethbridge, J., *Harrow on the Hooghly,* 1994

Linklater, E., *Country-Born* in Dunn, D. (ed.), *The Oxford Book of Scottish Short Stories,* 1995

Lively P., *Oleander, Jacaranda: Growing Up in Egypt in the 1930s and 1940s,* 1995 edn

Llewellyn-Jones, R., *A Fatal Friendship: The Nawabs, the British and the City of Lucknow,* 1985

Lovatt, H. and de Jong, P., *Above the Heron's Pool,* 1993

Low, D., *Britain and Indian Nationalism: The Imprint of Ambiguity, 1929–1942,* 1997

Ludowyk, E. F. C., *The Modern History of Ceylon,* 1966

Luker Ashby, L. and Whately, R., *My India,* 1938

Lumley, J., *Stare Back and Smile,* 1989

Lunt, J., *A Hell of a Licking: The Retreat from Burma 1941–2,* 1986

Lutyens, M., *The Lyttons in India,* 1979

Mack, E., *Public Schools and British Opinion since 1860,* 1941

Mackenzie, C., *Storms and Sunshine of a Soldier's Life,* 1884

MacMillan, M., *Women of the Raj,* 1996 edn

Maitland, J., *Letters from Madras,* ed. A. Price, 2003

Masters, J., *Bhowani Junction,* 2001 edn

Mathur, S., *An Indian Encounter: Portraits for Queen Victoria,* 2003

McCrum, R., *Wodehouse: A Life,* 2004

McLeod, R. and Lewis, M., *Disease, Medicine and Empire,* 1988

McLynn, F., *Stanley: The Making of an African Explorer,* 1989

Miller, J., *Freud: The Man, his World his Influence*, 1972

Monkland, Mrs, *The Nabob at Home*, 1842

Moore, B., *A Moment of Love*, 1965 edn

Moore, G. (ed.), *Diary of the Doctor's Lady*, Colina Brydon's Diary, 1980

Moorhouse, G., *India Britannica*, 1984

Morris, J., *Fisher's Face*, 1995

Murphy, R., *Collected Poems*, 2000 *The Kick*, 2002

Newson, J. and E., *Seven Years Old in the Home Environment*, 1976

Nightingale, F., *How People May Live and not Die in India*, 1864

NSPCC, *When we were Young*, 1989

Nugent, M., *A Journal from the Year 1811 till the Year 1815*, 1839

Orwell, G., 'Such, Such were the Joys' in *Collected Essays, Journalism and Letters*, 1970

Oxford Dictionary of National Biography, 2004

Pears, R., *Young Sea-Dogs*, 1960

Perham, M., *Lugard: The Years of Adventure*, 1956

Pickering, C., *Goodbye India*, privately published, 2004

Pictures in the Post: The Illustrated Letters of Sir Henry Thornhill, 1987

Pike, E. et al., *The Story of Walthamstow Hall*, 1973

Pollock, D. C. and Van Reken, R. E., *Third Culture Kids: The Experience of Growing Up Among Worlds*, 2001

Pollock, L., *Forgotten Children*, 1983

Porter A. (ed.), *The Oxford History of the British Empire*, 1999

Pugh, P., *Williamson Magor Stuck to Tea*, 1991

Quennell, P. (ed.), *Mayhew's Characters*, n.d.

(ed.), *Memoirs of William Hickey*, 1960

Rich, P. J., *Chains of Empire*, 1991

Richard, C., *Which One's Cliff?*, 1977

Ritchie, G., *The Ritchies in India*, 1920

Rivett-Carnac, J., *Many Memories*, 1910

Robb, P., *Clash of Cultures? An Englishman in Calcutta in the 1790s*, 1998

Roche, G., *Childhood in India: Tales from Sholapur*, 1994

Rodger, N. A. M., *The Command of the Ocean: A Naval History of Britain, 1649–1815*, 2004

Rorke, G., *A Child in Burma*, 2002

Ross, A., *Blindfold Games*, 1986

Royle, T., *The Last Days of the Raj*, 1989

Rushdie, S., *Midnight's Children*, 1982

Russell, W., *Indian Summer*, 1951

Rutherford, A. (ed.), *Early Verse of Rudyard Kipling*, 1986

Saki, *The Complete Short Stories*, 2000 edn

Sale, Lady, *The First Afghan War: Journal of the Disasters in Afghanistan, 1841–2*, ed. P. Macrory, 1969

Scott, P., *The Birds of Paradise*, 1967, edn
  A Division of the Spoils, 1977 edn

Scudamore, P., *Spike Milligan*, 1985

Shepherd, J. W., *The Cawnpore Massacre 1857*, 1886

Sherwood, M., *Lucy and her Dhye*, 1825

Slater, N., *Toast: The Story of a Boy's Hunger*, 2003

Slaughter, C., *A Black Englishman*, 2004

Spear, T. G. P., *The Nabobs*, 1932

Spencer A. (ed.), *Memoirs of William Hickey*, 1925

Spock, B., *Baby and Child Care*, 1979 edn

Spurling, H., *The Girl from the Fiction Department*, 2003
Paul Scott: A Life, 1990

Staines, J., *Country Born: One Man's Life in India 1909–1947*, 1986

Stark, H. A., *Hostages to India*, 1926

Steel, F. and Gardiner, G., *The Complete Indian Housekeeper and Cook*, 1898

Stevenson-Hinde, J. and Hinde, R. A., 'John Bowlby' in Smelser, N. J. and Baltes, P. B. (eds), *International Encyclopaedia of the Social and Behavioural Sciences*, 2001

Stoddard, S. et al. (eds), *Living on the Edge: Tales of Woodstock School*, n.d.

Stokes, E., *Innocents Abroad: The Story of British Child Evacuees in Australia 1940–45*, 1994

Stoppard, T., 'In Search of Childhood' in *The Independent*, 23 March 1991

Strachey, B., *The Strachey Line*, 1985

Taylor, S., *The Caliban Shore: The Fate of the Grosvenor Castaways*, 2004

Thackeray, W. M., *Roundabout Papers*, ed. J. E. Wells, 1925

Thompson, E., *The Life of Charles, Lord Metcalfe*, 1937

Thomson, M., *The Story of Cawnpore*, 1859

Tindall, G., *City of Gold*, 1982

Tinker, H., 'A Forgotten Long March: The Indian Exodus from Burma 1942' in *Journal of East Asian Studies*, 1975

Trevelyan, R., *The Golden Oriole*, 1987

Truby King, M., *Mothercraft*, 1934

Turing, S., *Alan M. Turing*, 1959

Turner, S., *Cliff Richard*, 1993

Vickers, H., *Vivien Leigh*, 1988

Vizram, R., *Asians in Britain: 400 Years of History*, 2002

Wagner, G., *Children of the Empire*, 1982

Walvin, J., *A Child's World: A Social History of English Childhood, 1800–1914*, 1982

Ward, A., *Our Bones are Scattered: The Cawnpore Massacres and the Indian Mutiny of 1857*, 1996

White, A., *Frost in May*, 1978 edn

Wilkins, E. G., *By Hands, Bullocks and Prayers*, 1987

Wilkins, J., *A Child's Eye View*, 1992

Wilkinson, T., *Two Monsoons*, 1976,

Williams, P., *Hugh Gaitskell: A Political Biography*, 1979

Williamson, T., *The East India Vade-Mecum*, 1810

Wilson, A., *The Strange Ride of Rudyard Kipling*, 1977

Wilson, A. N., *The Victorians*, 2002

Witting, C. (ed.), *The Glory of the Sons: A History of Eltham College*, 1952

Woodham-Smith, C., *Florence Nightingale*, 1964 edn

Woodward, F., *The Doctor's Disciples*, 1954

Woolf, L., *Growing: An Autobiography of the Years 1904 to 1911*, 1961

Yalland, Z., *Traders and Nabobs: The British in Cawnpore 1765–1857*, 1987

Younger, C., *Neglected Children of the Raj*, 1987

Websites

tckworld.com: Ann Baker Cottrell and Ruth Hill Useem, 'ATCKs maintain global dimensions throughout their lives'

www.ultimategrandparent.com

Index

Royer

DOROTHY

mumsy darling and h
big hug and b
give Baby am

BRITISH OVERSEAS AIRWAYS CORPORATION

Issued by

SUBJECT TO CONDITIONS OF CONTRACT INSIDE FRONT COVER
COMPLETE ROUTING THIS TICKET AND CON

NOT GOOD FOR PASSAGE

			LONDON			AI	109Y		R...
MISS A. PHYLON (un g)			BOMBAY	Y		IC	162Y	AI	
			COCHIN	Y		IC	165Y	AI	
			BOMBAY	Y		AI	162Y		
			LONDON	Y					

Master Teddy
Westmorland Wood
Homeward Bound
c/o P&O agent.
P&O Steamship
"Caledonia"
Portsaid
EGYPT

CE.14

An
LOCAL TI
CURRENCY
ENQUIRIES o
co
y's representative:
Mr Pointer

gladly be dealt with by th

ARRANGEMENTS FOR TO-MORROW
Monday, 17th July 1939
(DATE)

will be called at 0345
baggage will be collected at. 04
(local time)
(or launch) with

My dear Beloved Mother,
        You simply must
very well indeed, and am
small little walks on the
settled in Kasauli. Shei
excellent. We are sendin
photo of Mouse, and one e
one of the group, in which
Tiffer always puts out his
much sweeter than this.
again separately.   About
having found the adhesions
stretched, as the others h
collapse - a large area co
got to be forced into decer
very well in hand, and alt
gone now. Mummy I could no
separation from Tom is her
and we